UNDERSTANDING CULTURE.

For Inge
and our boys
Alex and Jonas

Understanding Cultures

Perspectives in Anthropology and Social Theory

Second Edition

Robert C. Ulin

First edition published 1984
Second edition published 2001

2 4 6 8 10 9 7 5 3 1

Blackwell Publishers Inc.
350 Main Street
Malden, Massachusetts 02148
USA

Blackwell Publishers Ltd
108 Cowley Road
Oxford OX4 1JF
UK

Library of Congress Cataloging-in-Publication Data

Ulin, Robert C. (Robert Charles), 1951–
    Understanding cultures : perspectives in anthropology and social theory / Robert C. Ulin.—2nd ed.
        p. cm.
    Includes bibliographical references and index.
    ISBN 0–631–22114–X (alk. paper)—ISBN 0–631–22115–8 (pb. : alk. paper)
        1. Ethnology—Philosophy. 2. Hermeneutics. 3. Cross-cultural studies. I. Title.

GN345 .U44 2001
306—dc21   2001025205

British Library Cataloguing in Publication Data
A CIP catalogue record for this book is available from the British Library.

Typeset in 10/12pt Sabon
by Kolam Information Services Pvt. Ltd, Pondicherry, India
Printed in Great Britain by TJ International, Padstow, Cornwall

This book is printed on acid-free paper.

Contents

Acknowledgments vi

1 Introduction 1

2 Anthropological Ancestors and Interpretation Theory:
Boas, Malinowski, and Evans-Pritchard 26

3 Peter Winch and Ordinary Language Philosophy 46

4 The Neo-Popperians and the Logic of One Science:
I. C. Jarvie and Robin Horton 63

5 Ordinary Language Philosophy in Question:
Steven Lukes and Alasdair MacIntyre 89

6 Beyond Explanation and Understanding:
The Hermeneutics of Hans-Georg Gadamer and Paul Ricoeur 107

7 Hermeneutics and Critical Anthropology:
The Synthesis of Practical and Critical Reason 139

8 Modernism and Postmodernism in Anthropology 182

9 Bounded Cultures – Bounded Selves:
The Challenge of Cultural Diasporas 204

Notes 239

Bibliography 258

Index 270

Acknowledgments

This book reflects a long intellectual journey and thus there are numerous colleagues and friends to thank for their influence, support, and encouragement. However, the common author's qualification is applicable here in that I assume full responsibility for the views and interpretations presented throughout this book.

There is little doubt that my experience as a graduate student at the New School for Social Research played a significant formative influence on my scholarly work and intellectual quests past and present. In particular, I owe debts to my late professors, Bob Scholte and Stanley Diamond. It was Bob Scholte who introduced me to the rationality debates during my first year as a graduate student. Bob shared his extensive bibliography on rationality with me and encouraged my work in philosophical anthropology and the ordinary language philosophy of the later Wittgenstein. From Stanley Diamond, I learned much about the Marxist tradition and the unrealized potentials of critical anthropology as a medium for challenging capitalist hegemony. Stanley strongly supported my intellectual pursuit of hermeneutics and critical theory and continued to be interested in my professional well-being long after I finished my graduate studies.

A number of other individuals have played less the role of mentor and more of colleague and friend. I am grateful to the late William Roseberry for his critical reading of the chapter on Marxism, an important chapter for its efforts to synthesize hermeneutics and critical anthropology. Shirley Lindenbaum, Rayna Rapp, Jeremy Nowak, and Helen Berger engaged me in conversation with respect to a number of theoretical arguments in the book and thus served as both sources of support and theoretical interlocutors. More recently, my friendship with David Miller was, and continues to be, a source of intellectual challenge. From David, I have learned much about the processes of signification and representation and, perhaps most important, the pleasure of interdisciplinary dialog and research.

John and Jean Comaroff provided the initial incentive to revise and update *Understanding Cultures*, believing that the book was theoretically unique in anthropology and thus could still benefit students and professionals. To John and Jean I also owe a special gratitude for supporting me through the trials and travails of my recent peripatetic career.

I would also like to thank Michael Herzfeld, who likewise supported the updating and republication of this book and who has always been there for me in various times of need. I have known Michael for over fifteen years and have enormous respect for his intellectual honesty, commitment to social justice in the academy and loyalty as a friend. Michael has that rare quality that motivates and inspires students, colleagues and friends. Thank you Michael.

Andy Lass and Allan Hanson served as readers for the three new chapters of this book. Their kind but trenchant criticism has done much to improve the quality of the book. I also thank Andy and Allan for their support over the years and for their companionship and intellectual challenge.

As most authors will acknowledge, editors play a very vital role in the development of a book project. In this capacity I would like to thank Jane Huber for encouraging me to proceed with this project and being tolerant of the occasional delays.

I also thank Sage Publications for permission to reprint a large portion of chapter 8 that originally appeared in 1991 in *Critique of Anthropology* under the title "Critical Anthropology Twenty Years Later: Modernism and Postmodernism in Anthropology." Likewise, a small part of chapter 9 originally was part of an essay entitled "The Current Tide in American Europeanist Anthropology: From Margin to Centre?" published in *Anthropology Today* in 1991. I would like to thank the Royal Anthropological Institute of Great Britain and Ireland for permission to reproduce those few paragraphs here.

Finally, I thank my wife Inge Meffert and our two sons, Alex and Jonas, for being tolerant of my emotional lapses during critical phases of the writing process. Inge has been a wonderful companion and source of support through various and sometimes turbulent periods of my career. Her acute mind, boundless spirit and sense of humor have taken me through more than one impasse. This book is dedicated to her and to our Alex and Jonas.

Robert Ulin
Kalamazoo, April 2001

1 Introduction

Any time an author revisits old theoretical grounds in producing a new edition of a book it is a welcome opportunity to reflect on intellectual directions that he or she has pursued over the years as well as the more general state of theory in contemporary anthropology and beyond. This Introduction will be directed, therefore, to two principal ends. The first is to discuss selectively some of the developments in contemporary anthropology and anthropological theory. The second is to revisit the themes of the original rationality debates so as to extend their purview to encompass the concerns of ethnographic writing and postmodernism that dominated in the 1980s, and the more recent issues of globalism, cultural borders, and cultural diasporas that have received wide interdisciplinary attention in the 1990s. It is likely, moreover, that these later issues will continue to engage scholars and to be dominant politically well into the twenty-first century.

The Anglo-American rationality debates, which served as the departure point for the first edition of this book in 1984 and as part of a larger effort in that work to synthesize political economy and cultural theory, no longer command the degree of attention that they did throughout the 1970s and into the 1980s. Many anthropologists have turned rather to poststructuralism, postmodernism and postcolonial theory for critical insights and have come to distrust the "grand narratives"[1] of modernism that inform the majority of positions represented in the rationality debates. However, I believe that the general themes presented through the rationality debates have not been surpassed in that sociocultural anthropologists in particular continue to be engaged with the theoretical and political issues and problems of understanding "the other" even if the direction of inquiry should be more the politics of representation than conventional epistemology. In fact, as I argue in chapter 9, as long as the historically produced political, economic, and social inequities that prefigure knowing on a global basis remain intact, the issues raised through the rationality debates will have an enduring relevance.

With respect to the general state of theory in anthropology, of which the above distrust of modernism is increasingly representative, the theoretical options are numerous and richly provocative. They range from attempts to revitalize structuralism to working through local articulations of culture with global processes, to rethinking the very foundational assumptions of the discipline – to name just some of the noteworthy. Moreover, anthropological theory has significantly influenced numerous disciplines and intellectual mediums, especially history, literary criticism, and cultural studies, and has exhibited more generally an increasing popularity and relevance to multicultural education and global initiatives, even if of the dubious sort.[2] However, not all of the developments have been quite so beneficial, since some anthropology departments have – like Duke and Stanford – split literally along ideological lines while others struggle to maintain a weak, even tenuous, union. Surely in question is the older and once-venerated vision of American anthropology as a four-field discipline (archaeology, linguistics, physical anthropology, cultural anthropology) integrated through the concept of culture as a mark of being distinctively human. As anthropologists turn away, furthermore, from the the potentially discipline-integrating questions of social evolution and comparative social development, which include culture as primary to the micro-discourses of postmodernism, the common ground between the four-fields tends to erode. How does one reconcile, for example, research on primate morphology and behavior with research on contested identities and cultural diasporas, the politics of language, and the archaeological evidence for state formation? Apart from the near ubiquity of intellectual fragmentation and practice, the above division in anthropology is compounded by a commitment on the part of some anthropologists to natural science as paradigmatic for the human sciences. The consequent long-standing tension resonates with and underlies all the contributions to the rationality debates and is thus a further testimony to their continuing importance.

No one can really predict whether or not the subdisciplines of anthropology will go their separate ways. After all, in Europe social anthropology, linguistics, archaeology, and physical anthropology have always been separate disciplines and presently in the United States physical anthropologists and archaeologists have their own vital professional associations, to which they seem more committed than they are to the American Anthropological Association.[3] However, it will take a greater vision than nostalgia provides to forge a new union in American anthropology. I suspect that such a union will require pursuing the large questions of the human condition in its multiplicity, even if the answers are necessarily multivocal and inconclusive, and a commitment pragmatically – and here ancestors such as Boas and Mead come to mind[4] – to challenge prejudice and social inequality in their multiple local and global forms. On the other hand, the theoretical and methodological issues of science, especially positivistic science, cut across the subdisciplines and thus one discovers tensions and challenges that are not simply subdisciplinary in nature and which in some circumstances have been remarkably constant.[5] This complicates the conversation both between and within subdisciplines especially in light of the hegemonic role assumed by natural science and instrumental rationality in the realm of human affairs.

The philosopher Edmund Husserl (1970), who is rarely cited in anthropology, recognized in the early twentieth century the ethnographic implications of natural science assuming a paradigmatic influence not only for scholarship but also for human experience more generally. While Husserl's phenomenology is marred, in my view, by locating the certitude of knowing in the solipsistic structure of the transcendental ego, he was a primary contributor to the idea of human experience as meaningfully constituted. The emphasis on the world as prefigured through human agency, or even human consciousness, was an important contrast to the empiricism of Hume and to regnant ideas concerning human nature at the dawn of the twentieth century. To Husserl and subsequent phenomenologists[6] more attuned to the social conditions of knowing we owe the concept of the "life-world". The concept of "life-world" has become familiar to anthropologists, especially those attuned to symbolism, as the intersubjectivity of meaning, the idea that human beings collectively create and inhabit a shared world of constituted meaning or experience. Husserl believed, moreover, that science was a potential threat to the "life-world" to the extent that scientific progress resulted in what he referred to as "the mathematization of nature." That is, the emphasis in science on abstract theories removed from experience and mathematical formulas, especially those of theoretical physics, potentially detracted from our collective ability to talk about a world shared, the realm of collective experience, and collective symbolic meaning.

Husserl's vision of a life of collective meaning imperiled by natural science, a condition which he identified as a crisis, is elaborated further in Hannah Arendt's *The Human Condition* (1958) and Jürgen Habermas's *The Theory of Communicative Action* (1984). Like Husserl, Arendt maintains that ordinary discourse and figurative language, what anthropologists generally refer to as tropes, are important to the having of a world in common. Technical language and especially the dependency of natural science on mathematics reduces the potential for human agents to establish the common grounds of understanding and consensus, both of which are essential to the building of community and political life. Habermas shares Arendt's belief that political or civic life is informed by the mutual understanding and consensus realized through ordinary language. However, Habermas sees the hegemony of science and its reliance on technical or instrumental rationality not only as a threat to "shared meaning" but also as a political challenge resulting in what he calls the "colonization of the life world." Stated simply, Habermas believes that the pervasiveness of science as paradigmatic of understanding in general is coming progressively to define the nature of human experience. Moreover, the the commitment of science to instrumental reason establishes a framework whereby the objects of scientific knowledge and research are constituted towards the end of technical control. This commitment to control, in turn, establishes science as a potentially powerful force in shaping social policy, while glossing over the political interests that normally compete in the public arena and define the nature of politics more generally.

While the divisions in contemporary anthropology and the political implications of science, especially technical or instrumental reason, are not, as noted, the primary focus of the rationality debates, I believe that the rationality debates lend themselves to a broad conversation that includes the issues raised by Arendt and Habermas as extensions of the "life-world" and the public arena. If we turn to Evans-Pritchard's classic work on the Azande, for example, we discover a critical engagement, albeit indirectly, both with the salient issues of evolution that marked the discourses of the late nineteenth and with early twentieth-centuries and positivist science as a model for understanding humans in their multiplicity. As I argue in chapter 2, Evans-Pritchard was a serious student of phenomenology and especially the hermeneutics of Dilthey, they led Evans-Pritchard to a rather significant departure, although not a complete one, from the reductive naturalized needs orientation of Malinowski and the essentialized structures of Radcliffe-Brown, the predominant paradigms of British social anthropology. Moreover, Evans-Pritchard's work on the Azande can be interpreted as a direct challenge to French philosopher Lucien Lévy-Bruhl's (1965) influential thesis on the "prelogical" mentality of indigenous peoples.

Lévy-Bruhl argued that indigenous peoples (he used the word "primitive") fail to distinguish categorically, as a natural endowment of mind, between animals and humans in their ritual life and thus do not have the requisite logic shared by westerners. The implication is that indigenous peoples are reflective of an earlier state of social evolution, an idea that was wide spread at the end of the nineteenth century and which came to serve as the civilizing ideology of western colonialism. Those committed to supporting colonialism could thus argue that, if not salvation, they at the very least were the harbingers of reason. Evans-Pritchard refuted Lévy-Bruhl's argument by presenting ethnographic evidence from the Azande that supported the logical coherence of their witchcraft accusations and consultation of oracles. According to Evans-Pritchard, the difference between the Azande and us is not a consequence of mind but rather their assumptions – from which they reason just as we do. He maintains that we and the Azande share the same logic or rationality but proceed from different assumptions about the natural and social world. The Azande thus manage a household just as we would and draw attributions of causation in a manner not dissimilar from ours. Needless to say, Evans-Pritchard's support of Zande rationality had the same practical potential as Boas's challenge to the racist immigration policies of the American government, although Evans-Pritchard's efforts did not alter the discourse of English colonialism.

Evans-Pritchard is an especially complex anthropological ancestor because his work bridges the incommensurable traditions of structural functionalism, of which *The Nuer* is illustrative, and a hermeneutic interpretation of Zande ritual practices. Moreover, although not generally acknowledged in American anthropology for this, Evans-Pritchard can be identified as an early supporter of historical anthropology.[7] However, it is Evans-Pritchard's rich elaboration of Zande intentions: an exploration of their "life-world", which sets him directly in opposition to colleagues in anthropology seeking to find the universal in the particular, the elaboration of law across cultures, human society in accord with nature – all of which was present in the British anthropology of the time. Nevertheless, as I argue in chapter 3, Evans-Pritchard would betray his own hermeneutic insights by rejecting the existence of Zande witches on empirical grounds. It is this rejection of Zande witches on empirical grounds that the Anglo-American rationality debates take their point of departure, one that commences with "the linguistic turn" in social theory as represented in Peter Winch's appropriation of the ordinary language philosophy of the later Wittgenstein. As we shall see, the linguistic turn has important theoretical implications for anthropology's relation to science which, in turn, has important implications for the subdisciplines.

The Linguistic Turn

Of all the social science disciplines, anthropology is perhaps the most engaged with language. The reasons should be self-evident in that anthropology has constructed itself historically as a mode of knowing whose primary object is the non-western other. Accessibility to other cultures, as Lévi-Strauss's classic *Tristes Tropiques* (1974) illustrates clearly, depends largely on understanding their languages and cultural idioms. Many graduate programs still incorporate a course on field linguistics as a fundamental part of training at the doctoral level and offer courses on applied linguistics, including sociolinguisitics, as well. Language is, furthermore, not only important to sociocultural anthropologists but also to archaeologists struggling to interpret the meaning and symbolism of material culture, and to physical anthropologists interested in questions of evolution as they pertain to the human fossil record. In short, language is a key medium for understanding human cultures past and present and because of its foundational relation to culture should occupy a central place in the discipline of anthropology.

That Evans-Pritchard's rejection of the empirical existence of witches has something to do with language may initially not be self-evident. However, this connection with language is precisely the line of argument pursued by philosopher Peter Winch in his *The Idea of a Social Science and its Relation to Philosophy* (1958). As noted above, Winch borrows from Wittgenstein's later rather than early period; this is because he is interested in presenting a theory of language as practice, a view of language that is thoroughly conversant with much of contemporary cultural anthropology. The early Wittgenstein (I do not go into detail here because much of this is described in chapter 3) was drawn to the label theory of language, a theory that presents words as corresponding to objects in the physical world. This theory is at fault for its formalism and for not taking into account human agency, a problem not dissimilar to the insufficiencies of the Prague School of linguistics, the formalism of De Saussure, or for that matter the digital logic of Lévi-Strauss. By contrast, and as a rejection of the essentialism of the label theory, the later Wittgenstein (1953, 1965) developed a theory of language games and forms of life whereby the physical and social world is composed of interrelated and potentially changing linguistic practices. The implications for science are quite interesting and significant in that for Wittgenstein the physical world and its material objects are a product of linguistic practice, and thus reject the schism between nature and nurture embraced by anthropology and the allied social sciences.[8]

If one considers that Winch's aforementioned book was published in the late 1950s, his appropriation of the later Wittgenstein was very innovative and has likewise proven to be influential in the social sciences. While the later Wittgenstein established a paradigm of linguistic practice, the specific connection of language to human agency and social interaction was not developed. Winch argued that just as we could understand words or concepts through their use in multiple language games so we could understand social interaction as a type of communicative practice. That is, the identity of what it is that people do as individuals and as members of a collectivity – group, village, town, nation – is based upon their shared, even tacit, assumptions that are communicatively embodied in a speech community. Winch's view of social action as communicative challenges both the essentialism and naturalism that can lead scholars to regard human action in lawlike terms, a common outcome of scientific practice.

As I discuss in chapter 3, Winch challenges Evans-Pritchard's assertion that Zande witches cannot be supported on empirical grounds. For Winch, empirical grounds are not a given but rather a consequence of linguistic and social practice, and so they are relative and must therefore be accounted for socially. Apart from the consequences for Evans-Pritchard's conclusions regarding Zande witchcraft, Winch's theory of social action as communicative practice establishes the basis for an anthropology or sociology of science. Empiricism, which is often taken as the bedrock of epistemology in the natural sciences and in significant areas of the social sciences, is regarded by Winch as relative to the intersubjective assumptions and methodological practices of natural science and therefore should not be taken as a universal – an Archimedean point from which to bring into question all that is particular. According to Winch, to understand Zande witchcraft we must come to grasp the assumptions and particular rationality that inform its practice. To dismiss the existence of Zande witches on empirical grounds is to commit a category mistake; that is, to apply assumptions or linguistic practices particular to western societies to societies where such assumptions are irrelevant or make no sense.

Some of Winch's adversaries in the rationality debates have argued that his theory of communicative practice presupposes that all human action is transparent. Winch's response to this charge invokes psychotherapy, healing through discourse, as a means of illuminating what is not transparent to actors in terms of their own actions and motivations. A therapist will assist a patient in working through blockages by reviewing with the patient the potential sources of problems sedimented symbolically in the past. The inequalities between therapist and patient aside, Winch maintains that the interpretations suggested by the therapist or patient must be mutually intelligible and make sense within the patient's actual and potential experience. Likewise, asserts Winch, an ethnographer must search for an interpretation of indigenous social practices that approximates informants' actual or potential experience. To Winch's credit, the informant's self-interpretations are taken seriously, a necessary precedent to recognizing the humanity of indigenous others.

Winch's appropriation of the later Wittgenstein as applied to a theory of communicative action has continuing importance for anthropology so long as the human past and present in its multiplicity remains the primary object domain. Although individual anthropologists may have preferences for other linguistically based social theories (e.g. Bourdieu, Foucault, Baudrillard, de Certeau), some of which I will take up later in this Introduction, Winch's work remains as a testimony to the enduring significance of language as practice to human agency and self-identity, as well as the relativity of rationality across cultures. Nevertheless, I continue to believe, as I argued in the original edition of this book, that Winch's theory is essentially contemplative of language games and communicative action because it does not question the historical, social and political-economic constraints under which individual and collectives engage each other in public space. It thus falls short of the reflexive potential that has long been a part of the critical practice of anthropology.

Friends and Foes

Winch's critique of Evans-Pritchard's assertion that the existence of Zande witches cannot be upheld on empirical grounds generated significant responses from both anthropologists and philosophers. What remains of interest to us here are the challenges that these responses pose both to the "linguistic turn" in social theory and to science and universal rationality as paradigmatic of human understanding in general. Many of the participants in the original rationality debates were critical of Winch's relativism and believed that "knowing" must rest on criteria which are verifiable, a condition that weighs heavily on the narrative and often anecdotal character of field research in sociocultural anthropology. Others, mostly in the minority, appreciated Winch's notion that rationality is a social construction but nonetheless upheld criteria of rationality that were not context-dependent, a key point of contention regarding science.

To his credit, I. C. Jarvie has done much to familiarize anthropologists with the work of philosopher Karl Popper, especially regarding science. The fact that Popper maintains, as does Jarvie, that the "truths" of science are tentative gives a complexity to his theorizing that is absent in many social scientists, who believe that the method and practice of science are foundational and therefore need not be questioned – positivism in its most vulgar form. In fact, following Popper, Jarvie argues against a naive empiricism – knowledge based on sense sensation – by asserting that theories are always informed by presuppositions that then must be subject to testing, or what Popper terms "falsification." Nevertheless, Jarvie, unlike Winch, upholds standards of objectivity grounded in the consensus of the research community. For Jarvie, empirically tested hypotheses are true because they correspond to a state of affairs in the world and thus, as by Evans-Pritchard, the existence of Zande witches can be refuted empirically.

Jarvie has also championed "methodological individualism," which places him at odds with many anthropologists trained in the Durkheimian tradition, especially the structural functionalism of British social anthropology.[9] According to methodological individualism, it is individuals and not institutions or collectivities that act. While (as I continue to believe) Jarvie has embraced as primordial an unexamined sense of self, he does at least entertain debate about the agency involved in social action in a manner that challenges reified visions of social institutions. What is missing is an appreciation of the social and historical contingencies through which the self is constituted.

While anthropologist Robin Horton does not counter Winch directly, his writings on indigenous modes of thought can be taken as a refutation of the sort of linguistic relativism supported by Winch and most theorists who champion the linguistic turn. Like Winch, Horton refutes Levy-Bruhl's contention that indigenous peoples are prelogical. However, quite unlike Winch, Horton argues that language socialization is preceded by preverbal schemata that are inborn and thus species-wide. Preverbal schemata include material object and causal concepts. The material object repertoire, in which there are ostensibly one hundred or so items, reproduces the label theory of language, with the exception that the label theory never regarded the relation between words and objects as primordial but rather as learned. The fact that causal concepts are inborn gives, for Horton, an unquestioned status to causal assertions as they relate to human behavior.

Horton, like Jarvie, borrows from Popper in arguing that societies are either open or closed. Open societies are capable of self-reflection and criticism while closed societies live by the determinations of tradition. For Horton, therefore, modern societies embrace the spirit of science and are able to bring their own beliefs and social practices into question, and thus are open. By contrast, the anomalies of beliefs and experience are never questioned in indigenous cultures, Zande oracles being exemplary, because of an absence of science and the predominance of tradition. Indigenous societies are thus closed. While perhaps not intending to, Horton's advancing of open and closed societies reproduces the Enlightenment bias against tradition as "anti-reason" and glosses over the fact that tradition itself is generally a product of invention, making a society's relation to tradition immensely more self-reflective than Horton allows.

Steven Lukes occupies an important position in the rationality debates in challenging Jarvie's methodological individualism. Following in the Durkheimian tradition where social facts are the predominant objects of social analysis, Lukes argues for the importance of social institutions as both limit and possibility of social action. According to Lukes, it is collective rather than individual life that is the foundation of social life, since one becomes an individual only through the mediation of family, tribe, nation or other institutions in their multiplicity. Moreover, according to Lukes, the emphasis on the individual in western society is recent and the product of historical factors associated with capitalism and the bourgeois state.

Lukes tends to support Winch in his assertion that there are culturally specific criteria of truth and rationality that one must invoke in order to understand, for example, Zande witchcraft or Nuer religious metaphors. However, Lukes distinguishes himself from Winch through arguing that culturally specific criteria of truth and rationality are ultimately tied to formal rules of truth and intelligibility that are shared by the human species.

According to Lukes, such formal rules, which are reminiscent of Lévi-Strauss's formalist rationality, are necessary in order for understanding between different cultures to be possible.

Lukes's position on universal criteria of truth and rationality is likely to resonate fairly widely with anthropologists who believe that the possibility of understanding the "other" depends on a cognitive faculty shared at some level. After all, no one really accepts the proposition that anthropologists and indigenous others live in radically separate worlds, even if such a potential was popularized throughout the 1970s through Carlos Castenada's books on the Yaqui shaman, Don Juan, or to some degree implied much earlier in the linguistic relativity of Sapir and Whorf. However, as I argued in the original edition of this book, understanding cultures is as much informed by the potential uses of language as it is through the conventional. That is, anthropologists and informants are always seeking common grounds of understanding through extending the horizons of their conceptual and linguistic practices, which is what we often refer to today as pushing the boundaries of discourse.

Alasdair MacIntyre's critique of Winch is similar to that of Lukes yet not entirely unsympathetic to Winch. Like Winch, MacIntyre maintains that criteria of truth and rationality are relative in that they have a history. Such a claim is very important to anthropology more generally since it creates the possibility of studying the history and culture of science; it thus counters the positivistic self-justification of science in scientific terms, and even pragmatic assertions that science should be the regnant epistemology because "it works".[10] However, like Lukes, MacIntyre contends that beliefs are propositions, collectively informed, about states of affairs in the world. The veracity of these beliefs can be judged ultimately by criteria that are extracontextual. Unlike Lukes, MacIntyre views extracontextual criteria as having a history but, from my point of view, one that is regretably evolutionary. The potential therefore to grasp truth and rationality historically is sacrificed ultimately by MacIntyre to the very assumptions that he originally brings into question.

The focus on Jarvie, Horton, Lukes, and MacIntyre is deliberate because they represent the predominant views on truth and rationality held in the social sciences. While my discussion is by no means exhaustive, and deliberately so, I have aimed to create a rhetorical tension between these four theorists that will establish the boundaries of the Anglo-American rationality debates in their historical version. The arguments against Winch and more generally ordinary language philosophy on the parts of Jarvie, Horton, Lukes, and MacIntyre, combined with my own belief that Winch lacks a perspective from which to bring language games into question, makes hermeneutics a potentially attractive alternative from which to defend the linguistic turn in social theory.

Hermeneutics Revisited

With little doubt, hermeneutics has played a seminal role in contemporary anthropological theory with virtually all ethnographers who incorporate discourse as a model for interpretation across cultures.[11] Hermeneutics occupies an important theoretical place in, for example Paul Rabinow's *Reflections on Fieldwork in Morocco* (1973) and Renato Rosaldo's *Culture and Truth* (1989), not to mention my own recent *Vintages and Traditions* (1996). Of the two hermeneutic philosophers discussed extensively in the first edition of this book, that is Hans-Georg Gadamer and Paul Ricoeur, it is Ricoeur who has been the most influential in anthropology. The reasons for Ricoeur's popularity have to do with a methodological emphasis that is absent in Gadamer and the fact that Ricoeur's voluminous writings, most of which are theoretically germane to the social sciences,[12] have been translated into English. Ricoeur's having held a joint appointment in France and the United States is perhaps another contributing factor. Nevertheless, in spite of being less known to anthropologists, Gadamer's insights into the general process of understanding continue to be of importance to all anthropologists and relevant to the general interpretive themes of the rationality debates. I will therefore discuss some of the reasons for Gadamer's continuing importance before turning to Ricoeur.

Gadamer provides a historical dimension to the linguistic turn which is absent in ordinary language philosophy as represented by the later Wittgenstein and Winch, and which resonates with recent trends in cultural theory. Gadamer argues, in a manner that suggests his Heideggerian training and the influence of Heidegger on contemporary hermeneutics, that "language is the being of man." Stated simply, for Gadamer, humanity is identified with a language community: to be human is to have a language; world and language are inseparable. This does not mean that Gadamer is insensitive to cultural differences nor does it indicate an indifference to the extraordinary number and variety of language communities. Rather, Gadamer's ideas on the centrality of language are fully conversant with the aforementioned tradition of grand theorizing that upholds the merits of speaking to the human condition in general. Moreover, Gadamer's emphasis is neither empirical speech events nor individual human agents, since he argues that our experience as social beings is necessarily prefigured by the language community of which we are a part. Our experience of self, other, and world is thus a product of the language we speak.

The connection between self, language, and world is for Gadamer profoundly historical in that he believes that tradition or past collective life as sedimented in language shapes and limits both actual and possible experience, what he calls effective historical consciousness. In this way he argues that "language speaks us"; our linguistically embodied past is consequential for the present as it becomes an emergent future. Tradition or collective life as sedimented in language becomes the historical and cultural horizon from which we or anthropologists engage the life-worlds of others. What we take to be ethnographic data or knowledge belongs neither to the anthropologist nor indigenous informants, but is a synthesis of their respective cultural horizons.

Regarding knowledge as a synthesis of cultural horizons is important to Gadamer's critique and ultimate rejection of method as the determining ethos of truth in the natural sciences and empirically based social sciences. For Gadamer, all knowledge is contingent, thus opening science to social and cultural elaboration. Although scientists, especially in the positivistic genre (the commitment to science's justification of itself scientifically), may believe that reproducible methods assure objectivity, Gadamer's version of hermeneutics shows that knowledge production in general is informed by cultural tradition as embodied in the intersubjectivity of language and thus cultural tradition shapes our horizon of expectations and possible experience.[13] For Gadamer, knowing is pre-judging, and consequently having a bias is precisely what allows us to know anything about either the natural or social worlds. Gadamer's hermeneutics gives theoretical support, therefore, to the historical and enduring importance of culture broadly conceived as the central integrative feature of anthropology.

Ricoeur's hermeneutics takes us in a somewhat different direction but nonetheless with an importance equal to that of Gadamer. As mentioned above, Ricoeur has a methodological emphasis that is absent in Gadamer's work. However, this is not the sort of methodological rigor that serves its own instrumental ends, for which Gadamer is critical of science, but rather a method that is employed in the interest of exploring the symbolic density of social life. Ricoeur (1971) distinguished himself early on through arguing that social life is symbolic and thus social action is like a text in that it contains the objectified meanings of social actors. The project of an interpretive theory was thus to decipher the sedimented meanings in a manner analogous to how an audience deciphers the meaning of a text.

Ricoeur's analogy between text and action is very important to anthropology because it allows us to distinguish between intentions and meanings. Questions related to intention, in spite of the warnings of Clifford Geertz (1973) – himself indebted to Ricoeur – often lead the investigator to probe the states of mind or intentions of authors, informants, or the agents of social action. As we should know by now, it is a specious assumption that we can ever get inside the heads of others to know what they thought when they created this or that object or performed a particular ritual or social action. However, pursuing the interpretation of meaning is another project altogether.

I will avoid the details of Ricoeur's theory here as they are elaborated in chapter 6. Essentially, Ricoeur argues that since texts are an object of public consumption the meanings they take on for the audiences to which they are directed are independent of the author's intentions. For Ricoeur, this assertion about the public nature of meaning, and symbols as conveyers of meaning, is applicable to all human products – art, literature, artifacts – and by extension to human action itself, hence the above analogy with text. The objective becomes therefore how we make sense of public meaning rather than subjective intentions. Ricoeur appeals to the formalism of structuralism and an early phenomenology in arguing that we bracket the outside references of the text in order to explore its inner relations. Whether we agree with the method or not (I was very critical of the method in the first edition of this book), the general idea that we look to public meanings to explore the opacity of social life remains a significant challenge for all of the human sciences.

In spite of significant merits, the hermeneutics of Gadamer and Ricoeur continue to be, in my view, insufficient to the critical potentials of anthropology. The notion of tradition, even in the version of effective historical consciousness, employed by Gadamer does not take into consideration that culture is often a contested arena. Moreover, if we are to make use of the concept of a language community, it is important to recognize that within and between language communities human agents are positioned in discourse differentially, a recognition that leads to both a politics of language and politics of culture. If anthropology as a discipline is to realize the critical potentials of embracing cultural diversity, anthropologists must be engaged with issues of local and global inequality and the construction of differentiated public arenas.

Ricoeur replicates to some degree the shortcomings of Gadamer's hermeneutics, especially in the formalism of his textual analogy. Again, as with culture, the constitution and interpretation of social meanings as embodied symbolically is subject to dispute. While Ricoeur is attentive to the multivocality of symbols, he does not raise the issue of power other than to advance a vision of symbols as practically effective in the public domain. Because Ricoeur, like Gadamer, is not concerned with concrete human agents, he does not address the differential position of human agents as they engage each other in history-making, perhaps yet further evidence that inert texts do not fully capture, even metaphorically speaking, the dynamism of social processes. For this reason, I turned to the Marxist tradition in hopes of establishing a more developed sense of differentiated human agency.

Marxism and Critical Theory Revisited

At the time that the first edition of this book was published in the early 1980s, Marxism or political economy occupied a significant place within anthropology and the social and human sciences more widely. Apart from its long-standing reputation for addressing questions of inequality anchored in work or labor, Marxism also appeared to articulate well with transformations in the world economy that followed the Second World War. Marxism seemed especially well equipped theoretically to explain globalization and the structural inequalities between developing nations and nations that were asserting their dominion as centers of finance capital. Today, much of this has changed and political economy in particular no longer appears to dominate research directed at the production and reproduction of inequalities. While this in part may result from the demise of the Soviet Union and the impression on the part of some scholars that capitalism has triumphed over socialism – a dubious assertion by any account[14] – I believe that there are reasons internal to Marxist theory itself that explain the loss of some of its luster.

As noted above, Marxist scholars, especially orthodox Marxists committed to political economy, have long pursued the critique of capitalism and social inequality through analyzing the process through which social labor is appropriated, a point of view which makes labor the principal formative and transformative process of the human species. This perspective, for example, underlies Eric Wolf's (1999) evaluation of power among the Kwakiutl, the Aztecs, and in National Socialist Germany, in spite of the fact that he has acknowledged the importance of culture as a medium of social control.[15] The Marxist emphasis on labor is both a measurable strength as well as a noteworthy weakness, especially when represented in terms of grand theory. There is little doubt that we can learn much historically about class formation and the structural inequalities of national and regional economies from a Marxist perspective, addressing as it does the distribution and allocation of social labor; we can do so especially in a contemporary context, where the primary interest is commodities and their circulation. However, the emphasis on social labor across times and cultures glosses over the mutual recognition and concerns of the public sphere, inclusive of contested culture, and thus advances a vision of the human condition as essentially informed by instrumental rationality. As I argue throughout this book, it is impossible to raise questions which are self-reflexive from an instrumental framework, that is, the types of questions that lead us to uncover the assumptions which inform knowledge claims. Moreover, an instrumental framework potentially overlooks the subliminal involvement of power in everyday experience or the life-world and ultimately regards cultural processes as derivative of social labor. It thus misses the generative potential of culture, including the cultural prefiguration of experience and social inequality.

The above critique of orthodox Marxism is not just applicable to the orthodoxy of political economy but also remains germane to the critique of structural Marxism represented in the first edition of this book. While Althusser may no longer be read with the eagerness that was typical of his reception in the 1970s and early 1980s, his work is of interest as much for what it overlooked as the theoretical argument it advanced. Althusser's work generated significant interest because it raised the perennial issue in Marxism of the relation between base and superstructure. Marxist ortho-doxy generally regarded culture or ideology, as noted above, as determined by the social relations of production, a conclusion that struck many social theorists, myself included, as too facile and reductive. Althusser, on the other hand, assigned a relative autonomy to culture by arguing that the economy was determinant in the "last instance," a conclusion that was appealing to some but still suggested to many others that the "base" ultim-ately structured cultural options or lived experience. In my view, Althusser's Marxism shares the general problem of structuralism in not being suffi-ciently attentive to human agency, a problem that renders the "last instance" unsuitable as a resolution to the question of how to reconcile political economy and culture. Without a notion of social agency as constitutive, culture becomes little more than labor's shadow.

The issue of social agency with respect to all the structural Marxists discussed in the first edition – Hindess and Hirst, Godelier, Terray, and Meillassoux – remains paramount, the lack of this concept is the main shortcoming of each of their theoretical positions. Hindess and Hirst are somewhat interesting in this regard because they argue in favor of "reality" as a product of theoretical discourse. While the incorporation of discourse is laudable as a critical alternative to naive empiricism, they fail to relate discourse to positioned actors, thus undermining the possibility of raising reflexive questions about the human interests that inform theory. Moreover, an absence of concrete reference to human agency as constitutive leaves Hindess and Hirst unable to address historical processes associated with a socially differentiated human arena in that human actors merely serve the ends of theoretical abstractions.

With Meillassoux, Terray, and Godelier, we encounter the ever-important issue of the applicability of modes of production analysis to indigenous societies. Generally, the French Marxist anthropologists have accepted the universality of modes of production analysis, with some fine-tuning to account for the central integrative role of kinship in indigenous societies. However, as Sahlins (1976) among others has argued, mode of production analysis is profoundly tied to a Marxist argument for the self-production of the species through the instrumentality of labor, thus glossing over the symbolic exchange of culture. Stated otherwise, mode of production analy-sis risks an economistic interpretation that is foreign to practice in indigen-ous cultures. Because he has taken on the theme of rationality directly, Godelier (1972) has participated less in this structuralist Marxist tendency.

In the first edition of this book, I turned largely to E. P. Thompson, Raymond Williams, and Jürgen Habermas to advance the cause of integrating political economy and cultural theory towards the end of a critical communicative theory. At the time, I thought it important to preserve the emphasis in political economy on history and economic constraints to human action – that is, the constraints ensuing from exploitation and the expropriation of social labor – while also turning to broader hegemonic themes that are produced and reproduced through culture. From E. P. Thompson, I was able to draw theoretically on a vision of historical process where human agents are not simply victims, moved totally by forces beyond their control, but rather, are engaged in the making and transforming of their quotidian lives. Such a view is not only important to understanding the multiple pathways and agencies of oppression, but it also draws our attention to resistance as a cultural practice.

Raymond Williams emphasizes cultural production in a manner that incorporates symbolism and the intersubjectivity of language as material process. Like Thompson, Williams is a scholar who is cited extensively in anthropology, the wide interest he arouses is surely due to his emphasis on material culture. Furthermore, unlike many theorists who regard language and symbolism as a largely mental or ideational process, Williams believes that language and culture are forms of material social interaction. In what amounts to a culturally informed Marxism – what is often referred to as neo-Marxism[16] – Williams goes further than many contributors to the "linguistic turn" in social theory by suggesting through his concept of "selective tradition" that interlocutors engage each other from differentiated social positions, thus opening culture to considerations of dispute and domination.

Thompson and Williams continue to be of importance to anthropology because they provide theoretical insights to what Sidney Mintz (1996) has called the "anthropology of everyday life." Both theorists emphasize the degree to which human agents are involved in the making of their social worlds and how the past operates effectively as both limit and possibility. Moreover, both Thompson and Williams are attentive to the traditional concerns of political economy in exploitation locally and beyond, while advancing a theory of culture that is nuanced and differentiated. In my view this is a real alternative to Tylor's complex whole and to the tendency of semiotics and interpretive anthropology to be removed from concrete material practice.

The influence that Jürgen Habermas has had on anthropology has been limited, for defensible reasons. There is little doubt that Habermas's project of creating a communicative theory of society with practical intent has much to contribute to anthropology, in spite of ethnographers who remain suspicious or generally critical of Habermas's commitment to "grand theory" and what he calls the unrealized critical potentials of modernism. Nevertheless, for anyone interested in the traditional concerns of the Anglo-American rationality debates in cross-cultural interpretation and the critique of positivistic science, Habermas has much to offer. Moreover, apart from Hannah Arendt, there are few theorists who equal Habermas's understanding of the implications of technology, science, and instrumental rationality for public policy, the politics of the public sphere and even for the meaning of individual and collective experience. With respect to the rationality debates, Habermas links rationality as differentiated to knowledge-constitutive interests. Instrumental rationality constitutes its objects of knowledge towards the end of technical control, while communicative rationality establishes a framework of knowing where mutual recognition and mutual understanding are predominant. Finally, critical rationality informs the self-reflexive potentials of knowing and orients human subjects towards the world with an interest in challenging exploitation and domination, an interest cultivated by the Enlightenment but, according to Habermas, still unrealized in contemporary society. In short, the comprehensiveness and critical nature of Habermas's theory provides for anthropology as a whole a number of theoretical options. They range from illustrating the contingency of knowledge to emphasizing the political and cultural consequences for contemporary life of the dominion of science and instrumental rationality. Moreover, his critique of domination is directed to critical theories as well, which he believes, like political economy, to be informed by instrumental rationality.

The major shortcoming of Habermas's grand theory is its reliance on cognitive or developmental psychology, on Lawrence Kohlberg to be precise,[17] to justify from an evolutionary perspective the reputed critical potentials of Enlightenment rationality. Like all evolutionary perspectives, Habermas's invoking of developmental sequences risks treating contemporary indigenous cultures in particular as timeless images of a distant human past, what Johannes Fabian (1983) has called the "denial of coevalness." That is, because Habermas's theory implies that indigenous cultures are representative of an earlier stage of cognition and thus rational development than societies that have embraced the Anglo-French Enlightenment, indigenous cultures are consequently regarded as non-contemporaneous. Such a theoretical move as Habermas's would, ironically, reproduce the very eclipsing of the public domain to which Habermas has directed his critique of instrumental reason. For this reason, some scholars may prefer Michel Foucault to Habermas as a source for critical theory, especially since Foucault's theory takes a subversive stand against Enlightenment rationality.

Although Foucault is referred to in the first edition of this book, it might strike some readers as curious that his theoretical corpus did not occupy a larger part, bearing in mind my own criticisms of positivistic social science and instrumental rationality. Surely Foucault's emphasis on discourse and the "disciplinary gaze" bears some resemblance to a communicative theory of social action? However, the decision to favor Habermas over Foucault in *Understanding Cultures* has less to do with shortcomings in Foucault and more with the foci of Habermas's critiques. Although Foucault's writings have ranged widely over topics from the medicalization of society to sexuality with great acuity and originality, apart from *The Order of Things*, his theoretical corpus is not as specifically directed as is Habermas's to the themes and issues embodied in and ensuing from the rationality debates. On the other hand, Habermas has long sought to establish the prerequisite conditions of human self-formation by outlining the normative bases of truth and mutual understanding through ordinary language. The ontological breadth of his theoretical project has led Habermas to confront both the hegemonic claims of positive science and the limitations of critical theory, including political economy. Moreover, Habermas (1976) has taken on directly the issue of rationality through his challenge to Popper and his followers, and has outlined clearly the limitations of structuralism for its lack of attention to praxis.[18] Habermas thus addresses many of the issues covered in the rationality debates and his theory of communicative action accords with my own efforts to synthesize political economy and cultural theory.

As for Foucault, I believe that his theory of discourse has some of the same insufficiencies as Gadamer's ontological vision of language. As a challenge to epistemology, and I may add a credible one, Foucault argues that the notion of the subject and humanity itself is a recent product of discourse. Such an assertion as this decenters the individual as the foundation of epistemology, an assertion that is commensurate with Agnes Heller's (1981) historicization of individuality and MacPherson's (1962) critique of Hobbes. However, by decentering the individual and by extension humanity itself, Foucault abandons human agency as constitutive. After all, to whom do we attribute the formation of discourses even if Foucault, following Nietzsche, argues for the problematic nature of origins? Moreover, with little or no reference to human agency as constitutive then the door is open to Foucault to gloss over the internal tensions and contested discourses that emerge from concrete social actors and their differential positions within the public arena, both local and global.

The other issue which Foucault raises with brilliance but not without problems is the ubiquity of power. I can hardly think of another scholar who has taught us more about the subtleties and discursive nature of power than Foucault has. It is very easy to ignore, for example, how regulations regarding the sale of food, the burial of the dead, or the organization of social space in the hospital are related to both the increased disciplinary power of medicine and the ability of the modern state to shape individual experience and practice. Foucault's emphasis on power is, therefore not only attuned to the negative consequences of social control but also to the positive potentials to create new conditions and life possibilities. We have clearly learned from Foucault to look for power in often ignored social spaces and public practices in a manner that is likely to influence scholarship for generations to come. However, Foucault's contention that power is ubiquitous does not go far enough in distinguishing politically, as Arendt (1958) has argued more generally, between the "power over" and the "power to." The latter refers to power as social control while the former involves the political capacity of human subjects to engage each other in the formation and shaping of the public sphere, even if public and private have been used – and they are not by Arendt – to obfuscate domestic labor and the "power" of women.

The above critique of Foucault is not meant as a dismissal, since his theoretical importance to contemporary anthropology and the human sciences is indisputable. Nevertheless, as with Habermas, it is important to acknowledge the limitations as well as the considerable merits. The tension perhaps between the "grand theory" of Habermas and the subversive discourses of Foucault, may suggest yet another alternative in Pierre Bourdieu (1977, 1984), although the potential theoretical options and favorites are far too numerous to review here. With Bourdieu, as with Habermas and Foucault, the emphasis is on a communicative understanding of social action. However, Bourdieu steers clear of assumptions of universal notions of rationality and avoids the potential problems associated with self-determining discourses. In fact, Bourdieu appeals to the very tradition of praxis that is so central to political economy and Marxism more generally, but puts a specific emphasis on culture, which is embodied in his notion of "habitus." With "habitus," Bourdieu has in mind the structured practices and dispositions defined subjectively and objectively that are representative of human subjects participating in fields of social action. The emphasis in Bourdieu is thus on human agency self-defining and defined. Moreover, Bourdieu maintains that human subjects participate in different fields of action which are governed by different logics, an assertion that refines the generality of action by accounting concretely for the differentiation of human actors themselves. With Bourdieu, fields of action governed by different logics challenge reified visions of culture and language by appealing to human agents located differentially in social space.

Bourdieu is also attentive to the multivocality of power, especially the symbolism of power as suggested through his concept of "cultural capital" (1984). By this, Bourdieu means acquired resources that serve symbolically and practically to secure privileges, economic or otherwise, within different fields of action and power. I found, for example, Bourdieu's concept of cultural capital especially useful (Ulin 1996) in discussing ethnographically the particular economic advantages of Bordeaux wine on the basis of a historically constructed and culturally mediated winegrowing hierarchy, a hierarchy that simply could not be grasped solely in economic terms. Thus with Bourdieu, we have a theoretical alternative, only partly explicated here, to the homogeneous concept of culture and glossing of power represented in the rationality debates, an alternative that could advance the synthesis of political economy and cultural theory in a manner attentive to concrete human agency. However, while Bourdieu's theory offers much to anthropologists interested in the localization and differentiation of power as manifested through cultural praxis and informed historically, he does not appear to address with the same vigor the larger questions of globalization and cultural diasporas, which have captured the attention of contemporary anthropology.

New Directions

Apart from this Introduction, this new edition of *Understanding Cultures* contains chapters entitled "Modernism and Postmodernism" and "Bounded Selves – Bounded Cultures," which were not present in the original. The intention of authoring a new edition is to make the rationality debates conversant with theoretical issues such as representation, ethnographic authority, cultural diaspora, and globalism that have emerged in the late 1980s and throughout the 1990s while also arguing for the continuing relevance of theories advanced by Winch, his adversaries, contemporary hermeneutics, political economy and cultural theory. This is an undertaking that follows from the encouragement of numerous colleagues who appreciated the breadth and depth of the original work but thought the original terrain could be expanded to incorporate new developments in social theory and more recent concerns in anthropology.

Since the publication of *Understanding Cultures* in 1984, there has been much debate in anthropology and social theory more generally regarding the ostensibly hegemonic implications of Enlightenment rationality and the aforementioned "grand theory," theory that addresses the human condition comprehensively, that the Enlightenment informs. Chapter 8, which is new to this volume, takes up the theme of grand narratives and the challenge that is presently posed by postmodernism, including its anthropological advocates. While not a self-identified postmodernist, Edward Said's *Orientalism* (1979) is a good example of an influential work that challenges grand narratives, even critical ones such as those developed by Marx, by showing the subaltern status of the multiplicity of eastern cultures when they are represented ideologically as homogeneous. Even more direct is the challenge to Enlightenment rationality and grand theory advanced through Jean-

François Lyotard's *The Postmodern Condition* (1984), a book that has been very influential in sociocultural anthropology. Lyotard believes that new technologies and specialized discourses have rendered superfluous foundational theories and universal criteria of truth, both of which he regards as the logocentric pretense of the Enlightenment. In the place of grand theory, Lyotard supports relative and local discourses, pastiche, and collage which are subversive of reason and the authority of grand narratives.

Jürgen Habermas (1981, 1984) has been foremost in defending grand narratives and challenging Lyotard's postmodernism. His communicative theory of society seeks to identify universal conditions which are presupposed in communicative action and which mark the reciprocal process by which competing knowledge claims are advanced and mutual understanding or consensus achieved (Bernstein 1983). Like Marx, Habermas's theory, or more exactly metatheory, reconstructs the process of human self-formation and thus allies itself with the Enlightenment interest in progressive transparency of the human condition and liberation. Against Lyotard's relativist and fragmented discourse, Habermas's reconstructive metatheory links the possibility of emancipation and the critical review of knowledge claims to practical action viewed from the idea of communication free from domination.

While there is no doubt a subversive interest in Lyotard's postmodern theory,[19] he appears to accept fragmentation and relative discourses at face value and does not therefore question how fragmentation is produced. From Habermas's perspective, fragmentation ensues from the context of advanced capitalism and the predominance of technical rationality and thus cannot assume the autonomy and removal from historical process that Lyotard's postmodernism suggests. Nevertheless, the emphasis on relative and fragmented discourses has been embraced by some contributors to the influential and challenging Clifford and Marcus volume, *Writing Culture* (1986), especially Clifford and Marcus themselves.

Writing Culture focuses significantly on ethnographic authority and writing, and the more general process of ethnographic representation. In most conventional ethnographies of the past, it was ethnographic realism that predominated – the having been there – and which established the authority of the text. We learn about indigenous others largely through what the ethnographer tells us as a self-appointed, and generally unquestioned, spokesperson for informants. However, as Hayden White (1978) has argued, and James Clifford more recently (1988), the authority of a text and its reputed claims to veracity are rhetorically constructed and so exploring the rhetorical construction of ethnographic texts is imperative. In fact, as Clifford and Marcus point out, and Clifford more exhaustively in his *The Predicament of Culture*, the rhetorical construction of texts invested in the authority of the ethnographer has much to do with the subaltern status of the informants represented. One potential but by no means ultimate solution to this problem is to foreground informants' voices, a strategy that is pursued by nearly all contemporary ethnographies.

Much of what Clifford and Marcus say about the classic ethnographies and the need to pursue new strategies of ethnographic writing is commendable. There are, I believe, significant gains from foregrounding informants' voices: the vividness of the accounts and the emergence of a multiplicity of differentially located voices, even if ultimately ethnographic authority is still vested in the author.[20] For this to be otherwise, indigenous cultures would have to author their own accounts or at the very least have a larger collaborative role, a role that is generally not available as a consequence of structural inequalities and of the way research has been traditionally defined. Moreover, the subaltern position of indigenous cultures is not likely to be changed through alternative strategies of representation without taking into account the structuring of the global economy, perhaps the very sort of ethnographic strategy that is rejected by Clifford and Marcus in their support for pastiche, collage, and local narratives.

The questions raised through ethnographic representation, new strategies of writing, and the challenge to grand narratives never entered into the original rationality debates; however, I believe that they are a logical extension of the general themes of rationality and cross-cultural interpretation upon which the debates focus. For example, to make grasping what others do problematic rather than assuming that human actions are transparent or amenable to universal laws raises the issues of both interpretation and representation. Struggling with what it is that informants convey and mean is an exercise in prefiguring their intentions and meanings, albeit not always consciously as directed to the potential audiences of ethnographic writing. Winch suggests indirectly the concerns of representation when he argues that "we" must extend our language games to understand those of our indigenous informants, implying that the "we" incorporates language games that the anthropologist shares with the general audience to whom ethnography is directed. Moreover, Winch's argument that rationality is particular to language communities contrasts with the majority of his adversaries, who support an empiricist epistemology of science; it reproduces in part the current dispute between the local narratives of postmodernism and the grand narratives of the Enlightenment tradition.

While the rationality debates touch upon and surely suggest current interpretive and representational issues, none of the original participants address broader contemporary concerns of globalism and cultural diasporas in that the epistemological framework of the debates is one that largely resonates with an earlier tradition of anthropology where "bounded cultures" and "bounded selves" were predominant.[21] Consequently, in revising *Understanding Cultures* I add a new concluding chapter in which I address the theoretical and methodological limitations of the prevailing image of the lone anthropologist who works as part muse and part scientist within culturally circumscribed spaces.

Winch's theory of language games maintains that cross-cultural interpretation should proceed from exploring the internal logic and meanings of defined speech communities. This assumes that the life-worlds of anthropologist and informants may be incommensurable. To the contrary, Winch's adversaries have generally argued that cultural differences can be subsumed under a common set of assumptions and principles shared by the human species and hence they tend to privilege the natural sciences as paradigmatic for cross-cultural interpretation. Although the theoretical conclusions and methodological assumptions are quite different, both Winch and his critics, from Jarvie to MacIntyre, maintain a vision of cultural difference that reinforces the homogeneity of culture and the general epistemological assumptions of a "knowing subject" and "known object," even though for Winch the "known object" approximates a "co-subject." The rationality debates do not prepare us, therefore, to address culture as differentiated and contested nor do they takes us very far in addressing globalism and post-colonial diasporas from which most of the most interesting and challenging questions to contemporary scholarship emerge.

Globalism and global theories draw our attention to the politics and power of interregional and international economic relations as historically composed and to the restructuring of capitalist economies following the World War II. This is the broader context to which anthropologists generally refer in trying to understand how cultures on the local level are affected by and respond to outside forces, a context that was generally ignored in village studies that predominated in the pre-and post-World War II years. Today, it is generally accepted in anthropology that in order to grasp local dynamics the ethnographer must look to the articulation of social practice on the local level with regional and global processes, without overlooking the capacity of individuals to influence political, economic, and cultural dynamics at the state level and beyond.[22] Moreover, it is generally believed that structured inequalities and continuing structural transformations of the global political economy adversely affect subaltern local populations and thus lead to the cultural diasporas of migratory labor and immigration to core areas of the global economy.

I maintain, however, that globalism and even world systems theory is not adequate to the task of grasping the complexity of cultural diasporas and the multiplicity of mediated identities both within and between nation states. In fact, globalism as a concept has been ideologically appropriated by multinational corporations and the nation state to legitimate the universalization of technology, science, and capitalist social relations. World systems theory, on the other hand, while attentive to the broader dynamics of political economy, disregards local-level social processes and the potential of local actors to shape and direct their destinies, an oversight that precludes a substantive understanding of local resistance. Short of a transformation in political praxis, what is required to grasp the density of cultural diaspora and diverse identities locally and beyond is, as I argue in the concluding chapter, an interpretive framework whose orientation is "multi-sited".[23] Multi-sited analysis includes, as George Marcus (1998) asserts, not only a multiplicity of distinct field sites but also research conducted with many distinct constituencies within a single geographical region, a theoretical and methodological move designed to address discordant narratives.

As with the foregrounding of informants' voices in ethnographic writing, which gained ascendancy in the 1980s, multi-sited research is becoming increasingly common because the pressing historical and contemporary questions – borders, identities, and cultural diasporas in particular – which inform research demand an approach that is sensitive to a multiplicity of cultural articulations. However, while multi-sited research may address many of the problems associated with bounded culture, it does not necessarily take on the "boundedness" of the ethnographer. This, I believe, is a long-standing problem of western society that likely has its origins in Renaissance culture and society (see Agnes Heller 1981) and, as Georg Lukács (1972) has argued, is associated with the eclipsing of community on the part of an incipient rural capitalism.

Addressing the problems of the "bounded self" in anthropology is likely as formidable a task as challenging the concept of "bounded culture," perhaps even more so. Unlike the natural sciences where collaborative research is the norm, anthropologists generally undertake research alone and likewise tend to publish their research as sole authors.[24] Moreover, young anthropologists are for the most part left on their own to conduct their first field research and even if some collaboration should be involved, as rarely happens, the dissertation is assumed to have one author and is even burdened with the expectation of originality. My point is not that anthropologists working alone cannot carry out very interesting and important research and then convey this research with insight and brilliance. Rather, I maintain that the demands of important research questions necessitate collaborative work and within a field context that is multi-sited. While I take pride in my own field research with cooperative winegrowers in south-west France (see Ulin 1996), I have no problem recognizing the considerable benefits that would have ensued from collaborative work. The terrain covered in that work is immense and the depth of analysis would have been improved by working with others.[25]

To conclude, the addition of a new final chapter on bounded cultures and bounded selves illustrates how inadequate the strict epistemological framework of the original rationality debates is in addressing the current issues of globalization and cultural diasporas, which result from political and economic transformations in the world. To raise questions today about understanding the "other" necessitates engaging the shifting grounds of cultural identity from a multiplicity of geographical and spatial frameworks. One must also take on the challenge presented through a view of culture as disputed or contested. The new parameters of anthropological inquiry that accommodate "peoples on the move" should not be regarded as conclusive nor should they be seen as an antidote to the fragmentation of the discipline. I continue to believe – and here I betray again my intellectual commitment to grand theory – that there is a relationship between cultural diasporas, globalism, and the fragmentation that challenges the unity of all contemporary professions. If I am correct in the premonition, then we need to look to political praxis rather than exclusively to intellectual praxis for indications as to how to link the power of "knowing" to social justice on a global scale. Short of such a demanding and monumental task that far exceeds any individual effort, the new edition of this book is offered, as was the original, hopefully, as a provocative contribution to an ongoing interdisciplinary conversation on cross-cultural interpretation and as a testimony to the important and enduring theoretical concerns that are raised through the rationality debates.

2 Anthropological Ancestors and Interpretation Theory: Boas, Malinowski, and Evans-Pritchard

The rationality debates have been until recently an exclusively English phenomenon. They have grown primarily out of internal issues raised in the analytical philosophy of science. The debates focus on the theories and methods involved in understanding and explaining human societies. The uniqueness of the debates stems from the linguistic turn in social theory as adumbrated in the writings of the later Wittgenstein. We shall see, however, that while the linguistic turn may give a new angle to reflections on rationality, the problems and issues raised were addressed by the ancestors of the anthropological tradition. In this chapter, therefore, I will show how the epistemological problems related to understanding other cultures have precedents in early anthropological theory. In order to bring the rationality debates into a fully Anglo-American and anthropological arena, I will focus my analysis on the epistemology of Boas, Malinowski, and Evans-Pritchard, although many other ancestors would have been equally suitable. I have also included a section on the epistemology of the politics of functionalist fieldwork, peripheral as it seems to the formal debates, because so much of early anthropological theory was formulated to meet the demands of colonial administration.

Boas

Franz Boas is indisputably the principal figure in the shaping of early American anthropology. Apart from Lewis Henry Morgan's (1972b) important work on the Iroquois, the first fully systematic fieldwork in the American tradition was carried out by Boas in Baffin Land among the Central Eskimo in the latter part of the nineteenth century. His fieldwork was significant in that it established the tradition of participant observation as an essential constituent of American anthropology. He taught his students and demonstrated to the nascent anthropological community that the means of studying non-western societies lay in participating in the social round of their customs and language; and he frequently spent from one to two years in residence. Furthermore, he integrated the methods of archaeology, linguistics, and physical and cultural anthropology in his studies of human societies, thereby distinguishing American anthropology by the four-field approach. George Stocking (1968: 199) has also argued that although Boas did not specifically develop a culture concept, he was a major force in overcoming the humanist notion of one culture as the progressive accumulation of scientific and aesthetic knowledge. He was among the first anthropologists to challenge this Eurocentric concept by arguing that human society is marked by a plurality of distinct cultures or traditions. In short, Boas contributed to anthropology both a method that is a hybrid of natural science and history and the concept of an object domain characterized by each society having its own unique culture and tradition. As monumental as this is in defining how anthropology as an organized method constitutes its objects of knowledge, it does not fully exhaust Boas's contribution to anthropology in particular and American society in general.

Boas's anthropology exemplifies the integration of professional and public life. His stance, for example, against nineteenth-century unilineal evolutionism within anthropological theory was paralleled by his opposition to racism and other social inequities within American society. He rejected the nineteenth-century evolutionary view of progress, which regarded existing native societies, on the one hand, as living representations of the dawn of humanity, and modern western civilization, on the other hand, as the quintessence of human development. The nineteenth-century evolutionary perspective, furthermore, was responsible for both the periodicity of museum classification and the specious rationalist assumption that similar cultural phenomena owed their generation to a uniform process of independent invention.

His opposition to the evolutionist notion of independent invention, however, did not ally him with the German diffusionist school of Father Wilhelm Schmidt. Boas's own views are distinguished from those of both the advocates of independent invention and the German diffusionists, in that he argued that similar cultural phenomena can be the outcome of diverse and extremely complex historical processes. He accused the diffusionists of reifying cultural traits by abstracting them from their concrete historical and cultural contexts. Once the traits had been thus abstracted, they could then be classified and compared according to the logical principles of untenable world-historical schemas. While also believing that cultural phenomena could be transmitted through diffusion, Boas always considered how the transmitted traits would be interpreted and contextualized in the cultural configuration of the receiving culture. He always emphasized, therefore, the importance of integrated cultural wholes over disconnected traits or complexes of traits, thereby exhibiting an interest in how, against a cultural, historical, and psychological background, the human subject would perceive and contextualize cultural traits. His critique of nineteenth-century evolutionary theory and the logical abstractions of the German diffusionist school was a primary force in restoring at the level of theory the integrity and value of diverse native cultures and traditions.

Boas opposed the social policies that were in part shaped by nineteenth-century evolutionary thought and social Darwinism. He extended his critique of evolutionary theory to encompass the racist attitudes and social inequalities of late nineteenth-and early twentieth-century American society. Nineteenth-century evolutionary thought served the interests of racism and social inequality – not to mention its primary role as the ideology of imperialism – by shattering the Enlightenment concept of humanitas. The nineteenth century introduced for the first time the notion that each race had its own separate history. Boas, using the methods of the four-field approach which he had helped to develop, demonstrated convincingly that there was no inherent relation between race, language, and culture and therefore no inferior races, languages, or cultures. His critical voice was a major factor not only in fighting unjust social policies but also in correcting the unilineal evolutionary perspective with its erroneous view of indigenous societies.

Boas shaped early American anthropology into a social praxis by endeavoring to make this new mode of inquiry responsive to important political and social issues whose historical antecedents had been responsible for the emergence of modern anthropology. Boasian anthropology, therefore, always maintained a critical emphasis. While his anthropology was critical, however, it was not dialectical or reflexive, as its epistemological foundation was too heavily tainted by a concept of psychological law and the methods of the natural sciences. Since it is the purpose of the rationality debates to explore epistemological issues in understanding human societies, I will limit my critical comments to what I consider to be Boas's epistemological faults. My critique, however, will not vitiate the overall critical intent of the Boasian tradition in anthropology.

While Boas's prolific publications cover a wide range of topics, it is his earlier writings which most clearly reflect his interest in the epistemological issues and questions that arise through anthropological praxis. His doctoral dissertation on the colors of seawater, for example, exhibits in this very early period his integration of natural and social science. He had become interested in the relation between the colors of seawater on the spectral scale and the human subject's perception of colors. The conclusions that he drew in his doctoral thesis constitute an implicit critique of naive empiricism in that he suspected that the cultural background of the human subject was an irreducible ingredient in the perception of colors. Boas's students had reported, furthermore, that one of his most salient reasons for doing fieldwork among the Central Eskimo was to attempt to verify his thesis on the cultural determinants of perception (Stocking 1968: 136).

Boas's essay "On Alternating Sounds" (1889: 47–53) was his first mature attempt to consolidate his critique of naive empiricism and the importance of culture in shaping perceptions. His apparent concern in this famous article, while the implications are more profound, is to elaborate what one experiences when one hears a new sound. The hearing of new or unfamiliar linguistic sounds is a situation with which the fieldworker is continually confronted. According to Boas, human subjects will classify a new sound in relation to the already known sounds of their language. This implies that a new sound is never given through a direct perception, as an unmediated presence, but, to the contrary, through what Boas refers to as an apperception. All mistakes, therefore, in the hearing of a new sound are attributable to wrong apperception. This means that a new consonant or vowel sound does not actually fluctuate or alternate but rather is subject to changing apperceptions on the part of the investigator who attempts to relate this new sound to what is familiar.

The implications of Boas's comments on the apperception of sounds can be transferred from the medium of language to cultural phenomena. Cultural phenomena, like linguistic phenomena, are not subject to direct and immediate experience but are also mediated through an apperceptive process. Stocking comments that according to this theory, cultural phenomena are conceived in terms of the "imposition of conventional meaning on the flux of experience" (1968: 159). This clearly demonstrates the nature of Boas's antagonism to Hume's theory of knowledge, which is based on the immediacy of sense perceptions, in contending that all sense perceptions are historically conditioned and transmitted by the learning process. It is this historically and culturally conditioned process that determines, for Boas, our very perceptions of the world. This is precisely what he was trying to confirm in his work among the Central Eskimo.

Stocking (1968: 144) notes furthermore that Boas spent much of his spare time in the Arctic reading and reflecting upon Kant's *Critique of Pure Reason*. While there are no references to Kant in Boas's voluminous writings, there are clear parallels between the two thinkers in regard to a critique of the underlying assumptions of Hume's empiricism. Boas's conclusions from his study of the Eskimo lent support to his view that the cultural background of the human subject contributes significantly to the shaping of human perception. His work, therefore, does not take for granted the relation between the human subject and what is referred to in the analytical philosophy of science as the objective world. This will become a crucial issue as we consider the rationality debates in later chapters.

Although Boas does raise the issue of the relation of human perception to the objective world, precisely what he means by this relation is more difficult to ascertain. While in Germany, Boas was a student of Adolf Bastian. Bastian is noted for his assertion of the psychological unity of mankind, an expression of the Enlightenment rationalism still prevalent in the nineteenth century. He claimed that the human mind is everywhere the same and not subject to historical or cultural variability. His position was significant in challenging the ethnocentric assumptions of evolutionary theory whereby the "savage" was thought to be our mental inferior, suffering from a prelogical mentality. It is likely that it was Bastian's theory of psychic unity, rather than the later encounter with Kant, that was the prevailing influence on Boas's work on the color of seawater.[1] If this is indeed the case, it raises serious questions as to what was Boas's understanding of the human subject: Did he develop a concept of a psychological subject as opposed to the subject of German idealism, for example, or the historical subject of the Marxist tradition? The pursuit of this important question, as well as a recognition of his natural science background, can provide a key to the epistemological foundation of Boas's fieldwork.

The major difference between a psychological subject and the subject of German idealism or Marxism resides in the way in which the relation between subject and object is conceived. In Hegelian philosophy, for example, objectified forms of social life are constituted through the intersubjective, formative process of human consciousness. According to this dialectical philosophy, the human subject and the universal forms of social life constitute a dynamic identity, thereby precluding absolute distinctions between an inner life and the external world. In the Marxist tradition, the division between subject and object is overcome by the intersubjective, self-formative process of social labor. In this tradition, as in the Hegelian, the external world is not taken to be preformed and thus given to a passively knowing subject. Knowledge, in the dialectical tradition, moreover, is not based upon the contemplation of the external world but, on the contrary, is grounded in mediation through historically specific social formations.

A psychologically oriented concept of the subject is significantly different from that of the Hegelian and Marxist dialectical traditions. The psychological view of the subject denies intersubjective human action its primary, world-constituting role by presenting a perspective of the human subject turned inward. Objectified forms of social life are no longer the consequence of human action but are generated by universal laws which express themselves through the activity of monological subjects. Knowledge claims, therefore, become based on either the contemplation of the world, as in the correspondence theory of truth, or the introspection of one's internal states. This concept of the psychological subject provides an inadequate epistemological basis for anthropology.

Jürgen Habermas, in his penetrating article "Towards a Theory of Communicative Competence," has developed a thorough critique of the monological subject that is fully applicable to the psychologically conceived subject. He contends that the notion of a monological subject, which is a historically more comprehensive version of the psychological subject, presupposes that meaning is generated from the context of the solitary speaking subject. This notion assumes that the way in which human subjects talk about and understand the world is not based upon consensus through discourse or other forms of social interaction but, on the contrary, is rooted in universal and uniform operations of the human mind. Habermas contends that the monological notion of the subject is based upon a priorism, which assumes that the inventory of ultimate meaning components, as the condition which makes semantic differentiation possible, precedes all experience. He refutes the idea of a psychological or monological subject by arguing that one cannot explain or understand human interaction which is intersubjective by means of a structure that begins with the isolated subject. The monological theorist makes an illicit transition, therefore, in attempting to generalize from the context of an isolated subject to the realm of human interactions, because the logic of the isolated subject and the logic of human interactions are incommensurable. Human subjects begin their lives in already established social structures and cultural traditions, and hence learn to understand themselves and their world through the intersubjectivity of the language they speak. The meaning of cultural traditions is not established through the logic of the isolated human subject but is, on the contrary, embodied in the irreducible context of social interactions. Human interactions, therefore, must be understood from the logic of the social and not an a priori logic of the individual.

While it is not my intention to demonstrate that Boas's epistemology was based upon a radical monism, I shall argue that, like the monological theorist, he cannot account for the disparity between universal psychological laws and the formative activity of human co-subjects. The contradictions in his epistemology are concealed in his linguistic writings. He clearly recognized the unconscious nature of linguistic phenomena, which means that the speakers of a language use grammatical conventions and rules without being aware of their formal properties. Speaking would become problematic if the interlocutors constantly had to reflect on grammatical rules. For Boas, the general concepts underlying language do not become conscious until the scientific study of grammar is initiated. The more interesting aspects of his theory emerge when we move beyond mere grammatical categories and consider principles according to which the world is classified. Boas says the following in relation to the categories of language:

> The categories of language compel us to see the world arranged in certain definite conceptual groups which on account of our lack of knowledge of linguistic processes are taken as objective categories and which therefore impose themselves upon the form of our thoughts. (Boas in Stocking 1968: 289)

Once the scientific study of language begins, we can demonstrate that objective categories are relative to the culture and language of which they are part. Boas then applies the unconscious nature of language to all cultural phenomena.

A means must be developed, therefore, to bring into reflective conscious-ness the unconscious nature of cultural phenomena. For Boas, this process of throwing light on cultural phenomena is history. He claims that to understand a given cultural phenomenon, we have to understand not only what it is but how it came into being. For Boas, therefore, all ethnology must be historical. There is, however, in his work a discontinuity between a historical understanding of how a given cultural phenomenon came into being, based on what I referred to previously as man's self-formative activ-ity, and the psychological processes of the human mind which are ultimately responsible for the generation of cultural phenomena.

Historical reconstruction for Boas does not take into consideration the native's point of view. He claims, rather, that the historical explanation of customs given by the native is generally a result of speculation and is by no means a true explanation (1940: 563). Having rejected the native's self-understanding, he establishes the task of ethnology as the inductive collec-tion of ethnographic data and their interpretation according to cultural context. This is nowhere more clearly demonstrated than in his ethnography of the Central Eskimo. This particular ethnography is a tiresome collection of Eskimo recipes, customs, and curiosities. The inductive nature of Boas's methodology seems to be a clear contradiction of his theoretical work on the color of seawater and fluctuating sounds, which makes the relation between subject and object a central thematic part of his epistemology. The contradiction is resolved, however, once we discover the psychological nature of his subject. Boas himself says that ethnology is oriented towards the discovery of the laws governing the human mind and that these laws are largely psychological in nature:

> My view of the study of ethnology is this: the object of our science is to understand the phenomena called ethnological and anthropological, in the widest sense of these words – in their historical development and geographic

distribution, and in their physiological and psychological foundation. (Boas in Stocking 1968: 63)

Earlier in the same essay he states:

> The longer I studied the more I became convinced that the phenomena such as customs, traditions and migrations are far too complex in their origin, as to enable us to study their psychological causes without a thorough knowledge of their history. (1968: 60)

While he is claiming that ethnological phenomena cannot lead us directly to an understanding of their psychological generation without the mediation of history, it is clear that these ethnological phenomena rest on a psychological foundation:

> From this we must conclude that human development follows certain laws, and to establish these is the second and more important goal of ethnology. (Boas in Stocking 1968: 68)

Boas was never able to reveal the substantive nature of the laws that are responsible for the generation of cultural phenomena. His failure to develop general laws as an ethnological goal was perhaps important for the strength of his historical method. If the informant distorts history through self-understanding, and is unaware of the unconscious psychological laws that generate cultural phenomena, we are left with the Boasian concept of a subject who is fully determined by unconscious psychological laws and therefore unable to contribute as a co-subject to the shaping of culture. Natives classify the world according to the unconscious logic of their language, and it is only the anthropologist equipped with the science of linguistics who can shed light on the nature of this process. An irreconcilable division appears to exist in the psychological concept of the subject, between the informant's interpretation of cultural and historical phenomena and the anthropologist's ability to reveal the actual processes through which these cultural-historical phenomena have developed their specific form – processes of which the native could not, according to Boas, be aware.

The question then arises as to what happens to the meaning of cultural phenomena if its generation is relegated to the unconscious process of psychological laws. It is my claim, despite Boas's rejection of Humean empiricism, that the Boasian concept of the human subject obscures the intersubjective nature and meaningful constitution of cultural phenomena, by irreparably dividing self-understanding from the meaning of human actions. In this respect, Boas as anthropologist and natural scientist are one. One of his principal interests was the inductive collection of cultural phenomena and the understanding of their development in a specific context. His emphasis on context, as I remarked earlier, places him in opposition to nineteenth-century unilineal evolutionism and its analogue, the comparative method. The strict science or scientistic epistemology of the comparative method and Boas's emphasis on psychological laws merge, however, in the following ways, when we consider how cultural phenomena are to be understood. First, both subordinate the world-constituting activity of the historical subject to the generation of cultural phenomena by lawlike processes. Second, both separate cultural phenomena from the intersubjective conventions and rules that give them their sense. Third, neither the natural science nor the Boasian approach recognizes that historical actors can use ordinary language, as opposed to the formal categories of scientific grammer, to reflect upon and bring into full consciousness the nature of cultural phenomena in specific, historical contexts. The reconstructed rules of formal grammer are limited to accounts of communicative competence and the study of the historical relation between languages, not the meaning of human actions.

Boas's emphasis on unconscious psychological laws is not, however, a peripheral feature of his work. Lévi-Strauss, for example, who also privileges unconscious mental processes in the shaping of perceptions and conceptions, claims to be indebted to this aspect of Boas's theory.[2] My emphasis on ordinary language, on the other hand, does not imply that human actors are always aware of the specific events or circumstances that establish a context for the expression of meaningful action. I want to contend nonetheless that human activity is constituted through the categories of ordinary language and hence that it is through this medium that human actors can potentially make conscious what is concealed or unconscious.

I have given this brief account of Boas's epistemology in relation to fieldwork because, while he raises the issue of the subject/object relation, which lies at the heart of the rationality debates, his resolution of this dichotomy does not provide a satisfactory epistemological ground for anthropology. According to his perspective, the social world is not meaningfully constituted as a consequence of historically specific human interactions but, on the contrary, is the outcome of unconscious categories of language as generated through uniform psychological laws. These unconscious categories are superimposed on the "objective" world and can only be brought into reflection through the development of scientific linguistics. While Boas would not support the notion that the social world is a product of monological subjects – a position whose weakness has been demonstrated in my reference to Habermas – it is latent in his concept of psychological laws as the foundation of cultural phenomena. The implications to be drawn from the theory of psychological laws, which are again contrary to the conclusions Boas would himself want to draw, are that these laws operate in all persons to an equal degree and that the cultural phenomena generated from them are an objectified expression of one's internal states. The notion of the sociocultural world as constructed through the cooperation and conflicts of historically acting subjects becomes subordinate to the formal laws of category formation. While Boas has probed the subject part of the subject/object relation, he has left the objective world unmediated by human activity. The inductive nature of his anthropology combined with his concept of the scientific study of language have systematically overlooked the degree to which the conventional use of language can itself reflect on linguistic categories. Boas, therefore, never recognized the reflexivity of ordinary language and hence did not develop a framework that could account for and reflect upon the epistemological assumptions of his own historiography.

The contradiction between Boas's epistemology, which probes the subject/object relation, and his inductive methodology, which rejects indigenous self-understanding, is resolved once we recognize that his notion of the subject is strongly psychologistic. By attributing cultural phenomena to psychological laws rather than to historically specific human interactions, he established the framework for a nonreflexive anthropology. This nonreflexive framework has further been exacerbated, as Fabian (1971) suggests, through a recent positivistic and scientistic emphasis in anthropology. The epistemological flaws of Boasian anthropology, together with the more recent positivism, account for the marginal impact of the rationality debates on the American anthropological community.

Malinowski

It is paradoxical that Malinowski's stated purpose of ethnology should be potentially more historical than that of Boas while his actual methodological procedures were thoroughly ahistorical. Malinowski, in contrast to Boas, states in *Argonauts of the Western Pacific*, his ethnography on the Trobriand Islanders, that the point of ethnology is to "understand the world the way in which the natives do." He claims that the final goal of ethnography is "to grasp the native's point of view, his relation to life, to realize his vision of the world" (1961: 24–5). This point of view stands in direct contradiction to Malinowski's actual method almost as startlingly as Boas's excellent ethnographic work on the Kwakiutl contrasts with his emphasis on psychological laws. Malinowski's actual procedures involved an almost total neglect of the native's "vision of the world." For example, elsewhere in the same ethnography Malinowski states:

The natives obey the forces and commands of the tribal code, but they do not comprehend them, exactly as they obey their instincts and their impulses, but could not lay down a single law of psychology. (1961: 11)

Indigenous social life is animated, therefore, by rules and regulations which are unquestionably unconscious. It is the task of ethnography to articulate this rule-governed but unconscious vision.

To comprehend what Malinowski means by rule-governed necessitates looking more closely at his notion of a social system. In the tradition of British social anthropology, a social system consists of the totality of institutions that compose a particular society. The relations of the various institutions to one another are modeled after the biological concept of natural system. The various parts that compose the whole in the natural system are conceived as maintaining a state of homeostasis or balance. This notion of natural system as balanced is teleological in that the system itself is seen to be selfregulating; each part of the system is designed to maintain the balance of the whole. Malinowski took this model from the natural sciences and applied it to social systems, so that various social institutions are understood as having a homogeneous relation to one another. The system itself is self-regulating and operates to maintain homogeneity. The role of institutions, furthermore, is reduced to the instrumental satisfaction of biological needs. Institutions exist both to regulate human populations on the basis of internal order and to adjust a given population to a natural habitat. For Malinowski, to understand the nature of a particular institution or cultural phenomenon the investigator must analyze its function within the total social system, the way in which the institution or cultural phenomenon is related to other such institutions or phenomena, and the relation of the system as a whole to the habitat. The difference between Malinowski and Boas becomes more apparent here. While Boas was interested in understanding cultural phenomena in their context, part of this comprehension involved the historical understanding of how the cultural phenomena achieved their particularity. Malinowski's concept of social system, on the contrary, is ahistorical. Malinowski claimed that because native societies are illiterate, oral traditions should be received with the greatest suspicion. Any attempt on the part of the anthropologist to reconstruct indigenous history on the basis of oral traditions would be at best conjectural. For Malinowski, then, history is equated with literacy.

Malinowski's methodology followed the canons of natural science. This is best shown by his principles of method stated in the introduction to *Argonauts*:

Ethnographic sources are of unquestionable scientific value, in which we can clearly draw the line between, on the one hand, the results of direct observation and of native statements and interpretations, and on the other hand, the inferences of the author based on his common sense and psychological insight. (1961: 3)

He makes a clear distinction between inferences and observation, which follows the distinction in natural science between the subjective views of the investigator and objective facts. This in part explains his contempt for theory. The fieldworker does not come equipped with a hypothesis to test or, for that matter, with well-formulated problems and questions. Rather, anthropology for Malinowski is an inductive science in which the field-worker plays the objectified role of data collector. Theoretical formulations should not take place in the field but rather within the walls of the investigator's study after returning from the field; these theoretical formulations can then provide a basis for problem formulation for later field-work encounters. This subordination of theory to method is clearly articulated early in the work on the Trobriand Islanders by three cardinal principles:

1   Student must possess real scientific aims and know the values and criteria of modern ethnography.
2   Student must put himself in good conditions of work by living without other white men among the natives.
3   The student has to apply a number of special methods of collecting, manipulating and fixing his evidence. (1961: 6)

It is the separation of theory from and subordination to method that ally Malinowski with the tradition of positivism in western social science. Within the British structural-functionalist school, Malinowski is a direct heir of Emile Durkheim.[3] This tradition conceives cultural phenomena as social facts, equivalent to nonintentional natural objects and hence capable of being grasped by a logic of one natural science.

The following positivistic attributes, without being all-encompassing, are clearly articulated or are latently embodied in Malinowski's methodology. First, using the inductive method, he presupposes that knowledge is rooted in the unmediated presence of sense perceptions. Second, his emphasis on anthropology as a natural science makes a claim for the value neutrality of the investigator in the collection of facts. Third, he makes no attempt to take seriously the native's own self-understanding of cultural phenomena. Malinowski, therefore, does not associate cultural and social phenomena with the a priori rules and conventions that give these phenomena their sense. Finally, his spatial and temporal separation of method and theory prevents investigators from reflexively confronting their own presuppositions and guiding interests.[4] Cultural phenomena are confronted as lifeless entities subject to the manipulation and classification of the social anthropologist. He does depart from the Durkheimian tradition in one respect that clearly differentiates him from such distinguished colleagues as Radcliffe-Brown. Rather than viewing institutions as the normative regulators of social life, Malinowski reduces these essential constituents of social life to the biological role of the satisfaction of needs. Biological needs and their satisfaction become the organizing principle of Malinowskian functional anthropology.

Evans-Pritchard

E. E. Evans-Pritchard was perhaps Malinowski's most important student. While in some respects he never transcended the fundamental assumptions of functionalist anthropology, the differences between student and mentor are striking. Evans- Pritchard, more over, is the fundamental protagonist of the rationality debates and for that reason alone deserves our attention concerning his concept of interpretation in relation to fieldwork.

Evans-Pritchard was one of the few anthropologists, American or British, who attempted to realize Malinowski's claim that ethnology could capture the native's vision of life. Contrary to Malinowski, however, he never advocated a division between method and theory, but rejected any form of anthropology that constituted itself as the collection of facts unmediated by theory. Despite his attempt to reconcile method and theory, nonetheless, his concept of theory was neither more nor less than the contemplation of social life.

Evans-Pritchard claims that the realization of Malinowski's goal requires the anthropologist to understand "a people's thought by thinking in their symbols" (1962: 79). As in the case of Boas, Evans-Pritchard brings language to the center of anthropological inquiry. He claims that as anthropologists learn native languages, they come to understand the "culture and the social system which are conceptualized in language" (1962: 80). A closer look at his view of language reveals, however, a functionalist orientation: the main purpose of language is to give expression to everything in social life. While it is true that language can function as a vehicle of expression, it is more than that. He makes no attempt to understand language as an activity through which agreement or consensus concerning the nature of reality is achieved. For example, Paul Ricoeur has asserted that metaphor, which plays a significant role in indigenous uses of language, not only provides an aesthetic form of expression but is capable of redefining the nature of the world. This world-constituting role of language is never broached by Evans-Pritchard. Rather, for him the referential function of language is primary. Consider the following:

... when one has understood the meaning of all the words of their language (in all their situations of reference) one has finished one's study of a society. (Evans-Pritchard 1962: 79–80)

On the other hand, he does recognize the significance of learning a language for anthropological fieldwork and is therefore critical of the exclusive use of interpreters.

Evans-Pritchard's place in functionalist anthropology is best expressed in his article "Fieldwork and the Empirical Tradition" (1962: 64–86). In this article, he lists four conditions of good fieldwork. First, the anthropologist must spend sufficent time in the field: generally from one to three years. In this connection, he is critical of early British fieldwork, which frequently had a duration of only one month. Second, the anthropologist should be in close contact with the people. One quickly recognizes the parallel here with his mentor Malinowski. Evans-Pritchard is advocating the notion of anthropologist as participant-observer which has contributed to the view that one is not in fact an anthropologist until one has undertaken a field project. Third, comprehending the native language and concepts is of central importance for the field experience. Fourth, and at the heart of the functionalist thesis, the anthropologist should study the "entire culture and social life" (1962: 80).

While his view of language shields him from Malinowski's highly reductive functionalism, which reduces cultural phenomena to the satisfaction of biological needs, for Evans-Pritchard a culture is homogeneous. Each part can only be understood in relation to its place in the whole and the degree to which it contributes to the existence of the whole. It is here most pointedly that Evans-Pritchard is in close agreement with his British colleagues. Theory is subordinated to the method of neutral observation, neutrality being the quality of participant-observation that he claims distinguishes the anthropologist from the missionary and colonial administrator. Inherent in this claim is the idea that the anthropologist does not and should not meddle in the affairs of natives. Evans-Pritchard makes the startling assertion that "an Anthropologist has failed unless, when he says goodbye to the natives, there is on both sides the sorrow of the parting" (1962: 79). The ideological claim of neutrality seems to have blinded this investigator to the exceedingly important fact that his study of the Nuer took place under the aegis of the colonial office which was located near the Nuer settlements. He makes no mention of the colonial office or its possible effects on Nuer society in relation to the outcome of his study. He has confused the apparently neutral aspect of his personal relation with the Nuer with the more determinate inequality of British imperialism, of which clearly he was a representative. It would have been necessary for him to have conceptualized theory dialectically, rather than contemplatively, in order to have made thematic the ideological content of his professed neutrality as an anthropologist.[5]

The above oversight on the part of Evans-Pritchard becomes even more interesting when we examine his views on the nature of anthropology as history. He quite rightly observes that all the early anthropologists were trained in the natural sciences, which had an enormous impact on their anthropological practice. For Evans-Pritchard, this means that the anthropologists working in this tradition conceived of anthropology as the creation of hypotheses to be tested by one's own observations in the field; he had his own mentor, Malinowski, in mind. He took the view, somewhat unpopular within British social anthropology, that anthropology had more in common with history than with the natural sciences. For Evans-Pritchard, anthropology should not involve the testing of hypotheses but rather should follow historical methodology by privileging interpretation. He departs, in this respect, from the ahistorical perspective of the functionalist school in his effort to follow in the tradition of the Geisteswissenschaften, as articulated by Wilhelm Dilthey in Germany in the nineteenth and early twentieth centuries. Dilthey was a key figure in the methodological development of the Geisteswissenschaften, owing to his view that the natural and historical sciences had distinctively different objects in nature and social life. The method of the science, consequently, had to fit its object.

Dilthey's formulation of the Geisteswissenschaften built upon the foundation of hermeneutics, which was rooted in biblical exegesis. The problem addressed by the Geisteswissenschaften was how to understand historically remote expressions of human social life. Dilthey's hermeneutic was applied not only to the analysis of texts, but also to the understanding of historical life in works, both artistic and social. He claimed that in order to understand a text or work, the investigator must reconstruct the place of the text or work in terms of the historical period in which it was generated. Distant forms of social life and texts, therefore, have their meaning only in the context of the period of which they are part. The methodology of the new Geisteswissenschaften became interpretation, as opposed to the classification of facts in the natural sciences. It was this context-dependent sense of interpretation that Evans-Pritchard had in mind in his concept of anthropology as a historical science. There are, however, differences between Dilthey's and Evans-Pritchard's methodologies that are significant for understanding Evans-Pritchard's place in the rationality debates.

While Dilthey can rightly be accused of developing a psychological hermeneutic based upon his concept of understanding through empathy,[6] we discover in Evans-Pritchard an even more subjective emphasis. Evans-Pritchard claims that it is the investigator's body of theoretical knowledge which determines his "interests and lines of inquiry" (1962: 87). This sense of theory, however, only confronts the object but in no way attempts to engage that object through mediation. He states that the anthropologist must be able to follow the cultural grain, which would seem to imply that the object in fact leads the investigator. The interesting notion of following the cultural grain bears some similarity to Dilthey's hermeneutic, in which the object poses certain questions and problems for the investigator, who then uses these "guiding interests" in the investigation.[7] The object's opportunity to engage the investigator in the dialectic of question and answer, however, is quickly silenced by Evans-Pritchard, who grounds his sense of interpretation in subjective personal experience. He claims, for example, that one can only "interpret what one sees in terms of one's experience and personality" (1962: 84). While it is true that the interests and disposition of the investigator play a significant part in selecting what is relevant and how it should be viewed, his notion of personal experience appears to neglect the degree to which his own sense of selectivity and interests is itself mediated, both by the social and historical tradition of which he is part and by the engaging of the cultural object.

For Evans-Pritchard, therefore, the identity of cultural phenomena is established independently of the questions raised by the investigator. His notion of anthropology as an interpretive art, which distinguishes it from the natural sciences, amounts to the superimposition of interpretations on a functionally interrelated world. He attempts to distance himself from his British colleagues and the positivistic implications of the Durkheimian tradition by claiming that there are no social facts but only ethnographic facts. The difference between his ethnographic fact and Durkheim's social fact is the degree to which the former emphasizes selection and interpretation as part of the process of recognizing the specificity of cultural phenomena. The ethnographic fact is still, however, reified: at best it is brought into active dialogue with a subjectivist personal history.

Epistemology and the Politics of Functionalist Fieldwork

The relation between fieldwork and politics is not addressed by the participants in the rationality debates nor by Malinowski or Evans-Pritchard. The process of self-criticism in British social anthropology has more recently been undertaken in an important work edited by Talal Asad, *Anthropology and the Colonial Encounter*. The contributors to Asad's volume trace the relation between colonial administration in Africa, India, and Fiji, and functional anthropology. They try to show that functional anthropology, with its emphasis on the homeostatic social system, develops in the context of and is well suited to controlling and governing indigenous societies. I will attempt to show that the notion of theory in functional anthropology has systematically eliminated the possibility of reflecting on the political interests that played such a dominant role in shaping anthropological practice in the colonies.

In the tradition of British social anthropology, as we have seen in the case of Malinowski, theory has traditionally been separated from the practice of fieldwork. The fieldwork process is thereby limited to the inductive collection of social or ethnographic facts. The functionalist anthropologist studies the entire social life of a given society, focusing on the interdependence and interrelationship of the various institutions in the ethnographic present. Theorization takes place after the anthropologist has left the field with a body of data. The role of theory in functionalist anthropology is then to organize the body of data into hypotheses which can be empirically verified through further field experience. Even Evans-Pritchard, who claimed that anthropological knowledge was based upon interpretation, limited his reflection upon theoretical activity to the investigator's personal life history and experience. He thus was unable to broaden his base of inquiry from the subjectivity of the investigator to the cultural and historical background of the British society of which he was part.

Many of the British social anthropologists had a humanistic self-understanding. They undertook studies of indigenous societies with the notion that a full understanding of the lives of native societies was necessary in order to insure fair and just governance on the part of the colonial office. In the case of Evans-Pritchard, this humanistic orientation became a mission. Humanism, however, accepted the civilizing ideology of the colonial office, albeit with resignation. Many of the British anthropologists never questioned the presence of the colonial office, while others, such as C. K. Meek and S. F. Nadel, actively shaped policy through dual roles as administrator-anthropologist. Evans-Pritchard, for example, while making reference to the glorious past of Zande kings in his classic work on their society, made no attempt to articulate the possible ways in which British colonialism may have exacerbated the expression of Zande witchcraft or altered the Zande society of which he was a participant-observer. The failure to recognize that sociocultural, political, and economic features of the colonizing society are a substantive force in shaping anthropological inquiry in the encounter of anthropologist and native is endemic to the nonreflexivity of functional anthropology, as exemplified in its dichotomy between inductive fieldwork and theory as hypothesis-formation.

The Malinowskian version of functionalism reduces the role of theory from its classical practical intent to a mere instrumental contemplation of social life. The classical world and the inductive method of modern science, the latter being the model for Malinowskian induction, share an objectivist concept of reality as having its own inherent order. The classical notion of theory, however, advocates knowledge of the inherent order of reality for the purpose of cultivating the just or good life. This notion of theory is informed by the framework of communicative rationality as based upon norms of reciprocal or mutual expectation. The functionalist concept of induction, in contrast, is directed towards the collection of facts for the purpose of forming verifiable hypotheses. These hypotheses are formulated in lawlike statements which are then considered by the functionalist anthropologist to be isomorphic with the objective conditions of reality. The functionalist theory accounts neither for the self-reference of the knowing subject epistemologically nor for how the facts that are collected are constituted. Furthermore, the functionalist emphasis on the homogeneous interrelation of institutions in the maintenance of the structure of the whole culture reduces the meaning of cultural facts to their role in the support of the structure. The intersubjective constitution of the meaning of cultural facts is reified as logically reconstructed rules for the technical maintenance of a total social system. Functionalist anthropology thus operates within a framework of instrumental rationality, that is, as a method whose technical rules of procedure are directed towards the objectification and control of reality.

The relation between objectification and control becomes apparent once we recognize the specious sense of totality implied in the functionalist theory of a homogeneous or integrated social system. The functionalist notion of a total social system conceives of the cultural whole as an already preformed, integrated structure, without considering how that system was formed or what forces may be operative in its change. This is in part attributable to the ahistorical perspective of British social anthropology, which conceptualized all indigenous history as speculative because native traditions are transmitted orally rather than through the written word. This, however, contradicts the notion that culture involves the transmission of tradition, for the concept of tradition implies continuity with a living past and hence history. The notion of history implicit in cultural tradition is not commensurate with the functionalist idea of an integrated but ahistorical cultural whole. In leaving the formative activity of human co-subjects and the conflicts and contradictions that arise in the course of human activity out of the functionalist concept of an ahistorical social whole, totality becomes coincident with nature. The functionalist can therefore reduce the meaning of human activity to its function in a virtual social system without considering either how the meaning of specific human activity becomes historically constituted or what the relationship of meaningfully constituted human activity may be to a self-reflective knowing subject.

According to the functionalist thesis, the anthropologist is neither ontologically nor epistemologically related to the reconstructed totality of native society. The anthropologist is viewed by functional anthropology as a neutral collector of facts, and therefore in no way mediates the totality of native society which is the object of inquiry. This methodological abstraction on the part of functional anthropology systematically eclipses the central communicative and reflexive feature of anthropological understanding. The purported neutral perspective of the investigator overlooks the determinations of the prescientific social life-world in all acts of understanding. It is not just the individual biography of the anthropologist, as Evans-Pritchard contended, that establishes the preconditions of entering into dialogue with native informants and other cultural traditions. The personal biography of the anthropologist is itself a manifestation of a cultural tradition. It is, then, the cultural tradition of the anthropologist that enters into dialogue with native traditions. The engaging of the native tradition makes anthropologists reflectively aware of the limitations and finitude of their own traditions. It is only through this process of reflection from the fullness of cultural tradition that the possibility of anthropologists' comprehending the social and political conditions of anthropological inquiry can be established. The objectification of the self and one's cultural tradition through the ideology of scientific neutrality, on the other hand, results in the objectification of native societies. Under functionalism, the anthropologist does not engage living cultural traditions that are constituted intersubjectively but, on the contrary, functional facts that contribute mechanically to the maintenance of the whole. Functional anthropology, therefore, informed by instrumental rationality produces knowledge that is technically utilizable.

The technically utilizable knowledge of functionalism and its suitability for the control of objectified reality are manifest in the historical relation of functionalist anthropology to colonial administration. The functionalist anthropologist as an adjunct to colonialism was only interested in the reconstruction of the ethnographic present insofar as successful governance was dependent upon understanding how indigenous societies operated, much as one understands the interdependence of parts in the functioning of a watch. This desire to understand the intricate functioning of the interdependent institutions of native society arose, however, as a practical consequence of administrative blunders. The British government was slow to learn that all societies did not operate on the principles of hierarchy and rational bureaucracy, so essential to capitalist society. Even the African proto-states were frequently organized on principles that decentralized political power. The British, in their initial attempts to rule by direct administration, frequently recognized the most ambitious persons rather than those who were truly representative of the people. The warrant court system among the Igbo is a case in point (Afigbo 1972). Anthropologists were supported to make a study of the total social life of subdued societies in order to increase the efficiency of British governance. The British had discovered that it was both expensive and inefficient to continue to rule native societies with principles that did not recognize or were not in concert with existing institutions. It is in this historical context that British functionalist anthropology was developed, along with its analogue indirect rule. British functionalist anthropology was none other than the application of Durkheimian sociology to the requirements of colonial administration. We discover, therefore, that while the manifest purpose of functionalist anthropology was the description and analysis of the total social life of native peoples, it concealed a process of objectification that produced knowledge that could be used to control and administer colonized peoples. The British anthropologists, with few exceptions, were simply unable to perceive the history of indigenous peoples apart from their own civilizing destiny.

Functionalist anthropology, as a method divorced from theory, was never able to raise the epistemological or political questions that were essential to a critical self-understanding of its role in the colonial domination of native peoples. This notion of method divorced from theory, or of contemplation as the role of theory, will be part of the ongoing dialogue of the rationality debates in the following chapters.

The problem of understanding another culture is directly related to the practice of fieldwork in native societies. The ancestors of anthropology, while occasionally recognizing the relation between knowing subject and object of knowledge, were unable to reconcile this dichotomy. They therefore could not formulate a firm epistemological ground for anthropology. Furthermore, the problem of epistemology in anthropology cannot be solved only at the level of thought, but involves the actual historical and usually unequal encounter of "primitive" and "civilized." A thorough historical and political understanding of the conditions under which epistemology in relation to fieldwork takes place is, therefore, an important part of cross-cultural understanding.

3 Peter Winch and Ordinary Language Philosophy

The process of interpretation lies at the heart of fieldwork and thus cannot be taken for granted in anthropological practice. As we have seen, while Boas and Evans-Pritchard recognized the problematic nature of interpretation, neither provided a satisfactory epistemological grounding for anthropological inquiry. This chapter will also make interpretation its central focus, but from the neo-Wittgensteinian contribution to the rationality debates as presented by the British philosopher Peter Winch. I will discuss the potential contribution of ordinary language philosophy to anthropological inquiry as well as criticize its shortcomings at the level of ideology.

Peter Winch's now famous article "Understanding a Primitive Society" is the departure point for the rationality debates. In this article Winch attempts to use the ordinary language philosophy of the later Wittgenstein to think both with and against Evans-Pritchard. He is in agreement with Evans-Pritchard in recognizing that interpretation should be the central concern of anthropology. He and Evans-Pritchard, furthermore, both claim that interpretation should be directed towards grasping the native's view of the world. They part ways when it comes to Evans-Pritchard's suggestion in *Witchcraft, Oracles and Magic among the Azande* that Zande notions of witchcraft and the efficacy of oracles are not in agreement with reality. This fundamental disagreement between Evans-Pritchard and Winch is over the question of whether or not it is possible to have a context-independent notion of reality from which the rationality of beliefs can be judged. In order to understand the nature of this conflict, it is first necessary to examine one of Evans-Pritchard's central concerns in the Zande book.

Evans-Pritchard's book on the Azande attempted to refute Lucien Lévy-Bruhl's thesis of the prelogical mentality of primitives. In *The Soul of the Primitive*, Lévy-Bruhl made the claim that the primitive's notion of the dual nature of a person as both beast and human was not just expressive, but, on the contrary, was literal. For example, a primitive man who ordinarily maintained his human form but during ritual occasions became a leopard actually believed that he had become this beast. Lévy-Bruhl considered such beliefs to be prelogical, as they violated Aristotle's logical criterion for identity. Evans-Pritchard tried to show in the Zande study that primitive societies were just as logical as our own but operated on different assumptions. Zande notions of witchcraft were consistent and therefore logical given Zande assumptions. Evans-Pritchard, furthermore, claimed that Zande assumptions of witchcraft, oracles, and magic were just as suitable for such practical activities as running a household as any of the western ways. The point of contention, therefore, between Winch and Evans-Pritchard is not over the logic of Zande life, as there is no disagreement on this matter. They clash over the latter's contention that even though the witchcraft beliefs are logical, they are not true. Evans-Pritchard, that is, presented Zande witchcraft beliefs as a logical fiction.

Evans-Pritchard is correct in stating against Lévy-Bruhl that what is logical is not necessarily scientific. Evans-Pritchard is wrong, as I believe Winch shows, in claiming that science is the only domain capable of providing truth. Language lies at the center of this controversy; Evans-Pritchard has presupposed that scientific statements in the form of hypotheses are the only form of discourse that concerns itself with and therefore corresponds to the objective facts of the world. The Azande, then, are not scientific in that statements concerning their various beliefs are not in the form of hypotheses or propositions, nor do they measure their statements empirically against an objective state of affairs.

Evans-Pritchard illustrated the nonscientific character of Zande beliefs by their concept of the inheritance of witchcraft. The Azande do not believe in witchcraft as a state of being; rather, they conceptualize witchcraft as an act. One way in which they can ascertain who is responsible for acts of witchcraft is through consulting their oracles; while there are no witches in the ontological sense, those who perform acts of witchcraft are thought to possess witchcraft substance in their intestines. A more direct method of evaluating the veracity of witchcraft accusations is through the performance of a postmortem autopsy. The autopsy would be requested by family members of the deceased suspect to clear the family name. It is necessary to find witchcraft substance in the intestines for the witchcraft accusation to be upheld. Winch quotes the following from Evans-Pritchard:

> To our minds it appears evident that if a man is proven a witch the whole of his clan are ipso facto witches, since the Zande clan is a group of persons related biologically to one another through the male line. Azande see the sense of this argument but they do not accept its conclusions, and it would involve the whole notion of witchcraft in contradiction were they to do so. (Winch 1972: 24)

Winch claims that the autopsy process, given Zande assumptions concerning the inheritance of witchcraft substance, should lead to irreconcilable contradictions, in that it would require only scattered incidences of witchcraft substance throughout the various lineages to prove that everyone was a witch. The contrary would be true, of course, if no witchcraft substance were found in a number of cases in different lineages.

Within the context of science, a contradiction of the above type would call the theory or hypothesis into question. One could claim, furthermore, that Zande notions of kinship, combined with the empirical results of autopsies searching for witchcraft substance, point to a logical fallacy in the Zande concept of witchcraft – the very sort of argument that Evans-Pritchard was trying to refute in relation to Lévy-Bruhl. Winch again quotes from Evans-Pritchard regarding this probable contradiction:

> Azande do not perceive the contradiction as we perceive it because they have no theoretical interest in the subject and those situations in which they express their belief in witchcraft do not force the problem upon them. (1972: 24)

Winch admits that it would seem practical at this juncture to make an appeal to the "superior" rationality of western science to expose a contradiction that the Azande simply do not perceive. The Azande, moreover, having had this contradiction pointed out to them, make no attempt, as Evans-Pritchard discovered, to remove it. Winch asserts that the western thinker who wishes to push Zande thoughts concerning the inheritance of witchcraft to their logical conclusion, thus producing a contradiction, is committing a category mistake. He bases this claim upon the notion that Zande witchcraft practices operate according to different rules from those that would lead the western scientist to identify these practices as contradictory:

> This suggests strongly that the context from which the suggestion about the contradiction is made, the context of our scientific culture, is not on the same level as the context in which the beliefs about witchcraft operate. Zande notions of witchcraft do not constitute a theoretical system in terms of which Azande try to gain a quasi-scientific understanding of the world. (1972: 26)

By "level," Winch is not implying that Zande practices and modern science are distinguishable in an evolutionary sense. He is attempting to relativize the supposed universality and privileged claims to truth of modern science by asserting that science, like Zande witchcraft practices, is the product of a particular society in a specific historical period and that the rules for the practice of science are based upon the normative consensus or agreement of a community of scientific investigators. Zande witchcraft and modern science are comparable only in the most abstract sense, as being rule-governed. They are radically different human activities when it comes to their fundamental assumptions and interests. It is in this respect that they are on different levels.

Winch's concept of following a rule, in the case of both science and Zande witchcraft, is derived from the later Wittgenstein's notion of language game. The concept of the language game will help us to follow the full sense of Winch's argument both against the privileged truth claims of science and against Evans-Pritchard.

The later Wittgenstein (1953, 1965) developed the concept of the language game as an implicit critique of the label theory of language presented in his early work, the *Tractatus Logico-Philosophicus*.[1] It was his project in his early period to put an end to philosophical puzzlement by developing a critique or analysis of language. As a result he attempted to create one language of a unified science. Karl-Otto Apel[2] has commented with respect to the project of the early Wittgenstein:

> Its claim (analytical philosophy) is not that of the older Positivists – that the realm of the mind itself can be reduced to the realm of nature and its laws – but rather that any knowledge obtained in the Geisteswissenschaften must be translatable into sentences of the one, intersubjective language about things and facts. (1967: 5)

The effort to create such a language was based upon Wittgenstein's concept of an isomorphic relation between the words in a sentence and objects in the world. This relation between language and the world was rooted in his label theory of language, a theory not unique to Wittgenstein, as it has predominated in western civilization since Plato. The label theory of language maintains that words are labels attached to objects in the world and acquired by ostensive definition. For example, if I want to teach a child the word *chair*, I point to the object and repeat the word until the child can do the same. The relation of the word *chair* to other words in a sentence in which it is used is supposed to be the same as the relation of the object chair to other objects in the objective world. Every possible sentence must be able to describe a possible state of affairs. Wittgenstein encountered problems with this concept of an isomorphic relation between language and the world when it came to describing belief sentences:

> The point about these belief sentences (even more obvious in the case of sentences of "indirect speech"), is, after all, that the truth of that which is believed, meant or said can remain undecided, while the sentence about the belief can nonetheless be true. (Apel 1967: 4–5)

Wittgenstein's solution to this problem was to claim that belief or intentional sentences are sentences about what Apel calls the "meaning of a sentence sign" (1967: 5). Wittgenstein's way of handling belief sentences was to avoid making reference to the psychologistic, subjective states of mind of the speaking subject. Such sentences are instead portrayed as the relation between "depicting facts and depicted facts" (Apel 1967: 6). What is clear here is that the intentionality of sentences uttered by the subject is replaced by sentences about the meaning of sentences.

The later Wittgenstein's concept of the language game rejects the principle of one language of a unified science, reflecting his realization that the referential function of language, implied in the label theory, is only one of the many things that we can do with language. The later Wittgenstein claims that language is an activity because speaking is something that we do. The contrast between label and language use becomes more striking if we think about words which are not proper names. For example, how could I possibly point to a "today" or "tomorrow," yet these words are part of everyday speech. Surely, they are not learned by saying a word and pointing to an object. Another example is the word *chair*, which I used to explain ostensive definition. The use of the word *chair* to refer to a four-legged object with a horizontal seat is certainly not the same as the use of *chair* in "to chair a meeting." The diverse uses of language in different social contexts according to conventional rules is what the later Wittgenstein means by language games. The number of language games is limited only by the number of different uses that we can make of language.

Wittgenstein frequently used the example of chess to draw an analogy between the playing of a game and the speaking of a language. Chess has formal rules which specify the various ways in which the players can move the pieces. These rules enable the players to distinguish a legitimate from an illegitimate move and are, moreover, intersubjective. Once the rules of chess are established, any two players following these rules at any time can be said to be playing chess. Knowing the rules of chess, however, as any chess novice quickly recognizes, is not sufficient to enable one to play. The novice learns to play through moving the pieces in all sorts of circumstances and coming to understand what is the right move in this or that context. The concept of following a rule, for Wittgenstein, does not mean the simple application in a mechanical fashion of that which is already patterned; understanding is essential to the concept of rule. The subject not only must be able to comprehend the sense of the rule but must also be able to apply it in appropriate contexts and in new situations. The application of the rule in appropriate and new contexts implies that the activity of playing the game is privileged over the formal rules, which are only grasped in a posterior reflection. The concept of training thus portrays what it means to learn to play chess more clearly than that of explaining formal rules. Consider the following in relation to the learning of language:

> The kind of training that is necessary to the acquisition of a natural language Wittgenstein says, requires "inducing the child to go on" in the same way in new and different cases. This is different from training for repetition which "is not meant to apply to anything but the examples given"; this teaching "points beyond" the examples given. (Pitkin 1972: 45)

Wittgenstein claims that the intersubjective nature of rules, which in the case of chess one learns through complex training, is applicable in the same way to language games. When I point, therefore, to the object and say "chair" and then encourage the child to do the same, I already presuppose that the child has fully comprehended what it means to point to and name an object (Pitkin 1972).

We are now in a better position to understand what Winch means when he says that Zande witchcraft and western science are informed by different rules. He claims that the rules of scientific investigation involve the researcher's relation both to the phenomena studied and to other scientists. The logic of science proceeds by depicting a world of facts and things formulizable into universal hypotheses that are capable of being verified: hence the importance of the experiment. The knowledge-constitutive rules of science, furthermore, are directed towards the production of knowledge which is technically utilizable. While it is clear that the scientific community works according to certain specifiable and communicable rules of procedure and explanation, scientists make no such assertion about the objective world which they depict through the self-same rules of procedure and explanation.

Zande witchcraft practices also have communicable rules, but not for the purpose of formulating nomological hypotheses based upon empirical verification nor for the strict purpose of producing technically utilizable knowledge. In contrast to the language games of science, Zande statements concerning witchcraft are intentional and thus bear a closer resemblance to the belief sentences that were problematic for the early Wittgenstein. Following the later Wittgenstein, Winch claims that Zande statements concerning witchcraft cannot be translated into the language games of science without reifying their intentionality.[3] Scientific description, by emphasizing universal hypotheses, exhibits no interest in interpreting how witchcraft is constituted – a task that would involve comprehending the intersubjective rules through which witchcraft derives its sense or meaning. Witchcraft acts are not just physical movements of the body but follow clearly defined rules in both their practice and mutual intelligibility. The main distinction, therefore, between the objects depicted by natural science and those described by anthropologists is that the objects of anthropology are also human co-subjects.

Despite Evans-Pritchard's claim that anthropology is an interpretive art, he ultimately reifies Zande witchcraft beliefs by claiming that they are not in agreement with reality. He treats Zande witchcraft beliefs and practices as an ethnographic fact in a manner which he believes distinguishes him from the British tradition of structural anthropology rooted in the Durkheimian social fact. The strength of the Durkheimian position is that its basic category of analysis is society and the social structure, as opposed, for example, to contract theory, which is based on the agency of the isolated individual. The weakness of the Durkheimian position is twofold. First, while society shapes the individual, the social fact stands totally outside the realm of human action. Human society and social institutions are reified in that they are sustained without a world of intentional human actors. Second, as can be ascertained from the *The Elementary Forms of the Religious Life*, Durkheim is interested in formulating the universal structures of social life of which the human actor is unconscious:

> I consider extremely fruitful this idea that social life should be explained, not by the notions of those who participate in it, but by more profound causes which are unperceived by consciousness, and I think also that these causes are to be sought mainly in the manner according to which the associated individuals are grouped. Only in this way, it seems, can history become a science, and sociology itself exist. (Durkheim in Winch 1958: 23–4)

Evans-Pritchard's ethnographic fact conflicts with the social fact most directly in regard to its claim for the universality of human social structures. Evans-Pritchard argues that there is no universality to social institutions, since they differ in relation to specific cultural contexts. He supports his claim with his ethnographic research in Africa among peoples of diverse sociocultural integration and his view that the identity of a social institution is based upon the role that it fulfills within the total culture. As societies change historically, so do their social institutions and the elements of which they are composed. The ethnographic fact reflects social life in its specific historical manifestation, while the social fact, on the contrary, portrays human association in all contexts and historical periods as governed by universal principles.

The methodological similarities and differences between the social and ethnographic fact are interesting. Durkheim favors the notion of one language of a unified science as the only way that "history becomes a science, and sociology itself can exist" (Durkheim in Winch 1958: 23–4). Evans-Pritchard contends, on the other hand, that ethnology is more akin to history in its privileging of the art of interpretation, rather than the classi-

fication of facts as in the natural sciences. For Evans-Pritchard, interpretation means no more than the engaging of the cultural object according to
the selectivity of one's personal biography. The social and ethnographic fact
are methodologically in agreement in jointly claiming that the intentionality
of social life is subordinate to the "more profound causes which are unper-
ceived by consciousness" (Durkheim in Winch 1958: 23–4). This is precisely
what Evans-Pritchard implied when he claimed that Zande witchcraft practices, while logical, are in the end fictional.

Implicit in both Durkheim's concept of social fact and Evans-Pritchard's
concept of ethnographic fact is the idea that social life, institutions, and
structures are rule-governed but that these rules stand apart from the formative activity of co-subjects. Winch's concept of rule provides a suitable
alternative that avoids the serious consequences of reification. His concept
of rule is intersubjective and conventional, without being a mechanical
following of what is pregiven. The human subject must be able not only
to understand the rule but to use it in new social contexts. Winch therefore
claims that while rules arise through social relations, they cannot then take
on a life of their own apart from the continued interactions of human
subjects. It is important to note that although rules are constituted in
language, they do not merely refer to or name social relations. Such a
concept would contain the same fallacy as the label theory of language.
Winch asserts that social relations are inherently communicative:

> A man's social relations with his fellows are permeated with his ideas about
> reality. Indeed, 'permeated' is hardly a strong enough word: social relations
> are expressions of ideas about reality. (1958: 23)

He here implies that actions in the world, or social relations, are always
intersubjective events with respect to their intention, form, and consequence.

The contrary notion – action conceived as a private event – has been
articulated in contract theory. Viewed historically, the notion of society as
based on a social contract originating with an isolated subject coincides
with the creation of civil society in the late eighteenth century. The presupposition that one can establish a social contract through agreement
already signifies that one can distinguish agreement from disagreement.
To agree or disagree is to follow a convention; how else could one determine
that one was doing the same thing on other occasions. But, to reach agreement with another presupposes that one shares with the other the same
sense of what it means to agree. It is therefore absurd to understand the
notion of agreement, as all contract theories suggest, as part of one's private
language and, consequently, as a private act. The concept of reaching
agreement already presupposes a conventionality that is social to the core.

While the human subject, then, can have reasons for acting in the world that are related solely to individual biography, the sense or meaning of the act, as well as the sense of its consequence, is always within a conventional or intersubjective framework. Human acts are never totally reducible to physical movements such as, for example, the relation between subatomic particles in physics, nor to the solely private intentions of the actor. This does not of course imply that human actions do not have unforeseen consequences. If this were the case, then it would be impossible to do anything new. There must, however, be a logical connection between what is conventional and the doing of something new, just as in the language game the rule can be extended to new social contexts.

Winch has been criticized by some of the participants in the rationality debates for his claim that all action originates in an intersubjective framework. These theorists mistakenly atribute to Winch the notion that human actors are always fully conscious of their motivations. They in turn argue that if human actors in fact are not conscious of their actions, how can they be counted on to explain their actions in a meaningful sense? This argument leads to the conclusion that the unconscious nature of social life must warrant a context-independent analysis analogous to the formation of explanatory hypotheses and classification of facts in the natural sciences.

Winch counters this critique with the assertion that most certainly not all motives for acting are transparent to the actor. He appeals to psychoanalysis – therapy through the medium of discourse – to illustrate the intersubjective nature of even unconscious motives.[4] The classic patient of psychoanalysis visits the therapist because some process unresolved in the past persists and manifests itself in the present. The purpose of therapy is to use discourse to overcome the blockages of the past and achieve integration in the present. Frequently, the therapist will suggest interpretations of present life that are reflective of the patient's past life. The patient will in some cases either affirm the therapist's interpretations or deny them. It is important to note that the sense or meaning of the therapist's interpretation must be, at the very least, intelligible to the patient. This is the case because the patient's interactions which are interpreted by the therapist have a limited range of possible meanings that are established through a mutually intelligible repertoire of cultural meanings.[5] Reflection through ordinary language on the repressed dimensions of one's life can thus uncover unconscious processes and motivations that are intersubjective and open up the possibility of individuation. It is vital to recognize that the repertoire of mutually shared cultural meanings is not something that individual actors carry around in their heads. These cultural meanings are, as Winch has so emphatically expressed, implicit in social relations and interactions.

The example of psychoanalysis provides an important entry into a social science grounded in ordinary language and yet another perspective from which the critique of Evans-Pritchard can be deepened. Winch has distinguished himself from the later Wittgenstein primarily through his notion that ordinary language can be used to reflect upon itself. This is significant in that it helps to overcome some of the strongest arguments against a context-dependent social science by claiming that the unconscious motives of human subjects can be made conscious through reflection in an ordinary language that is mutually shared by a given community. Reflection on unconscious motives does not imply that they are brought to language without prior linguisticality but does presuppose that these unconscious motives are already conventional or rule-governed. The intentional nature of both conscious and unconscious motives provides a particular challenge to anthropology. According to Winch, the anthropologist operates with two distinct and often contrary sets of rules that are what the later Wittgenstein called forms of life:

> Human life as we live and observe it is not just a random, continuous flow, but displays recurrent patterns, regularities, characteristic ways of doing and being, of feeling and acting, of speaking and interacting. Because they are patterns, regularities, configurations, Wittgenstein calls them forms; and because they are patterns in the fabric of human existence and activity on earth, he calls them forms of life. (Pitkin 1972: 132)

What is clear from the concept of form of life as developed by the later Wittgenstein and utilized by Winch is the fact that the conventional nature of human social life as mediated by language is not just an intellectual attitude or world view, but is a way of acting or being in the world. There are, furthermore, different culturally specific forms of life. Anthropologists, therefore, who go to the field are equipped with their own rules for doing anthropology but confront native societies which have different sets of conventions or forms of life. When Winch accuses Evans-Pritchard of category impositions, he is implying that the categories by which Evans-Pritchard has addressed Zande social life are not in phase with activities as understood by the Azande themselves. Winch wants to claim that the meanings of Zande actions are only intelligible within the repertoire of language games that compose the Zande form of life. It will be instructive to consider examples from another classic by Evans-Pritchard, *Nuer Religion*, to appreciate the full impact of Winch's argument.

Evans-Pritchard contends that the Nuer god, Kwoth, is a transcendent high god, thus creating an antinomy between sky and earth. When Evans-Pritchard, however, explains how the Nuer themselves conceptualize Kwoth, we are presented with a significantly different picture. The Nuer speak of Kwoth in relation to the wind, the breath of life. The wind not only portrays a heavenly image but also sweeps the face of the earth. We inhabit a sea of air, hence the wind is both heavenly and of the earth without the contradiction implied by Evans-Pritchard.

The second example from *Nuer Religion* comes from the chapter entitled "Sin." Having interpreted Kwoth as a transcendent high god, Evans-Pritchard proceeds to interpret interdictions as laws in the Judeo-Christian sense. The violation of an interdiction is therefore interpreted as a violation of God's law, which will certainly bring its just consequences. Evans-Pritchard is not wrong in recognizing that the Nuer have interdictions but is mistaken in interpreting these restrictions on action within the rules or form of life applicable only to a covenant made with a "jealous" god. Sin does not come into existence until the institutionalization of moral and ethical universalism, which is contrary to the concreteness and particularity of Nuer religious life.[6]

I have used a Winchian analysis in these two examples to show how Evans-Pritchard's category impositions derive from the form of life of the Judeo-Christian religious tradition and, when applied to the Nuer, distort the meaning of their religious life. The forced imposition of categories is symptomatic not only of having the wrong intellectual attitude towards the Nuer but also of failing to understand their religious life in terms of how they act, think, and speak. For Winch, a similar distortion is made by Evans-Pritchard when he states that Zande witchcraft beliefs are not in agreement with reality. Winch claims that agreement with reality is dependent on the use and sense of language as constituted through the language games and forms of life of a given language community:

> To ask whether reality is intelligible is to ask about the relation between thought and reality. In considering the nature of thought one is led also to consider the nature of language. Inseparably bound up with the question whether reality is intelligible, therefore, is the question of how language is connected with reality, of what it is to say something. . . . To assume at the outset that one can make a sharp distinction between 'the world' and 'the language in which we try to describe the world', to the extent of saying that the problems of philosophy do not arise at all out of the former but only out of the latter, is to beg the whole question of philosophy. (1958: 11–13)

Evans-Pritchard has begged the whole question of anthropology in his assertion that modern western science is the sole arbiter concerning what is and is not agreement with reality. He has failed to recognize that science is a form of life with its own particular language games and intersubjective rules of procedure which establish criteria for valid knowledge claims. Winch claims that the rules of science are suitable for the instrumental manipulation of the material world and the classification of objectified facts and things. The formal and abstract nature of modern science, which has no interest in capturing or reconstructing the intentional nature of everyday life, condemns not only Zande witchcraft but many of the practices and procedures by which we live our daily lives. While Evans-Pritchard has claimed that anthropology is interpretive and should strive to "capture the native's vision of life," his view of language as neutral has prevented him from recognizing the inextricable connections among social relations, language, and the world. He has therefore reconstructed the logical coherence of the Zande rules, but without "raising questions about the point which following those rules has in the society" (Winch 1958: 27).

Winch and Ordinary Language in Critical Perspective

Winch's concept or use of the later Wittgenstein's "forms of life" reinstates the classical problem of interpretation at the center of anthropological inquiry but with a more profound conception of the role of language in social life. In contrast to Boas (1889), who stated that a formal science of linguistics was necessary to reveal the unconscious rules of language, Winch asserts the primacy of the power of ordinary language to reflect upon itself. This is to a degree presupposed every time a rule is applied in a new social context. Winch further shows that language is more than the intellectual attitudes used by a given community to describe an unchanging objective world.[7] For Winch, acting, speaking, and thinking are all mediated through the language games that compose the form of life of a given community. It is therefore inconceivable to have a world apart from our understanding of the world in language. Winch's perspective, then, makes it imperative that the anthropologist attempt to understand native practices and beliefs in the context of the form of life from which they are generated:

> Seriously to study another way of life is necessarily to seek to extend our own
> – not simply to bring the other way within the already existing boundaries of
> our own, because the point about the latter in their present form, is that they
> ex hypothesi exclude the other. (1972: 33)

Winch does not imply that, indigenous and modern societies share no common rationality that would make their forms of life mutually intelligible. On the contrary, according to Winch the speaking of a language and rationality are interdependent, thus making it possible for anthropologist and native to understand each other.[8] Since it is the anthropologist, however, who wants to understand the indigene, it is the anthropologist who must extend the use of language in an effort to capture the meaning of native practices and beliefs. Winch is simply trying to draw our attention to the epistemological problem that our concepts and categories for describing the world only have sense with respect to the social relations and institutions of our society. Many modern institutions, such as our concept of civil law as rooted in private property, exclude such indigenous practices as the corporate use of land and the arbitration of disputes through custom. The use of our economic and legal categories to describe indigenous societies simply reduces them to reflections of ourselves, which defeats the whole purpose of anthropology.

Despite the fact that Winch has called for a communicative theory of society which is critical of all attempts to translate sentences or activities of the Geisteswissenschaften into one language of a unified science, he allows the dialectical moment of communicative theory to escape by privileging solely the categories of the native. Alasdair MacIntyre has criticized Winch on this very point but, as we shall see in chapter 5, his solution is also inadequate. Winch has shown that the idea of science as context-independent is untenable insofar as scientists work with social categories that are the products of historically and culturally specific social relations. He implies, however, that anthropologists should abdicate their categories so as not to distort meaningful action as constituted in native societies. In order for him to maintain the dialectical nature of understanding, it would be necessary not to abdicate but to utilize the social categories of the investigator as a historical and socially effective standpoint from which to engage the cultural object. It is not just the lives of natives and anthropologists in their own cultural contexts which are communicative, but the encounter between these distinct forms of life as well. This dialectical-communicative encounter is a synthesis of distinct forms of life, much as a conversation between two communicators is a synthesis through their mutual understanding. The critical anthropological dimension of this encounter is sustained to the extent that the engaging of distinct forms of life brings the relativity, without relativism, of the anthropologist's way of speaking, thinking, and acting into full, historical, context-dependent perspective. By abdicating the categories of the anthropologist or by stretching them, which may amount to the same thing, thereby privileging the native's categories, Winch is left in the same abstract position as the natural scientist or the social scientist who studies culture according to a scientistic self-understanding:

> This methodological approach [i.e., Winch's] can actually be legitimate and fruitful from the point of view of the Geisteswissenschaften, but it also shows how much Winch's assumption of the language game, only understandable by and in itself, is really a mere theoretical abstraction, which is strictly applicable only in mathematics – thus bearing witness to the origin of Wittgenstein's thinking in logic and mathematics. (Apel 1967: 56)

There is an element of irony in Winch's privileging of the native's categories, or abstract contemplation of language games, in that it suspends the very reflexivity of language which distinguishes his concept of the language game from that of the later Wittgenstein. This loss of reflexivity when he moves from within a cultural tradition to the encounter of cultural traditions tends to reduce the communicative nature of his theory to the instrumentality of method. The abdication of the investigator's categories implies on Winch's part that anthropologists have full control of their linguistic categories, to the degree that they could be suspended through subjective choice. We should keep in mind that for Winch the suspension of linguistic categories is tantamount to suspending our ways of thinking, acting, and speaking. The suspension or in some cases extension of our categories becomes the epistemological method through which the cultural object is known. This presupposes that the method of knowing in no way interferes with what we are attempting to know – the very presupposition that is made by scientism through the purported neutral objectivity of the investigator.[9] I am not claiming that Winch has merely produced another scientistic method, but that his communicative framework fails at the very point where it could make a significant contribution to anthropological theory – that is, the dialectical, reflexive character of understanding through ordinary language. Winch's failure to follow through with his own project can best be exemplified by what he does not recognize and criticize in Evans-Pritchard's study of Zande society.

Winch claims that the social relations between human subjects are expressions of ideas about reality. He furthermore claims that self-understanding can be achieved through the inherent reflexivity of ordinary language, thus making conscious unconscious but intentional features of social life. He overlooks, however, the disjunctures that can arise between individual motivations and self-understanding through institutionalized ideological distortions of social reality. This appears to be the case with Zande witchcraft practices and beliefs. Winch and Evans-Pritchard fail to make the historical and sociopolitical background of Zande witchcraft a substantive part of their interpretation. The Zande society which Evans-Pritchard studied and which has become the center of attention in the rationality debates was created through conquest. Zande society is by no means homogeneous, therefore, being composed of some 180 clans spread over parts of the Southern Sudan, the Congo, and Uganda. The present-day tribal name of Azande includes both the conquerors and the conquered. Evans-Pritchard claims that the original Azande were located in the vicinity of the Valley of Mbomu in the Congo and that they migrated to their present-day homelands sometime during the late eighteenth and early nineteenth centuries. It is not known specifically why these migrations took place apart from the fact that Arab slavers had pressured Zande society considerably throughout the eighteenth century. It has been documented by the Italian explorer Casati and the German explorer Schweinfurth that these waves of Zande migrants led by their Avongara rulers conquered the politically decentralized peoples of the Southern Sudan, thus forming a unified kingdom ruled by the Avongara nobility.[10]

Evans-Pritchard relates that both the Avongara nobility and the Zande commoners participate in witchcraft beliefs and practices. It is, however, important to note that neither Winch nor Evans-Pritchard seems to recognize the significance of the fact that while the Avongara can accuse commoners of witchcraft, they are themselves immune from accusation.[11] This discrepancy between nobility and commoners cannot be accounted for simply by a distanced and abstract review of the language games used by the Azande in their own self-understanding of witchcraft practices and beliefs. If we are to use a communicative framework to understand social reality, we must attempt to understand not only what is communicated, which in itself is abstract, but how the relations of the communicators affect what is said and mutually understood. Zande witchcraft practices, therefore, while normative and intersubjective, are still subject to political constraints that give the social relations of Zande society their specific form. In other words, the norms of Zande society, which are expressions and objectifications of social relations, become distorted because their social relations are class-based.[12] These norms, generated in the context of stratified social relations, then become the basis on which the Azande develop their own self-understanding and sociocultural identity. Zande witchcraft, therefore, operates in at least one respect as a form of ideological distortion and cultural domination that both conceals the hostilities of the conquered Azande from Avongara rulers and deflects them to a purely internal confinement among the commoners. My emphasis on social control with respect to Zande witchcraft is feasible in light of the fact that the original decentralized Azande had their total way of life transformed by the conquest. The institutionalization of witchcraft, therefore, in the form which it has taken in Zande society legitimizes unequal distribution of authority in the society.

This does not negate everything that Winch has said about Zande witchcraft, nor does it vitiate his critique of Evans-Pritchard's scientism.[13] Winch's assertion that the identity of a social phenomenon is dependent upon its sense as generated within a culturally specific form of life helps the anthropologist to avoid an overly simplistic and distorted equating of various expressions of witchcraft, such as European and Zande. European and Zande witchcraft are supported by entirely different institutional orders and rules according to which the diverse practices articulate their sense.[14] While Winch is correct in recognizing that social relations express ideas about reality, he overlooks the degree to which social relations are subject to historically specific social, political, and economic forces.

The ahistoricity of Winch's analysis of forms of life and language games and the abdication of the investigator's categories have further implications for the communicative nature of anthropological inquiry. As soon as Winch has suspended the culturally specific categories of the anthropologist and privileged those of the native, it no longer becomes possible to reflect upon the interests which determine the nature of the investigation.[15] Empirical and knowledge-constitutive interests are lost in the process because the suspension of the anthropologist's categories eliminates the knowing subject, thereby producing the situation of a known object without a reflexive subject. This was the very situation created by Evans-Pritchard in his claim to neutrality on the part of the anthropologist as compared to the missionary or colonial administrator. Winch makes no attempt to probe the way in which the presence of the British colonial office altered the social context from which witchcraft practices derived their sense. The British colonial office undermined the class structure on which witchcraft was based, in two swift moves. First, the British colonial office militarily destroyed the power and nature of the Zande kingship, thereby making future kings the agents of the colonial office. Second, through the policy of indirect rule, the class structure and government of the Azande were maintained at the price of accountability to the colonial office. Moreover, to effectively govern a subordinated population the British found it necessary to limit the mobility of the Zande population, thus making it more difficult to obtain the rare *benge*[16] substance used in the oracles to determine culpability for witchcraft acts. While all of these circumstances are described by Evans-Pritchard, they are in no way incorporated into his or Winch's interpretation of Zande witchcraft, despite their overwhelming importance in specifying the nature of Zande social relations. Winch's abstract subject, furthermore, provides no perspective from which to examine either presuppositions in terms of formulated questions and problems or the historical relations between the society represented by the anthropologist and the society under study. Yet these provide the concrete context from which interpretation is initiated and dialectically unfolds.

It is the abstract nature of Winch's method that lessens its suitability as an epistemological framework for anthropological fieldwork. While Winch has criticized the Durkheimian school of sociology for supporting a concept of society that postulates structures or institutions without active human subjects, he is equally culpable for holding that we can have social relations and forms of life without historical subjects. He is unable, as a result, to ascertain the specific social forces that shape social relations and the cultural meanings which they express.

Winch's concept of social theory is equally abstract in advocating the contemplation of language games and the forms of life of which they are a part without considering their historicity. Consequently, he speaks, for example, of forms of life in modern society as if they were complete in themselves. Art, religion, and science are all forms of life, therefore, which do not have rules or conventions that overlap. He does not raise the question as to whether the fragmentation of these modes of inquiry, which are also modes of speaking, thinking, and acting, in any way mirrors the general fragmentation of social life. He is unable to recognize, for example, the historical relation between religion and science: the fact that the eschatological and utopian visions of the former persist in the latter.[17] His theory lacks the very efficaciousness that his communicative notion of social relations implies: that subjects, through their interaction, which already presupposes a framework of conventionality and agreement, both interpret and shape the world. He overlooks the Marxist dictum that the shaping of the world is not always of the actor's choosing; that the possibilities for action are limited by concrete social and historical forces, such as the predominance of the market in capitalist societies. These objective limits on human action are then objectified in language and become opaque symbols through which actors attempt to understand themselves. It is necessary for social theory, not merely to contemplate, as Winch has suggested, but to mediate social life to reveal both the social forces that shape social relations into their specific forms and the specific ideas about reality that are expressed by these social relations.

Despite its many problems, Winch's communicative theory based on ordinary language is a cogent and formidable opponent to scientistic anthropology. According to Winch social action is only intelligible within the context of a given language community which is normative or rule-governed. What is most significant is his recognition that social science investigation itself operates in a context of rule-governed procedures that is mediated by an intersubjectively valid language. This challenges the simple equivalence of modern science or social science and rationality, and shows clearly that the use of language and its associated forms of life is problematic and cannot presuppose a value neutrality. We are now in position for a direct confrontation with the neo-Popperian contributors to the rationality debates.

4 The Neo-Popperians and the Logic of One Science: I. C. Jarvie and Robin Horton

Philosopher I. C. Jarvie and anthropologist Robin Horton owe a self-proclaimed debt to Sir Karl Popper, in spite of the qualification that I alluded to in the Introduction with respect to Jarvie's methodological individualism. Jarvie and Horton are the two most formidable proponents of the Popperian tradition represented in the rationality debates and thus deserve our careful consideration. Jarvie's importance to the rationality debates lies in both his application of Popperian philosophy of science to a critique of positivist induction and his antagonistic stance to Winchian ordinary language philosophy. Horton has clearly been inspired by Popper's notion of open and closed societies, which, with some revisions, he has used to characterize both the continuity and the differences between traditional and modern societies. Horton opposes Winch's implied distinction between modern and traditional societies based upon different forms of life and consequent rationalities by claiming that there is only one rationality, which is best exemplified in modern western science.

Jarvie and Objectivism

In *The Revolution in Anthropology* (1964) Jarvie criticizes the inductivist field method of the Malinowskian tradition of anthropology. He argues that anthropology has been trivialized by a fieldwork technique that advocates the mere recording and cataloguing of facts.[1] The inductivist collection of facts is naive in that it is based on an epistemology which grounds knowledge in sense perceptions, a perspective which, as Jarvie points out, has been thoroughly criticized since Kant.[2] Jarvie emphasizes that induction has mistakenly been identified with empiricism, a view that he wishes to correct by means of Popper's objectivist methodology. Jarvie claims that all individuals are immersed in social contexts to the extent that to be human is to have presuppositions. These presuppositions must not be avoided but must be used by the fieldworker as a basis from which to formulate problems that may then be taken to the field for research. It is the formulation of clear problems that enables the anthropologist to distinguish relevant from irrevelant facts. Hypotheses are then tested empirically to discover if they illuminate facts which are given and therefore relevant to the research problem. Jarvie, following Popper, argues that objectivity is not grounded in the untenable notion of a presuppositionless social science nor in the object itself, but is guaranteed through the method of forming hypotheses which withstand repeated attempts at refutation. The research community is vital to this process, as it is the community of investigators that either upholds or refutes a hypothesis. Objectivity resides, in Jarvie's sense, in hypotheses which are publicly recognized as having withstood empirical testing and are true because they correspond to actual states of affairs in the world. The intent of these intersubjectively held hypotheses is to account, where possible, for the lawlike nature or regularity of social phenomena by establishing causal relations between facts.

The notion that all social life is permeated by presuppositions is central to Jarvie's and Popper's methodology. Jarvie, furthermore, claims that presuppositions are what distinguish human beings as objects of knowledge from nature, although he maintains that both human social life and nature can be explained and grasped by the same objective method of hypothesis formation. He asserts that actions are affected by presuppositions or by what the actor believes, and that since beliefs affect actions, they in turn affect the way the world is. He is careful to distinguish idiosyncrasies of individual belief from what the community holds to be true, which he characterizes as the objective world just as he has presented the research community as the ground of objectivity. Jarvie contends that the whole social fabric is woven from the beliefs that are held in common by a community. For example, in *Concepts and Society* (1972) Jarvie takes this idea to its limit by claiming that the entire class system in American society is maintained simply because individuals believe that there is a class system and therefore act accordingly.

Although Jarvie's assertion that the American class system is reducible to belief appears to be an indefensible overstatement in light of conventional social class theories, we can understand how he arrives at this conclusion once we appreciate the position from which he initiates social inquiry. He contends that British anthropologists and sociologists of the Durkheimian tradition are mistaken in attributing aims or goals to institutions or collectivities. According to Jarvie, only individuals have aims or goals and are therefore capable of action. Since action is the object of the proper study of social life and only individuals are capable of purposeful action, then individuals and not institutions or social wholes become the standpoint from which to initiate the investigation and explication of social life. The initiation of social inquiry from the perspective of the individual has become known in the Popperian tradition as methodological individualism, although Popper distanced himself from this perspective towards the end of his life (he died in 1994). Methodological individualism is then employed by Jarvie, and the Popperian tradition, as the core of a more extensive project known as situational logic. We shall see that in relation to social life, situational logic provides the factual material from which hypotheses are formulated.

The acting subject of methodological individualism and situational logic is characterized by the investigator as typified and therefore as formulating conventional aims that can then be subsumed under explanatory laws. Jarvie recognizes that individuals do not act in a social vacuum, so that actions may become interactions and have unforeseen consequences. Institutions, furthermore, are dependent on the conventional interaction of individuals but are not necessarily based upon the conscious design of actors. Institutions and other social actors are perceived by Jarvie as a "Hobbesian" limit to individual action:

> A man can be viewed as in pursuit of certain goals or aims within a framework of natural, social, psychological and ethical circumstances. Circumstances constitute the means of achieving his aims and constraints on that achievement. The individual's appraisal of how the aims within the circumstances can be achieved is called sorting out the logic of the situation. (1972: 4)

It is his intent to use the hypothetico-deductive method of intersubjectively verifiable hypotheses to reconstruct the aims of individual actors (what Habermas has called "purposive rational action"[3]) while recognizing social institutions and norms only as limits or means to the realization of the actor's aims. Jarvie, following Popper, has called this methodological reconstruction of aims "situational logic." Situational logic, therefore, conceives of the individual as rationally deliberating alternate strategies to achieve goals or aims within a given context that includes norms, other people, and material, social, and psychological circumstances that both limit and provide the means of realizing the goals. Despite the fact that Jarvie has claimed that social institutions are not consciously designed by human actors and that action has unforeseen consequences, he characterizes all human action as goal-oriented. It is because Jarvie has initiated his social inquiry from the structure of an isolated individual in pursuit of aims that he fails to recognize that a social structure composed of intersubjective institutions, which are not merely means or limits but are constitutive of social life, can prevent the individual from realizing a goal such as the elimination of the class system by simply withdrawing belief in that system. Even to the extent that elimination of the class system becomes a quasi-collective aim in Jarvie's sense, he still overlooks the degree to which the class system can be supported by such institutional structures as the law, police, or school systems.

Jarvie claims that the hypothetico-deductive method of situational logic is suitable for sociological or anthropological analysis because human action itself is deductive. Human action is deductive because the proper strategy for realizing a goal is deduced from the context of the actor's immediate situation. The hypothetico-deductive method, which was originally developed in the context of the natural sciences, is therefore appropriate to explain human actions. Jarvie warns that his sense of the hypothetico-deductive method should not be confused with Descartes's concept of deduction, as it does not imply the notion of eternally true a priori axioms. The social scientist must create hypotheses that do not describe raw facts but rather describe the actor's statement or account of facts. These hypotheses must then be able to survive the criticism of the investigative community, and will be accepted as true until it can be shown that they do not correspond to an objective state of affairs in the world.

Jarvie *contra* Winch

Given the above portrait of Jarvie's methodology, we are now prepared to examine his five-point criticism of Winch, also developed in *Concepts and Society*. The five-point criticism will also illustrate how Jarvie perceives the relevance of his method to anthropology.

Jarvie's first critical point is addressed to Winch's claim that rationality is associated with a form of life and that different forms of life imply different rationalities. He insists that the Azande and the anthropologist share some sense of rationality although admittedly a poor one. His assumption of shared rationality is based on both his belief in the unity of the human mind and his view that modern western science has the most developed form of rationality and thus establishes a standard by which to judge other societies. He does not associate rationality, as does Winch, with the ways of thinking, speaking, and acting in a given language community, but upholds the critical spirit of science as the ultimate measure. According to Evans-Pritchard, who is often quoted by Jarvie, the Azande do not repudiate their oracles despite repeated failures, because they are not capable of thinking outside of their concepts and will therefore blame failures on unsuitable conditions such as bad *benge* substance. Jarvie claims that both the Zande oracle beliefs and the beliefs of modern scientists are theoretical statements in that both attempt to explain a state of affairs in the world. The difference between the beliefs of the modern scientist and the Azande is the former's willingness to question, revise, and if necessary reject theoretical statements. Jarvie, furthermore, distinguishes between a weak and a strong sense of rationality. In his view, rational action is goal-directed and rational belief is based on verifiable evidence capable of withstanding the criticism of a community of investigators. The first sense of rational action described by Jarvie is tautological; as we have seen in the first section of this chapter, he supports the notion that all action is goal-directed, therefore rational. He considers actions to be rational in the strong sense only if they are supported by verifiable rational beliefs. The Azande, therefore, have some sense of rationality in that their action is goal-directed. He would claim that the Zande sense of rationality is weak, however, because it is based on mistaken beliefs that could not withstand criticism. Implied in his argument is the notion that the mere fact that a society survives indicates the presence of some sense of rationality.

In defense of Winch, I do not think that Jarvie's first point of criticism has a firm basis in what Winch has argued. Winch has clearly indicated that the very speaking of a language is inherently rational in that it is rule-governed and intersubjective. He indicates, moreover, that rules are not merely followed mechanically but are applied in new and original circumstances. Certainly anthropological fieldwork calls for the application of rules in new social contexts, thus pointing to the open horizon of language and the possibility of mutual communication between native and anthropologist. The focus of conflict between Jarvie and Winch, therefore, is not over whether anthropologist and native share a concept of rationality, but over the sort of rationality they share.

In his second point Jarvie asserts that Winch's association of rationality with a form of life implies, at least in indigenous societies, that two forms of life cannot coexist in the same society, especially if the forms of life are rooted in radically antithetical assumptions. The example given by Jarvie is the coexistence of native healing and modern medicine. He argues that the principles supporting the germ theory are not compatible with explanations of illness rooted in the disturbance of the social harmony of the group or transgression against the ancestors. Yet many traditional societies have sustained these contradictory views by claiming that, while the germ theory may explain the cause of disease, social disharmony or transgression against the ancestors explains why one person is stricken instead of another.

It is true that Winch betrays an overly provincial view of indigenous societies in suggesting that they necessarily have one unified world view and that contradictory perspectives cannot be maintained. Jarvie's perspective, however, does not provide an alternative to Winch's method of interpretation. Even in a society that had a mixture of both traditional and modern healing, it would not be legitimate to use the categories of the germ theory to explain what the natives were doing when they consulted an oracle, for it would not get to the root of the meaning of consulting the oracle or any related activity. Jarvie also overlooks the social significance of his contention that modern and traditional healing can be sustained in the same society: the presence of modern medicine often reflects the unequal relation between former colonies and the metropole. Certainly, it is not presuming too much to suggest that indigenous societies accept modern medicine for other than purely efficacious reasons or because it represents the truth in a way that cannot be grasped by native beliefs.

Jarvie's third point has particular relevance to Zande society. He claims that societies in all periods of history have been pluralistic, a fact that Winch has not accounted for in his notion of the language community as a unity. By pluralism, Jarvie has in mind multilingualism engendered by a diverse range of cultural contacts such as gift exchange and long-distance trade. While Winch claims that a society can have more than one form of life, it is clear that his examples pertain more to the fragmentation of knowledge than to multilingualism and cultural diversity.

The traffic between languages is not quite the neutral arena suggested by Jarvie's notion of pluralism and Winch's concept of forms of life. The ability of language games to be applied in new social contexts covers Winch insofar as he wishes to account for the reciprocal encounter of forms of life in cultural contact. Many encounters between cultures are marked, however, by a lack of reciprocity in exchange, which at the communicative level discloses itself in the inequality of interlocutors. The presence, therefore, of several spoken dialects in a single culture does not imply their equality. The political struggle for dominance among dialects in a single society can also be recognized in the state formation process. An attempt is often made to extend the hegemony of political institutions through the cultural medium of adopting a unified dialect for market and juridical matters. Zande multilingualism, therefore, was not pluralistic in the sense of an equal play of dialects in a single society, but, on the contrary, reflected the political use of language arising from the Avongara conquest of a decentralized indigenous population.

Jarvie's fourth point emphasizes that modern western and Zande societies are both part of one pluralistic world culture. Contrary to Winch's concept of the different rules of intelligibility associated with dissimilar forms of life, Jarvie views cultures as distinct in degree but not in nature. He makes favorable reference to Evans-Pritchard in support of his position:

> Evans-Pritchard, too, in his classical study of Azande witchcraft (1937) does not attribute different aims to the Azande than to the rest of mankind; the differences lie in the situation – if you like, the "reality orientation." (1972: 11)

It is never clearly specified by either Jarvie or Evans-Pritchard what aims or goals we have in common with the Azande apart from the somewhat functional and teleological maintenance of a social order. Jarvie does not mean that because we share aims or a world culture with other societies, all peoples are equal. Quite to the contrary, his philosophy of history takes our own society as the pinnacle of human progress:

> Certainly primitive societies have their good and interesting sides, and they have things to teach us. That doesn't at all affect the fact that man has made objective progress in improving his society and that we in the West seem at this stage to have the best society in recorded history. (1964: 14)

Jarvie's criterion of progress is the critical rationalism of the deductive scientific method, which when coupled with technology has been utilizable for the control of both nature and human society. The truth and objectivity of this method are guaranteed, as we have seen, by the mutual consensus of a community of investigators who continually subject their lawlike hypotheses, which draw relations between facts in the world, to unrelenting criticism. Jarvie's notion of knowledge as rooted in science amounts to a philosophy of history because the development of the human species itself is understood as a gradual progress towards the manifestation of the critical spirit of the hypothetico-deductive method. This ultimate manifestation of the standard of truth in the scientific method then becomes the perspective from which not only all prior periods of history but also other cultures are both described and judged. The unity of the human mind characterized by various stages progressing toward the realization of truth and objectivity in the scientific method makes the interpretation of other cultures nonproblematic for Jarvie.

Furthermore, Jarvie claims that rationality itself has been enhanced through the general proliferation of literacy, which has given us an unquestionable past with which to compare the present. He unreflectively asserts the truth of the written word against the ambiguity and potential deception of the spoken. He has, however, apparently ignored his own dictum that presuppositions determine actions and thus the way the world is. He does not account for why presuppositions should be absent from written history or why, if presuppositions are in fact objectified in written history, they should necessarily be true. Since, for Jarvie, what is publicly held is true, the public nature of written history must then ensure a true account of events. Yet oral history is also publicly held, although Jarvie seems unwilling to absorb this into his account of truth. He ignores the fact that historical events and texts both are open to multiple interpretations, which are frequently contradictory depending upon the historical horizon of the interpreter. He furthermore overlooks the fact that history is written by concrete persons, originally by the priest-guardians of temples, and that the presuppositions expressed in historical writings are all too often, and I may add inevitably, the manifestations of class or dominant-group interests.[4]

Jarvie's notion of a pluralistic world culture entails that any society that shared or could understand our sense of critical rationality would then be willing to abdicate its mistaken beliefs:

> if the native had never heard the arguments in favor of scientific explanation ... it would only be non-rational if, faced with all the arguments, and able to appreciate their force, the native still refused to accept that a Western scientific explanation was any improvement on their own. (1964: 138)

Jarvie has devitalized the whole sense of pluralism as cultural diversity by arguing that if natives knew better they would find it beyond their rational capacity to reject our philosophy of history manifested by the scientistic self-understanding of the human species. Herbert Marcuse also recognized in *One Dimensional Man* (1964) the possibility of one world culture based upon scientistic rationality and technology; he did not view this social process as progress, however, but rather characterized it as the dialectics of world domination.[5] Marcuse, and more recently William Leiss (1974), articulated a view of science, not as the contemplation of nature, in Jarvie's sense, but as a social process that dialectically transforms nature and thus human society to meet social needs. This dialectical framework exposes a science that is dedicated to the control of objectified processes as also dedicated as a result to the control and therefore domination of social life.[6] The political implications of one world culture, a notion antithetical to Winch's forms of life, never occur to Jarvie.

Jarvie's fifth and final objection to Winch's ordinary language philosophy is that the world is extralinguistic. He bases this on the assertion that western science makes hypotheses about the world which are either true or false. According to Jarvie, language is only important as the fundamental social institution through which investigators reach consensus. Science is therefore the privileged medium through which reality should be explored. He claims that he is not supporting the view of science for science's sake, but of science employed to further human knowledge. This appears, however, to contradict the following:

> Truth and consistency are qualities we attribute to statements apropos their relationship to this 'external world." Inconsistent statements cannot possibly be true together of any world; true statements are true of this world. That the Azande do not have explicit notions corresponding to these, show little interest in them, etc., is simply an empirical fact. These ideas are great discoveries in the history of mankind. They are accepted in a wide diversity of cultures. . . . They are at the core of what I earlier referred to as a universal standard of rationality. Diffusion is not perfect and so they are not to be found everywhere yet. But I predict that, like industrialization, they will be. (Jarvie 1972: 53–4)

Jarvie's argument is tautological in that it appeals to a universal standard of rationality, which is none other than the scientific method, in order to justify science. He avoids the whole issue of science's accountability for its own categories by appealing to the politics of power to explain the diffusion of the scientific method. For example, he claims that our standards of rationality are better than those of the Azande because the anthropologist travels to Zande society and can make sense of their world, but the Azande do not know how to make sense of the anthropologist's world. He assumes that anthropologists have understood Zande society simply because we as modern westerners have rejected Zande beliefs in witchcraft, thereby exhibiting the self-evident superiority of scientific explanation. Even if we grant that Evans-Pritchard understood a great deal about Zande society, and I see no reason why we should not, he made it his central ethnographic aim to understand the world in the native's terms through a method of interpretation which he understood as an art. This is, of course, contrary to Jarvie's hypothetico-deductive method of creating lawlike, verifiable hypotheses that view a typified actor in pursuit of goals limited by the circumstances of norms and institutions. It is because he views action as separate from belief that Jarvie is able to dismiss the self-understanding of the Azande and privilege the categories of the western anthropologist, which take science as the very paradigm of rationality.

Horton: Continuity and Evolution

Robin Horton's contribution to the rationality debates is not as systematic as that of I. C. Jarvie. Horton, furthermore, has nowhere attempted to refute or address directly the issues raised by Peter Winch. He has attempted, rather, to outline both the social and the psychological preconditions of continuity between traditional and modern thought. It is in relation to this asserted continuity that we can recognize the challenge to ordinary language philosophy.

Horton has claimed in two essays, "African Traditional Thought and Western Science" (1970) and "Lévy-Bruhl, Durkheim and the Scientific Revolution" (1973a), that anthropological interpretation has been marked by a liberal credo which he calls the "lost world." This view, he says, is best exemplified by the anthropologist who, disenchanted and alienated by modern society, characterizes all organic-traditional societies as utopias. Such societies are distorted by this interpretation in that they are conceptualized as the inverted image of western society. Horton claims that the lost world perspective owes its origins not only to the social preconditions of alienation in modern society but also intellectually to problems raised by Lévy-Bruhl in the early part of the twentieth century and to a misreading of

Durkheim's *The Elementary Forms of the Religious Life* (1965). Lévy-Bruhl is cited for his portrayal of the logical contradictions in primitive beliefs, a view which he later refuted. Horton argues that many liberal anthropologists, such as Leach and Fortes, have attempted to defend indigenous cosmologies from their seeming irrationality by claiming that traditional beliefs should not be taken literally but symbolically. This is contrary to Lévy-Bruhl's contention that primitive beliefs must be treated literally because treating them as metaphor vitiates their claim to grasp reality. Horton resolves this conflict by asserting that erroneous beliefs are not a sign of inferior intellect; western science itself has progressed by means of the refutation of theories and establishment of new paradigmatic models to inform research. He claims that deeper reflection on the growth and nature of our own theories is a prerequisite for understanding the evolution and continuity of theory formation in traditional and modern societies.

Horton cites Durkheim as furnishing evidence for the continuity between traditional and modern societies, inasmuch as both primitive religion and modern science transcend common sense in order to draw relations between unobservables:

> By the use of such ideas about an unobservable order of things (what Durk-heim calls "a world of ideals"), we can grasp causal connections which common sense could have never dreamed of.... But such ideas, so crucial to the development of higher thought, could never have occurred to us had it not been for the primal religious situation.... So it is that we can find the vital germ of the most elaborate sciences in the first stirrings of the most primitive religions. (1973a: 262)

Horton contends that students of Durkheim have tended to emphasize his dichotomy of sacred and profane to the neglect of this perception of continuity. Horton thus characterizes the liberal anthropologist as portraying traditional societies in a framework of "contrast-inversion" rather than a perspective which he calls "continuity-evolution." We will see how Horton's continuity-evolution perspective is in direct opposition to the concept of language and world-constitution represented by Winch. Winch's position, moreover, cannot be subsumed under Horton's category of contrast-inversion, owing to its radical refutation and rejection of Durkheimian sociology.

From his continuity-evolution perspective Horton, like Jarvie, does not perceive the interpretation of non-western societies as problematic, since their concept formation is merely expressed in a different idiom and therefore differs only in degree and not in kind from western science. The rationality of western science is not essentially different from the rationality of theory formation in traditional societies. Horton, however, unlike Jarvie, does not accept the unqualified superiority of western society:

> Yet as a man, here I am living by choice in a still – heavily – traditional Africa rather than in the scientifically oriented Western subculture I was brought up in. Why? Well, there may be lots of queer, sinister, unacknowledged reasons. But one certain reason is the discovery of things lost at home. An intensely poetic quality in everyday life and thought, and a vivid enjoyment of the passing moment – both driven out of the sophisticated Western life by the quest for purity of motive and the faith in progress. How necessary these are for the advance of science; but what a disaster they are when they run wild beyond their appropriate bounds! (1971: 170)

It is paradoxical that this statement comes from the same man who has characterized the liberal anthropologist as searching for the lost world. Shakespeare himself could hardly have created a more tragic figure, one who on the verge of vision retreats to the lost world to mourn the passing of poetry. Despite Horton's recognition of the poetic in indigenous societies, however, his views on language are shaped by a contradictory faith in the progress and necessity of science. It is over the medium of language that his most serious confrontation with Winch, and the primitive, occurs.

Horton describes language socialization as a secondary process external to but built upon the primacy of preverbal schemata. In this respect, he owes a self-acknowledged debt to the Swiss structuralist and developmental psychologist, Jean Piaget. Piaget claims that the development of internal brain-neurological processes coordinates visual, tactual, and kinesthetic stimuli. This process is not entirely innate, as the developing child is always in interaction with a human and natural environment. Piaget's developmental schema is a version of neo-Kantian rationalism in that it posits universal stages of both cognitive and moral development. These stages are not dependent on consensus or intersubjective agreement but on physiological processes which universally draw relations between things and categories of things, both natural and social, in the world.

Horton, in turn, claims that adults have, as part of their linguistic repertoire, fundamental "material-object and causal concepts" which have preverbal and presocial foundations. According to Horton, this material-object or observation language is both universal and ahistorical, and is responsible for the constitution of the "given" with which he claims any theoretical framework must articulate or correspond. There are approximately 100 to 200 material-object words that Horton claims are the same from language to language. The concept of material object presupposes that there is a direct or immediate relation between a word and an object in the world.

The language that serves as the intersubjective basis of theory formation is not constitutive but descriptive and therefore neutral.

Horton's concept of language presupposes two levels, one a correlate of universal brain structures and the other socially contingent and serving as the basis of theory formation and description. The language associated with brain structures is not a private language, since its objectivity is grounded in the common physiology of the human species. What Horton calls the "given," the social and natural world, is the consequence of a biologically rooted object language and not social convention. The question then arises as to how we can move from the level of a biologically rooted material-object language, which is universal but not intersubjective, to the level of meaningful social interaction, which in anthropology is the foundation of cultural life. Horton's concept of language suggests that the intersubjective meaning components of cultural life, which permit the identification of causal relations between objects in the world, are part of the basic biological equipment of the solitary speaking subject. These intersubjective meaning components, which in turn make it possible to differentiate between meaningful objects, are postulated by Horton, moreover, as a priori in that, being both preverbal and presocial, they precede all experience. Differentiation or relation between actual or possible objects of experience presupposes, however, not merely the biological response of a solitary human subject but also the mutual interaction of co-subjects able to differentiate or relate in the same manner. Hence the notion of differentiation presupposes intersubjective rules that are linguistically mediated and part of a socially transmitted cultural learning process. It is contradictory, therefore, if we are to maintain that objects of actual or potential experience are meaningful, to move, as Horton does, from the context of a singular speaking subject to the intersubjective framework of either theory formation or the constitution of cultural life. It is absurd, furthermore, for Horton to assume that preverbal schemata are conceptual, since being conceptual already presupposes a framework of mutual intelligibility – an argument made by the early Wittgenstein against the possibility of private languages.

In view of Horton's concept of language, it is not difficult to understand why he views anthropological understanding as nonproblematic. The objective world is constituted, according to him, through causal associations established at the preverbal and presocial levels and mediated through the biological developmental process of the human species. Because the human species shares the same biological equipment and hence the same material-object language, anthropologist and native are both part of the same unmediated world. The second level of language is neutral and thus facilitates the process of copying reality, or theory formation. Given the neutrality of the second level of language and the objective determination of the material-object language by the biology of the human species, it becomes impossible a priori for the anthropologist to superimpose western categories in the distorting way that Winch has suggested. This does not mean that theories cannot be mistaken; hypotheses can fail to correspond to natural, causal relations that are for Horton preverbally and presocially established. According to Horton, however, cultural life is in a constant state of flux and must be transcended by theory formation to grasp the "unobservable order of things."

Horton's concept of language provides the groundwork for his concept of theory, which has been expressed in eight related theses in the aforementioned article, "African Traditional Thought and Western Science." I will review only some of these theses in terms of their major presuppositions, as they tend to repeat and therefore emphasize the same themes. His concept of theory elaborates his continuity-evolution theme and thus sheds light on his conception of anthropological understanding.

Horton's major thesis asserts that the role of theory is explanatory:

> The quest for explanatory theory is basically the quest for unity underlying diversity; for simplicity underlying apparent complexity; for order underlying apparent disorder; for regularity underlying apparent anomaly. (1971: 132)

He claims that his notion of theory applies not only to the canons of modern western science but also to indigenous explanations of reality. This version of theory asserts the subsumption of particular events and circumstances under universal deductive laws that are capable of predicting and therefore explaining individual occurrences of these laws. His notion of theory also presumes that particular manifestations of human behavior can be explained through lawlike hypotheses in a manner which is analogous to a universal concept of human nature. The progress of science is then marked by the development of increasingly fewer hypotheses with greater ranges of applicability. The population-pressure thesis within anthropology – cultural ecology – provides an example of such a generalized law which is meant to explain the development of increasingly more complex levels of sociocultural integration.[7]

Horton claims that a scientific hypothesis is not different in kind from an indigenous religious or cosmological concept that attempts to explain a wide range of circumstances in the social and natural world:

> gods of a given culture form a scheme which interprets the vast diversity of everyday experience in terms of the action of a relatively few kinds of forces. ...Like atoms, molecules, and waves, then, the gods serve to introduce unity into diversity, simplicity into complexity, order into disorder, regularity into anomaly. (1971: 133–4)

It is my contention that Horton has confused two distinct forms of knowledge and rationality: instrumental and communicative. The hypotheses of western science, whose leading interest of knowledge[8] is instrumental rationality, put forward lawlike statements that are intended to be capable of predicting individual events and circumstances. Hypotheses are then either confirmed or refuted through induction, which takes the form of feedback-controlled action according to the experimental method. The knowledge gained from this method may be used both for the reformulation of mistaken hypotheses and for the technical control of objectified processes and events.

The process of theory formation in Horton's sense, however, is not understandable according to the technique of feedback- controlled instrumental rationality. Hypotheses are formulated through the mutual discussion and consensus of a group of investigators, thereby grounding theory in the sociocultural life-world of ordinary language communication or communicative rationality. Horton reveals some comprehension of the grounding of theory in the sociocultural life-world when he claims that all theoretical developments have their point of departure in the world of common sense.

Communicative rationality, on the other hand, claims that the sociocultural life-world can only be grasped symbolically through the mutual expectation and reciprocity of ordinary language. There is no sense of control implied in communicative rationality; native peoples would be horrified to think that their cosmology implied the primary utilization of their gods and ancestors for control of the natural and social world.[9] As I have shown in my discussion of Winch, the beliefs of indigenous peoples and modern scientists are based upon fundamentally antithetical rules and forms of life and, as argued above, interests of knowledge.

Although Horton claims that theory has its point of departure in common sense, he argues that it is capable of grasping broader connections: "Theory places things in a causal context wider than that provided by common sense" (1971: 135). Common sense is tied to the world of observables and is therefore limited in the connections that it can grasp. Theory concerns itself with unobservables, hence is able to transcend the limits of common sense. Theory begins where common sense runs into problems, but is not opposed to common sense: "Common sense and theory have complementary roles in everyday life" (1971: 140).

While it is true that both common sense and theory can draw causal relations between events, things, or objects, in the world, Horton fails to recognize that causality is a concept and therefore frequently used in different language games with different meanings. He claims that all societies, traditional and modern, establish causal relations in precisely the same manner, since causal relations are constituted through the preverbal and presocial material-object language. The universality of causality in theory is then based, according to Horton, on the dependence of theory on causal links established at the material-object level. Common sense is also capable of grasping causal connections but with a more restricted range of generalizability. In accordance with his label theory of causality, he asserts that the native uses the concept of causality in the same manner as the western scientist in explaining such things as the causation of illness. According to Winch's ordinary language philosophy, on the other hand, the use of cause in native concepts of illness involves different rules and consequently forms of life than the scientific use of causality.

Let us follow out Horton's example of native conceptions of the causality of disease and compare it with Newton's law of gravity. Horton himself suggests that natives almost always attribute a social cause to illness. The social cause is usually a consequence of transgression of tribal custom or retribution resulting from neglect of the ancestors. In either case, illness is attributed to the transgression of an intersubjectively recognized moral sanction. The relation of individuals to each other or to the ancestors as mediated through moral sanctions is inherently intentional. Newton's law of gravity, in turn, presents us with another sense of causality when applied to the explanation of falling objects. When I release an apple from my hand and it falls to the ground, it would not be incorrect to claim that gravity caused the apple to fall. The law of gravity could also be applied as a theory to all falling objects with the same sense. The law of gravity does not imply intentionality but rather a mechanical relation between a force and an object.

The form of life suggested by the moral realm is appropriate, then, for understanding the meaning of actions and beliefs associated with native concepts of illness. The concept of causality as a mechanical relation between nonintentional but lawlike relations between objects is only applicable within the instrumental rules and procedures of natural science. Horton has committed a category mistake, in Winch's sense, by applying a concept of causality which has sense only within the language games of natural science to explain the native's self- understanding of beliefs associated with illness. That he accepts the nonintentional nature of causality with respect to human actions is clearly illustrated by the following:

> Indeed, as one who has hankerings after behaviourism, I am inclined to believe that it is this idiom, and this idiom only, which will eventually lead to the triumph of science in the sphere of human affairs. What I am saying, however, is that this is more a reflection of the nature of reality than a clue to the essence of scientific method. (1971: 153)

Horton claims, despite his insistence that indigenous theories account for causality and therefore have explanatory value, that the method of modern science is clearly more able to grasp causal connections. This is in part due to the fact that natives live for the most part in the world of common sense and only resort to the mystical or theoretical when common sense fails. Modern science operates more consistently and systematically within a theoretical framework and has developed experimental techniques by which theories can be either affirmed or rejected.

Throughout his treatment of the issues that I have briefly reviewed, Horton has repeatedly emphasized the continuity- evolution theme in relation to modern and traditional societies. While he has been careful to distinguish common sense from theory in all societies, he confuses the analytical notion of theory in western science with traditional notions of cosmology. It is my contention that he is guilty of the same lack of reflection for which he chastises the contrast-inversion anthropologists. He has failed to reflect upon transitions in the concept of theory in our own tradition. For example, Aristotle's concept of theory in the Greek tradition was directly related to praxis or the leading of the just or good life. This certainly contrasts with the notion of theory in modern science as the formation of universal laws for the purpose of drawing casual relations between objects and events in the world. The Greek sense of theory had a moral-practical-communicative interest, as opposed to the instrumental interests of western science. While an indigenous cosmology and modern western science are both interpretations of the world, the interests in pursuit of which each engages either actual or possible objects of knowledge cannot simply be taken for granted or treated as epiphenomenal. Since indigenous cosmologies have no interest in the control of objectified processes in either the natural or social world through the establishment of causal relations by feedback-controlled experimentation, it simply makes no sense to postulate continuity between native cosmologies and the theories of modern science. This need not imply that indigenous peoples, as Horton fears, have inferior intellects. The establishment of the communicative realm shows that the range of human experience and knowledge exceeds the limits of the scientific method.

Horton and Popper: The Open and Closed Society

Despite Horton's emphasis on the continuity-evolution theme, he contends that there are differences between the world outlooks of traditional and modern societies. Following Karl Popper's example in *The Open Society and Its Enemies* (1966), he characterizes traditional societies as closed and modern societies as open. He has stated that he intends to use the concept of open and closed societies in a narrower sense than Popper, claiming that individuality and achieved status do not necessarily develop with the open predicament and can therefore be found in closed societies as well. According to Horton, traditional societies can be characterized more specifically in contrast to modern societies:

> What I take to be the key difference is a very simple one. It is that in traditional cultures there is no developed awareness of alternatives to the established body of theoretical tenets; whereas in scientifically oriented cultures, such an awareness is highly developed. It is this difference we refer to when we say that traditional cultures are 'closed' and that scientifically oriented cultures 'open.' (1971: 153)

He has accepted the contrast between open and closed societies on the basis of Popper's notion of science as rational criticism, a view already developed in my section on Jarvie. The Popperian notion of science is critical of all claims to absolute truth or certainty. Every hypothesis is held tentatively until it can be shown inductively that it is unable to account for a fact in the world; the anomaly may then be used to refute that hypothesis. Horton has claimed that theories in traditional societies are not held tentatively and therefore that no effort is made towards refutation.

To support his view of traditional societies, Horton appeals to Evans-Pritchard's study of Zande witchcraft. In the case of divination, Horton relates that failures or anomalies do not bring the diviner's practices into question, as the practices are based upon beliefs of absolute validity. He uses his notion that theory gives a sense of order to chaos to justify his interpretation that, having no theoretical alternatives in Zande society, the natives hold tenaciously to their beliefs in order to avoid the anxiety associated with having no accepted beliefs.

Horton's argument is both tautological and functional in a quasi-Malinowskian sense. It is tautological in that a society which has no alternatives cannot by definition challenge its accepted beliefs, since to do so would imply that it did have alternatives. Human society, furthermore, always presupposes some sort of social order, language, and intersubjectively held beliefs. Belief versus chaos is therefore a pseudodichotomy with no basis in any society. Horton's argument is functional in that it instrumentalizes beliefs by reducing their intentionality to the avoidance of anxiety. What they mean then becomes secondary to their function in some social order.

I do not believe that Horton is wrong in recognizing some differences between traditional and modern modes of thought, as these distinct forms of society are characterized by very different social orders.[10] I do believe that Horton's use of the concept of open and closed societies is ideological and bears no resemblance to Winch's use of the concept of different forms of life. By ideological, I mean that Horton's and Popper's characterization of science as the epitome of the open predicament conceals an inherently conservative research process, and mystifies the social preconditions of science by grounding its method and criteria for objectivity in the consensus of the investigative community rather than the prescientific social life-world.

Since Horton has borrowed the idea of science as a model for the open society from Karl Popper, let us begin our investigation of the ideological features of science and the open society by examining the legitimacy of Popper's claim that scientific research is an open process. Popper's portrayal of science as the rational criticism of deductive hypotheses has been cogently challenged by the philosopher of science Thomas Kuhn in a series of articles published in *Criticism and the Growth of Knowledge* (1970).[11] Kuhn, in opposition to Popper, characterizes science as an inherently con-servative process, only periodically marked by new insights leading to scientific revolutions. Kuhn claims that the growth of science has not been the result of a cumulative and evolutionary growth of knowledge, each layer being built upon a prior layer. Rather, scientific research is guided by inter-subjective models, or paradigms, which provide normative rules, methods, and procedures for selecting and interpreting both actual and potential objects of knowledge. Scientists trained in various disciplines are schooled in the major paradigms of their subject of inquiry. Anomalies ordinarily are not used to refute the paradigm but are attributed to the experimental error of the investigator. Kuhn claims that it is the exception, rather than the rule of science, when a series of anomalies cannot be rationalized by experi-mental error and a new paradigm is presented with a more comprehensive range of applicability. He argues that in most cases the new paradigm constitutes a radical refutation of the old – Einsteinian versus Newtonian physics, for example – and is not simply derived from its predecessor. He claims that Popper's notion of open and rational criticism is a rare occur-rence and that such "heroic science" should not be taken as the normal practice and procedure of science. Kuhn's view of science is not unlike Horton's view of Zande oracles, which are upheld because of their absolute validity. Science and Zande oracles are not based upon the same rationality, of course; but science, despite its periodic revolutions, is not in reality the open forum of rational criticism that Horton, following Popper, would lead us to believe.

While Horton and Popper have repeatedly emphasized the objective nature of intersubjective consensus within the scientific community, they have not made an attempt to relate this community of investigators to society as a whole. Consequently, they have assumed that, since it is the scientific community which operates on principles of rational criticism, this selfsame community has come closer than any other conceivable commu-nity to producing knowledge that is in agreement with reality.

Furthermore, Horton and Jarvie assert that the institutionalization of rational criticism provides a means to recognize and replace mistaken hypotheses, thus avoiding overly dogmatic assertions. The methodological procedures arising from rational criticism allow science to evolve as a dynamic process. Because science also produces knowledge which is technically utilizable, it affects both the nature and quality of social life. It is the relation between science and the quality of social life in particular that lies behind Jarvie's praise and Horton's recognition of the necessity for scientific progress.

I have shown, however, that the instrumental methods and procedures of science are not sufficient for the self-explication of science, since the rational discussion of hypotheses that leads to their acceptance or refutation takes place in ordinary language. Hence, while scientists are capable of objectifying the world through hypotheses that seem only to draw relations between facts, scientific practice itself is guided by rules and conventions of mutual expectation that directly link the scientific community to the larger society and thus, in Winch's sense, to other forms of life. I do not mean that the average layman can immediately understand advanced nuclear physics, which operates within the context of formal languages such as higher mathematics. Often these scientists are capable of communicating the nature of their activity only to other specialists, through obscure mathematical formulas. I am, however, suggesting that scientific practice, as it operates within a wide range of possible social goals, is clearly understandable to the average person, despite attempts by scientists and state bureaucrats to conceal policy decisions behind a veil of specialization. For example, I am not well-versed in the principles that enable an astronaut to be sent to the moon. I do, however, have a clear understanding of what it means to spend federal funds on the escalation of the space race as opposed, for example, to community hospitals. Because the application of science affects the nature and quality of social life, scientific practice in both its means and consequences is as much moral and political as technical. Horton has masked the ideological thrust of the notion of the scientific "open" society by disguising political and moral questions as purely technical. He fetishizes science in a way that resembles Marx's description of the fetishism of commodities, whereby the social nature of political economy is disguised as the mere exchange of goods.

Horton's characterization of traditional societies as closed still requires critical comment. This conception has contributed to the mystification of tradition, in that rituals and myths are often portrayed as passively accepted, with no room for alternatives or choice. According to Horton, choice and alternatives only arise with the philosophy of science and epistemology, which present clearly articulated rules and norms for the validity of knowledge claims. The mechanical acceptance of myth, lore, and ritual can only be derived through a behavioristic understanding of human action and tradition, a view which Horton claims is in agreement with reality. In indigenous societies, however, traditions are not merely handed down without question but require active interpretation and recreation through the ritual life of the people. Rituals, furthermore, provide a vehicle for the expression of ambivalences felt towards the community as well as a medium through which to create and recreate the meaning of life crises:

> In primitive society, the ritual drama is a culturally comprehensive vehicle for group and individual expression at critical junctures in the social round or personal life cycle, as these crises are enjoined by the natural environment or defined by culture. In such ceremonies, art, religion and daily life fuse, and cultural meanings are renewed and re-created on a stage as wide as society itself. (Diamond 1974: 150)

The division of labor, which in many indigenous societies creates distinctions between men's and women's work as well as between generations, is not highly specialized, which accounts for the individual's knowledge of and participation in a wide range of social activities. The conflicts, diversity, and unity of indigenous social life are all expressed in native cosmologies, which as world views can be comprehended and articulated by all members of the society.

Horton has characterized indigenous cosmologies as expressive of a personalistic idiom which illustrates the value orientation of mutual human relations characteristic of many native cultures. It is this personalistic world view of indigenous societies, his closed predicament, that he compares to the impersonal idiom (but open predicament) of modern western science. The impersonal idiom values material over human factors, a condition described by the Hungarian Marxist Lukács as reification.[12] While Lukács understands the impersonal idiom as a symptom of alienated labor and domination, Horton interprets the personal/impersonal idioms merely as different value orientations of humanity that bear no relation to an unchanging reality.[13] Furthermore, he was wrongly compared native cosmologies, which have the comprehensiveness of world views, with modern science, which, rooted in instrumental rationality, is capable of expressing only a fragment of human experience and knowledge.

Horton and Jarvie have also suggested that oral traditions are much more susceptible to distortion than literate traditions. I contend that although the process of disseminating oral traditions from elders to juniors is controlled by the former, oral traditions are part of a common repository of knowledge shared by an entire culture. Oral traditions are not merely memorized by younger men and women, but consist of common themes which are cast into the personal mold of the storyteller without loss of meaning or distortion. The handing down of oral traditions through the storyteller provides many occasions for the questioning of tribal traditions.

Horton's concept of open and closed societies is symptomatic of a culture which, having inherited and radicalized an Anglo-French concept of criticism, is unable to reflect upon and thus come to terms with itself as a tradition. Endless dichotomies are created thereby which project our own sense of frustration and lack of integration onto all societies that do not share our sense of destiny and world view. The limitations of the dichotomy of open and closed are exhibited somewhat latently by Horton in the following:

> But the layman's ground for accepting the models propounded by the scientist is often no different from the young African villager's ground for accepting the models propounded by one of his elders. In both cases the propounders are deferred to as the accredited agents of tradition. As for the rules which guide scientists themselves in the acceptance or rejection of models, these seldom become part of the intellectual equipment of the members of the wider population. For all the apparent up-to-dateness of the content of his world view, the modern Western layman is rarely more "open" or scientific in his outlook than is the traditional African villager. (1971: 171)

His behaviorism here emerges again, in that it is not just the African who is shaped by the authority of tradition but the modern westerner as well. In his view, only the scientific method of instrumental rationality and hence the scientific community can rise above tradition.

Jarvie and Horton: Positivists or Objectivists?

The central core of difference between the neo-Popperians Jarvie and Horton and the ordinary language philosopher Peter Winch is the formers' rejection of and the latter's insistence on maintaining a distinction between explanation and understanding. Winch's distinction between explanation and understanding is based upon his perception of a radical difference between the objects of the human and the natural sciences and the necessity of insuring the suitability of method to object. While Jarvie and Horton do not argue for the identity of explanation and understanding, they do advocate, following Popper, a unity of method for the human and the natural sciences. Jarvie, in particular, views understanding as ancillary to the explanation of objectified processes and things. Understanding is portrayed as psychological and subjective and as therefore an unsuitable foundation for a critical science. In contrast to understanding, explanation takes the form of deductive, intersubjectively valid hypotheses subject to either affirmation or falsification and under which the particularity of events and experiences is subsumed. Jarvie and Horton emphasize that both explanation and understanding are permeated by presuppositions and standards, which, they claim, distinguishes their use of those concepts from the induction of the positivists. They have therefore followed Popper's self-proclaimed objectivism to distinguish their method from the inductive positivism of the Vienna Circle.

In a series of debates which took place in Germany throughout the 1960s, Adorno (1976b) and Habermas (1976) took issue with Popper's self-proclaimed objectivism. Habermas, in particular, showed through his contribution to the debates that the Vienna Circle inductivist positivism, which Popper takes as the definitive statement, did not totally exhaust the project of positivism as originally developed by Comte. If the Vienna Circle view does not exhaust the project of Comtean positivism, as Habermas argues, then it becomes interesting to evaluate Popper's claim that the hypothetico-deductive method is not positivist against von Wright's excellent comprehensive definition of positivism:

> One of the tenets of positivism is methodological monism, or the idea of the unity of scientific method amidst the diversity of subject matter of scientific investigation. A second tenet is the view that the exact natural sciences, in particular mathematical physics, set a methodological ideal or standard which measures the degree of development and perfection of all the other sciences, including the humanities. A third tenet, finally, is a characteristic view of scientific explanation. Such explanation is, in a broad sense, "causal." It consists, more specifically, in the subsumption of individual cases under hypothetically assumed general laws of nature, including "human nature." (1971: 4)

None of the above tenets in any way departs from the general program developed by Popper and employed by Jarvie and Horton as an argumentative position in the rationality debates. The continuity, therefore, between the neo-Popperians and Comtean positivism is unquestionable.

Jarvie's and Horton's views on anthropological understanding can be summarized thus: (1) methodological monism, (2) the separation of standards and facts, (3) the subsumption of intentionality under causality, (4) the advocacy of universal-general laws, and (5) the reduction of epistemology to methodology. Before concluding this chapter, I wish to challenge the neo-Popperians on several remaining issues.

Jarvie and Horton both claim that there is a regularity to social life that can be articulated through general laws of intersubjective validity. In Jarvie's case, this regularity is exposed through situational logic: typified actors review alternate strategies of means and ends to realize purposeful goals and aims in specified situations. He regards institutions and norms, in contrast to Winch, not as constitutive of social life but rather as instrumental means or limits that facilitate the achievement of the aims of individual actors. For Horton regularity is established through causality at the preverbal and presocial levels. He therefore understands institutions and norms behavioristically as determining the beliefs or views of individuals. For Horton institutions come and go but the basic causality of social life remains unchanged.

For both Horton and Jarvie, theories maintain their autonomy with respect to both the natural and the social world because they are seen merely as verifiable methods for copying reality. Verifiable hypotheses establish standards of objective research and thus are distinct from the facts that they attempt to grasp. This notion of the relative autonomy of standards and facts allows Jarvie and Horton to assert that one objective method is suitable for both the natural and the social sciences.

The notion of the relative autonomy of standards and facts has profound consequences both for social theory and for participant-observation in anthropology. In regard to social theory, Jarvie's and Horton's concept of theory as method reduces the traditional role of theory as critique of social life to the criticism of hypotheses. This reduction furthermore transforms the classical role of theory in the development of moral and practical life to a more instrumental control of objectified processes and things. The Popperian and neo-Popperian analytical philosophy of science has thus devitalized the dialectical constitution of theory as mediation in favor of a crippled and methodologically abstract contemplation.

The Popperian concept of theory assigns the anthropologist as participant-observer a role analogous to that of a laboratory technician – testing hypotheses and recording facts. We have already seen how the reification of the intentional nature of human actions, by reducing them to causal relations between objectified facts, makes interpretation for the Popperian anthropologist nonproblematic. The reductionist nature of Popperian anthropology is partly accounted for as a confusion of instrumental and quasi-biological aims of individual actors with rule-governed and linguistically mediated intentional actions of human co-subjects. The fieldworker must not be satisfied simply with inquiries into what an individual actor is doing in a given situation, but must attempt to understand how that act is constituted and has its meaning within the intersubjective framework of the forms of life of that language community. Institutions are never merely means or limits to the realization of individual aims but are constituted by meaningful, intersubjective norms. While institutions can serve the empirical interests of ruling groups, as in the case of Zande witchcraft, the normative constraints of such institutions are still embodied in the medium of ordinary language and therefore require the reflexivity of the communicative framework for their meaning and ideological distortions to be understood.

The issue of reflexivity is at the heart of the controversy between an ordinary language and dialectical approach to anthropology and Jarvie's and Horton's positivistic separation of standards and facts. It is only through reflection that the relation between knowledge and interests can be ascertained, as well as the inherent limitations to questions that arise in the course of social inquiry. We have seen in chapter 3 that reflexivity in ordinary language is the very condition that distinguishes Winch from the later Wittgenstein. Popperians would perhaps protest that certainly the rational discussion of hypotheses involves reflection. It is, however, an abstract reflection, limited to discussion of formal rules of objectivity and methodological procedure and insulated therefore from prescientific origins in the social life-world. The neo-Popperian objectivist methodology is unable to account for either the meaning or the origin of scientific hypotheses. Reflection on the conditions of possible knowledge is replaced by the philosophy of science, which reduces epistemological questions to questions of technique or methodology:

> Positivism marks the end of the theory of knowledge. In its place emerges the philosophy of science. Transcendental-logical inquiry into the conditions of possible knowledge aimed as well at explicating the meaning of knowledge as such. Positivism cuts off this inquiry, which it conceives as having become meaningless in virtue of the fact of the modern sciences.... Hence, transcendental inquiry into the conditions of possible knowledge can be meaningfully pursued only in the form of methodological inquiry into the rules for the construction and corroboration of scientific theories. (Habermas 1971: 67)

Positivism is able to limit its reflection to methodological questions and avoid metareflection on science as only one of many possible theories of knowledge because, as Jarvie has claimed, it can best "do the job." This argument is circular in that science is used to justify the validity of its own knowledge claims. As I pointed out earlier in this chapter, a scientitic understanding of science is unjustified, because scientific activity and discourse are rooted in the social life-world of ordinary language communication and therefore require a communicative framework of self-understanding. The self-reflecting ego, furthermore, which characterizes epistemology from Kant through Hegel and Marx, is eliminated in objectified scientific methodology. The ego that self-reflectively knows itself through objectifications in language and the world comes equipped, through an intersubjective process of individuation, with both a personal biography and a cultural tradition. Science looks upon the empirical interests of an ego with personal and cultural history as potentially contaminative to the objectivity of the scientific method. It is, however, both personal and cultural history that contribute to the very meaning of scientific practice, despite being systematically eliminated from the standards of scientific method. Science is unable to grasp itself as a tradition and thus to comprehend the connection between its a priori transcendental interests and its actual and potential objects of knowledge.

The reflexivity of Winch's ordinary language philosophy is clearly within the epistemological tradition and hence challenges anthropology to reflect upon the foundations of its knowledge claims. Winch, furthermore, provides another angle from which to develop a critique of the separation of standards and facts. Winchian epistemology makes the claim that the so-called facts of science can only be grasped through a conscious act on the part of an ego. We must keep in mind that for Winch an ego is never isolated but is immersed in a linguistically mediated form of life. Insofar as the grasping of facts is intersubjective, they are mediated by language games acquired through the socialization process in a particular culture. With respect to epistemology, consciousness never merely copies facts but rather is responsible for their constitution through a complex, linguistically mediated sociocultural learning process. Validity claims to knowledge, then, cannot be justified through an abstract, methodical separation of standards and facts, but must be reflectively related to the forms of life of the language community through which both standards and facts have their sense and are mediated:

> The ethnographic situation is defined not only by the native society in question but also by the ethnological tradition in the head of the ethnographer. The latter's presuppositions are operative even before entering the field. Once he is actually in the field, the native's presuppositions also become operative, and the entire situation turns into complex intercultural mediation and a dynamic interpersonal experience. (Scholte 1974: 438)

The loss of reflexivity in the positivist philosophy of science has serious consequences for the participant-observer in anthropology. The methodological procedures and the questions asked of informants both have their sense and origin within the form of life of the investigator, not the native society. If anthropologists do not comprehend the meaning of their social practices and recognize that questions pose a limited framework of possible answers, then their life-world will simply be reproduced in native cultures. The process of understanding does not involve merely the contemplation of an objectified subject but the mediation of subject and object through the engaging of two distinct forms of life. Jarvie and Horton have vitiated epistemology by substituting an objectivist methodology that makes no attempt to ground knowledge claims in historically specific, intersubjective life-worlds.

The reduction of reflexivity to intersubjectively verifiable hypotheses also permeates Jarvie's use of Popper's situational logic. Popper rejected holistic theories of society because from this perspective it is impossible to develop a verifiable methodology. According to Jarvie, social wholes, like institutions, do not have aims. Social science must therefore attempt to reconstruct and objectify the aims of individuals in given situations. The frame of this reconstruction is limited to only those factors that enhance or inhibit the actor's attempt to realize a goal. Both the actor's aims and the circumstances contributing to their realization or inhibition are treated by the investigator as facts whose causal relations will be established through hypotheses. Situational logic, however, provides no means by which to relate specific events to other aspects of society or to meaningfully comprehend a particular event as part of a determinate history or tradition. As a method, therefore, it is not suitable to its object.

In this respect, there is ascertainably a convergence between the autonomy of Winch's language games and the autonomy of events reconstructed by situational logic. We have seen in the chapter on Winch how the notion of the autonomy of language games and forms of life prevented him from recognizing the disjuncture between Zande self-understanding of witchcraft and the objective determination of witchcraft as disguised institutional domination. Situational logic likewise fails to contribute to our understanding of Zande witchcraft, because it does not take the intentionality of the intersubjective rules of witchcraft seriously, nor does it provide a framework which even facilitates the understanding of witchcraft within the context of Zande social history.

The very concept of social whole that Jarvie rejects is capable of transcending the limitations of his positivistic methodology. Positivist social scientists find the concept of totality methodologically useless because they fail to realize that totality is epistemological as well as methodological. The concept of totality, as it has been articulated by the neo- Marxist Adorno, presupposes that reality is mediated by a self- reflecting ego who is inextricably part of the research process and therefore of the totality. Totality, furthermore, presupposes that societies are structured dialectical wholes, producing and reproducing themselves through their individual moments without being reducible to them. Totality is different from other holistic concepts, such as epoch, in that it recognizes and accounts for contradictions in social formations:

> Social totality does not lead a life of its own over and above that which it unites and of which it, in its turn, is composed. It produces and reproduces itself through its individual moments. (Adorno 1976b: 107)

Totality does not imply the mechanical repetition of a social whole, as the totality is both sustained and transformed through human activity. Jarvie's and Horton's neo-Popperian methodology is vitiated, then, by a social totality which cannot be grasped by the individual moments of situational logic or the behavioristic reification of social institutions.

5 Ordinary Language Philosophy in Question: Steven Lukes and Alasdair MacIntyre

The social sciences have not traditionally concerned themselves with the concept of truth. Truth has been either ignored or banished from their domain and interest as a remnant of a prescientific past.[1] Truth belongs to the realm of metaphysics and therefore has no place in positive science. As we have seen in the previous chapter, truth is not welcome in Popper's objectivist methodology, where all hypotheses are held only tentatively. A de-emphasis of the concept of truth is also well exhibited in Leach's and Beattie's interpretation of seemingly irrational indigenous beliefs.[2] Both Leach and Beattie insist that it is a mistake to interpret indigenous beliefs literally, since they are not attempts to explain objective phenomena but are merely symbolic or expressive. In contrast, Steven Lukes and Alasdair MacIntyre claim, although separately, that native beliefs make assertions about the world and can therefore be evaluated for their truth content. That is, native beliefs can be evaluated as propositions and judged as to whether they correspond to a state of affairs in the world. In this chapter we will consider Lukes's and MacIntyre's concept of truth in relation to their notion of context-independent criteria for rationality.

Lukes *contra* Jarvie

Steven Lukes, in an article entitled "Methodological Individualism Reconsidered" (1970), confronts Popperian situational logic from the standpoint of a Durkheimian concept of the social. Lukes begins his critique by relativizing the universal claims of situational logic to account for social life as rooted in the goal-oriented action of autonomous individuals. He argues that the principles of methodological individualism can be traced to the contract theory of Hobbes, the Enlightenment concept of individualism, and nineteenth-century utilitarianism. According to contract theory social wholes, governments, and institutions mediate the competing aims and interests of individuals for the good of the social whole. Within contract theory, other human beings are conceived as limits in the "war of all against all" rather than as means of realizing human freedom. Consequently, social union can only be achieved through individuals' abdicating their rights to the Leviathan in exchange for protection. Hobbes's concept of humanity thus reflected the politics of the seventeenth and eighteenth centuries and the emerging bourgeois society.

Lukes contends that the nineteenth century was marked by an interest in collective phenomena, exhibited by the utilitarian philosophy of John Stuart Mill. Collective human actions and passions were conceived, however, to be governed by laws of individual human nature. The utilitarian philosophy is remarkably similar to Popper's notion of the individual as reviewing alternate strategies of means and ends to realize goals that are lawfully posited by human nature. The weakness of this position has been well articulated by Hannah Arendt:

> The trouble with the utility standard inherent in the very activity of fabrication is that the relationship between means and end on which it relies is very much like a chain whose every end can serve again as a means in some other context. In other words, in a strictly utilitarian world, all ends are bound to be of short duration and to be transformed into means for some further ends. (1958: 153–4)

Lukes demystifies methodological individualism, which Jarvie has advocated as a suitable method for anthropological research owing to its agreement with objective reality, by showing that it can be accounted for both sociologically and historically. The putative universality of methodological individualism is thus divested of the immunity of pure science and exposed as historically particular and ideological.[3]

Lukes claims that methodological individualism reduces social facts to explanations rooted in individual facts:

> Some thinkers have held it to be equally truistic (indeed, sometimes, to amount to the same thing) to say that facts about society and social phenomena are to be explained solely in terms of facts about individuals. This is the doctrine of methodological individualism. (1970: 77)

Statements concerning social wholes are consequently meaningless and unintelligible, because they do not correspond to any empirical state of affairs in the world. The methodological individualist attributes ontological status only to individuals and claims that institutions are merely models formally constructed by the investigator. Lukes cites Jarvie's discussion of the army as an example of the methodological individualist position.

According to Jarvie, the army as a social whole is visible and comprehensible only through statements about the acts and beliefs of individual soldiers. Lukes convincingly shows that while it is true that an army is composed of individual soldiers, the existence of the soldier as soldier is contingent upon his being a member of a social institution known as the army. The very meaning of soldier is relational and therefore institutional. Because the meaning of being a soldier is contingent on the institutional nature of the army, the army cannot simply be reduced to a means or limit to fulfilling the aims of particular soldiers. Lukes asserts that it is absurd on Jarvie's part to attempt to explain a social phenomenon on the basis of individual motives or intentions. Citing Durkheim's rules of sociological method, he claims that social phenomena must have social explanations.[4] Social phenomena or institutions, according to the Durkheimian paradigm, have a coercive influence on individuals that frequently transcends personal choice. For example, the child born into a French family in Paris has little control over what language will be spoken. It would be nonsensical to explain the social fact of a French-speaking child in terms of individual aims or goals as Jarvie's position implies.

Lukes furthermore contends that visibility does not distinguish individuals from institutions and that institutions therefore have an equally strong ontological claim. While institutions may exist in the heads of investigators as models, they also have objective empirical existence in the world. The institution of the court, for example, is observable through the concerted action of a judge, jury, lawyers, defendant, and plaintiff. Lukes also shows in this particular example that while the court is empirically visible, the motives of individual actors are not.

Despite his trenchant criticism of methodological individualism, Lukes does not reject individuals as subjects of social inquiry but rather reconsiders their significance from a modified Durkheimian perspective. His alternative to methodological individualism avoids the mutually exclusive extremes of viewing social reality solely from the perspective of social wholes or of autonomous individuals. According to Lukes, social reality is irreducibly established through the reciprocal interaction of institutions and individuals. In this respect, his position is an improvement over the Durkheimian tradition, which all too frequently reifies social institutions by suggesting that they lead lives of their own apart from human actors. Lukes's perspective, however, maintains continuity with the Durkheimian tradition by contending that the interaction of institution and individual is a nonintentional social fact. His challenge to Jarvie, therefore, resides in the privileging of social fact over the reductionist individual facts of methodological individualism. Jarvie's and Lukes's differing methodological positions converge, however, in their belief in the objectivistic facticity of the social world. As a result the meaning of social inquiry is not essentially different for Jarvie and Lukes; an absence of intentionality characterizes human activity in both theories. It is the intentionality of human actions which clearly distinguishes the positions of both Jarvie and Lukes from Peter Winch's ordinary language philosophy.

Lukes *contra* Winch

In his essay "On the Social Determination of Truth" (1973) Lukes makes the claim that there is no substantial basis for Winch's assertion that all criteria of truth and validity are context-dependent and therefore culturally variable. He goes so far as to contend that the very possibility of understanding between native and anthropologist is based upon mutual criteria of truth and rationality which are universal. According to Lukes, the existence of universal criteria of truth and rationality does not imply that there are not in fact some criteria which are culturally specific:

> I shall suggest that some criteria of rationality are universal, i.e., relevantly applicable to all beliefs, in any context, while others are context-dependent, i.e., to be discovered by investigating the context. (1971: 208)

He insists, however, that culturally specific criteria are necessarily parasitic on universal criteria. Culturally specific criteria of truth and rationality only make sense when viewed as "operating against the background" (1971: 203) of universal criteria, since universal criteria are the ultimate logical constraints to which all human thought is subject.

The relationship between universal and particular criteria of truth and rationality is exhibited, according to Lukes, in Evans-Pritchard's (1956) discussion of Nuer religion. According to Evans-Pritchard, the Nuer contend that twins are birds. He insists that the Nuer hold this belief not metaphorically but literally. The Nuer equivalence of twins and birds is, furthermore, completely rational when comprehended according to the fundamental premises of their religious cosmology; twins are identified with birds because both have an essentially spiritual nature. According to Lukes, the logical rules which permit us to make sense of this seemingly irrational Nuer belief are only discoverable through examining the premises associated with Nuer religion. He claims, however, that the criteria of rationality associated with Nuer religion are not sufficient to establish the truth of their religious beliefs. According to Lukes (1971: 209), all beliefs must fulfill the following conditions in order to sustain a claim to truth and rationality: (1) the criteria of context-dependent rationality must not violate the universal laws of logic such as noncontradiction, negation, and identity; (2) the criteria of truth and rationality must be empirically verifiable.

The main weakness, from Lukes's perspective, of Winch's notion of the social determination of culturally specific criteria is the failure to recognize that the rules which arise in the course of social life and make interpretations of culturally specific beliefs and practices possible are logically tied to formal rules of logic and intelligibility shared by the human species. Luke's concept of formal rules of logic and intelligibility situates his position within a rationalist tradition that includes such eminent anthropologists as Claude Lévi-Strauss. He furthermore contends that the notion of universal criteria of truth and rationality permits the anthropologist to raise such important questions as the difference between scientific and prescientific cultures, as well as providing the necessary standpoint from which to judge all local beliefs.

The question of whether universal criteria of truth or inteligibility are necessary for cultural comparison to be possible is inevitably an issue to which a science rooted in the comparative method must address itself. It can only be raised, however, from a perspective that does not take the rules of interpretation for granted. As we shall see, while Lukes concerns himself, in order to overcome Winch's relativism, with the epistemological question of the grounds for the validity of knowledge, he does so at the expense of adhering to positivism.

Lukes claims that Winch's notion of understanidng social life is relativistic in that his criteria of truth, rationality, and what counts as real are thought to be internal to the language games shared by a speech community. He furthermore interprets Winch's concept of rationality as conformity to norms. For Lukes, criteria of rationality and reality are not norms but extralinguistic and extraconventional standards by which the intelligibility and validity of particular beliefs are judged. According to his position, these standards of rationality and validity cannot be viewed even as social facts in the traditional Durkheimian sense, for that would reduce their status from transcendental to institutional or conventional in nature.

Lukes not only assigns an importance to the rule-governed or normative aspects of language games that is not present in Winch's conception, but he also falls subject to the rationalist problematic by divorcing universal standards of logic and rationality from the intersubjectively valid language in which they are objectified. His notion of rationality is a priori in that he posits a homology between the cognitive processes of the human mind and the structure of the objective world. Like all rationalists, Lukes is unable to illustrate how it is possible to make a transition from a priori criteria, which are present in the cognitive structures of all isolated egos before they are subject to the mediations of language and sociocultural learning processes, to the intersubjectivity of social life, which is the outcome of the formative process of human co-subjects. Furthermore, the internal/external dichotomy which Lukes reinforces with his notion of context-independent criteria of rationality ignores the fact that meaningful discussion of criteria of logic or truth necessarily involves drawing them into the context of specific language games and consequent forms of life. As Winch has stated: "criteria of logic are not a direct gift of God, but arise out of, and are, only intelligible in the context of, ways of living or modes of social life" (1958: 100).

Lukes also claims that Winch has no theory-independent reference for such terms as *world*, *nature*, and *reality* and therefore has no theory-independent criteria of truth. Here he unknowingly makes a distinction between the criteria and the content of truth. According to Lukes, it is only through the criteria of formal logic and empirical verification that a given belief can be considered true. All beliefs which are expressed in language are treated as propositions whose truth value is external to their meaning and therefore extralinguistic. The truth value is measured purely by the internal consistency of the proposition as it does or does not correspond to the formal rules of logic and by whether or not the proposition corresponds to a state of affairs in the world, which it signifies. Lukes claims that contextual interpretations are useful only insofar as they give the investigator some sense of what the beliefs mean to those who hold them.

Winch, on the contrary, makes the claim that such terms as *reality, world*, and *nature* have no sense apart from the language games in which they are used. In his view, the meaning of the concept of truth itself can vary depending upon in which of many possible language games it is used. For example, the notion of truth as correspondence between statement and fact derives its meaning intersubjectively through the form of life and associated language games of modern science. The concept of truth in aesthetics, however, does not depend upon correspondence to some objectified sense of reality but, on the contrary, upon whether through its saying it exhibits an aspect of human experience as embodied in some particular tradition.[5] Since the language games and form of life of modern science do not exhaust the full range of human experience, the Nuer belief that twins are birds is true to the degree to which it expresses the Nuer religious tradition. Winch does not have a theory-independent notion of truth, reality, or world because the criteria that establish the sense of these concepts are themselves part of language games and forms of life.

Lukes extends his critique of Winch by appealing to the authority of Marx and Lukács. According to Lukes, both Marx and Lukács have emphasized that social factors cause beliefs. His interpretation of Marx and Lukács is, however, reminiscent of a nondialectical Feuerbachian materialism. Marx and Lukács never claimed that social factors cause beliefs but rather that historically specific social preconditions give rise to beliefs which then interact dialectically with the material conditions from which they arose. The dialectical nature of the material conditions of life and thought, to be sure, in no way contradicts Winch's central thesis that the relation between beliefs expresses the social relations between men. The problem arises, as I have pointed out in my own critique of Winch, with respect to ideological distortion. Lukes has obviously appealed to Marx and Lukács to support his belief that context-independent criteria of truth are necessary to the critique of ideology. He uses this notion, however, in a way which is clearly distinct from that of Marx or Lukács. His concept of context-independent criteria of truth presupposes a scientistic dichotomy of subject and object which is overcome in the Marxist tradition by the concept of mediation through praxis or the self-formation of the human species. In the Marxist tradition, the criteria through which ideology is exposed are never completely divorced from specific historical contexts. Marx (1964) and Lukács (1971), contrary to Lukes, understand ideology as beliefs which both reveal and conceal social reality. Lukes is correct in arguing against Winch that a society's self-understanding does not always correspond to the objective conditions of its social life. He opens his own theory, however, to a penetrating Marxist critique by suggesting that the criteria according to which beliefs are judged have no basis in historical context. In this respect, his appeal to the Marxist tradition supports Winch's position, which has a concept of mediation, more emphatically than his own.

Lukes places language at the center of his philosophical critique of Winch, but subordinates it in significance to reality shared a priori between native and anthropologist. Consider the following:

> the existence of a common reality is a necessary precondition of our under-standing G's language. Though we need not agree about all "the facts," the members of G must have our distinction between truth and falsity as ap-plied to a shared reality if we are to understand their language, for if, *per impossibile*, they did not, we and they would be unable even to agree about the successful identification of public, spatio-temporally located objects. (1973: 238)

The reality which the anthropologist and native share is not created through a mutual effort to understand each other or the social and historical conditions that bring their two societies into contact. According to Lukes, the reality shared by anthropologist and native is the unmediated world of nature, of which consciousness is a part because of the constraints of formal logic to which all human thought is subject. Human thought, therefore, following its own internal laws will uniformly structure the world according to universal coordinates of space and time. Lukes implies that the isomorphic relation between thought, language, and the objective world is functional in that it allows human actors to predict both natural and social events.

We do not have to search far within anthropology to find that his "universal" spatiotemporal coordinates vary widely from culture to culture.

Benjamin Lee Whorf's (1956) now-famous study of Hopi verbs shows clearly alternative possibilities of conceptualizing the relation of time to space.[6] We can also discover considerable variation within the western tradition among concepts of time and space. For example, the concept of space as extension did not come into existence until the development of modern geometry. Likewise, E. P. Thompson (1967) has shown that the concept of linear time in western societies is attributable to the form of work discipline imposed on a newly proletarianized population in the early period of capitalism. The multitude of historical and cross-cultural examples vitiates Lukes's claim that native and anthropologist share a common, unmediated world. The possibility of mutual understanding between native and anthropologist is, then, not attributable to an a priori common world but rather to the inherent openness of ordinary language, as articulated by Winch, to being applied in new and original ways.

Lukes develops a sociological critique of Winch through his concept of rational criticism. He claims that the good historian or social theorist should attempt to understand beliefs not only internally but also through external criteria that expose ideology and its social role. His contention that the social theorist must be able to account for the social significance of ideology is his strongest argument against Winch. Through comprehending why ideological beliefs are held, we establish the possibility of transcending these beliefs. While Winch convincingly argues that social relations express ideas about reality, he provides no perspective from which to ascertain whether the ideas expressed reflect social relations of domination. Lukes, however, seriously cripples his argument by equating rational criticism with the superior cognitive powers of scientific thought. The transcendental interests of science in the control of objectified processes of nature and society do not provide an adequate framework within which the objects of domination can become co-subjects in their own emancipation and transformation of society. The transformation of society requires self-reflection on the structures and ideologies that support domination as well as a program of praxis involving cooperation and mutual understanding. Both self-reflection and praxis transcend the limitations of science, rooted as it is in the interest of control. It is therefore not fully possible to comprehend the social role of ideology in the manner which Lukes has suggested.

MacIntyre *contra* Winch

Alasdair MacIntyre's critique of Winch in several ways parallels that of Lukes in that MacIntyre also understands beliefs as propositions that make assertions about some state of affairs in the world. MacIntyre differs from

Lukes, however, in that the extracontextual criteria by which the rationality and veracity of beliefs can be judged are not transcendental or universal. MacIntyre views criteria of rationality and truth as having a history and hence, while extracontextual, as sociological or anthropological. He contends that Winch's concept of criteria is too closely tied to use and context, thus providing no standpoint from which to evaluate social change or how particular criteria come to be. This, as we shall see, is important in that it moves toward developing an interpretive anthropology that recognizes the significance of understanding social phenomena in light of social history. MacIntyre, however, undermines the significance of his own insight by characterizing history according to a quasi-evolutionary framework. His theory of history is quasi-evolutionary, as opposed to evolutionary in the full sense, in that it does not represent human societies as having progressed or developed through a series of necessary stages of sociocultural integration. It is permeated nevertheless by the evolutionary notion of progress, which is then applied to epistemology. He claims, for example, that within the context of Zande society, their witchcraft beliefs appear perfectly rational and true to any Azande. He even agrees with Winch and Evans-Pritchard that, given the social preconditions of Zande society and the assumptions that support their religious cosmology, contradictions do not call their beliefs into question because the Azande are not capable of thinking outside their concepts and hence have no interest in the matter.

MacIntyre is unable, however, to agree with Winch that there are no extracontextual criteria according to which Zande beliefs can be shown to be inconsistent and the existence of witches insupportable. According to MacIntyre, these extracontextual criteria have been brought into existence through human history. While it is true that the Azande do not have science, contrary to what Horton has suggested, modern western societies have institutionalized the critical spirit and practices of science. Science, furthermore, is a living monument to the progress of humanity, and by its standards we can assert positively that there are no witches. MacIntyre insists that his view of the progress of human knowledge is not ethnocentric in that changing social conditions in modern-day Africa have brought witchcraft beliefs into question by Africans themselves.

MacIntyre's critique of interpreting concepts according to use also exposes the disjunctures that can exist between the beliefs currently held in a society and the social preconditions which gave birth to those beliefs and may long have been transcended. This issue converges with Lukes's interest in explaining the social role of ideology. MacIntyre's solution, however, to this potential disjuncture is reconstructivist history. According to MacIntyre, it is the history of a practice or belief, and not merely its synchronic use, that gives it its sense. Consider MacIntyre's example in relation to taboo:

What I am quarrelling with ultimately is the suggestion that agreement in following a rule is sufficient to guarantee making sense.... There are the cases where the anthropologist, in order to interpret what people say, has to reconstruct imaginatively a possible past situation where expressions had a sense which they no longer bear. Consider theories about what taboo is. To call something taboo is to prohibit it, but it is not to say that it is prohibited.... So some theorists have constructed from the uses of taboo a sense which it might once have had and a possible history of how this sense was lost. One cannot take the sense from the use, for the use affords no sense.... (1971a: 68)

The meaning of taboo, at least in some cases, is not dependent on how it is described in discourse by native informants but rather is comprehensible through understanding why the natives profess to believe in and obey the taboo despite frequent and overt violations of its interdiction. According to MacIntyre, historical reconstruction will provide the investigator with knowledge of social processes and causes which determine the meaning of particular phenomena and are not perceived by the actors. The anthropologist's understanding of native beliefs and concepts will not, therefore, always correspond to the natives' interpretations. This ability of the investigator to comprehend unpreceived social processes and causes provides an adequate standpoint, according to MacIntyre, from which to criticize native activities and criteria of understanding. His suggested methodology avoids the serious relativist consequences of historicism in that the reconstruction of the histories of societies also implies critique on the part of the investigator with criteria that are themselves historically determined. While the relativist problem is avoided in MacIntyre's historical reconstruction, the disjuncture that he suggests between use and meaning is latently positivistic.

MacIntyre makes use of an objectivist concept of meaning in his method of historical reconstruction. He agrees with Winch, on the one hand, that social science investigation must begin with the actors' concepts or understandings of social phenomena. He claims, for example, that it would have been impossible for Durkheim to have explained suicide in a given society without comprehending how that society distinguished death through self-infliction from other causes. He contends, however, that Winch's method of ordinary language philosophy exhausts its potential once the problem to be investigated has been identified. In contrast to the Winchian concept of meaning as use, the objectivist criterion of meaning asserts that the sense of a given social phenomenon is ascertainable through its cause. Causes are not reducible, according to MacIntyre, to reasons or intentions held by actors or groups of individuals. The meanings of social phenomena, with respect to rules of intelligibility, are external to their actual or potential constitution by a language community. MacIntyre's reconstructivist history therefore attempts to transcend the limitations of actors' self-understanding by elaborating the social processes which cause or determine the meaning of social life. His method does not presuppose that a given actor and a social scientist could not agree on the meaning of a given event or process. He insists, however, that it is necessary to go beyond the informant's interpretation, so that ideology or false consciousness can be discovered where it is manifested.

By contending that the concept of causality is necessary for both the identification and the critique of ideology, MacIntyre rejects Winch's distinction between the natural and social sciences as based upon distinct objects of knowledge and hence divergent methodologies. He claims that Winch's concept of meaning as use only accounts for an unconstrained relationship between a given individual and society. The concept of causality, on the other hand, more adequately accounts for a relationship between an individual and society marked by constraints, as for example in a society with distinct social classes. While it is true that Winch's characterization of language games and forms of life best grasps those social situations that are domination-free, MacIntyre's recognition of this fact is based upon reasons that I consider insupportable. For example, Winch has nowhere characterized meaning simply in terms of the reasons given by an actor for performing a particular action. He has clearly shown in his example of the psychiatric encounter (1958) that a subject's self-understanding can often be out of phase with the objective conditions of his or her existence. The reasons given by a patient to explain particular actions or events can therefore be grossly distorted. Winch's most important point is that the explanations given to the patient by the psychiatrist, even if not fully comprehensible to the patient, must originate and unfold from mutually shared language games and forms of life. Consider the following:

> Again, a psychoanalyst may explain a patient's neurotic behaviour in terms of factors unknown to the patient and concepts that would be unintelligible to him. Let us suppose that the psychoanalyst's explanation refers to events in the patient's early childhood. Well, the description of those events will presuppose an understanding of the concepts in terms of which family life, for example, is carried on in our society; for these will have entered, however rudimentarily, into the relations between the child and his family. (1958: 89–90)

The patient's distorted self-perception can be understood only in relation to a specific context of social relations and the concepts which those social relations express. Although Winch does not make this comparison, the patient's distorted self-perceptions are not essentially different from the distorted self-understanding characteristic of ideology in society. As Habermas (1971) has suggested, self-reflection through the inherent intersubjectivity of ordinary language can provide a basis from which ideology can be recognized and potentially overcome.[7]

Social life, according to Winch, can never in any absolute sense be characterized as constraint-free, as the most fundamental constraint to which all humans are subject is the finite character of the language they speak and through which they understand themselves and the world. While it is true that human beings frequently have reasons or motives for acting, it is not these subjective intentions alone which give actions their sense. This sense is always codetermined through the intersubjectivity of language games and consequent forms of life. It is not inherent in the concept of language games and forms of life that ideology cannot be recognized where manifested, as MacIntyre has suggested. Winch's failure to account for ideology is more comprehensible as a result of his treatment of language games and forms of life as ahistorical and autonomous, which exhibits the limitations of the theorist rather than of language itself.

MacIntyre furthermore contends that a society's or culture's language games are not sufficient to account for ideology because there are peoples who exhibit ideology without having any such concept. Under these conditions, a concept of causality can show how status differentiations are maintained by the social structure and how beliefs arise to justify these differentiations. The concept of causality in this case would attempt to explain lawful regularities in the social structure in a way not unlike that in which regularities exhibited in nature are explained. MacIntyre cites the authority of Hume to defend the complementarity of causality in nature and society:

> He [i.e., Winch] makes this remark in the context of his discussion of predictability; and what he does not allow for in this discussion is that in fact the behavior of agents may exhibit regularities of a Humean kind and be predictable just as natural events are predictable, even although it can also be characterized and in some cases must also be characterized in terms of following and deviating from certain rules. (1971b: 121–2)

It is the predictability of human events which allows MacIntyre to speak of them in terms of causality. He does, however, appear to concede something of Winch's position by concluding that the following or breaking of rules may also be important. The crucial question is whether the concept of causality as used in either natural or social science is able to comprehend the full significance of what it means for human activity to be predictable. I contend that the concept of causality is itself logically tied to the behavioral system of instrumental rationality and is therefore unsuitable as a means or end by which to identify or transcend social constraints. I shall also argue that MacIntyre's attempted universalization of the concept of causality can be accounted for by the propositional notion of truth, which he shares with Lukes.

The concept of causality employed in natural science presupposes a sequential temporal relation between two entities whereby the entity that is prior in time is conceived as an agency or cause that produces the second entity or effect. The relation between the two is hypothesized as being predictable and describable by general universal laws. This relationship, furthermore, is usually characterized as mechanical and nonintentional. The concept of causality is thus contingent upon the range of language games and social practices through which it obtains its sense. Because of the emphasis on predictability and the nonintentionality of the agency with respect to its effect, the concept of causality within the language games of science lends itself to a process of objectification and control of reality. As Habermas (1971) has argued, the process of objectification and control is the leading interest of knowledge that informs the practice of science.

MacIntyre contends that the logic which orients the research procedures of scientific experimentation can also be used to explain events in the social world. In this respect, he defends the notion of one logic of a unified science. He tries to demonstrate several ways in which causality can be shown to be operating in the social world. His first example is intended to illustrate in what ways reasons can be understood as the causes of actions. He distinguishes between reasons that are consciously held by an actor and bring about a particular action and reasons that bring about certain actions but are not consciously held. The former case, according to MacIntyre, is intentional because of the internal connection between the reasons provided by the agent and the circumstances which produced the action. The latter, on the other hand, is causal because the reasons which were shown to produce an action are not the reasons or interpretations that were provided by the agent of the action.

> the question inevitably arises as to whether the possession of a given reason may not be the cause of an action in precisely the same sense in which hypnotic suggestion may be the cause of an action. (1971b: 117)

Causality, as portrayed by MacIntyre, implies external control in that the disjuncture between reasons and action presents a situation whereby human subjects are not the agents of their own action. It is the importance of control in the production of human action that he has in mind when he argues that causal description is applicable to the social sciences. There should be no question, therefore, that he recognizes an instrumental relation between an agency or cause and its effect.

Another example used by MacIntyre to demonstrate the suitability of causal description for social science is taken from Erving Goffman's *Asylums* (1961). According to MacIntyre, an individual incarcerated in one of the total institutions described by Goffman, such as a prison or mental hospital, must undergo an ordeal of initiation that substitutes the inmate personality for the personality possessed prior to institutionalization. Every detail of the inmate's day is controlled to meet the needs of the institutional bureaucracy. The question arises as to whether the logic that articulates the instrumental relation between cause and effect in natural science is simply reproduced in the total institution or other situations marked by social control. MacIntyre has himself indicated, but I do not think clearly recognized, the noncomplementarity between causality in the natural and the social sciences by asserting that predictability in causally determined social situations is essentially characterized by the concept of following or not following a rule. The concept of following a rule is important to situations which are predictable because it enables the investigator to judge whether the activity currently observed counts as the same as what was done on other occasions. Recognizing that rules are implicit to the observed is what leads Winch to claim that social scientists must account for not only their own methods of procedure but also the intersubjective rules of the object of knowledge, which is also a subject. The relations, therefore, between reasons and actions which MacIntyre characterizes as causal are not simply the outcome of a sequentially determinate process but involve, on the contrary, the relations between objectified human intentions. These relations, as we shall see in the chapter on hermeneutics, exhibit logical connections between signifieds, thus nullifying MacIntyre's dichotomy between intentional reasons and those not consciously held. Winch's emphasis, furthermore, on dual sets of rules implies that social science is necessarily a dialectical activity mediating between investigator and informants.[8]

Winch's notion of the two sets of rules involved in social science practice does not assume that human subjects cannot be objectified and thereby controlled through processes of political domination or economic exploitation. Social control does not imply, however, that human subjects are objectified in any absolute sense. If absolute control or determination were possible, as implied by the mechanical relation between cause and effect in natural science, the dialectical opposition to domination and exploitation – for example, in resistance movements – would not be possible. The overcoming of domination requires an interest in emancipation, which presupposes a context of cooperation that transcends the limitations of the language games and form of life whose principal interest is the control of objectified processes and things. MacIntyre's insistence on the importance of causal description in social science as a logic of one unified science contributes to the very condition of control that he wishes to identify and overcome.

MacIntyre's propositional theory of language and truth is responsible in the main for his concept of one unified science. As I stated in the section on Lukes, the propositional theory of language holds that language is only referential inasmuch as words or sequences of words are labels attached to objects or states of affairs in the world. This theory has contributed to the long and widely held view that reality is external to linguistically mediated activity on the part of human co-subjects. As I have shown in my discussion of Winch, however, what does or does not count as real is dependent on the sense that language has, through language games and forms of life. The notion that language is external and merely approximates reality is what enables MacIntyre and Lukes to treat human actions as reified things, not essentially different from objects in the material world. Reasons, then, occur in the heads of subjects and act as external forces on actions which are extralinguistic and thinglike. MacIntyre, though, is not as consistent as Lukes in holding this reified view of human activity. He contends that roles which are normative are constituted by human actors because the identity of the actor with the role makes them an unconstrained form of human activity. Situations which involve constraints are not constituted by human actors and are therefore subject to causal description. MacIntyre's position is philosophically inconsistent in that all human activity, whether constrained or not, is intersubjective and hence has an inherent linguistic-ality that transcends the finiteness of instrumental description.

In conclusion I want to credit MacIntyre with what I consider his strong-est point of criticism against Winch's position. MacIntyre contends that it is impossible to use any criteria other than our own in order to understand indigenous societies. He claims, furthermore, that Winch, in attempting to develop an interpretation theory that is context-dependent, is inconsistent by virtue of his unrecognized substitution of the context of the investigator for that of the native. This creates a somewhat embarrassing situation for Winch in that, while the native is tied to a specific context of language games and forms of life, the anthropologist is excused from such particu-larity. By privileging the categories of the native over those of the anthro-pologist Winch has systematically eliminated the reflexive dimension of anthropology: the necessary mediation through which anthropologists come to understand their own practice. Winch has attempted to answer this criticism by claiming that the anthropologist will frequently have to use western social science categories but that these categories, in order to avoid distortion, must be logically tied to the object being studied. He does not, however, adequately address the problem, which (ironically) he originally raised of mutually exclusive language games and forms of life.

While MacIntyre has very acutely recognized the problems inherent in the idea of anthropologists surrendering their categories of understanding, his solution to this dilemma is equally problematic. He claims that since we cannot surrender our own criteria of knowledge, we might as well be honest about it and simply go ahead and make use of our standards. He invokes the authority of functionalist anthropology by contending that it is after all possible for different institutions to satisfy the same needs:

> Goldschmidt argues for the recommendation: Don't ask what an institution means for the agents themselves, ask what necessary needs and purposes it serves. He argues for this not because he looks for functionalist explanations of a Malinowskian kind, but because he believes that different institutions, embodying different conceptual schemes, may be illuminatingly seen as serving the same social necessities.... It is because I believe writers such as Goldschmidt are correct in saying that one must transcend such a framework that I believe also that Winch's book deserves close critical attention.

What possible social necessities can MacIntyre have in mind that are universal to humanity? Social necessities are not simply given but are, as Marx argued, produced, reproduced, and most importantly created under historically specific social relations.[9] Many institutions, furthermore, such as the best friend in native cultures, are not found in class societies. If it is true that different institutions, as MacIntyre has suggested, serve the same needs and do so satisfactorily, how then do we explain social change? Even the family, which both creates and satisfies needs for nurturance, is based upon a fundamentally different logic, and hence sense, of production and reproduction in its extended-communal form in native societies, as contrasted with its nuclear form in modernity.[10] The critical question with respect to institutions is not their cross-cultural translatability to meet hypothesized universal needs but rather the incommensurability of institutions in different social formations. Furthermore, MacIntyre has reduced the normative character of institutions to the instrumental satisfaction of needs. This, it is interesting to note, reduces the meaning of institutions to their use, the very case that MacIntyre wishes to make against Winch.[11]

Lukes and MacIntyre

While Lukes and MacIntyre have differing notions of how the criteria of truth and rationality are constituted, they agree on the necessity for context-independent criteria as a means to avoid the serious consequences of relativism. Both theorists distance themselves from neo-Popperian positivism by rejecting methodological individualism in favor of the social body as the basic unit of social science analysis. Both also distinguish themselves from the neo-Popperians by rejecting the tentative nature of truth assertions as exhibited in intersubjectively verified hypotheses. MacIntyre, as we have already seen, takes a position that does not support the a priori nature of Lukes's claim for the universality of the formal rules of logic. In contrast to Lukes, he asserts that the universal, context-independent criteria of rationality and truth are attributable to the historically related progress of human knowledge.

This important difference between them, however, does not make their respective theoretical positions irreconcilable. Despite a very pointed critique of language games and forms of life, neither Lukes nor MacIntyre totally rejects Winch's thesis. Both are able to recognize the social significance of acknowledging the informant's point of view as a limited ground from which to initiate social science investigation. Lukes attempts to transcend Winch through the privileging of universal criteria, while MacIntyre advocates the explanatory power of the concept of causality. Both, however, support the notion of the logic of one unified science, which, as I have indicated, is common also to a positivistic understanding of human action.

Their views of human action are positivistic in that intentionality is confined solely to the initial stages of social science investigation, and the rules of interpretation which they advocate coincide with the formal procedures and self-understanding of modern science. Scientific self-understanding restricts the domain of human activity and its comprehension to the control of objectified procedures and events. Its logic not only prevents the anthropologist from comprehending the meaning of the native's activities but also inhibits full comprehension of the meaning of anthropological practice. As I have already shown, the scientistic outlook, through its a priori interest in control, contributes to rather than undermines structures of domination. An interest in the emancipation from or demystification of ideology, moreover, by requiring a praxis that is necessarily grounded in critical reflection and cooperation, transcends the limitations of control.

Lukes's and MacIntyre's context-independent criteria of truth and rationality also involve a view of theory as contemplation. This view has become predominant with the development of a scientistic understanding of the world, which emphasizes the division between a knowing subject and a known object as the exclusive paradigm of research. According to this paradigm the knowing subject is conceived as a potential contaminator of the purity of the object. The truth or potential value of the investigator's observations depends upon how closely they correspond to the object-in-itself, regardless of whether the object is part of the natural or the social world. Despite the fact that both Lukes and MacIntyre insist that the investigator or anthropologist must not only describe local beliefs but must also be able to judge their veracity, neither reflects seriously upon the concrete totality which mediates the relation between subject and object. Their concept of judgment is abstract in that the activity of judging is external to and in no way enters into the context of the known object. The judgment does not mediate the object and hence leaves the world unchanged.

The concept of theory as contemplation – the perspective supported by most of the contributors to the rationality debates – did not come into existence merely with modern science. As I mentioned previously, the ancient Greeks also held a correspondence theory of truth. The Greek concept of truth, however, was contemplation with moral or practical intent, which is clearly absent in the modern scientistic version. Contemplation in Greek society had practical consequences in the leading of the just or good life, which cannot be subsumed under behavioral systems of instrumental action. On the contrary, the Greek concept of truth is grounded in the mutual expectations of human action or a communicative sense of rationality. It is precisely the moral or practical intent of truth that has been banished from the realm of positivistically oriented natural and social science. In the expectation of creating a communicative anthropology with moral and practical intent we will look towards hermeneutics. It will provide a basis from which to transcend the current obsession of social science with instrumental methods and in this regard provide a theoretical framework better able to comprehend the breadth of human experience that characterizes the object of anthropological practice.

6 Beyond Explanation and Understanding: The Hermeneutics of Hans-Georg Gadamer and Paul Ricoeur

Hermeneutics originated in textual analysis, most notably in biblical exegesis. During the latter part of the nineteenth and early twentieth centuries, the German philosopher Wilhelm Dilthey adopted hermeneutics as the methodological foundation of the Geisteswissenschaften in an attempt to provide the human sciences with the precision and certainty that had characterized the enormous prestige and success of the natural sciences. According to Dilthey, all human activity becomes externalized or objectified in works of culture. He claimed that this general process of the externalization of human activity in cultural products parallels the process through which an author externalizes his intentions in a text. Hermeneutics, therefore, as the art of textual interpretation did not have necessarily to limit its scope to texts but could also be used as a method by which the meaning of all cultural products could be interpreted. Through hermeneutics one attempts to understand authors and their texts as expressions of particular historical epochs, thus leading to the now-famous hermeneutical slogan "understanding an author better than he understood himself." Texts and cultural products became for Dilthey the key to understanding the subjective intentions and historical life of remote societies. His emphasis on both the importance of context-dependent interpretation and the necessity for establishing distinct methods for the human and natural sciences based upon their respectively different objects is compatible with Peter Winch's project of ordinary language philosophy. Unlike Winch, however, he makes a strong appeal to the logical reconstruction of psychological motives.[1]

Despite the original grounding of hermeneutics in textual analysis, Dilthey's extension of the hermeneutic method to the human sciences can potentially make a major contribution to anthropology as an alternative to the positivistic and scientist self-understanding of human cultural forms. This potential contribution transcends, however, the limitations of Dilthey's psychological hermeneutic; we will therefore turn to Hans-Georg Gadamer's philosophical hermeneutics and Paul Ricoeur's hermeneutics of suspicion.

The anthropologist unfamiliar with the history of hermeneutics will perhaps question what a science that originated in biblical exergesis can contribute to the study of the human species as found in enormously diverse cultural settings. I contend that Dilthey's attempt to develop a hermeneutical method capable of understanding historically remote texts or other cultural expressions is paralleled by anthropological fieldwork in the anthropologist's efforts to make sense of native customs and beliefs. Both the textual scholar and the anthropologist are confronted with the difficult task of appropriating that which is alien or not one's own. Despite the fact that anthropologists frequently work outside their home environments and are generally able to enter into dialogue with their objects, which are also subjects, the process that characterizes the comprehension of human actions and cultural products is not essentially different from the interpretation of a text as a life expression. The understanding of other cultures, which is the issue in question in the rationality debates, is a classic example of the hermeneutic problem, which only arises in cases where the meaning of a statement or cultural product is not immediately apparent and thus requires interpretation.

Gadamer claims that Dilthey's concern with emulating the success of the natural sciences by developing hermeneutics as the method of the human sciences eclipses the more radical question of what characterizes understanding in general, whether in the natural or the social sciences. Gadamer is not, however, asserting one logic of a unified science as do the neo-Popperians, but, on the contrary, is challenging the epistemological bias that grounds the certainty of all knowledge in subjectivity. All methods, whether in the natural or the human sciences, presuppose, according to Gadamer, that the conditions of possible knowledge are established by the knowing ego. This is not only true, he contends, for the reflexive philosophies such as Hegel's but is also true for the case of the transcendental interests of science in the control of objectified processes and things. Following in a tradition of hermeneutics established by Heidegger, he wishes to raise again the question of being or *dasein*, which he claims has been lost with modernity's emphasis on epistemology. According to Gadamer, it is understanding or "standing in history" which characterizes the ontological condition of the human species.

The universalization of understanding as the being of man overcomes the serious historicist limitations of Dilthey's method and consequently of Winch's method as well. Dilthey's hermeneutical method is historicist in that cultural products are understood only in the context of the historical period of which they are part, and do not take into consideration the relations between different historical epochs. For example, if I am trying to understand the meaning of Flaubert's *Madame Bovary*, I do not simply try to comprehend the text against the background of nineteenth-century France with the expectation of recapturing the subjective intentions of the author. According to Gadamer's hermeneutic, the reconstruction of Flaubert's subjective intentions would be abstract, as I would necessarily have abdicated my own historicity, upon which my possibility of understanding is not only a priori dependent but essentially constituted. Winch, as we have already seen, is subject to an equally abstract and untenable historicist fallacy owing to the suspension of his own forms of life and language games on behalf of the privileging of those of the natives.

Gadamer claims that the historicity of humanity's being in the world is manifested through tradition. Tradition accounts for both humanity's finitude and openness to possible futures. It is not simply cultural artifacts from the past which are sedimented in the cultural repository of the present, nor is it an autonomous historical realm that has a life apart from concrete human activity, as with Kroeber's concept of the superorganic. Tradition requires active appropriation, perpetuation, and transformation by human co-subjects. We must not lose sight, nevertheless, of the fact that for Gadamer tradition is ontological, which means that we come to grips with tradition through already living within tradition. From within tradition we understand our world and each other. According to Gadamer it is this irreducible lived tradition that came into question during the Anglo-French Enlightenment. That pivotal period in western society, which witnessed the birth of modernity and thus of anthropology, elevated reason as the final judge of the value and legitimacy of all beliefs. Despite the enormous diversity within the Enlightenment, ranging from Rousseau's critique of civil society to Hume's empiricism, its unity is recognizable in the replacement of the authority of tradition by the authority of reason.[2] Gadamer judges the victory of reason and, consequently, of subjectivity as a misleading abstraction, for even the avowed universality of reason and its potential for critique must be concretely grounded in tradition:[3]

> Reason exists for us only in concrete, historical terms, i.e. it is not its own master, but remains constantly dependent on the given circumstances in which it operates. (1975: 245)

While Gadamer (1975) has shown that the Anglo-French Enlightenment is responsible for the debasement of tradition, he accuses the Romantic period which followed the Enlightenment of further distorting it. The Romantic period of the nineteenth century attempted to restore tradition to its former place of importance by opposing the logocentrism of the Enlightenment. As a consequence of this distortion, we have become heirs to a concept of tradition that opposes itself to reason, with profound consequences for the development of anthropology, which historically has attempted to claim traditional cultures as its sole object domain. For example, the Romantic concept of tradition as opposed to reason is implicit in Popper's and Horton's antinomy between the critical spirit of open societies and the unquestioned authority of tradition in closed societies. The seemingly opposite but in fact complementary view is exhibited in Lévy-Bruhl's (1965) romanticization of the "noble savage" as nonrational.

The combined Enlightenment – Romantic antinomy between tradition and reason has also become manifest in scientistic anthropology and threatens to eclipse the significance of tradition in regard to anthropological self-understanding and the understanding of other cultures. According to the scientistic perspective, progress in science is marked by the continual revision of knowledge whereby questions that are not empirically verifiable are discarded in favor of testable hypotheses in increasingly narrower and more fragmented areas. Thus tradition, the continuity with a viable and effective past, is rejected for the novelty of the rationalized growth of knowledge. The scientistic turn in anthropology, which itself is a manifestation of an unacknowledged cultural positivism, has increasingly emphasized quantitative technique and universal laws, matched by a de-emphasis on theory. Cultural ecology – the search for abstract universal laws of social development – and componential analysis – the mathematization of language – are just two cases in point. As anthropology becomes more immersed in scientific method and technique, with its self-understanding either directly opposed to or unaware of tradition, it gradually loses sight of its own knowledge-constitutive interests.

The degrading of tradition as an effective part of anthropological practice is exemplified by a conspicuous de-emphasis on meaningful discourse concerning the nature of culture such as the famous debates between Kroeber and Sapir in the 1920s.[4] This paucity of dialogue on culture is paralleled by a consequent vanishing of the meaning of cultural traditions in other societies as a principal object of inquiry. The Enlightenment heritage of anthropology, as well as questions raised by ancestors such as Morgan or Boas, appears as a curiosity in the light of scientistic anthropology, a fading memory of a now-transcended past. The Anglo-French Enlightenment and Romantic views of tradition have together contributed, as part of a much broader cultural process in western society, to the effacement of the meaning of anthropological practice as constituted through its heritage.

Gadamer has attempted to correct the Romantic distortion by contending that tradition constitutes all understanding and is therefore not opposed to reason. He claims that human actors are not simply a passive reflex of tradition but that tradition is transmitted as part of a sociocultural learning process that requires for its perpetuation the active participation and understanding of human co-subjects. The meaning of historically transmitted culture is not immediately apparent but requires active mediation between the concrete tradition which the subject has already appropriated or is irreducibly a part of and the culture which is being transmitted. He contends that tradition is not accepted blindly out of a nonrational reverence for its age, but because it represents legitimate authority. According to Gadamer, the authority of tradition can be comprehended through an act of concrete reason which discloses the superior knowledge and wisdom of tradition as well as our own finite limitations:

> It rests on recognition and hence an act of reason itself which, aware of its own limitations, accepts that others have better understanding. Authority, in this sense, properly understood, has nothing to do with blind obedience to a command. Indeed, authority has nothing to do with obedience but rather with knowledge. (1975: 248)

Tradition is therefore not opposed to freedom or knowledge but actually becomes a legitimate medium through which one can realize freedom. It is hence a prejudice of the Enlightenment and Romantic eras that asserts that there are no rational grounds to support the authority of tradition.

Gadamer makes the claim, in spite of the Enlightenment rejection of tradition, that tradition is operative in all acts of understanding. He furthermore contends that the positivist notion that the point of view or concepts of the investigator contaminate the research process is an illusion of modernity and yet another example of the modern era's obsession with control. He argues that the point of view of the investigator cannot be suspended by an act of subjective self-assertion, as that would imply individual control over the very grounds of social and historical existence. On the contrary, as I have already emphasized, he insists that the prejudices of the investigator are a precondition of the possibility of understanding. According to his view, it is the foundation of human existence, or the being of man, to stand in history and therefore to have an attitude towards the world. Human actors are always oriented with respect to the world and each other through prejudices. Gadamer contends that the current low regard for prejudice or prejudgment is another consequence of the Enlightenment attitude towards tradition:

> And there is one prejudice of the enlightenment that is essential to it: the fundamental prejudice of the enlightenment is the prejudice against prejudice itself, which deprives tradition of its power. (1975: 239–40)

Prejudices are significant inasmuch as they are the cultural anticipations which make possible our understanding of texts, cultural products, human actions, and ourselves. It is our prejudgments which draw us into the now-famous hermeneutic circle, which as we shall see is not a vicious circle. The hermeneutic circle is implicit even in science, for to be able to formulate a meaningful question means that some knowledge of the object or problem must be anticipated.[5] Prejudices are neither suspended nor dogmatically maintained but are corrected or modified through the dialectical movement of understanding in the relationship of part to whole.

Let us turn to the model of a text, in true hermeneutic fashion, to understand how prejudices are historically operative in the dialectic of part to whole. The translation of a foreign text provides us with the most immediate example of the parallel anticipation that takes place in fieldwork. When translating a foreign text, an experienced translator will first read it as a whole before attempting to work on any one sentence or part. The translator has an anticipation of the meaning of the whole text which will act as a guide in making sense of individual parts. Then, as the translator moves from sentence to sentence, she or he will come to recognize that while the concept of the whole is necessary for grasping the sense of the parts, the parts will contribute jointly to a codetermination of the meaning of the whole, thereby leading the translator to correct her or his initial anticipations. This dialectical relationship between part and whole will unfold continually throughout the translation. The initial anticipations of the whole, which are continually active yet always being reformulated, make the meaning of the text as a whole more than the simple sum of its parts.

The anthropological fieldworker also proceeds with anticipations from which problems or questions to be researched derive. Through interacting with informants and other members of the foreign culture, the fieldworker will also reconsider initial anticipations as a consequence of concrete experiences. And, as in the case of the text, the correction of anticipations does not contribute to their elimination but rather to their reformulation, from which further questions to be asked or problems to be researched can be articulated. It is precisely the fact that anticipations can be corrected dialectically which prevents hermeneutics from becoming a vicious circle.

It was Gadamer's recognition of the significance of prejudgement, the voice of concrete tradition, that led him to reject Dilthey's methodological distinction between the natural and the social sciences. Although Gadamer recognizes that the natural and the social sciences have distinct objects in nature and social life, he does not agree that these distinct objects call for different methods of investigation. He shows that in some respects Dilthey's attempts to create a separate method for the human sciences merely reproduce the objectivism of science. Dilthey's objectivism derives from the suspension of his own historical particularity and prejudgments in order to recreate the intentions that are objectified in cultural products. The parallel with science should be apparent; it is the scientific ideal to formulate reproducible experiments that are not contingent upon the attitudes or personal views of the experimenters. Gadamer contends that the suspension of the prejudgments which are the essential constituent of all knowledge, whether in natural or social science, creates a situation in which the prejudgments of a particular tradition are dogmatically defended. The dogmatic assertion of one's prejudgments systematically eliminates the possibility of their dialectical reformulation and thus prevents the disclosure of the radical otherness of the object of knowledge.

Gadamer's critique of Dilthey should be a strong warning to anthropologists. If they are truly interested in understanding other societies both cross-culturally and historically, they must be prepared to allow the otherness of the object/subject to assert itself. This can only be accomplished if the prejudgments of the anthropologist are not eliminated from the inquiry, as they are the irreducible ontological foundation from which to engage the otherness of the cultural object in the dialectical process of understanding.

Gadamer contends that the elimination of prejudgments robs tradition of its power; they are what makes historical consciousness an ongoing, dynamic, dialectical process. He has referred (1975) to the dialectical movement of consciousness as "effective-historical consciousness." We have already seen that Dilthey's concept of the historical nature of consciousness is commensurate with the reproducibility of objectified intentions in remote historical epochs. According to this view, the creative moment of historical consciousness is subordinated to the mere imitation in the mind of the investigator of the meaning of past events or cultural products. Recreating the truth of past meanings is therefore dependent on the quality of the reproduction. Gadamer argues that the reproducibility of past meanings silences history and tradition by limiting the audience for which the meaning of the event or cultural product was produced to the historical epoch of its generation. To abdicate our prejudgments is to cease having an attitude towards the world, which for Gadamer is to abdicate the very ground of our being or humanity:

> A person who does not accept that he is dominated by prejudices will fail to see what is shown by their light. It is like the relation between the "I" and the "Thou". A person who reflects himself out of the mutuality of such a relation changes this relationship and destroys its moral bond. A person who reflects himself out of a living relation to tradition destroys the true meaning of this tradition in exactly the same way. Historical consciousness in seeking to understand tradition must not rely on the critical method with which it approaches its sources, as if this preserved it from mixing in its own judgements and prejudices. It must, in fact, take account of its own historicality. To stand within a tradition does not limit the freedom of knowledge but makes it possible. (1975: 324)

The life of tradition, that is, of cultural meanings transmitted by either written or oral communication, is above all, as Gadamer has stated, a "moral bond" and therefore dependent upon an audience which it can speak to and engage beyond the horizon of its own existence. There are two prerequisites for the meaningful transmission of tradition. First, in order for tradition to address an audience that is larger than its own historical epoch, the meaning of events or cultural products must be separable from the subjective intentions of their agents. Winch has shown how this is possible through associating the constitution of meaning with nonpsychological forms of life and language games that are inherently intersubjective. Second, the potential audiences to whom the meaning of cultural events and products is addressed must themselves already be possessed by or, as Gadamer states, stand in tradition. The anticipations and prejudgments of these potential audiences are then employed to engage the remote or alien cultural form. Effective-historical consciousness, therefore, implies that the life of tradition does not lie dormant in the historical epoch of its generation but is capable of producing effects in the present as it is taken up by the lived tradition of other historical epochs:

> I have already pointed out above, that effective-historical consciousness is something other than inquiry into effective-history of a particular work as it were, the trace the work leaves behind. It is, rather, an awareness of the work itself, and hence itself has an effect. (1975: 305)

Effective-historical consciousness operates according to a principle described by Gadamer (1975) as the "fusion of horizons." The fusion of horizons is the engaging of distinct traditions, which characterizes every act of understanding and through which meaning and truth are disclosed. In order to grasp this concept, it is essential to recognize that the fusion of horizons is not a method but rather a delineation of the universal principles of hermeneutical understanding.[6] The fusion of horizons is a dialectical process through which, as I come to know the cultural object in its radical otherness, I also come to know myself as a historically finite being. The meaning of an alien cultural product is neither solely a part of my horizon nor solely a part of the horizon of the object I wish to understand but is disclosed through the fusion of horizons.

Language is central to Gadamer's concept of the fusion of horizons, in that this process closely resembles the form of a conversation and also that the disclosure of meaning takes place in language. The fusion of horizons follows the format of the dialectic of question and answer. The horizon of the cultural object which the investigator wishes to understand is viewed by Gadamer as an answer to a question. This puzzling assertion is clarified by

John Hogan in an article designed to introduce the English-speaking public to Gadamer's *Truth and Method*:

> For the logic of question and answer, Gadamer is indebted to R. G. Colling-wood. For Collingwood history is not the past as past but rather the past as formulated in the consciousness of the historian. In order "to understand an historical event, one must reconstruct the question for which the historical actions of persons were the answer". The point is that history cannot be understood merely as facts. Understanding comes when history is seen as the reasons why such facts took place. (1976: 9)

The horizon of the investigator is the finite tradition of anticipations and prejudgments from which questions to be directed to the alien cultural life-expression will be generated. The fusion of horizons follows the structure of discourse in that neither the horizon of the alien cultural form nor the horizon of the investigator controls the disclosure of meaning. The individual who attempts to control a conversation quickly brings it to an end. Conversations develop dialectically in the sense that the logos, or logic, of the discourse leads the interlocutors.

The rules of speech apply equally to the dialectics of understanding in that the coparticipation of distinct traditions is required in the fusion of horizons. In a conversation where understanding has become problematic, questions and answers are exchanged between interlocutors until mutual understanding is achieved. These questions and answers are not simply cast aside when they have exhausted their usefulness but, on the contrary, flow into the mutual understanding arrived at in speech. Through the engaging of traditions, the investigator directs questions to the alien cultural form in order to disclose the possible questions to which the alien cultural form is an answer, thereby allowing the questioned to speak for itself. This format of question and answer mirrors the process of the dialectical relation of part to whole in textual translation which was described earlier. Each question or anticipation elicits a response from the cultural object which in turn leads to new questions and the reformulation or retracting of anticipations, until the meaning or sense of the whole discloses itself:

> The unfolding of the totality of meaning towards which understanding is directed forces us to make conjectures and to take them back again. The self-cancellation of the interpretation makes it possible for the thing itself – the meaning of the text – to assert itself. (Gadamer 1975: 422)

The remote cultural form or product does not literally speak to us but addresses us through disclosing its being, or what Winch has characterized through ordinary language philosophy as ways of speaking, thinking, and acting which are not our own.

The conversational or linguistic nature of all understanding, as exhibited in the fusion of horizons, shows that the question of interpreting other cultures raised through the rationality debates can be grasped as a distinctively hermeneutical problem. While Gadamer's concept of understanding is most sympathetic to the ordinary language tradition of the later Wittgenstein as represented by Winch in the rationality debates, his emphasis on ontology serves as a radical point of distinction. There is, however, no major difference between Winch and Gadamer with respect to either the essential linguisticality of the world or the unity of subject and object in language. For Winch and Gadamer, having a world is dependent on sharing an intersubjectively valid language. Consider the following from Gadamer's *Truth and Method*:

> To have a "world" means to have an attitude towards it. To have an attitude towards the world, however, means to keep oneself so free from what one encounters of the world that one is able to present it to oneself as it is. This capacity is both the having of a "world" and the having of language. Thus the concept of "world" or "environment" (Welt) is in opposition to the concept of "surrounding world" or "habitat" (Umwelt), as possessed by every living thing. (1975: 402)

Language is not only at the center of human social life, but in Gadamer's theory is raised to a philosophical anthropology in that language is what distinguishes humanity from all other living things. The differences between Winch and Gadamer begin to emerge, however, once we focus our attention on the former's concept of the autonomy of language games in contrast to the latter's emphasis on language as the medium through which we participate in the universality of being.

Winch has used the concept of forms of life to support the notion that native activities derive their sense and are only intelligible from the repertoire of indigenous language games. He furthermore contends that where it is necessary for the anthropologist to employ a western category, this category must reproduce the original native intention. Forms of life are presented by Winch, however, as if there is no necessary historical continuity within the development of one form of life nor any necessary relation between different forms of life. If we truly are trapped by our concepts, as Winch suggests by his notion of autonomous forms of life, then both the anthropological and the historical enterprise are reduced to skepticism in the attempt to understand or appropriate what is alien. The portrayal of forms of life as radically autonomous systematically precludes the possibility of common discourse between forms of life or of metadiscourse concerning forms of life in general. The possibility of communication is not tied, as Winch argues, to the immediacy of a single form of life but is, on the contrary, capable of exhibiting a "trans-form of life" potentiality. Winch's position within the rationality debates is thus entirely consistent with the Wittgensteinian rule that "the limits of my language are the limits of my world" (Wittgenstein 1961: 57).

In contrast to Winch's view as to the autonomy of forms of life, Gadamer argues for the universality of language as ultimately identified with being: "Being that can be understood is language" (1975: 450). While Winch contends that language is what radically distinguishes human groups, Gadamer asserts, to the contrary, that language is essentially what humanity has in common. Language does not merely establish the limits of my world, but is, rather, the necessary medium through which a language community is open to new possibilities of understanding and being:

> Every such world, as linguistically constituted, is always open, of itself, to every possible insight and hence for every expansion of its own world-picture, and accordingly available to others. (1975: 405)

According to Gadamer, all that has been, is, and will be manifests itself through language, so that without language all being or existence would be eternally silent. Language is the principal constituent of philosophical hermeneutics, as all interpretation, which for Gadamer is the same as understanding, takes place in language. Linguisticality permeates tradition, effective-historical consciousness, and the fusion of horizons, all of which, as we have seen, have the structure of discourse.

Gadamer's concept of language differs from those of other theorists who have emphasized language as discourse in that he does not surrender the primacy of ontology in the speech event. For example, in spite of the fact that all speech events originate from an agent or sender and are directed to a hearer (e.g., Hymes 1974), Gadamer contends that neither the sender nor the hearer has control over the discourse. As in the case of the fusion of horizons, all discourse is dialectical, meaning that the speech event leads both the sender and the hearer, who participate mutually in its unfolding. The predominance of the dialectical nature of discourse over the autonomy of the individual speaker is revealed by Gadamer's contention that there is a sense or degree to which "language speaks us" (1975: 421).

While the historical finitude of humanity comes from living in the midst of tradition, language is universal. Gadamer's claim for the universality of language does not, of course, ignore the obvious fact that diverse peoples throughout the world speak many unrelated languages and that these languages, as Herder claimed, shape world views. The universality of language means that all that has been said or will be said is potentially understandable to every language speaker and hence all language communities. I shall again turn to Gadamer's notion of the fusion of horizons and the case of Zande witchcraft to show how the concept of universal linguisticality provides a framework for interpretation.

It was Winch's contention that Evans-Pritchard superimposed western scientific categories on Zande society in his rejection of their witchcraft claims. Winch suggested that we must follow the sense of Zande categories in order to understand their witchcraft practices. The methodological problem arises, however, as to how we can follow the sense of Zande concepts without translating these concepts back into our own language games. If translation into our concepts is unavoidable, then how can we understand the meaning of Zande witchcraft practices without distorting them? This is the central question to which all contributors to the rationality debates have addressed themselves.

Anthropologists may be disappointed to hear that Gadamer's concept of the fusion of horizons does not provide a methodological solution to this problem. He has developed a specifically philosophical hermeneutics that concerns itself with the universal preconditions of understanding, which are prior to and presupposed by the application of all methods. According to the principles of the fusion of horizons, it is not within the purview of the anthropologist to choose which categories will be used to make sense of Zande witchcraft phenomena, since it is a necessary condition of human existence to stand within the determinations of a finite tradition. The possibility of understanding Zande witchcraft depends necessarily upon entering into dialogue with the Zande beliefs through the tradition of the anthropologist. There is nothing arbitrary about this procedure, as the tradition which the anthropologist represents is itself intersubjective. Furthermore, the meaning disclosed by Zande witchcraft practices will not be the capricious fiction of the native informant nor of the anthropologist. The meaning of Zande witchcraft unfolds through the mediation of the traditions of anthropologist and native. The anthropologist, as an investigator, attempts to bring to light the question to which Zande witchcraft is an answer, for the purpose of disclosing the reasons that brought witchcraft into being. Hermeneutics is primary to this process of disclosure in that these reasons are not "mere facts" but rather the meaning of social events. The anthropologist puts forward interpretations and corrections of interpretations until the meaning of the whole is disclosed. The disclosure of the meaning of Zande witchcraft in turn broadens the horizon of the anthropologist. What makes Gadamer's thesis quite different from that of Winch or Evans-Pritchard, is that the meaning of Zande witchcraft is not established for posterity, to be verified or falsified by future generations of fieldworkers. As we have seen, meaning is manifested through language and is potentially open to all existing and future language communities.

Because the meaning of Zande witchcraft discloses itself through a dialectical process, there is no assurance that it will remain unchanged as it is engaged by the diverse horizons of historically finite traditions.

Some anthropologists will doubtless interpret Gadamer's philosophical hermeneutics as another in a long line of idealistic continental philosophies that have since been superseded by positive science with verifiable methods. Positive science has proceeded under the conviction that through its methods scientists can extricate themselves from the contingencies of the historical life-world. These historical and cultural contingencies, as Gadamer shows, have been identified by science as obstacles to knowledge. Positive science has failed, however, to demonstrate how its views concerning method, knowledge, and truth are themselves not reflections of historically determinate tradition. The notion of attitudes or methods that are somehow exempt from social and cultural contingencies is idealistic, in that these contingencies are the very social substance, no less necessary than the human brain, of our existence. Gadamer's philosophical hermeneutics is, in contrast, closer to realism than idealism, in that historically finite tradition is the necessary precondition for the very possibility of knowledge and social life. Rather than prescribe what should be the case when an anthropologist understands another culture, Gadamer's hermeneutics provides a framework that uncovers the universality at the heart of all human understanding.

Gadamer's philosophical hermeneutics also exhibits a close kinship with critical anthropology, although the ontological dimension of the former falls short of the emancipatory reflexivity of the latter. It is my contention that philosophical hermeneutics and critical anthropology have a common interest in human freedom, inasmuch as their object domains – the appropriation or understanding of cultural and historical diversity – have the practical intent of establishing alternative visions of what it means to be human, and thus open up the possibility of a wide range of futures. The ontological domain of philosophical hermeneutics tends to make its emancipatory interest less apparent than the clearly manifest interest in emancipation shown by critical anthropology. The emancipatory interest of philosophical hermeneutics is nonetheless ascertainable in Gadamer's call for the recovery or restoration of tradition. Only through the recovery of tradition can we come to recognize that our present is a manifestation of a still-effective past as directed towards an unformed future. This recognition of the significance of tradition and effective history is a potential ground for overcoming what Lukács (1971) has called the fragmentation of knowledge. An emancipatory anthropology begins by recognizing that as a method of inquiry it does not stand above its own social and cultural history nor does it have as a praxis a future that will be distinct from that of western civilization. The fusion of horizons, furthermore, reveals the emancipatory potential of all knowledge.

Through the dialectical engaging of diverse traditions, we become aware of our own historical finiteness and the radical distinctiveness of other traditions as we participate in the universality of human existence.

The crucial difference between philosophical hermeneutics and critical anthropology is the latter's grounding in reflection. The distinction between Gadamer's philosophical hermeneutics as an ontology and the critical theory of society as reflexivity is articulated in Jürgen Habermas's review of the German edition of Gadamer's *Truth and Method* (1975). Habermas contends that the finite character of philosophical hermeneutics is exhibited in its failure to expose different forms of domination as they are embodied in the normative institutional structures of various traditions. He shows that Gadamer, ironically, has rejected the critical nature of reflexivity which is part of our own western tradition stemming from the Anglo-French Enlightenment. Gadamer has thus raised an abstract notion of tradition against a concrete contribution from his own heritage. While the fusion of horizons as a dialectical encounter makes us aware of the historical finiteness of our own tradition, it does so only in a normative sense. Critical anthropology must therefore not be satisfied with a hermeneutics of the life-world of tradition but must be able to penetrate, by means of reflection, the density of social life to reveal the ideology and domination embedded in normative structures of society. The project of moving from a hermeneutics of ontology to a hermeneutics of reflection has been undertaken by the French philosopher Paul Ricoeur, to whose hermeneutics of suspicion or depth semantics we now turn.

Hermeneutics of Suspicion

Paul Ricoeur makes the claim in his hermeneutical work *Freud and Philosophy* (1970) that the modern era has been marked by three philosophies of suspicion: Freud, Marx, and Nietzsche. The philosphies of suspicion distinguish themselves from earlier philosophies in the western tradition by their common emphasis on the nontransparency of immediate consciousness. We shall see that Ricoeur's interpretation theory is clearly within the domain of philosophies of suspicion in that the symbol, which is for Ricoeur the privileged object of hermeneutics, has unfathomable depth and opacity.

There are similarities and differences between the hermeneutics of Gadamer and Ricoeur. Both accept the essential finiteness of humanity as well as the linguisticality of the world. Furthermore, both share the view that all existence would be eternally silent if it did not manifest itself in language. A principal difference between them, which leads to a series of further distinctions, lies in Gadamer's acceptance and Ricoeur's rejection of the equivalence of language and being. Gadamer's position leads to the conclusion that all existence is transparent, since all that can be said can be understood. Ricoeur maintains, on the contrary, that because symbolization is grounded in life, or what he calls the bios,[7] the depth of human existence is only partially reflected in language.

In order fully to comprehend Ricoeur's hermeneutical theory of symbols, it will first be necessary to make an illuminating detour by way of his concept of metaphor. His theory of symbols challenges noted anthropological theories such as that of Clifford Geertz (1973), who at times conceives of symbols formally as maps or blueprints that provide strategies for possible action. While Geertz's theory has renewed interest in the concept of culture, its equating of symbols with strategies dichotomizes thought and action – a problem that can be transcended through Ricoeur's version of hermeneutics. We shall also see how Ricoeur's theory of symbol and metaphor provides a solution to puzzling riddles uncovered by Evans-Pritchard in his studies of the Azande and Nuer and drawn into epistemological debates by the rationality theorists.

Ricoeur works through the structure of the metaphor to arrive at a theory of symbols because he perceives the double structure of metaphor to be a key to the semantics of the symbol. He contends that many of the contemporary theories of metaphor, anthropological versions among them, are permeated by a positivistic self-understanding. The positivistic understanding of metaphor is attributable, at least in part, to the influence of Russell and the early Wittgenstein, who worked jointly at eliminating the ambiguities of ordinary language by attempting to make it more denotative. Positivistic self-understanding has accordingly privileged the denotative content of metaphor over the connotative, which has become epiphenomenal. Ricoeur claims that this emphasis on denotation has led to the belief that only the denotative function of metaphors is cognitive and therefore semantic. The connotative aspect, according to the positivist theory of metaphor, cannot be semantic, as it consists only of emotive evocations. The figurative aspects of metaphorical expressions have, then, no semantic value or meaning. This interpretation of metaphor has thus led to a reduction of the connotative or figurative element to mere ornamentation contributing nothing new to our understanding of the world.

An example of the positivist theory of metaphor within the discipline of anthropology is furnished by Leach and Fortes's contention, mentioned earlier, that the Nuer belief that "twins are birds" is merely figurative or ornamental. their position should be viewed against the background of Lévy-Bruhl's equally positivistic perspective. He claimed that the Nuer metaphor should be taken literally on the basis of an equivalence of subject and predicate as signified by the presence of the verb *to be*. From this perspective he made his well-known assertion that primitive peoples have a prelogical mentality. Leach and Fortes were attempting to rescue the beliefs of native peoples from classification as prelogical by contending that such metaphors could not possibly be understood literally without reducing them to nonsense. The fact that native societies had successfully adapted to many, diverse environments was evidence enough for Leach and Fortes that indigenous peoples are rational and hence logical. While intending to preserve the integrity of native thought, however, they reduced the entire mythopoetic realm to a mere colorful embellishment of the denotative character of speech. Both the literal and the ornamental interpretations of metaphor thus silence its creative potential.

Ricoeur contends that the positivist theory of metaphor is the metaphor of the word, another version of the label theory of language. On the contrary, all metaphor belongs to discourse, or to what he calls the metaphor of the sentence. It is the structure of the sentence that establishes a tension between the denotative or literal signification and the connotative or figurative signification. Ricoeur contends that this tension not only sustains the structure of the metaphor but also provides the dynamic behind its creative potential. By recognizing the tension between literal and figurative inherent in all live metaphors, he exposes the misconceived methods of interpretation that have been applied to the puzzling rationality of mythopoetic discourse. According to Ricoeur, the tension between the subject and object in a metaphorical expression is not merely a tension between two words or labels for objects in the world but, on the contrary, a manifestation of the resistance of two interpretations asserting themselves. This conflict of interpretations at the level of metaphor is resolved by the self-destruction of the literal signification, which then passes into a new signification:

> The metaphorical interpretation presupposes a literal interpretation which self-destructs in a significant contradiction. It is this process of self-destruction or transformation which imposes a sort of twist on the words, an extension of meaning thanks to which we can make sense where a literal interpretation would be literally nonsensical. (1976: 50)

Metaphor exhibits a dialectical structure through which the resolving of inherent contradiction leads to the creation of meaning. The fact that the inherent structure of metaphor leads to the creation of meaning makes metaphor not merely denotative or literal but predicative or world-constituting.

Ricoeur contends that tension metaphors are not translatable because they create their own meaning by sustaining and resolving their inherent contradictions. It would not be possible, therefore, to restore literal signification to "twins are birds." The interpreter can at best paraphrase the signification of a tension metaphor. Even paraphrasing, however, cannot capture the full depth or meaning of the original signification. This accounts for the many untranslatable metaphors in prose, poetry, and written and oral traditions.

The power of metaphor depends upon its ability to signify ever-new meaning. Ricoeur claims that metaphors can lose their power and thus become dead metaphors either by overrepetition or by the reduction of the sustaining tension between subject and predicate to mere equivalence or resemblance. Metaphors of resemblance are metaphors of substitution, whereby the predicate can be substituted for the subject without exhibiting dissonance of meaning. In contrast to metaphors of resemblance, Ricoeur argues:

> In this sense, a metaphor is an instantaneous creation, a semantic innovation which has no status in already established language and which only exists because of the attribution of an unusual or an unexpected predicate. Metaphor therefore is more like the resolution of an enigma than a simple association based on resemblance; it is constituted by the resolution of a semantic dissonance. (1976: 52)

The double structure of the metaphor, with its tension between the literal and figurative significations, has now prepared us to encounter Ricoeur's theory of the double structure of symbols.

In a series of articles published as *Interpretation Theory: Discourse and the Surplus of Meaning* (1976), Ricoeur breaks with his earlier theory of symbols developed in *The Symbolism of Evil* (1969). This theoretical break arises from a changed outlook in regard to the relationship between the symbol and language. In *The Symbolism of Evil*, Ricoeur used symbol and metaphor synonymously, claiming that both belong to discourse. He has retracted this earlier view and now contends that while the symbol manifests itself through language, it has its origins in the bios, through which it receives its determinate power. The grounding of the symbol in the bios puts it beyond the control of humanity or the conventionality of metaphor:

> Metaphor occurs in the already purified universe of the logos, while the symbol hesitates on the dividing line between bios and logos. It testifies to the primordial rootedness of Discourse in Life. It is born where force and form coincide. (1976: 59)

That the symbol resides on the border "between logos and bios" means that it has both semantic and nonsemantic features. Let us first explore the nonsemantic features of the symbol, then the semantic.

At the level of bios, the symbol does not yet have form; it is shapeless force or power without voice or speech. By the concept of bios I take Ricoeur to mean the undifferentiated force of life which is the foundation of all existence. The concept of bios, while having metaphysical implications that might make some social scientists uncomfortable, is not as abstract in Ricoeur's application as it might first appear. Ricoeur is trying to show that symbols do not simply arise through human conventions or culture but, on the contrary, have prelinguistic origins. Through the symbol, he attempts to transcend the familiar dichotomy between nature and culture by rethinking this relationship dialectically. His project is not essentially different from that undertaken by the anthropologist Mary Douglas in her book *Natural Symbols* (1973). Ricoeur's phenomenological hermeneutics, however, is radically different from Douglas's structural treatment of symbols, which relies extensively on Basil Bernstein's elaborated and restricted codes.[8] According to Ricoeur, the bios is manifested in psychoanalysis as desire or energy, while in religion it is manifested as the sacred. He thus implies that the nonsemantic aspects of symbols are exhibited in "areas of our experience that are open to different methods of investigation" (1976: 57).

It is in his study of Freud (1970) that Ricoeur most clearly exemplifies the manifestation of nonsemantic features of symbols. He shows that most traditional interpretations of Freud emphasize the energetics of his system. Freudian theory, which draws very heavily on a medical model, is concerned with the channeling of libidinal energy through a series of cathexes and anticathexes. It is the libido, according to Ricoeur, which gives rise to the various representations that serve as the material for psychoanalytic interpretation. Repressed libidinal impulses or psychic conflicts, for example, become represented and thematic in oneiric activity. Ricoeur's interpretation of Freud is unique in that, while acknowledging the medical model's emphasis on energetics, he contends that the symbolic representations deriving from the libido require hermeneutical interpretation. It has been the tradition in Freudian analysis, on the contrary, to explain symbolic representations only in relation to libidinal energies. Ricoeur holds that since psychoanalytic representations manifest themselves in discourse, which means that they have intersubjective meaning, a depth semantics must be given priority over a mechanics of energy systems. He thus views psychoanalysis as a prime example of a method of investigation that discloses the life of symbolic activity on the border of "energetics and semantics" or "desire and culture."

Ricoeur argues that although symbols derive much of their force or power from the nonsemantic realm of the bios, they can become objects of reflection only if they manifest themselves in speech or discourse. He claims that all symbols are polysemic or multivocal and that their interpretation necessarily requires a depth semantics. The double structure of metaphors provides a means by which to comprehend the multivocality of symbols, since at the semantic level they share an essentially complementary structure.

Symbols can be distinguished from signs in that they are not exhausted in their signifying. The multivocality of symbols is most easily perceived in a religious framework. For example, in the Christian tradition the crucifixion of Christ gives rise to a concatenation of further significations such as the redemption of man or suffering. Ricoeur uses the example of the symbolism of evil to trace hermeneutically a series of transformations in the western symbol of stain from contagion to the embodiment of stain in the covenant with the consequent new signification of sin. Symbols are thus inherently ambiguous in that the literal signification gives rise to an infinite series of multiple significations. It is the infinite multivocality of symbols which leads Ricoeur to conclude that symbols transcend all elaboration or classification by conceptual language:

> This bound character of symbols makes all the difference between a symbol and a metaphor. The latter is free invention of discourse; the former is bound to the cosmos. (1976: 61)

The power of the symbol, therefore, is not sustained solely by the inherent tensions between literal and figurative expression; metaphor is only the surface semantics of the symbol. Of the literal and figurative significations, it is the literal signification which is primary in pointing to the symbol's multivocality.[9] Symbols, then, also possess a double structure of literal and multivocal meaning, which Ricoeur characterizes as the "symbol giving rise to thought." Depth semantics or the hermeneutics of suspicion becomes for him a method of concrete reflection whereby one moves from the immediacy of a symbol's literal signification to other significations which constitute its surplus of meaning:

> Symbolic signification, therefore, is so constituted that we can only attain the secondary signification by way of the primary signification, where the primary signification is the sole means of access to the surplus of meaning. (1976: 55)

He claims that the semantic aspects of symbols, which overlap with the double structure of the metaphor, provide the material for linguistic and logical analyses of signification and interpretation.

It is not simply the emphasis on the multivocality and opacity of symbols that makes Ricoeur's theory important for the understanding of social life. He contends that the power of the symbol lies in its ability to assimilate both aspects of reality and ourselves to itself. The ability to assimilate various aspects of reality to itself expresses the condensation of the symbol. In indigenous societies, the condensation of the symbol assimilates such disparate phenomena as the land, cycles of the seasons, the ancestors, and the people themselves in rituals devoted to the earth deity (Uchendu 1965). The assimilative powers of the symbol are also manifested by major cultural representations in the western world. For example, in his *Meaning in History* (1949), Karl Löwith outlines how the symbolism of eschatology, which has its origins in the Judeo-Christian tradition, persists in modern philosophies of history as a meaningful representation and framework from which to interpret experience. The assimilative nature of the eschatological symbol is also revealed more concretely as it becomes thematic in the utopian expectation that modern science will provide a better world – a myth shared by most of us in western society (Leiss 1974). Ricoeur's theory of symbols thus provides a penetrating perspective from which to explore the unfathomable depth of lived symbols as they shape the destiny, histories, and traditions of various cultures and societies. While Gadamer's hermeneutics has emphasized that there is a sense in which "language speaks us," Ricoeur emphasizes the great degree to which symbols articulate traditions and also, therefore, in a sense "speak us."

By subordinating the role of the individual to the power of the symbol, Ricoeur is not reifying tradition or the symbol. He and Gadamer direct their critical comments to the self-representation of modernity as absolutized "homo faber."[10] Ricoeur contends that human actors do not, as individuals or groups, control the formation of symbols, that is, symbols are not simply conventional constructions arrived at through intersubjective consensus. Symbols, as shown by all mythopoetic uses of language, are what tie us to the cosmos. Symbols thus exhibit a twofold double structure. The primary double structure is the symbol's prelinguistic, nonsemantic origin in the bios coupled with the semantic feature that manifests itself in discourse and reflects back on the bios. The other double structure is what the symbol shares with the metaphor and hence what accounts for the creative potential of all symbols.

Ricoeur has developed a hermeneutical method rooted in dialectical, concrete reflection, through which symbols and hence the meaning of human actions can be interpreted. He argues in an article entitled "The Model of the Text: Meaningful Action Considered as a Text" (1971) that interpretation theory must take notice of developments in scientific linguistics. He has in mind the distinction between *la langue*, language, and *la parole*, speech, which was introduced by Ferdinand de Saussure (1966). According to Ricoeur, language, as an internalized system of signs and relations between signs, is both atemporal and nonreferential. It thus lacks both a subject, that is, a person speaking, and specific reference to a person addressed. Language makes no assertions about the world. Discourse or speech, on the other hand, implies a temporal relation to the present with respect to both a speaking subject and those addressed by the speaker. Discourse, furthermore, is referential in that it communicates and asserts something about the world. Ricoeur argues that language, viewed as an internal system of atemporal and nonreferential signs, meets the requirements of an objective science. The concept of language as system can equal the rigor of objective (natural) science in that the study of the internal relations of signs requires a distancing from or suspension of the contingencies of the investigator, the intentions of the speaking subject, which are not part of the system, and the world of co-subjects. It thus becomes possible through the suspension of all referents and social contingencies, which is inherent to the method of structural linguistics, to study objectively the internal relations of texts, symbols, and human actions.

We shall see shortly that, while for the structural linguist the study of the internal system is an end in itself, Ricoeur makes the objective standards of the structural method the mediating term in his dialectic of explanation and understanding. He claims that it is unnecessary and even misleading for the social sciences to attempt to mirror the objective standards of the natural sciences. Rather, the objective standards of the social sciences are given in the science of semiotics, for it is in signs that all human activity becomes externalized. I shall explicate Ricoeur's method, then, with the particular intention of exposing the untenable dichotomy between understanding and explanation that lies at the heart of the rationality debates.

Ricoeur remarks that discourse has a fleeting character in that it disappears without trace at the end of a speech event or conversation. Recognition of the frailty of discourse has led many hermeneuticians, including Gadamer and Ricoeur, to regard the invention of writing favorably. Ricoeur claims, following Dilthey, that the text allows for the possibility that an author's intentions may become objectified and hence be on record for future readers. The intentions of the author share many of the features of discourse in that they assert something about the world and have a fleeting character. Our distance in space and time prevents us, however, from reproducing these original intentions. While the intentions of the author are of short duration, however, Ricoeur contends, reinforcing Gadamer's claim, that the meaning of a text transcends the finite period of its production. The text thus shares some of the characteristics of both language and discourse. The internal relations of the text resemble the systematic relations of semiotics, while the objectification of meaning in the text parallels discourse in asserting something about the world. Ricoeur (1971: 536) claims that a similar process of objectification, which he refers to as the dialectic of "event and meaning," takes place in human actions.

The analogy between text, either written or oral, and action should be of particular interest to anthropologists whose research is undertaken among pre-or nonliterate peoples. Events, like an author's intentions or temporal discourse, are also fleeting in that they appear and then disappear. The meaning of an event, as recorded in memory, oral tradition, or historical documents, can therefore be autonomous with respect to the temporal actions that are the conditions of its generation. This autonomy of meaning with respect to the immediate intentions of the actor holds whether the anthropologist was witness to the event or had it recounted through an informant. According to Ricoeur, the objectification of meaning in a text as autonomous with respect to the intentions of the author is exactly paralleled by the objectification of the meaning of actions or events as autonomous with respect to the intentions of the actors. It is this form of objectification that makes Ricoeur conclude that meaningful human action can become the object of a science:

> My claim is that action itself, action as meaningful, may become an object of science, without losing its character of meaningfulness, through a kind of objectification similar to the fixation which occurs in writing. By this object-ification, action is no longer a transaction to which the discourse of action would still belong. It constitutes a delineated pattern which has to be inter-preted according to its inner connections. (1971: 538)

Ricoeur turns to the science of semiotics to disclose the internal relations of objectified meaning in either actions or texts. This reliance on method clearly distinguishes his approach from Gadamer's dialogical fusion of horizons.

Ricoeur's hermeneutical method unfolds through a dialectic of under-standing, explanation, and comprehension. He elaborates this dialectic by first developing the relation between understanding and explanation, then proceeding to explanation and comprehension. I will follow the movement of his dialectic.

Ricoeur, like Gadamer, maintains that there is a difference between the ostensive nature of intentions, best exemplified in a conversation, and the referential character of a text. The referential character of a text is what it is about or its meaning, which is addressed to a horizon or audience beyond the scope of its generation. Our inability to reproduce the original intentions of an author leads Ricoeur to choose the relation of reading to writing as the paradigm for the relation between understanding and explanation. The medium of writing enables an author to externalize his or her intentions in the totality of a text. Reading, of course, is the activity by which a human subject interprets the externalized signs of an author embodied in a text. Ricoeur contends that the relationship of reading to writing also describes the process by which we attempt to interpret human actions, which also become objectified in signs – for example, in historical records or oral traditions.

He compares the first step of interpretation to guessing, which is his own version of what has been traditionally referred to as *verstehen*. This stage of Ricoeur's theory is very similar to what Gadamer means by initial anticipa-tions that guide the relation of part to whole in translation:

In more general terms, a text has to be construed because it is not a mere sequence of sentences, all on an equal footing and separately understandable. A text is a whole, a totality. The relation between whole and parts – as in a work of art or in an animal – requires a specific kind of "judgement" for which Kant gave the theory in the Third Critique. (Ricoeur 1971: 548)

The judgement referred to is an attempt to grasp a sense of the whole; Ricoeur also believes that it moves between the poles of skepticism and dogmatism. This does not imply that the understanding of a text is a capricious process. Ricoeur contends that a text, like a symbol, has a multi-vocality that renders it open to different readings. These multiple readings amount to what he has called the conflict of interpretations.

Arriving at a "correct" interpretation does not involve measuring an interpretation against the facts, as is implied in the correspondence theory of truth, nor does it involve verification as required by all positivist and neopositivist theories of knowledge. Ricoeur contends, on the contrary, that the conflict of interpretations opens itself to a process of rational argumentation or validation, as, for example, in juridical procedures:

To show that an interpretation is more probable in the light of what is known is something other than showing that a conclusion is true. In this sense, validation is not verification. Validation is an argumentative discipline comparable to the juridical procedures of legal interpretation. (1971: 549)

The range of possible interpretation is, nonetheless, limited by the totality of the text. Not all interpretations are equal or even conceivable. He implies that the process of argumentation can and should strive towards achieving a preferred interpretation or consensus.

Ricoeur contends that this initial step in the logic of interpretation also applies to human actions, which like texts exhibit multivocality. His discussion of human actions departs somewhat from his discussion of texts in that he specifically addresses the modern human-action theorists who, like MacIntyre, have been influenced by Hume's notion of causality. These theorists, as I explained in the chapter on MacIntyre, distinguish between purposes, of which the actor is aware, and motives, which are unconscious and the causes of actions. I argued that the concept of cause was taken from the language games of science and presupposed a mechanical, temporal relation between an antecedent and its consequent. Ricoeur has shown that the relation between antecedent and consequent is a relationship between a series of signs and hence exhibits a logical, not merely a mechanical or temporal, relation. The relation, therefore, between cause and effect must be understood in terms of reasons, which is a task for a depth semantics or hermeneutics of suspicion. Human actions, however, like texts, are open to only a limited range of interpretations.

The second part of Ricoeur's dialectic, from explanation to comprehension, is a critical method which clearly distinguishes him from Gadamer's philosophical hermeneutics. Ricoeur claims that it is the momentary subordination of process to system which makes semiotics or structural linguistics the critical dimension of his hermeneutical method. Semiotics suspends both the ostensive and referential dimensions of texts, or of events or actions, in favor of the purely internal and logical relations among the signs which constitute the system. The notion of system is atemporal or, according to Ricoeur, "virtual." He believes that the method of structural linguistics is critical in that it has the inherent tendency to create a distance between human actions and their referents or texts with their multivocality, while placing in abeyance the prejudgments and contingencies of the investigator. This is desirable because this distancing, whereby referents are suspended, allows the multiplicity of appearances of the object of knowledge to disclose itself. Ricoeur has interpreted this process of distancing or suspension in structural linguistics as Husserl's phenomenological epoché,[11] thereby transcending and distorting the finite boundaries of the structural method. Consider the following:

> The first way of reading is exemplified today by the different *structural* schools of literary criticism. Their approach is not only possible but legitimate. It proceeds from the suspension, the *epoché*, of the ostensive reference. To read in this way means to prolong this suspension of the ostensive reference to the world and to transfer oneself into the "place" where the text stands, within the "enclosure" of this worldless place. According to this choice, the text no longer has an outside, it has only an inside. (1971: 554)

Among the structuralists Ricoeur has in mind as interpreters of texts is Lévi-Strauss. Lévi-Strauss has become famous for his structural interpretation of native myths through the alleged disclosure of their internal logic. He proceeds by grouping together a series of sentences, according to their logical relation, into what he calls "mythemes" (Ricoeur 1971: 555). These mythemes acquire their value in relation to other mythemes, yielding the binomial opposites such as raw and cooked for which Lévi-Strauss has become famous. The principal factor that Ricoeur overlooks in comparing the structuralist suspension of referents to the phenomenological epoché is that the latter is designed methodologically to get at the meaning of a constituted object by allowing the phenomenon itself to appear in its multiplicity. The structuralist method, as illustrated by Lévi-Strauss's mythemes, adheres to the rationalist principle that all objects of knowledge must conform to the universal operation of reason that is part of the functioning of the human mind a priori.[12] While for Husserl the constitution of meaning is primary, Lévi-Strauss argues that meaning is epiphenomenal with respect to structure. The epiphenomenal character of Lévi-Strauss's concept of meaning is clearly illustrated and then critiqued in Stanley Diamond's essay "Anthropology in Question":

> Lévi-Strauss the ethnologist is actually saying that he is not interested in meaning (significance), which he regards as merely (and always) phenomenal. For him, the primary phenomenon is not meaning but non-meaning, which lies behind meaning and to which, he believes, meaning is reducible. But the reverse is not true; that is, non-meaning is never "reducible" to meaning. In short, Lévi-Strauss is concerned with the primary or underlying structures of non-meaning, which nonetheless govern meaning. Lévi-Strauss, so to speak, reverses the focus of the phenomenologist; he had substantially dismissed phenomenology in *Tristes Tropiques*. (in Diamond 1974: 95)

Ricoeur, however, does not conclude his theory of interpretation with Lévi-Strauss's structural method. On the contrary, he only uses structuralist method as the mediating term on the way towards comprehension. In this respect, he thinks both with and beyond Lévi-Strauss. He contends, as we have already seen from his interpretation of Freud, that it is possible for Lévi-Strauss only to repress or suspend meaning, not to vitiate it completely. According to Ricoeur, myth itself is already an interpretation of symbols and is thus in some respects the meaning of meaning. Myth, furthermore, has an essential referential feature, which means that it discloses or articulates something about human existence and the world. To deny the referential character of myths is, for Ricoeur, to reduce them to senseless mathematical games:

> To eliminate this reference to the *aporias* of existence around which mythic thought gravitates would be to reduce the theory of myth to the necrology of the meaningless discourses of mankind. If, on the contrary, we consider structural analysis as a stage – and a necessary one – between the naive interpretation and a critical interpretation, between a surface interpretation and a depth-interpretation, then it would be possible to locate explanation and understanding at two different stages of a unique *hermeneutical arc*. (1971: 557)

We see, then, that Ricoeur begins the dialectic of interpretation with a guess, a naive interpretation, which is corrected through the critical approach of the structural method. The structural method, as the critical moment in the dialectic, leads to the final disclosure of meaning in objective comprehension. As with Gadamer, the final moment in this dialectical process, when applied to cross-cultural understanding or remote historical periods, reveals alternative expressions of the human condition.

The Limits of Semiotic Mediation in the Context of Hermeneutics

While Ricoeur clearly recognizes the limitations of the traditional hermeneutic approach, or what appears as the stage of naive interpretation in his method, his emphasis on semiotic mediation does not contribute to the critical potential of his interpretive theory. Although the critical moment of semiotic mediation has been developed to transcend the limitations of traditional hermeneutics, it shares with this interpretive process an inability to account for how power, as it arises in the form of historically specific social relations, shapes and limits communicative interactions.

Ricoeur has established a second stage of semiotic mediation in his dialectical interpretative theory for three reasons. First, like Gadamer, he makes the linguisticality of human actions primary by contending that the medium of language is what enables all phenomena to become expressible and thus provides an ontological basis for understanding. Human actions and life products are multivocal and therefore in need of mediation to disclose what is concealed in their signifying. Second, the text is a whole composed of a multiplicity of interrelated parts. It cannot be viewed as a series of sentences but, on the contrary, must be construed. Third, since human activity becomes objectified in the signs of language, an interpretation theory can be built upon a logic of the human sciences that does not reproduce the methods of the natural sciences but is capable of equaling their rigor. It is not, then, the multivocality of human actions alone which accounts for Ricoeur's development of a depth hermeneutic, but all three points taken together.

Although his critical moment is modeled on the structural analysis of texts, one must not lose sight of the important ways in which Ricoeur distinguishes himself from such contemporary structuralist theorists as Roland Barthes and poststructuralists such as Jacques Derrida. Barthes, for example, who builds on the earlier linguistic tradition of de Saussure and Hjelmslev and goes beyond that of Lévi-Strauss, develops a semiotic theory of culture. The intent of Barthes's theory is to reconstruct how systems of signification operate in accordance with general structuralist principles of internal opposition and the inter-relation of systems. For Barthes, the process of signification does not belong to language alone but includes all cultural products, both material and social. Through the study of semiotic systems such as the fashion industry (1967), he attempts to articulate a code that links signifier and signified, or the planes of expression and content. Like Ricoeur, he is critical of the label theory of language, as can clearly be seen in his semiotic concept of meaning. For Barthes, the production of meaning does not result from a simple correlation of signifier and signified but, on the contrary, is relational. The meaning of a signified is dependent on a value which it obtains in its setting by virtue of the relation of the signified to other signifieds. Meaning, hence, implies the simultaneity of signifier and value. The importance of this structuralist concept lies in its presenting us with a non-psychological theory of meaning. While Barthes rejects meaning through correlation, he accepts a substitution theory of metaphor. According to this theory, the original unit can be replaced by units to which it has a paradigmatic relation, established through memory, convention, or social practice. The problem with the substitution theory, as Ricoeur has argued, is that it eclipses the world-constitutive potential of metaphor by collapsing the tension between previously unrelated concepts. It is, however, the specific meaning which Barthes and Derrida give to the concept of relation that most pointedly distinguishes their respective versions of structuralism and poststructuralism from Ricoeur's hermeneutics of suspicion.

The concept of relation is used by Barthes and Derrida to describe only the virtuality of systems and their interrelation. Derrida claims that the ego, which has played such a central role in modern western metaphysics, is not a fixed content but a series of relations between self, other, language, and world. Since what is traditionally referred to as the ego is caught up in a series of transitory relations, it makes no sense, according to Derrida, to identify the ego as the genesis of self-reflection and constitution of the social world.[13] Although Ricoeur accepts the structuralist emphasis on opposition and virtual system as the method of his critical moment, it is precisely to the reflection of the substantive ego in the process of its historical self-formation that he returns in the third step of his hermeneutical method. Furthermore, unlike most contemporary structuralist theorists, he does not dichotomize in an absolute sense process or history and the atemporality of system or structure. Quite to the contrary, it is human agency in the process of history that generates the material of semiotic mediation.

Although we cannot appeal to the many critiques of structuralism as a means of bringing Ricoeur's method as a whole into question, it may be said that his use of the semiotic method as a critical moment is based upon two specious assumptions which he shares with structuralism. The first is the notion that the text has a pure interiority; the second postualates that the knowing ego can stand inside the pure interiority of a worldless text, that is, its condition of being nonreferential.

Ricoeur builds his claim that a text has a pure interiority upon the assumptions that the objectified signs of the text can be separated from the meaning intentions of historical agents and that the knowing ego, by performing a quasi-phenomenological epoché, can suspend the referential dimensions of the text. The separability of the subjective intentions of actors from the intersubjectivity of meaning is precisely what makes remote historical periods or alien life expressions accessible to us. Through the semiotic method, we suspend the significations of the text and attempt to reconstruct its internal architecture. According to Ricoeur, it is the knowledge of the text's internal structure or logical coherence that enables us to claim that we have explained the text, although not yet understood it. The restoration of the text's reference draws us into a deeper understanding of the world that it discloses while simultaneously casting light on our own world.

While it is to Ricoeur's credit to argue that the logic of a text is generated in the context of human history viewed as a process, the suspension of this process through the semiotic method creates problems with respect to the critique of ideology and the practice of a critical anthropology. Historical contingencies are not obstacles to knowledge but, on the contrary, are what make knowledge and a critical understanding of social life possible. By historical contingencies, I have in mind the ostensive references of human actions or their relation to concrete contexts. These contexts may include any number of constitutive factors, such as gender relations, social class, cultural tradition, and social and political institutions, which provide the limitations within which human interactions dialectically unfold. As Ricoeur himself has indicated, human actions and discourse share a common referential feature. With this in mind, we have been able to understand human actions and interactions, not as a complement of the nomological classification of facts in the natural sciences but as a communicative event. Although the structure of communication may imply mutual understanding, we cannot for that reason presuppose that it is based upon reciprocity. The hermeneutic emphasis on a mutually shared cultural tradition has tended to accentuate the reciprocity of communicative interactions and has thereby overlooked the degree to which some interchanges between interlocutors may reflect asymmetrical social relations.

Although Ricoeur's view of semiotics rejects the notion of an a priori closed system, the logical oppositions which he intends to disclose through his method are drawn internally, within the text, and thus raise to the level of reflection the abstract conditions of a closed system. Once internal contradictions are divorced from the historical process of their generation, they become reified and hence cease to be dialectical. Real contradictions and oppositions occur only in the process of history. The working out of these contradictions through the lives of human co-subjects is what accounts for their transcendence or movement in history. Within a closed system, the possibility of transcendence or the resolving of contradictions is vitiated, as the finite structure of the system can only produce significations that are self-referential. In other words, in a closed system there is no past and future. The logical relations which Ricoeur identifies within a virtual system can be only functional at best because the oppositions and contradictions disclosed cannot be resolved and must therefore operate towards the continual maintenance or identity of the system. Because critique becomes identified for Ricoeur with the self-referential, logical coherence of a text, constructed solely on the basis of its internal structure, then the movement to comprehension, or the restoration of the text's reference on a new level, merely reproduces its immediacy – the very limitation for which he has criticized naive consciousness.

A text, whether in written, oral, or action format, has neither a pure interiority nor pure exteriority. Significations owe their generation to human practical activity and hence belong fully to the historical process. A critical theory of mediation, as Marx demonstrated,[14] not only discloses the concealed logic of a social system but also demonstrates how this logic can be accounted for historically. Only within the concrete self-formative activity of human co-subjects can logic and history converge, and hence only in this realm does critique have its roots. Ricoeur's theory of semiotic mediation therefore displays the same shortcomings as an exclusively hermeneutic approach to the social sciences. Neither is able to account for inequalities in human interaction nor for concrete institutional limits on human action.

As I have shown, significations are always referential and therefore belong to the historical process. Signs whose reference has been suspended cease to be significations and take on the characteristics of empty categories. Ricoeur himself has claimed, in reference to the important work of John Searle (1967), that a communicative act or signification has both a propositional content and an illocutionary force. The propositional content is the act of saying whereby we convey a message. The illocutionary force, on the other hand, is what we do by saying. According to Ricoeur, the meaning of a communicative event must include both its propositional content and its illocutionary force.[15] To suspend the illocutionary force of a communicative event in order to reflect upon the propositional content, as is implied, for example, in the semiotic method, is to disregard how significations are used in specific contexts, that is, their social praxis. The logic of a situation does not arise simply from the review of propositional contents but, on the contrary, from how actions and interactions are constituted meaningfully. It is precisely the illocutionary force of communicative acts that is disregarded by the semiotic method, which suggests that the significations analyzed are without their full intentionality.

Just as it is not possible for a text to have a pure interiority, so it is not possible for a knowing ego to be drawn into a worldless text. By knowing ego, Ricoeur is not referring to the solipsism of the earlier phenomenological tradition.[16] The knowing ego is for Ricoeur immersed fully in the intersubjectivity of language and cultural tradition. The questions raised by the knowing ego are not drawn simply from the individual's life history but also from the historicity of the prescientific social life-world. As Ricoeur himself has said, the process of knowledge in the social sciences is necessarily self-reflexive. The knowing ego which is thus drawn into the worldlessness of the text, in Ricoeur's sense, defines a context that is neither internal nor external but dialectical. The knowledge of the pure interiority of a text already presupposes that the human subject is inextricably immersed in a historical and cultural milieu subject to the limitations of particular social relations and institutions. The very ontological conditions from which epistemological reflection departs are contrary to the internal and external process of mediation that has been suggested by Ricoeur as a necessary moment in transforming a naive into a critical interpretation.

While Ricoeur has drawn our attention to the important parallels between the interpretation of texts and the interpretation of human actions and events, the process of semiotic mediation that serves as the middle term in his dialectical process of understanding is unable to account for the social conditions under which texts are produced or the social constraints to which symbolic interactions are subject. Although it is beyond the scope of this chapter to develop these implications fully, the shortcomings of Ricoeur's method might have been foreseen if he had asked the question complementary to his original question, that is, how can the interpretation of human actions illuminate our understanding of texts? This directs our attention to the historical process or the concrete conditions of human self-formation. It is not that structure is a fiction but, rather, that structure exists in history. System owes its existence to process; thus we must look to process to disclose the social contradictions and relations of power that are concealed in the significations of communicative interactions.

Another objection to the analogy of texts and human actions, as well as the privileging of writing by both Ricoeur and Gadamer, is raised by Jacques Derrida in *Of Grammatology* (1974). Ricoeur and Gadamer privilege writing over discourse because of the fleeting character of discourse. However, they leave other attributes of the relation between discourse and writing unexamined. By implying that writing is more permanent than discourse, there is a tendency on their part to present the telos of writing as simply providing an arena of objectification for what is temporary. Derrida contends that writing has been completely misunderstood in western society because, in serving as the arena for the objectification of discourse, it has itself become an activity that is only derivative. He claims that the immediacy of discourse has led to its close association with logos or reason.

Writing, argues Derrida, should not simply be equated with the development of alphabets, and therefore consequent to discourse, but on the contrary, should be recognized in the history of the species as the leaving of a mutually intelligible trace. The cave paintings of Les Eyzies qualify as a form of writing and hence have as close an association to the logos as the discourse which they most likely predate. There is a tendency for Gadamer and Ricoeur tacitly to functionalize writing by comparing the temporal dimensions of its very specific and limited form in the alphabet to the temporal attributes of discourse. While the analogy between the text and human actions is not challenged fully by Derrida's concept of writing, the implications of this concept warn against taking the text in the full sense as a paradigm for interpreting human actions.

The constitution of symbols and their meaning, whether through social interaction or in the form of texts, always reflects the character of power relations in a historically specific social formation and cultural tradition.[17] Symbolic interaction and texts must be comprehended not only from the perspective of what is communicated, that is, their propositional content, but also from that of the social conditions in which communication takes place. By emphasizing the importance of sociohistorical process in the interpretation of texts and symbolic interactions, I am not regressing to an interpretive theory that ties meaning directly to an unmediated context. On the contrary, we must always keep in mind, as Ricoeur has made clear, that the meaning of texts or events is always mediated by questions raised hermeneutically from the changing horizon and cultural tradition of the investigator.

Conclusion

Although I have argued that Ricoeur's moment of semiotic mediation is faulty insofar as it locates oppositions or contradictions in the worldlessness of the text rather than in the historical process of human self-formation, this should not obscure the merit of his analogy between the interpretation of texts and human actions. He has shown how it is possible, by rejecting the methodological implications of an explanation/understanding dichotomy – how emics and etics have come to be used in contemporary anthropology to distinguish types of theoretical constructs – to develop an interpretation theory with critical implications based on the logic of the human sciences. Anthropologists who resort to an exclusively explanatory or etic position through drawing nomological hypotheses fail to recognize that cultural phenomena are intentional in that they owe their generation and identity to the historically constitutive activity of human co-subjects. On the other hand, anthropologists who privilege understanding conceptualize this process as a logical reconstruction of the subjective intentions of actors or, in a more complex sense, the identification of meaning with context. Ricoeur argues that the pursuit of an exclusively explanation-or exclusively under-standing-oriented theory is based upon an epistemological reduction. The privileging of theories based upon natural-science explanation reduces the intersubjectivity of meaning to the classification of facts, while theories based upon understanding reduce the dialectical movement of meaning to the ostensive reference of context. In either case the critical potentialities of anthropology are vitiated because the reflexive dimension of the interpretive process is absent.

Ricoeur's theory, therefore, is important for anthropologists because it combines an emphasis on mediation, or the critique of naive consciousness, with the conception of human actions as intentional, communicative events. It thus goes a long way towards satisfying some of the deepest objections raised by the scientistic outlook against the method of *verstehen* while retaining the latter's emphasis on a hermeneutic understanding of social life. His theory, without resorting to the objectivism of the natural sciences, pursues the logic of a method that is in concert with the unique object/subject of the human sciences.

7 Hermeneutics and Critical Anthropology: The Synthesis of Practical and Critical Reason

We have seen in the previous chapter that the hermeneutic perspectives of Hans-Georg Gadamer and Paul Ricoeur leave us short of a fully developed critical interpretive framework. While Gadamer's emphasis on the mediations of tradition in his concept of the fusion of horizons points to the primacy of presuppositions and history in the interpretive process, his subordination of the self-reflection of epistemology to an ontological hermeneutic ignores the power constraints to which communicative interactions are subject. It is not possible within an ontological hermeneutics to distinguish truth claims that are based upon normative consensus or reciprocity from those that are ideological. Ricoeur's theory promised to transcend the limitations of the ontological hermeneutic by introducing a dialectic of explanation and understanding into the critical method of semiotic mediation. Although the process of semiotic mediation has proved its value in the formal analysis of texts, the restriction of its field of critical review to a virtual system of objectified signs prevents the interpreter, or self-reflexive subject, from grasping the concrete historical determinations that account for the generation and transformation of objectified human interactions. While the intention of the semiotic method is to disclose what is concealed in the process of signification, the suspension of the contingencies of the knowing subject, the phenomenological epoché, and the constituted object of knowledge reproduces within hermeneutics an objectivism analogous to the natural sciences. As I have shown in the last chapter, when Ricoeur moves from the moment of semiotic mediation to the stage of critical understanding, he comes dangerously close to reproducing immediacy.

These problems do not, however, vitiate the overall importance of hermeneutics for the development of a critical interpretive theory within anthropology. On the contrary, hermeneutics emphasizes the reflexive character of all interpretive processes in that knowledge of the radical other, whether human interactions, informants, or texts, discloses the uniqueness or historical particularity of the interpreter's cultural tradition. The hermeneutic method, furthermore, demonstrates that meaning is not reducible to subjective intentions nor to the context of its generation, as the meanings of objectified intentions are necessarily open to all actual and potential horizons of interpretation. Gadamer, through emphasizing the relation between historical events and the questions to which they are an answer, poses a direct challenge to empiricist history and its facticity of the given. His notion of the historicity of tradition and the communicative character of all interactions, together with Ricoeur's concept of the power of symbols to assimilate and shape human destiny, portrays the irreducible moral and cultural dimension of all interactions – that human interactions are informed by a process of communicative rationality, that is, by norms of mutual expectation.

While self-reflection, effective historicity, and the cultural character of all interactions are indispensable ingredients of the process or totality that defines interpretation, they are not sufficient, at least as articulated in the hermeneutic tradition, to account for the complexity of interactions that are marked by social inequality. In other words, hermeneutics operates with a concept of tradition and communicative interaction that presupposes reciprocity between interlocutors. The point here is not to reject the hermeneutic project, but to transform its practical intent, the phenomenology of the sociocultural life-world, into one that is critical and emancipatory. I will argue in this chapter that the transformation of hermeneutics into a critical interpretive theory can be accomplished by absorbing the communicative dialectic into the materialist dialectic of social being. The articulation of this transformation will require steering a course between two Marxisms which have grown to maturity in the post-Second World War era and which are among the major theoretical influences on contemporary critical anthropology. These are structuralism, represented by Althusser and his many disciples, and what I call the historical-culturalist perspective – an outgrowth of Lukács, Gramsci, and certain members of the Frankfurt School, represented here in the works of E. P. Thompson and Raymond Williams. We shall see that the absorption and transformation of hermeneutics through an encounter with this tradition will also involve critical examination and reformulation of certain leading concepts as they have been articulated by these two schools of Marxist social theory. I will present the Marxist concepts of social formation and hegemony as a means of deepening the hermeneutic concept of tradition, while showing how the hermeneutic concept of culture can correct tendencies in Marxist theory to equate the concept of interaction with the instrumental process of labor.

Structuralist Marxism and Interpretive Theory

In *History and Class Consciousness* (1971) George Lukács attempts to formulate a unified vision for Marxism. He contends that Marxism is not an empirical science dependent upon a process of verification but, on the contrary, a critical theory informed by the concept of totality and grounded in the method of mediation. He furthermore claims that the failure of Marxism to predict events in the world is not a sufficient reason to reject its theoretical intent, as Marxism is most fundamentally a form of historical praxis. Lukács's very notion of a unified theoretical praxis, however, serves as the object of the structuralist critique of Marxist humanism. According to Althusser and Balibar in *Reading Capital* (1970), the humanist position is guilty of reducing Marxism to the historical conditions of its existence and of equating relations of production to Hegelian intersubjectivity. Rather than claiming that a social formation, or in Lukács's sense a totality, owed its generation to the formative activity of human co-subjects, Althusser argues that human subjects are only vectors or functions in the structure of the relations of production. Since the object of knowledge for Althusser is the outcome of a theoretical mode of discourse, as well as the means through which the real object is appropriated, historical events are conceived as contemporaneous. He claims that history itself must be explained and is therefore subordinate to synchronic theoretical articulation. The primacy of the synchronic in Althusser is obvious in his concept of structural causality, *Darstellung*, according to which the structure is present or immanent in its effects. While this concept accounts for the continual reproduction of a social formation, we shall see that it also presents problems with respect to social transformation.

Twentieth-century Marxism provides us, therefore, with two oppositional traditions: one emphasizing the world-constitutive activity of human subjects and the historical determinations of concrete totalities, the other subordinating the significance of human subjects and history to an articulated hierarchy of synchronic structures that are the product of a theoretical mode of discourse. Althusser and Balibar do not, however, employ the concept of structure in a fashion that resembles British social anthropology or the structuralism of Lévi-Strauss. In British social anthropology, as exemplified by Radcliffe-Brown (1965), structures are used to describe actually existing, empirical social relations. Lévi-Strauss (1963), on the other hand, claims that structures are not reducible to the visible but are, on the contrary, the generative logic of social life. His treatment of structure is rationalist in that the existing structures of social life are conceived as homologous with structures of the human mind. For Lévi-Strauss, the diversity of empirical structures, myths, and cultures throughout the world

are merely variations on a common theme, a surface semantics of an underlying universal logic.

Structures, according to Althusser, are the product of theoretical practice,
as they are neither empirically given in the world nor a priori reflections of
the structure of mind. As I pointed out earlier, he distinguishes between
"real" objects and objects of theoretical knowledge. When the "real" objects
are social relations, they are considered to be ideological because they
consist only of the imaginary relations that human subjects have to their
world. The transformation of raw material, which for Althusser is never
simply given, from its ideological or imaginary form into an object of
scientific knowledge is a three-part process. The first stage, or "generalities
I," consists of the concepts and abstractions that will serve as the basis of
theoretical practice. These concepts in themselves have no more intrinsic
value than the individual phonemes of a language. They must be brought
into some systematic or articulate relation, what Althusser refers to as
"generalities II." "Generalities II" defines the field or problematic as the
theoretical mode which articulates the relation of concepts to each other
and determines the nature of each concept by its place or function in the
system. The third stage, "Generalities III," is the production of theoretical
knowledge itself. Structures, in short, do not exist as given entities in the
world but consist of articulated combinations of elements that are the
product of a determinate problematic or theoretical mode of discourse.

Althusser develops the concept of structure one step further in contending
that the different structures which compose both a mode of production and
a social formation are not equally determinant. In contrast to the Hegelian
notion of expressive totality, which predominates in humanist versions of
Marxism, Althusser argues that a social formation consists of an interrelated hierarchy of asymmetrical structures.[1] In any given social formation,
the alignment of contradictions with respect to different regions of social
practice, such as the political or economic, will determine which structure is
"in dominance." The most puzzling aspect of his notion of the structure in
dominance is his contention, despite the variability of dominant structures,
that in the last instance the structure of the economy is determinant. This
emphasis in Althusser's theory, which he claims is true to the spirit of Marx,
has led to a rigid idea of a social formation as consisting of an economic
base and political, cultural, and ideological superstructures. We will see, in
the section on the cultural-historical trajectory in Marxism, how the Althusserian division between base and superstructure is inadequate not only for
grasping indigenous social formations, where productive relations are not
distinct from kinship, but also for understanding the logic of interaction and
reproduction of the capitalist system.

Althusser's concept of social formation as a hierarchy of structures, in
spite of his emphasis on the dominance of the economic in the last instance,

shows that there are multiple determinations of varying importance that limit and shape human interactions. His notion that the theoretical object of knowledge must be constructed, as well as his idea that the disparate elements and concepts of reality must be articulated according to their immanent connections in the problematic of a theoretical field, clearly shows the untenability of atomist and empiricist concepts of a reality that is simply given.

Although I have only touched on some of the salient contributions that Althusser has made to Marxist social theory, it will be necessary to consider other well-known adherents to Marxist structuralism in order to appreciate the diversity within this school. Two of the most controversial theoreticians, Barry Hindess and Paul Hirst, have in a number of provocative works including *Pre-Capitalist Modes of Production* (1975) and *Modes of Production and Social Formation* (1977), initiated a critical dialogue with Althusser and have therefore contributed to an internal critique of structuralism. They also warrant our careful attention because they address the theoretical limitations of such noted Marxist anthropologists as Meillassoux, Rey, and Dupré.

Hindess and Hirst's perspective is difficult to summarize, not only because of the breadth of their intellectual concerns and the diversity of the traditions that they address, but also because they continually qualify, contradict, and retract positions which they have articulated,[2] both from work to work and within individual texts. The coherence of their work can nonetheless be perceived in their consistent application of a formal concept of theory and their vehement antiempiricism and antirationalism.

Hindess and Hirst, following Althusser, reject the empiricist presupposition that facts are simply given in the world and can therefore be grasped through intersubjectively verifiable hypotheses. In their view the given must always be constructed or constituted through a definite theoretical or ideological practice.[3] The facts of the sciences, for example, are produced through a scientific mode of discourse. While their critique of empiricism at this level is commendable, serious problems arise when they extend their antiempiricism to a rejection of all epistemology.

According to Hindess and Hirst, epistemology presupposes a dichotomy between the knowing subject and the object of knowledge.[4] Knowledge claims in the empiricist tradition are built upon the elements of human experience, which are raised to the level of hypotheses which either do or do not correspond to the objective facticity of the world. They argue that empiricist epistemology, apart from not raising the question of how these facts are produced, undermines the scientificity of knowledge claims by reducing their universality to the contingency of human experience.

Hindess and Hirst also focus their critique on rationalist epistemology as it is disclosed in the works of Althusser. In rationalism, the link between the knowing subject and the object of knowledge is based upon an a priori homology between the human mind and the order of the objective world. The relations between concepts, therefore, are supposed to be able to express the essence of the real.[5] At the epistemological level, Althusser's notion that the "real" object can be appropriated through the object of knowledge is rationalist and therefore unacceptable to Hindess and Hirst because it does not specify how the given can be appropriated except through a priori definition. Hindess and Hirst also contend that Althusser's notion of a mode of production is rationalist, in that it is thought to produce the conditions of its own existence as its effects. This perspective on reproduction, which is attributable in part to the influence of Spinoza's rationalism, makes it systematically impossible to envision a transition from one mode of production to another. Because the effects produced through the structure of a mode of production are not distinct from the conditions that account for its existence, the mode of production will maintain its identity through its cycles of reproduction. In contrast to the presuppositions of rationalist epistemology, Hindess and Hirst claim:

> On the contrary, in the absence of such extra-discursive (and yet specifiable) objects, the entities specified in discourse must be referred to solely in and through the forms of discourse, theoretical, political, etc., in which they are constituted. (1977: 19)

The concepts of constitution and discourse are keys to Hindess and Hirst's notion of theory. By discourse, they are not referring to the speech event of the sociolinguists, since they use discourse in a sense that makes no reference to interlocutors. They argue, rather, that all concepts are abstract and are defined, as in semiotics, both by the place they occupy and by the function they perform within a determinate field or system of concepts. They claim, furthermore, that concepts have no existence outside of the knowledge process through which they are produced. The validity of concepts, in contrast to the empiricist and rationlist traditions, is based solely upon the internal coherence or consistency of the concepts that compose the field or system. Although Hindess and Hirst do not agree with Althusser's a priori distinction between science and ideology,[6] they are fully in agreement with his notion that theoretical practice, which in Althusser's case produces scientific knowledge, stands completely outside the contingencies of a social formation.

That theoretical practice is not part of a concrete social formation is essential for understanding their explicit rejection of history. Locating a sequence of events in space and time is not sufficient for Hindess and Hirst because this sequence must be explained by grasping the adequacy of its concept. Because the field of concepts that compose a theoretical articulation is nonreferential and self-constituting, history is superfluous to the logic of the social sciences:

> The study of history is not only scientifically but politically valueless.... Historical events do not exist and can have no material effectivity in the present. (1975: 312)

For Hindess and Hirst, in short, theory is a mode of practice in knowledge whereby concepts are produced and organized into coherent and consistent articulations. The objects which are constituted in theoretical discourse are exclusively self-referential and should not be taken as paradigms for any existing social formation or sequence of related historical events. Because this form of theoretical practice is nonreferential, its validity claims are supported solely through their internal consistency.

Hindess and Hirst label all theoretical traditions as empiricist and rationalist whose epistemological claims to validity are grounded or mediated by some form of human experience in the world. The problem with this approach is that it combines and treats as equivalent many incommensurable social theories. There are not only important differences between these social theories with respect to knowledge-constitutive interests, but significant distinctions that must be recognized within the historical development of individual traditions. We shall see that even their own theoretical geometry manages to transgress the boundaries of such an all-encompassing definition of empiricism and rationalism.

Hindess and Hirst's autonomous and formal concept of theory as a mode of practice in knowledge provides the basis for their treatment of modes of production and social formation. They contend that it is not their project, as it was Althusser and Balibar's in *Reading Capital*, to construct a general theory of modes of production. They argue that such a theory is idealist in that the possible combinations of its elements are supposed to be able to depict the relations between actual historical events. In the case of Althusser and Balibar, the elements are identified as the labor force, the object and means of labor, and those who are not direct producers and therefore appropriate surplus labor. In Balibar's general theory, these elements can be combined through two principles, referred to as the technical and the social division of labor. The first principle involves the relations of real appropriation or the production process, while the second incorporates property relations or the exploitation process (Glucksman 1972). The mode of production as defined by Althusser and Balibar is universal and ahistorical, since the elements are present in all social formations and differ only in content as they are articulated within alternative combinations of production. Against a general theory, Hindess and Hirst argue that the concept of a mode of production, as well as other concepts in Marxist theory, is only a theoretical means, whose elements can be recombined based on how surplus labor is extracted, to produce a determinate mode of production. They define the mode of production in the following way:

> A mode of production is an articulated combination of relations and forces of production structured by the dominance of the relations of production. The relations of production define a specific mode of appropriation of surplus-labor and the specific form of social distribution of the means of production corresponding to that mode of appropriation of surplus labor. (1975: 9–10)

The forces of production are the mode of appropriation of nature through which a raw material is transformed into a determinate product. According to Hindess and Hirst, it is not possible to define the relations and forces of production as separate entities, but only as they are combined within an articulated mode of production.

Hindess and Hirst use their concept of mode of production to evaluate whether the primitive-communist, ancient, slavery, Asiatic, and feudal modes of production consist of an articulate combination of relations and forces of production. The key ingredient in this evaluation is the mode of extraction of surplus labor, which draws our attention both to the control of the labor process in the organization of production and to the distribution of the social product.

One of the strengths of the above formulation is that it enables Hindess and Hirst to show the weakness of Meillassoux's technicist conception of the mode of production in his study of the Guoro (1964). Meillassoux argues that the process of appropriation in indigenous societies can take one of two distinctive forms: simple or complex redistribution. Simple redistribution is found most commonly in societies with a band form of social organization, where there is little marked division of labor and membership in the band is fluent. Although division of labor between the sexes exists in band societies, the division of labor between age groups is minimal because age statuses are not maintained. Cooperative labor is temporary under simple redistribution as there is no permanent labor organization. The product of labor, which in most cases is an animal kill-ed in a hunt, is divided among the band according to a hierarchy of statuses.

Complex redistribution, according to Meillassoux, is different from sim-ple redistribution in that it is found in societies with larger and more stable populations and is based on a production process that is organized accord-ing to the cooperative labor of the village, lineage, and lineage segments. In his study of the Guoro society, for example, he describes how hunting with nets involved the cooperation of all men in the village while certain agri-cultural activities only required the cooperation of a lineage segment, or in some cases an age set. Complex redistribution, furthermore, permits a more specialized division of labor, particularly with respect to artisans or craftsmen, and, in addition, accounts for the support of nonproducers such as children and elders. Although the division of labor is more developed in societies organized according to complex redistribution, the division of labor and the process of exchange, which in its commodity form is limited to exchange between societies, are held in check by the collective appropriation of surplus labor. Hindess and Hirst, however, regard the evolution from simple to complex redistribution as progressive in that it leads both to an improvement in the instruments of production and an increase in the productivity of labor.

The problem with Meillassoux's analysis of simple and complex redistribution, according to Hindess and Hirst, is that he conceives the mode of production in such a way that it can be deduced from the division of labor mandated to execute a specific technical task, such as hunting or agriculture. They claim that the processes of both simple and complex redistribution discussed by Meillassoux involve the collective appropriation of surplus labor and hence constitute a single mode of production.

Hindess and Hirst claim that they can determine the adequacy of any one of the modes of production without making reference to concrete social formations or the history of their development. The grasping of a mode of production unfolds through a process that involves only the review of the logical connections between concepts. The objectivity of the mode of production, as I explained earlier in regard to their formal notion of theory, is guaranteed by the internal consistency of its theoretical articulation and the absence of social contingencies.

Their formal concept of mode of production as presented in *Pre-Capitalist Modes of Production* has provoked a number of critical responses from both Marxist and non-Marxist scholars.[7] The general consensus of these critiques, apart from diverse particulars, is that Hindess and Hirst take an Althusserian version of theory to its point of absurdity by implying that there is no relation between the level of theoretical articulation and concrete social interactions. One must keep in mind that, at least for Althusser, the necessary telos of theory is the appropriation of the real through the object of knowledge. In their later *Auto-Critique* Hindess and Hirst modify their position somewhat by claiming that it was never their intention to deny the existence of social relations. They contend that they were simply trying to explicate the inadequacy of the correspondence theory of truth or what they refer to as the "category of the concrete as an object of knowledge" (1977: 7). This retreat from their more radical rejection of the given leaves them with a theoretical articulation that is closely tied to the Althusserian project and hence its problematics.

Hindess and Hirst's notion of a mode of production as a logical relation between abstract concepts also generates problems, as did Althusser's, in regard to accounting for social transformations. Their solution to this problem, if not clearly rationalist, is certainly teleological. They take Marx's polemical comments from the *Communist Manifesto* literally and hence introduce the class struggle as a universal ingredient of social change. Not only is the universality of class struggle controversial in Marxist literature, one wonders how Hindess and Hirst can draw upon it, since their formal notion of theory rejects both history and the human subject's participation in the social world. Their articulation of the class struggle is teleological and rationalist; it exists only *in abstracto* as the necessary link between formal categories or integrated systems.

The relation of the mode of production to social formations in their work is difficult to grasp because once again they alter their position from *Pre-Capitalist Modes of Production* to the *Auto-Critique*. According to Hindess and Hirst, a social formation consists of a unity of economic, ideological, and, in some cases, political levels. The political level is qualified as they equate political life with the state.[8] They argue that the structure of the economy is determinant since it is the mode of production that determines not only which level dominates in the social formation but also how the political and ideological levels intervene in the economic. As Rod Aya states in his critical review of *Pre-Capitalist Modes of Production*, Hindess and Hirst's liberal view of a social formation as consisting of relatively autonomous modes reifies social relations by ordering them into a hierarchy of abstract regions. For example, in their discussion of the primitive-communist social formation. Hindess and Hirst make the claim that kinship can be derived from the economic reproduction of society because kinship, while only a possibility in band societies, is a necessity among sedentary agriculturalists. I contend, however, that kinship in indigenous societies integrates a number of regions of human practical activity. It organizes not only the process of production but also the reproduction of culture through a highly complex sociocultural learning process. Human activity discharged through the institution of kinship synthesizes the instrumental or strategic action of the production process with reciprocal norms of mutual expectation in the transmission of culture. Hindess and Hirst's treatment of the primitive-communist social formation not only reifies social relations but also tends to transform the social reproduction of culture into a function of the logic of production. We shall see that they are not alone among the structuralist Marxists in substituting the instrumental rationality of production for the communicative rationality of culture.

In *Auto-Critique* Hindess and Hirst reject the concept of mode of production because they believe that its emphasis on economic class relations cannot account for more complex interactions such as petty commodity production and merchant's capital. They suggest that this concept be replaced by the theory of social formation conceived as "determinate sets of economic class relations, their conditions of existence, and the forms in which these conditions are secured" (1977: 55). While this definition of social formation avoids the problems arising from the notion of a hierarchy of levels, the logic of the social formation is still tied in a determinate manner to the instrumental rationality of production.

Hindess and Hirst's concept of theory as it informs their notions of mode of production and social formation not only departs form Marxist tradition in its rejection of epistemology, but also, in its abstract and self-validating formulation, is commensurate with the scientistic self-understanding of society. Their antiempiricist and antihistorical perspective can be viewed as a departure from Marxist tradition, as Asad and Wolpe have argued (1976), because it was never Marx's project to reject the given. Marx claimed, on the contrary, that reality is only incompletely manifested in the visible and hence it is incumbent upon a critical theory to seize and transform the given. This is also implicit in Marx's concept of praxis, whereby the participation of human co-subjects in the world not only transforms nature through the objectification of labor but also, through the course of human interactions, transforms human nature and society. Marx referred to this dialectical process, which also challenges the subject/object dichotomy, as the humanization of nature and naturalization of man (1967a: 177). It is interesting to note that the concept of praxis, which is so central to Marx's theoretical articulation, is absent from that of Hindess and Hirst.

Hindess and Hirst's eclipsing of the historical dimension of both the constituting subject and constituted object of knowledge vitiates the critical potential of their concepts of mode of production and social formation. As we have already seen, the mode of production and social formation exist for them only at the level of the clarification of logical constructs within an atemporal system. As they discuss the various modes of production we discover, as Asad and Wolpe have shown, that they substitute concrete social formations for logical proofs of their theory (1976: 479–80). This should come as no surprise, since Marx's development of various concepts of modes of production reflects dialectically his historical research into concrete societies. The concepts which Hindess and Hirst attempt to clarify at the logical level for consistency are thus permeated by historical connections. A mode of production cannot be rejected because of its inconsistencies at the abstract level alone but rather because of its inability to articulate the historical connections of the concrete. When the concept of mode of production is raised purely to the abstract level, its ties to the historically concrete are ruptured so that the social world is left unmediated. This is precisely the outcome of Hindess and Hirst's theoretical articulation in regard to the primitive-communist social formation. While they are able to illustrate in a formal sense that production in indigenous societies is based upon the collective appropriation of surplus labor, they leap to the a priori and insupportable conclusion that domination cannot exist in the primitive-communist social formation.

Hindess and Hirst offer a theoretical perspective that exacerbates problems already present in Althusser's voluminous works. The clarification of concepts exclusively at the abstract and formal level contributes little to the serious Marxist scholar's attempt to penetrate the opacity of social reality. It seems to me that if anthropology can be regarded as a historical science whose purpose is to grasp human societies in a diversity of social forms and milieus, then Hindess and Hirst, by rejecting the concreteness of social interaction, block this potential. They do not, however, exhaust the scope of a Marxist anthropology, as a more concrete and ethnographic version of structuralism has been developed by Maurice Godelier.

Godelier, along with a group of other Marxist anthropologists such as Terray and Meillassoux, has been acclaimed for his application of Marxist method to indigenous societies. His work on the processes of state formation, for example, is an important contribution to the anthropological literature on modes of production. His *Rationality and Irrationality in Economics* (1972) addresses the many rationalities that characterize social systems as well as providing a method through which the diverse logics of social life can be grasped. Godelier, more than any of the other Marxist anthropologists, provides us with a perspective from which to draw the issues of the rationality debates into a fully Marxist theoretical framework.

Contrary to Althusser, Hindess, and Hirst, Godelier argues that history is important for the understanding of social formations. He discloses the orthodoxy of his structuralism, however, in his claim that the history of a social phenomenon can only be known once the internal logic of the social system of which it is part has been fully articulated. History, for Godelier, is neither the reconstruction of chronologies nor a process through which human co-subjects constitute their world. It is, rather, the origin of a social phenomenon as deduced a posteriori from the logic of a social system. This concept of history merely reverses the emphasis of Lévi-Strauss, who claims that historical understanding is an initial step in uncovering the concealed logic of social life.[9] The justification for subordinating history to logic or process to system resides, according to this school of Marxist anthropology, in the authority of Marx's analysis of the capitalist system.[10] According to structuralist interpretation, it was necessary for Marx first to reconstruct the logic of the capitalist social formation before he could address its origins. For Godelier, therefore, one must grasp the internal logic or mode of production of an indigenous society before coming to terms with the history of its development.

The method which Godelier employs to reconstruct the internal logic of a social system adheres closely to the Althusserian project in its antiempiricism and adversarial stance towards Hegelian intersubjectivity. Like all structuralists, he believes that social reality is opaque and that therefore the object of knowledge must be constructed. In addition, he argues that empiricism is related to a Popperian version of methodological individualism in that both theoretical positions base the constitution of the social world on the isolated ego's experience. Godelier contends, on the other hand, that the constitution of social reality can only be accounted for through the determinate interrelations of structures and their conjunctures. Unlike Hindess and Hirst, he accepts the Althusserian notion of structural causality as the means by which a social formation develops its specific identity and thus its objective limits.

Although Godelier is critical of the methodological individualism of the empiricist tradition, there is a surprising convergence of his notion of theory with that of the neo-Popperians. This convergence does not lie in his rejection of the immediacy of social reality but, rather, in his notion of reconstruction as a model. According to Godelier, a model is not reducible to social reality, since it consists of formal logical relations between concepts which, although implicit in the world, are concealed by the immediacy of the given. In order to penetrate the opacity of social reality, the theoretician must reconstruct the logic of a social formation through the hypothetico-deductive method. Godelier argues that this method can be applied to social formations to analyze economic structures and their interrelations, to deduce the possible combinations of these structures so that new forms can be anticipated, and, finally, to define the essential structure of the economic system.

While certainly there is merit in attempting to disclose the concealed logic of economic systems, it is questionable whether this can be accomplished by means of the method-model relation that Godelier suggests. The hypothetico-deductive method, as we saw in the case of I. C. Jarvie, is based upon the formulation of verifiable hypotheses capable of establishing nomological relations between objective phenomena in the world. The truth conditions of these hypotheses rest with the consensus of the investigative community. The relationships between concepts expressed in a hypothesis, furthermore, are claimed to be isomorphic with objective conditions in the world: the concepts express the essence of the real. The a priori rationalism that Godelier absorbs from the hypothetico-deductive method is exhibited clearly in the following:

> These deductive operations are based on the logical necessary relations between the categories, and this ideal logic "reproduces" the actual logic of the concrete capitalist system. (1972: 158)

As with Althusser's notion of the appropriation of the concrete or Lévi-Strauss's concept of the complementary structures of mind and social life, Godelier supports a homology between thought and reality.

The problem with Godelier's reliance on the hypothetico-deductive method and the concept of model, apart from its rationalism, is that it counters his own attempt to mediate the appearances of economic systems by substituting a positivist notion of critique for one that is dialectical. The hypothetico-deductive method involves a critique of language inasmuch as its intent is to create statements that are capable of surviving repeated attempts at falsification. Hypotheses that are accepted as conditionally true merely reproduce at the level of thought the objective conditions of the world. The use of this method within a Marxist theoretical framework exposes its limits in that it can merely, at best, systematically express reality and its contradictions, thereby leaving the world unchanged. A dialectical method of critique, on the contrary, is reflexive. It reconstructs the human interests that make knowledge of the social world possible and discloses the historically concrete determinations that account for the formation and reproduction of social phenomena. The concept of model or paradigm, which predominates in contemporary social science and which is commensurate with the hypothetico-deductive method, establishes an essentially conservative modus operandi for the social sciences in that its goal is the clarification of isomorphic concepts rather than a reflexive critique of social life.

While Godelier resorts to a positivist notion of science in order to demonstrate the necessity for constructing the given – a fact also substantiated by his notion of the invariant laws behind structural transformations – his contribution to the rationality of economic systems, despite certain limitations that I will discuss, is essentially more critical. The anthropological literature on indigenous economies is laden with images of the native as an acquisitive, rational calculator.[11] Unfortunately, all too many anthropologists have taken the presence of the market and hence the process of exchange as a sign of the universality of homo economicus.[12] Godelier argues, however, that there is no specific economic rationality, logic of production, or law that can be taken as intrinsic to the diverse social means by which societies obtain their subsistence and thus guarantee their reproduction. On the contrary, the rationality of production is immersed in the wider rationality of social systems.

Godelier does not use the concept of the rationality of a social system in a way commensurable with the language games and forms of life that I discussed in relation to Peter Winch. In contrast to Winch, Godelier has utterly dismissed intersubjectivity as a constituent of social systems, since, as he asserts, it is the unintentional properties of economic and social systems that determine their rationality. He argues, moreover, that the rationality of social systems cannot be reduced to the goals or intentions of individual actors, as the objective of individual actions can only be deduced from the interrelations of structures which constitute a social system. For Godelier, the rationality of a social system is the hidden logic articulated by the interrelations of structures that constitute the system. His notion of structure, as we have seen for all the structuralists we have considered, makes no reference to the formative activity of human co-subjects. Structures, on the contrary, are objective social relations animated by the laws or rational principles that articulate their hierarchical interrelation within a determinate social formation:

> These laws exist and express the unintentional structural properties of social relations, their hierarchy and articulation on the basis of determined modes of production. . . . In order to arrive at this profound logic we must go further than a structural analysis of forms of social relations and modes of thought and try to decipher the "effects" of structures on each other through the various processes of social practice and place them in the hierarchy of causes determining the functioning and reproduction of economic and social formations. (Godelier 1977: 2)

By claiming that there are diverse rationalities that compose economic and social systems, Godelier challenges the universal rationality and implied notions of human nature of formalist economic theory, thereby establishing a basis for a comparative economic anthropology. He furthermore avoids the dilemmas of a completely relativistic rationality, as well as the problematics of the hermeneutic notion of communicative reciprocity, by emphasizing that a social formation consists of a hierarchy of social relations determined by a hierarchy of causes which are articulated through the organization of production.

The political, economic, and ideological structures of a social formation are sometimes presented within the structuralist Marxist tradition in an alternate version as the economic base and ideological superstructure. This alternate formulation predominates in Godelier's *Rationality and Irrationality in Economics* and his *Perspectives in Marxist Anthropology* (1977):

> In order to obtain this synthetic definition, a Marxist perspective requires a number of scientific steps, for example:
> (1) identify the number and nature of the different modes of production combined in a specific way in a specific society and which constitute the economic basis of that particular epoch;
> (2) identify the different elements in the social and ideological superstructure which in origin and function correspond to the different modes of production. . . . (1977: 63)

He argues, for example, that because kinship functions in a multiplicity of roles, it is part of both the base and the superstructure. As part of the superstructure kinship organizes such activities as the ritual cycle, healing, religion, and political functions, while as part of the base it organizes and controls the process of production. He agrees with Hindess and Hirst that kinship as the relations of production should not be equated with the division of labor mandated by technical tasks, so that a new mode of production is articulated in each case:

> The most common error, among Marxists, is to confuse the study of the production process with the study of the labour process, and to invent as many modes of production as there are labour processes. (1977: 24)

The organization of the production process, for Godelier, incorporates the forces of production in terms of technology and the division of labor and the social relations of production in terms of the appropriation and control of the means and products of production. For Godelier, the social relations of production are always primary.

Since Godelier, like most structuralist Marxists, identifies the material conditions of life in the organization of production as determinant, it is kinship in the form of the relations of production that conditions ultimately all the dimensions of the ideological superstructure. Homo faber, viewed as that which makes us distinctively human, underlies not only the generative logic of the species but also its diverse sociocultural manifestations. A social formation, therefore, cannot be fully articulated by means of the components of its ideological superstructure because, as Godelier argues, these components merely correspond to the economic base and, moreover, are permeated by the imaginary relations that human subjects have to each other and to their world. The ideological or imaginary nature of the superstructure is clearly expressed by Godelier in the case of religion:

> Therefore, in origin and content, religion is the spontaneous and illusory representation of the world, yet this representation is such that, by its very content, from within, it establishes and demands a corresponding practice and observance. (1977: 179)

He contends that the economic base provides the scientific content of both history and anthropology:

> Marx's answer to the problem of the differential causality of various instances of social life – in other words "the mode of production of material life conditions, in the last analysis, the process of social, political and intellectual life in general" – seems to us to be the essential hypothesis to be taken up and

systematically explored in order to renew the scientific content of history and anthropology. (1977: 29)

Because the structural interrelations at the level of production determine the form and character of a social formation, Godelier contends that economic facts must be reconstructed to disclose the scientific laws or hidden rationality of social systems.

By claiming that the economic base fully conditions the ideological superstructure and at the same time provides the scientific content of anthropology, Godelier supports, with Jarvie and Horton, a logic of one unified science. In other words, the laws disclosed by the organization of production are adequate to grasp all regions of human practical activity. The logic of religious beliefs, for example, which Godelier accepts as efficacious to the extent of motivating certain actions, is ultimately translatable into the logic of production or science of economics. This position is contrary to that of Ricoeur whereby different areas of human coparticipation in the world, or forms of life in the Wittgensteinian sense, are amenable to diverse logics of inquiry. Ricoeur has shown, for example, how it is not possible to fully understand oneiric activity solely in terms of a Freudian system of energetics, since all dream activity is embodied or objectified in symbols which require interpretation through a depth semantics or hemeneutics of suspicion. In similar fashion, the processes of production and reproduction, as well as the constitution of the ideological superstructures, are not intelligible simply in terms of the mechanics of the logic of production. The principal level of analysis missing from Godelier's model is the exchange of symbols, or communicative interaction, upon which the possibility of production and reproduction rests, although this seems to be a problem rectified in his recent work on gift giving (see Godelier 1999).

Although Marx scarcely wrote about language, he clearly recognized the importance of symbolic exchange in the production process. In a now-famous section of *Capital* (1967a: 178) Marx compared the labor of a bee to that of a man. While a bee is able to build a hive, this possibility depends upon the bee's inner nature. A man, on the contrary, is able to develop a concept of a project prior to its execution. While the concept may be original, its intelligibility for its generator and for others is dependent upon its objectification in the intersubjectivity of language. The separation of concept from execution develops within the context of the capitalist division of labor and its reified social relations; thus it is the historically specific form that labor takes under capitalism that masks its communicative features. For Marx, labor was not only the instrumental appropriation of nature but also the cooperation of human co-subjects through mutually intelligible symbols.

Another example of the importance of symbolic exchange as a mediator of the production process is provided by Malinowski's description (1961) of the Trobriand canoe builder. This example also illustrates how labor takes on a particular expression and meaning with respect to its cultural medium. The canoe builder held a position of status in Trobriand society since the canoe was the technology necessary to link the islands involved in the important socioeconomic Kula exchange. The building of a canoe was learned through apprenticeship and required considerable skill to make the craft sea-worthy. As Malinowski claims, however, it is not technical knowledge alone that ensures the quality of craftsmanship. The canoe builder, while practicing his trade, would also perform a series of elaborate chants, songs, and incantations that were recognized as essential to the task at hand. Although in Godelier's model the technical aspect of building would be considered part of the base, the songs and incantations as superstructural, technology and magic are woven inextricably into the symbolic process that characterizes this Trobriand trade.

The process of production is thus permeated with ideas, concepts, and cultural assumptions that do not merely correspond, as part of the superstructure, to the productive base, but, on the contrary, are essential to its constitution and meaning. The production process, which is social to the core, is hence possible only through mutually intelligible communicative exchanges. This is not to say that the expropriation of surplus value is not of primary importance in explaining social-class divisions or the specific nature of some social formations but, rather, that the division between base and superstructure inhibits our ability to recognize the processes of production and reproduction as symbolic interactions. It is not only superstructural activities such as rituals and politics that become objectified in symbolic ordinary language communication, but all human activities including production and reproduction. It is the social character of the production process, as a series of symbolic interchanges, that enables the anthropologist to distinguish, even at the level of formal rules or laws, the alternative rationalities of economic and social systems. Although Godelier has emphasized that there is no specific rationality to an economic system apart from its embodiment in the rationality of a social system, his position is compromised by the assertion that one unified science modeled on the logic of production can outline the formal structural interrelations which characterize a specific social formation. His assertion is furthermore contradictory in that it makes superstructural entities, as well as the social dimension of production, a function of an economic teleology or rationality – the same sort of reduction for which Godelier chastizes formalist economic theory. The concept of one unified science based upon the logic of production, which Godelier absorbed from Althusser's a priori distinction between science and ideology, is thus unable fully to grasp the multivocal communicative exchanges upon which the possibility of cooperative labor and hence production rests.

An alternative and more reflexive version of rationality, which challenges Godelier's equivalence of kinship to the relations of production, has been presented by Jean Baudrillard in his *Mirror of Production* (1975) and Marshall Sahlins in his *Culture and Practical Reason* (1976). Apart from indicating the inconsistencies in Godelier's argument, it is Baudrillard's intention to argue that the Marxist distinction between use value and exchange value is tied to a utilitarian, productivist logic that counters the emancipatory potential of a critical theory.[13] Sahlins, on the other hand, draws heavily from Jürgen Habermas's *Knowledge and Human Interests* (1971) in order to show how the instrumental rationality of production is unable to account for the creation and transmission of culture. A brief review of the central arguments of these two works will, I believe, summarize the salient problems with the structuralist Marxist positions and hence set the stage for my discussion of the historical-culturalist alternative.

Baudrillard claims that Godelier's notion of theory has an insufficiently developed dialectic. According to Baudrillard, the only dialectic present in Godelier's work is the self-validation of theory through formal simulation of the object (1975: 72). This conception of theory, however, is fully commensurate with scientism in that it can account neither for its own development reflexively nor for its hermeneutic relation to the knowledge-constitutive interests of the sociocultural life-world. Baudrillard argues, furthermore, that Godelier, like Althusser, fragments the integrated totality of a social formation into its functions and then recombines them under the dominance of the economic. This formal recombination of functions is taken to be scientific:

> Godelier exhibits a theoretical mania for fragmenting the object into functions in order to dialectize them "historically" – in fact, to structuralize them under the hegemony of one of them – and to reconcile the whole under the sign of science! (1975: 73)

The fragmentation of the object of knowledge is nowhere more apparent than in Godelier's analysis of kinship systems. According to Baudrillard, Godelier's claim that kinship functions in indigenous societies as both base and superstructure elevates this dichotomy to a position of universal validity with respect to all existing societies. That is, once Godelier has claimed that kinship operates as both base and superstructure in native societies, he has also conceded that any indigenous social formation can be analyzed in terms of these two autonomous domains. Baudrillard suggests that what Marx took to be unique to the capitalist social formation in terms of the primacy of the economy, Godelier extends to all precapitalist social formations. He argues, furthermore, that since Godelier contends that the relations of production in indigenous societies are not distinguishable from social, political, religious, and kinship relations, it is impossible therefore to conceive of the relations of production as individual and determinant entities within the indigenous social formation. This would be possible only through a contradictory assertion that social or political relations are in the end nothing more than relations of production, which would mean that they are not what their concept implies. Baudrillard concludes that if there are no relations of production, then there cannot be a primitive mode of production.

Marshall Sahlins, building upon his earlier *Stone Age Economics* (1972), also challenges the structuralist Marxist equivalence of kinship relations to the relations of production. He argues that religion, economics, politics, and ideology do not manifest themselves as distinct systems in native societies. He also contends, in agreement with Baudrillard, that there are no specific "social relations that can be assigned to any one of these distinct functions" (1976: 6). On the contrary, it is kinship which organizes and orders all sets of social relations in indigenous societies:

> Tribal groups and relations are "polyvalent" or "multifunctional": they order all the activities which in Western civilization are the subject of special institutional developments. (1976: 6)

According to Sahlins, Godelier and other structuralist anthropologists such as Terray and Meillassoux transform the actual into the formal by translating kinship into the relations of production. Sahlins believes that this mode of translation or transformation contravenes Godelier's project of reaching the real through the scientific.

Following Habermas (1971), Sahlins also attempts to relate the formative process of the human species in terms of human practical activity both to knowledge-constitutive interests and to forms of rationality. The fact that these interests are related to the formative process of the species makes them transcendental rather than empirical. Being transcendental, however, they are no more abstract than the universality of labor that Marx claims with respect to the formation and transformation of the species. The process of labor does not involve a mere activation of the physical body in a metabolic exchange with a natural habitat. Labor, on the contrary, is informed by the knowledge-constitutive interest of instrumental rationality or technical rules of procedure for the objectification and control of reality. In other words, labor is not merely part of the base in the structuralist sense, but is also cognitive or superstructural in that it constitutes its objects of knowledge. Godelier's discussion of rationality is limited exclusively, therefore, to the realm of instrumental rationality, inasmuch as he insists that the rationality of a social system is ultimately conditioned by the processes of production and reproduction. To the extent that Godelier discusses means/end rationality, according to which ends are defined as alternative logics of production, he is still tied to empirical interests which are not explained in terms of how they are constituted. Moreover, as Hannah Arendt has explained in *The Human Condition* (1958), the problem with means/end rationality lies in its utilitarian nature, in that any constituted end can become a means in an endless chain.

While the process of instrumental rationality addresses the dimension of human experience that owes its existence to the formative property of social labor, it is unable to account for the production and reproduction of culture. Both labor and culture can be characterized as necessarily involving symbolic exchange, but the latter does not constitute its objects of knowledge in the interest of technical control. Culture, on the contrary, is based upon the knowledge-constitutive interest of communicative rationality or norms of mutual expectation. The validity of these norms is grounded in mutually understood intentions and publicly recognized obligations. Culture is embodied in the medium of ordinary language communication, or what Clifford Geertz refers to in *The Interpretation of Cultures* (1973) as ordered systems of meaning and symbols. Mutual understanding and obligation are therefore what distinguish the communicative rationality of culture from the instrumental rationality of production. For Habermas, the formation of the species, as well as the articulation of forms of social integration, are dependent upon both production and culture, neither of which is reducible to the other.

Sahlins (1976: 134–5) therefore claims that Godelier, Terray, and Meillassoux obscure the cultural properties of productive relations and of social relations in general by ontologizing historical materialism in work and hence its material specifications. This version of Marxist theory vitiates the cultural dimension of historical materialism by transforming thought and communicative interaction into functions of the behavioral system of instrumental action.

Although many important differences distinguish Althusser, Hindess and Hirst, Meillassoux, and Godelier with respect to a Marxist anthropology, theoretical similarities can be identified: the privileging of system over process and structure over intersubjectivity, and the primacy of the logic of production in the construction of a social formation. These similarities are sufficient to consider structuralist Marxism a coherent school. By grounding the materialist dialectic in the logic of production, the structuralist Marxists are able to chart the hierarchical social relations that are attributable to control over the extraction and distribution of the surplus product. This is, as I have emphasized, an important dimension which is missing from an exclusively hermeneutic approach based upon the reciprocity of communicative interactions. The inevitable problem, however, with limiting the materialist dialectic to the logic of production is, as I have shown for Baudrillard and Sahlins, that it prevents our appreciating either the cultural properties of production or the communicative rationality that informs all human interaction.

Historical-Culturalist Alternative

E. P. Thompson, in his polemical work *The Poverty of Theory and Other Essays* (1978), discusses in detail the salient epistemological and political problems that follow from an Althusserian version of structuralism. He presents his own perspective by developing the notions of praxis and historical methodology within a Marxist theoretical framework. His emphasis on the human subject's making of history, the importance of cultural tradition, and the limitations of political economy should prove to be heuristic for the anthropologist struggling to incorporate into fieldwork a dimension of critical historiography. His perspective on historiography, as we shall see, supports the view that a social science must be appropriate to its object/subject of knowledge.

Many of the points that Thompson raises against the Althusserian position are not original and can be found in earlier critiques by both structuralist and nonstructuralist theorists.[14] For example, although Thompson emphatically dismisses Hindess and Hirst as Althusserian offshoots, his challenge to Althusser's idealism is fully compatible with their critique (1975) of Althusser's rationalism. All three agree that Althusser's notion of theory presents a self-confirming conceptual universe to which the material of social existence must conform. The originality of Thompson's critique lies, rather, in his relating of epistemology and praxis to historical interpretation.

The category of experience, which Althusser has rejected because of its empiricist and historicist presuppositions, is central to Thompson's interpretive theory. The category of experience not only provides the link to the concrete with respect to the participation of human co-subjects in the world but also mediates between social being and social consciousness:

> It is by means of experience that the mode of production exerts a determining pressure upon other activities: and it is by practice that production is sustained. (1978: 98)

It is not the relationship between concepts, therefore, which determines humanity's existence in the world but rather the real interactions of human subjects under historically specified conditions. The mode of production becomes reified unless it exerts its determining influence on social life through the conflicts and cooperation of historical agents. The category of experience, however, is dialectical: it is not simply by means of a nonreflexive historical agency that modes of existence are realized, rather it is through the praxis of determining historical subjects that social life unfolds.

The notion that historical subjects are as much determining as determined is important for grasping Thompson's concept of historical interpretation and its distinction from periodicity or chronology.[15] Thompson adheres closely to Marx's dictum, itself critically absorbed from Vico, that "men make their own history but not always according to conditions of their own choosing." This important statement implies that historical experience has an intentionality, inasmuch as past events can be regarded as the outcome of a complex process of meaningfully constituted actions. Thompson argues, furthermore, that there are no strictly objective facts that speak for themselves. On the contrary, he refers to historical facts as witnesses to real events and social processes. They must be probed or questioned to discover what they conceal in their representation. One is reminded of Collingwood's (1956) rejection of objectivist history, in which he claims that the historical record is an answer to a question and hence that the purpose of historiography is to ask the right questions.

Although Thompson emphasizes the degree to which human co-subjects shape the world through lived experience, the intentionality of historical life is not without limitations. These limitations are of several sorts and disclose both the similarities and differences between Thompson's method and hermeneutics. Gadamer, Ricoeur, and Thompson recognize that lived historical experience has both a retrospective and a prospective determination. The retrospective dimension of lived historical experience is the ontology of cultural tradition. The mutual expectations that collectively represent social identity or are internalized in the form of personal identity are informed by the historicity of a shared cultural tradition. Both the identity and meaning of a specific action or event, as well as its possible interpretations, are dependent upon a symbolically constituted past whose horizon extends into the present. Not only, therefore, is actuality mediated by cultural tradition, but also what counts as the possible. The persistence of a lived cultural past in limiting and shaping the future is the prospective dimension of historical experience.

The retrospective and prospective dimensions of cultural traditions as they shape historical experience have been discussed by Thompson in "Time, Work-Discipline and Industrial Capitalism" (1967). In this important essay, he illustrates the persistence of rural cultural patterns in a recently proletarianized peasantry. He shows that an incipient process of proletarianization must contend with a labor force that is tied to a predominantly subsistence economy and to the temporal rhythm of the countryside. The cultural patterns of the countryside made it very difficult for the nascent capitalist to rationalize the workday and ensure that his work force would appear regularly. The actions of human co-subjects that become objectified in the historical record have their source in the historical determinations of cultural tradition. While it is through lived culture that human actions and events obtain their sense, culture must also be grasped as a limit on the possible. Furthermore, it is the dialectic of limitations and possibilities as expressed through culturally mediated historical experience that defines the uniqueness or particularity of historical contexts.

If the ontological determinacy of culture were presented as the principal limit on the human subject's shaping of the social world, there would hardly be a basis upon which to distinguish Thompson's historiography from orthodox hermeneutics. While Thompson privileges the intentionality of historical experience, this does not exhaust his notion of social history. He is critical of more conventional historiography, which traces the course of human events through reconstructed chronologies of famous rulers or military conquests. History written from the point of view of elites not only conceals the determinate activity of subordinate sectors of the population with respect to the process and outcome of historical events but also substitutes what is partial for an account of the whole. Anthropologists must, of course, confront this issue in taking into consideration the social status of their informants or the partiality that may be concealed in missionary accounts, colonial records, myths, and oral traditions. Social history differs from conventional periodicity and hermeneutic reciprocity in emphasizing the concrete lived dimension of multiple social groups and their interactions. Because social historians try to capture human subjects in the course of their daily lives, they portray history as a process.[16] Viewed in this way, history is not dependent upon the correspondence or noncorrespondence of conceptual structures, as it is for Althusser and Godelier, but is realized, on the contrary, by means of the alignments and conflicts of human agency. Thompson's version of social history is distinct, however, in that he not only articulates the daily lives of diverse social groups and their interactions but also, most importantly, reviews the nature of these interactions and history in the making in terms of exploitation and domination.

The fact that Thompson emphasizes the self-formative, intentional activity of human co-subjects in the constitution and transformation of historical process contributes to the uniqueness of his views on social history in regard to exploitation and domination. For example, in his classic *The Making of the English Working Class* (1966), he argues that proletarians were not simply victimized nor were they made by social forces outside their participation. This is not to say that the working class was fully aware of the complex social processes which intersected in the development of capitalism nor that proletarians alone should be held responsible for creating sociopolitical and legal institutions that enhanced the penetration of the market into wider areas of social life. Thompson maintains that exploitation in the form of the expropriation of surplus value or domination as manifested by the internalization of a specific form of work discipline is the outcome of a process that the working class has itself helped to shape. This is exhibited concretely in his (1966) descriptions of the many clubs, societies, and organizations which were created through working-class alliances and which served in some cases as a source of political resistance while in others as a means of capitalist socialization. The Methodist Church, for example, through its doctrine not only provided the well-known notion of a calling but also stimulated working-class political action.[17] The ruthlessness of capitalist exploitation, revealed by Marx's critique of political economy, and its mode of social control, did not create the working class, therefore, without the unwitting assistance and participation of its occupationally diverse members. The effectiveness of the capitalist organization of production was dependent not only upon control of the work place but also upon the reproduction of the worker's household. The point of Thompson's argument is to show that the capitalist form of social control cannot be deduced from abstract Marxist categories or formal institutions but only as it is lived through the real interactions of the working class in its relation to capital. To deduce the working class, which amounts to viewing proletarians sheerly as victims, from the formal categories of the capitalist mode of production is to transform a historically lived relation into a static or reified entity.[18]

By demonstrating that exploitation and domination are historically lived relations, Thompson shows that the creation of the working class or any subordinate population is not the reflex of a lawlike, determinate historical process. Once the concept of the working class is accepted as a lived relation, it also becomes possible to show how the self-formation and reproduction of working-class culture, as it contributes to the historical process of capitalism, can under certain circumstances contribute to further domination of the proletariat. This is certainly the case in advanced capitalist societies, where members of the working class have internalized the value of radical individualism, thereby undermining the possibility of political organization and resistance.[19]

The introduction of historical agency as the constitutive dimension of a sociocultural formation contributes to the density or multivocality of social life and hence makes the issues generated through interpretation increasingly more challenging and problematic for the social scientist. The social scientist must not only grasp hermeneutically the cultural determinations that are expressed through lived social interactions but must also be careful not to overlook the possible objective power constraints to which social relations are subject. As we have seen, the question of exploitation and domination is complicated by the fact that those who are subject to its injustices can also contribute to its reproduction. We shall shortly see, however, that Thompson is prepared methodologically to confront the subtleties of exploitation and domination.

Thompson also makes use of the constitutive significance of the historical actor, apart from its retrospective dimension, to emphasize the importance of contemporary political praxis. While he accepts the fact that there are objective historical, sociocultural, political, and economic constraints to which human actions are subject, he also believes in the potential for oppressed groups to organize and forcefully articulate their demands. His argument is related historically to disputations within the Marxist tradition about the role of the party, as well as to Althusser's contention that social change follows from resolving at the structural level the internal contradictions of a social system. Althusser contends that the level of understanding that typifies popular consciousness is ideological and should therefore be distinguished from the scientific apprehension that is intrinsic to the Marxist analysis of a social formation. Because ideological consciousness tends to persist even after a socialist revolution. Althusser justifies the exclusive leadership of party elites by their scientific grasp of reality. The working class, furthermore, plays only a passive role in the revolution and the rule which follows, in that their activity is determined by existing structures and their conjunctures. In *The Poverty of Theory* Thompson argues that Althusser's legitimation of elitist party rule, protected by the veil of a vague scientificity, necessarily leads to the kind of political repression that characterized the Stalinist era.[20] Thompson's views are not simply articulated from a theoretical perspective but also reflect his analysis of the history of the working class in England. The popular consciousness of the working class in England not only reflected aspects of capitalist ideology but also manifested an awareness of the objective conditions of society, as attested to by the many pockets of resistance. The historical actor, according to Thompson's view, has not only contributed to the constitution of past social formations but also has an important part to play in the transformation and emergence of the new.

Thompson's emphasis on the self-formation of the social world through the activity of human co-subjects is grounded in the category of lived experience. It is this dimension of his theory that most clearly distinguishes it from the structuralism of Althusser and his disciples. As I mentioned previously, it is lived experience which mediates between social being and social consciousness, a point that has been made provocatively in Michael Jackson's (1998) anthropological synthesis of Sartre's existentialism and Merleau-Ponty's phenomenology. Rather than view human existence as a series of distinct levels determined by the instrumental action of production, Thompson maintains that the relation between social being and social consciousness is dialectical. By social being, he means the material interactions of historical existence. Social consciousness refers to concepts, mutual expectations, and cultural values through which human actions obtain their identity and meaning:

> For we cannot conceive of any form of social being independently of its
> organizing concepts and expectations; nor could social being reproduce itself
> for a day without thought. (1978: 8)

According to Thompson, all change occurs within social being, which in
turn gives rise to altered experience. Altered experience then exerts a determination on social consciousness in the sense that it provides the stimula-
tion for abstract intellectual activity and, moreover, confronts the human
subject with new questions. The dialectic does not terminate with a transformed social consciousness, as social consciousness is implicated in the
organization and reproduction of social being. It is the formative motion of
consciousness – reduced in Althusser's theory to a reflex of the infrastructure or ideology – in conjunction with the historicity of lived interactions as
mediated by experience, that accounts for Thompson's notion of the human
subject's participation in the social world. The dialectic of social being and
social consciousness is a reflexive process in that it is possible for the human
subject to grasp the objective social and historical conditions woven into
human activity in the world. Hence, the determinations of social being with
respect to social consciousness are never for Thompson absolute.

The method employed by Thompson to disclose the social determinations
of exploitation and domination within a given social formation combines
important aspects of hermeneutics with British empiricism. Although he
maintains that historical evidence has an existence independent of the
investigator, he does not believe that facts speak for themselves. He does
not, however, follow the hermeneutic trajectory in asserting that facts are
constituted through their dialogical relation to the investigator. Facts, for
Thompson, are constituted only insofar as they represent the objectified
meaning intentions of past events and actions. His approach converges with
hermeneutics in that it emphasizes the historical and cultural determinations of intersubjective human activity and does not subordinate questions
of historical interpretation to method.

Thompson argues that historical evidence must be interrogated, an
approach not unlike Ricoeur's (1971) dialectic of skepticism and dogmatism. Like Ricoeur, he is prepared to make assertions and correct or retract
them until a sense of the whole begins to emerge. Unlike Ricoeur, however,
he asks questions of historical evidence that relate to power and its sociocultural reproduction. He considers the issue of who writes history, for
example, to be of the utmost importance. Since writing is a specialized
technology that was usually practiced, until quite recently, by elites, the
question should be raised as to whose views are embodied in the historical
record. The question of who writes history is also significant for societies
which are stratified in other ways than social class or have recorded their
history in oral tradition or myths.

The fact that historical events have been recorded in oral tradition or written documents does not mean that their mode of portrayal is true or accurate. Apart from the question of who writes history, the social historian must also attempt to reveal for what purpose the material in question was recorded. In some archaic states, for example, accounts of battles were written to celebrate the power and duration of elite rule. Thompson maintains, however, that the accuracy of historical records can be judged from existing adjacent evidence. With respect to my example of the Azande, the adjacent evidence which assists the anthropologist in grasping critically the multivocality of witchcraft practices is the oral history of nobility conquest – a history which reveals the transformation of a decentralized society into a society based upon the political organization of the state. The historical record is opaque, which makes its interpretation problematic. According to Thompson, the researcher must strive to relate and integrate a wide range of complex materials by moving between a sense of the whole and particulars. It is the dialectical relation of part to whole in the interpretive process that leads us to portray historical interpretation as a hermeneutic process.

Thompson also believes that it is important to ask whether the historical evidence under consideration is a social or cultural phenomenon. Social and cultural phenomena raise questions of value, since they involve an actor's attitudes and beliefs. This category of historical evidence is the most difficult to interpret critically as it is most directly linked, if only under certain conditions, to ideology. Yet, as Thompson emphasizes, it is impossible to think of social and cultural reproduction, as well as material interactions, apart from sociocultural concepts and ideas. He argues that value-bearing evidence can be contrasted with value-free evidence such as wages and indices of mortality, which are amenable to statistical computation. Value-free, however, is a poor choice of concept in that it not only ties his distinction to the problematics of Weberian epistemology but it also tends to obscure important questions as to the meaning of statistical facts.

Thompson's method of historical interrogation includes an attempt to ascertain how the historical evidence in question is linked in both a linear and a lateral series. A linear series means history as it has actually occurred in a sequential temporal framework and as it is reconstructed and revised through the narrative of the historian. Thompson is careful to add that a narrative view of history does not imply that it can be fully known. A lateral series is a specific instance of historical evidence as it occurs in a number of different forms of social relation, such as the political and the social, which enables us to grasp a "provisional 'section' of a given society in the past – its characteristic relations of power, domination, kinship, servitude, market relations and the rest" (1978: 29). The lateral series contributes to the view of a sociocultural formation in its individual moments as an integrated whole – a perspective we shall consider in regard to the Marxist concept of totality.

While both Thompson and Ricoeur share a knowledge-constitutive interest in disclosing what historical evidence conceals in its signifying, Thompson's method does not involve an abstract review of the internal significations objectified in the historical record. For Thompson, critique involves the mediation of historical contingencies, whether cultural, political, or economic, by penetrating more deeply the interconnections of historical reality in the process of its development. This form of mediation operates through a historical logic appropriate to its object of inquiry. He defines historical logic as the following:

> a logical method of inquiry appropriate to historical materials, designed as far as possible to test hypotheses as to structure, causation, etc., and to eliminate self-confirming procedures ("instances", "illustrations"). (1978: 39)

Although the language that Thompson uses to describe historical logic echoes neopositivist interpretive theory, there are some important respects in which it is distinct. He rejects, for example, the formulation of nomological statements and the use of analytic logic as applied to historical interpretation. According to Thompson, nomological statements and analytic logic imply an unchanging reality that can be broken down into unambiguous terms. He argues that historical reality is a process of continual movement or disorder permeated by ambiguities. Testing a hypothesis is not the confirmation of a law but, on the contrary, involves the careful review and reformulation of a historical narrative. His use of causation, furthermore, should not be confused with the mechanical sense acquired by this concept in the social sciences. Since for Thompson all events are the outcome of historical agency, the relation between events is logical and meaningful rather than merely sequentially determinate.

Thompson's concept of verification is sufficiently ambiguous to lead one to conclude that it is as much latently positivistic as hermeneutic. While his notion of historical logic involves a critical dialogue with and interrogation of historical evidence, he also supports the epistemological independence of the past with respect to the inquiry of the researcher in the present. Consequently, a historical narrative can only be evaluated for its truth content according to whether or not it corresponds to the determinations of the evidence. There are some significant problems with this method of verification which it shares with all correspondence theories of truth. Although Thompson argues that facts do not speak for themselves, he ignores their hermeneutic relation to the researcher in regard to confirming their veracity. This leads him to the specious conclusion that the questions raised by the researcher in no way affect the ontological status of past events. No serious researcher would actually contend that past events can be relived in the present. Thompson seems to forget that past events are never an in-itself but always a for-us, which means that the ontological dimension of past events changes with respect to qualitatively different questions raised by the investigator.[21] Anthropologists have come to recognize the importance of the type of question raised in relation to the constitution of reality, as evidenced, for example, by the development of a feminist trajectory in ethnology. Cultures previously portrayed only through the eyes of men have been totally recast by ethnographies that address the role and status of women. Ricoeur also asserts that the past would remain eternally silent if it did not have the power to signify in the horizon of the present. The ontological status of past events or of other societies will always reflect the changing questions through which they are drawn into dialogue with the present. Because Thompson ignores the dialogical dimension of historical research when he argues for the independence of past events, he also overlooks its reflexive potential.[22]

Using the concept of totality articulated by Georg Lukács (1971), Thompson builds a critique of absolutized versions of political economy. The concept of totality represents society as an integrated whole on the basis of the necessary interconnections of the social phenomena that underlie its appearances. Appearances must be mediated to ascertain what they conceal in their givenness. Reality viewed as a totality is not, moreover, a formalized or already made whole; it is a society or culture grasped in the process of its genesis and development.[23] The underlying interconnections, in the process of development, provide the context within which seemingly disconnected appearances and historical events can be critically interpreted. The sense of the whole in the Marxist concept of totality is dialectical in that by means of its contradictions, as they are lived through the real interactions of historical subjects, social transformations unfold. Thompson departs somewhat from Lukács's view, however, in not recognizing that the knowing subject is part of the totality being interrogated.

Although Thompson argues that there is an interconnectedness underlying the superficial appearances of reality, he conceives of social formations as consisting of distinct domains or circuits of social life. At this juncture of his argument, Thompson's analysis is not essentially different from Althusser's thought that a social formation consists of relatively autonomous political, economic, and ideological structures. As I have explained, the principal difference between Thompson and Althusser lies in their different respective emphases on historical agency and structure. In addition, Althusser, unlike Thompson, portrays social formations as consisting of distinct hierarchical levels, among which the economic is ultimately determinant. Thompson's concept of totality, on the other hand, takes account of the interrelatedness of the economic, political, and cultural realms without reducing any one to a determinate function of the others. While recognizing the primacy of the market in capitalist society, he still maintains that the reproduction of the economy does not determine absolutely the reproduction of culture or the character of political institutions. This is because he insists that the reproduction of material interactions, even with regard to the social relations of production, is not possible without cultural concepts and ideas.

Thompson also argues, like Baudrillard and Sahlins, that culture and the economy reproduce themselves according to different logics:

> But historical materialism (as assumed as hypothesis by Marx, and as subsequently developed in our practice) must be concerned with other "circuits" also: the circuits of power, the reproduction of ideology, etc., and these belong to a different logic and to other categories. (1978: 68)

While the reproduction of the economy is based upon the instrumental logic of production, the reproduction of culture and ideology depends upon socialization and the symbolic constitution of experience, that is, what I referred to in the previous section as communicative rationality. Political economy, while taking account of the instrumental process through which the human species appropriates nature and hence transforms itself, is informed by a different logic than the internalization and reproduction of cultural norms. By disclosing the process of exploitation or the means by which surplus labor is extracted from a population, political economy demystifies only those interactions that are related to production. As Thompson has emphasized, there are other mediums of social intercourse that, when taken collectively with the relations of production, constitute the totality of capitalist social relations. It is thus possible for social control to be concealed and reproduced in other regions of human practical activity. If exploitation, as the extraction of surplus labor, does not exhaust the types of social control, then it is possible to conceive of domination outside the production process.

Thompson's argument that political economy, in contrast to historical materialism, cannot disclose capitalism in the totality of its social relations is suggestive in several respects. The reproduction of the economy in capitalism, as the works of members of the Frankfurt School and others have shown,[24] is not dependent simply on control of the production process but also on the role of the state in legitimizing capitalist social relations and mediating its periodic crises. Capitalism's claim to legitimacy is thus dependent upon the mediations of the political realm – an arena which is open to competing claims and hence is not simply a function of the ruling class.[25] In addition, the reproduction of capitalist social relations has become increasingly responsive to the generation of needs through the culture industry.

Advertising has played a crucial role in the generation of ideal self-identities which, when internalized in a normative sense, give rise to consumerism. Consumerism operates as a form of social control in that it substitutes privatized needs for social objectives and thus contributes to the depoliticization of the public realm. The reproduction of the totality of capitalist social relations is dependent upon a medium of social control that intersects culture, political life, and personal and social identity, as well as the economy.[26] It is important to recognize that for Thompson these diverse regions of human interaction cannot be subject to total domination due to the human capacity to reflect upon and resist mediums of oppression.

Thompson's distinction between exploitation and other circuits of power is particularly relevant for anthropologists whose research is undertaken in societies where the market has not emerged as a separate and predominant institution. As Baudrillard has pointed out with respect to Godelier, the social relations of production are not distinct from kinship relations in indigenous societies. This has led numerous theoreticians, including Hindess and Hirst, to conclude that there is no exploitation or basis for class divisions in societies where the economy is redistributive. While it is true that there may not be exploitation, in the sense of the appropriation of surplus labor, in redistributive indigenous economies, this does not preclude the presense of other forms of domination. This has certainly been the argument of feminist anthropologists, for instance, who contend that male domination in its historically specific forms is not tied immediately to the relations of production. Thompson's recognition that social control operates through a multiplicity of possible circuits of power that are historically variable should draw the attention of social scientists to the problems that can arise through collapsing domination into the categories of political economy exclusively.

The importance of Thompson's method is that it illustrates the self-formative or constitutive dimension of human interactions while also taking into consideration the many regions of social intercourse through which social control is produced and reproduced. It also emphasizes, contrary to the neo-Popperians and structuralist Marxists, that the constitution and reproduction of social life are based upon different rationalities and hence require alternative logics of interpretation. Thompson's shortcomings, on the other hand, are his empiricist epistemology and his insistence that historical evidence exists fully independent of the investigator. Both these problems can be surmounted in part by incorporating the Marxist cultural theory of Raymond Williams, with its emphasis on the constitutive significance of language.

Raymond Williams contends in his *Marxism and Literature* (1977) that there is a tendency in the Marxist tradition to reduce the process of material interaction to labor, thereby obscuring the constitutive significance of cultural tradition and language. The failure of some Marxists, particularly the structuralists, to identify the constitutive potential of cultural tradition and language with the material social process is in part attributable to the way in which culture has been conceived in the western tradition. The concept of culture was originally applied to the cultivation of crops and animals and only much later to the development of the human faculties. Williams relates that in the eighteenth century, culture was synonymous with civilization. During the latter part of the eighteenth century, however, the notion of civilization was criticized by Enlightenment philosophers such as Jean-Jacques Rousseau. Rousseau challenged contemporary ethnocentric notions of civilization by claiming that the inequality of men could be attributed to the process called civilization. With the assault on civilization in progress, the concept of culture gradually retreated to the safety of humankind's inner or spiritual life. Culture became associated with religion, aesthetics, and personal life and, Williams argues, opposed to civilization or society. In the nineteenth century, it was Herder who wrote about culture as a social process that shaped distinct ways of life. Herder's perspective was unique in that he was among the first authors to address culture in its plural rather than singular sense.[27] Although the concept of culture as referring to distinct and various ways of life spread throughout American anthropology in the early twentieth century, its idealist formulation as a process opposed to civilization or society continued to be influential. The notion that culture is a set of practices, beliefs, concepts, and ideas, as distinct from material interactions, has therefore been absorbed into certain versions of the Marxist tradition through our western intellectual heritage.

The dichotomy between culture and material interactions is reproduced in Marxist structuralism as base and superstructure, while for E. P. Thompson it takes the form of the dialectics of social being and social consciousness. It is Williams's intent to bridge this dichotomy by developing a linguistic theory of social being. The concept of social being developed by Williams regards material interactions as communicative interchanges subject to cultural, historical, and power determinations. His position is distinct from those of the Marxist theoreticians whom we have considered in that culture, as it is embodied in the symbols of ordinary language communication, is part of the process of material interaction rather than its correlate or dialectical relation. He argues that the distinction in historical materialism between culture and production, language and reality, and social being and social consciousness merely shifts the emphasis of the idealist theory of culture. Once these dichotomies are reinforced, culture in its communicative sense can only be grasped materially as physical sounds.

Williams's theory of culture as communicative interchange intersects Winch's concept of language game, Gadamer's hermeneutic ontology, and the semiotic theory of culture. Williams, like Winch, contends that the interactions between human co-subjects are expressions of ideas about reality. These ideas are not merely external to human material interactions, but are intrinsic in that it is the objectification of human activity in symbols, with their inherent linguisticality, which enables both participant and investigator to distinguish one act from another. For Williams and Winch there are no strictly physical or material acts apart from the linguistic conventions through which they obtain their sense. Williams and Winch do not employ the concept of linguistic conventions to refer to formal grammatical rules but rather to mutually intelligible, intersubjective norms shared by a speech community or cultural tradition. There is for Williams, hence, an immediate link between the linguisticality of human actions and culture. He maintains not only that material interactions are communicative but that speech events themselves are also material. This is because a speech event or discourse, as Gadamer has also emphasized, is constitutive in that it discloses the meaning that the world has for us and hence shapes our participation in it:

> Language is then, positively, a distinctively human opening of and opening to the world: not a distinguishable or instrumental but a constitutive faculty. (Williams 1977: 24)

Williams, like Gadamer, contends that speech events and all communicative interactions are manifestations of a determinate historical and cultural past as it continues to shape the present and future. He compares communicative interaction to Marx's notion of practical consciousness, arguing that language permeates all human activity including production and is therefore intrinsic to the formation, reproduction, and transformation of human societies.

Williams, in short, defines social being as human practical material activity that manifests itself through the process of signification. His notion of signification touches upon but does not absorb the semiotic theory of culture. He maintains, like Roland Barthes, that all events, actions, and human products signify through the use of formal signs. A sign for Williams is a fusion of a formal element, the signifier in the semiotic sense, and that which is signified, or its meaning. He distinguishes himself from the semioticians, however, by rejecting the notion that meaning is derived from the interrelation of signs that compose a system. For Williams meaning is a social product or the outcome of human practical activity. Like E. P. Thompson, he privileges the world-constituting activity of human co-subjects. The process of signification therefore owes its existence, development, and transformation to human practical material activity. Williams argues that disjuncture of the sign and human material activity tends to reduce the former to the fixed content of a signal.

Williams's association of signification with human practical material activity becomes problematic when he describes language as a means of production:

Signification, the social creation of meanings through the use of formal signs, is then a practical material activity; it is indeed, literally a means of production. (1977: 38)

The concept of means of production in Marxism refers technically to the social division of labor and technology. Since Williams makes a point of arguing that there has been a tendency in Marxism to reduce production to the instrumental rationality of the labor process, it is ironic that he translates what he himself had defined as the constitutive dimension of signification into the aspect of production that is most amenable to the labor process. Since he uses the concept of constitution interchangeably with the concept of production, even though he qualifies production as human practical material activity, he should be particularly careful not to be seduced by the very instrumental trajectory within Marxism of which he is critical.

Perhaps Williams's most salient contribution to our treatment of rationality in regard to a critical interpretive theory emerges from his work on culture and domination. Although it overlaps substantially with the perspective applied by E. P. Thompson to his analysis of the English working class, Williams's cultural theory owes more to the Italian Marxist Antonio Gramsci. Gramsci maintained that the reproduction of capitalist social relations was attributable not only to the control of production but also to internalized cultural norms. He described the mutually intelligible norms which serve the reproduction of capitalist social relations as cultural hegemony – a process we shall consider further in regard to Williams's contribution to cultural theory.

Much of the recent work in cultural theory, including that of hermeneuticians and other theoreticians who privilege discourse, emphasizes the uniformity of a tradition or speech community. We have already seen in the case of E. P. Thompson that the representation of a tradition or speech community in the historical record is problematic in that the researcher must be sensitive to whose views are being disclosed. Williams challenges the notion of a uniform tradition and the hermeneutic concept of communicative reciprocity, contending that the representation of cultures, traditions, or speech communities is selective. He argues, against the concept of uniformity of tradition, that culture or tradition should be understood as an interrelated configuration of archaic, residual, and emergent cultures. Archaic culture refers to past patterns that are no longer effective in the present but may serve as sources of historical identity. Residual culture, on the other hand, refers to lived patterns that also originated in the past but continue to affect interactions in the present – a concept reminiscent of Tylor's notion of survivals. Emergent culture refers not only to existing expectations, values, and interactions but also to the process through which new meanings and relationships are continually created. The notion of a culture or tradition as uniform thus masks the synthesis of old and new which constitutes the lived meanings, expectations, and interactions of a concrete society. The notion of tradition itself is also selective in that societies which are transformed through conquest, as we saw in the case of the Azande, or which develop hierarchical differentiation internally, potentially may conceal a plurality of traditions in what appears to be a singular culture or unified tradition.[28] Furthermore, considering the many modes of intercourse between societies, it is likely that every cultural tradition is an amalgam.

It is not the concept of emergent culture that distinguishes Williams's theory from hermeneutic interpretive theories but rather the meaning that he attributes to selective tradition in its relation to cultural hegemony. He defines selective tradition as the interconnected practices and expectations that are taken as representative of the whole of social life but are in fact partial to the legitimation of the existing social order. In complex societies marked by class divisions, the tradition that predominates, which as we have seen may only be one of a plurality of possible traditions, serves the hegemony of the ruling elite. A selective tradition is, however, not so much instrumental as constitutive, in the sense that it contributes to the formation of personal and social identity and hence shapes interaction in the world. Williams does not mean by his concept of selective tradition that all tradition is ideological; the concept applies only to social formations and historical contexts where the reproduction of social relations and cultural practices supports the hegemony of a class, group of elites, or, in certain cases, gender. Tradition, on the other hand, can exercise a neutralizing or protective determination, as in the formative period of capitalism, for example, where local custom stigmatized the incursion of foreign merchants.[29] A selective tradition, therefore, while pervasive, is not all-determining. The limits of a selective tradition are dependent upon specific historical circumstances, the existing form of social integration, and the distribution of authority in the society under question.

The concept of selective tradition is more inclusive than the notion of ideology because it transcends the arena of consciousness to incorporate the whole lived social process. Williams hence associates the notion of selective tradition with cultural hegemony defined in the following way:

> It is a whole body of practices and expectations over the whole of living: our senses and assignments of energy, our shaping perceptions of ourselves and

our world. It is a lived system of meaning and values – constitutive and constituting – which as they are experienced as practices appear as reciprocally confirming. (1977: 110)

The strength of Williams's position, in contrast to structuralist Marxism as well as to features of Thompson's theory, is that through the concept of cultural hegemony, manifested in a selective tradition, a connection is established between a communicative notion of social being and social control. The process of social control by a hegemonic group can, under historically variable conditions not amenable to nomological treatment, be built into the very mutual expectations and practices of human material activity through which co-subjects produce and reproduce social life. Williams's cultural theory assists us in developing and strengthening the notion of tradition in Marxism, which is sometimes inert. His perspective also provides us with a perspective from which to address the disjunctures that may arise in a social formation between cultural values and social practices, in that cultural values are themselves regarded as material interactions. It is not that ideas and social relations should be taken as out of phase with each other, but rather that contradictory and competing communicative social practices can coexist in a single social formation. Williams's notion of a communicative social being, in summary, incorporates the hermeneutic emphasis on language and the historical determinations of culture while taking into account the power constraints to which they may be subject.

Like Gramsci, however, Williams is primarily a theorist of the formative and mature periods of capitalism. We must therefore ask to what extent his notion of cultural hegemony is applicable to precapitalist social formations and indigenous societies. In capitalist societies, commodity relations have become the general form of social relations; hence it is possible to see how cultural forms of domination penetrate a wide range of distinct social activities and institutions. In precapitalist social formations and particularly in indigenous societies, tradition and cultural customs limit the degree of influence that an individual or group can exert on society. In a native culture the skillful hunter, for example, will have authority only with respect to the hunt. The big man, on the other hand, or for that matter the feudal lord, may have wider influence but still cannot operate capriciously, as a sense of responsibility to his constituency is mandated by custom. The fact that the influence of groups and individuals is more limited in precapitalist societies does not preclude a cultural form of domination that is autonomous with respect to the social relations of production. Certainly this is the case among some African peoples who practice the custom of clitoridectomy – a custom which has even been institutionalized in some modern hospital settings. The argument has been made that this practice serves a specific form of male domination. I believe that the question of the applicability of the concept of cultural hegemony to precapitalist societies can in part be answered by distinguishing cultural hegemony from cultural domination. While both concepts imply a process of social control by means of lived meanings, expectations, and social relations, the notion of cultural hegemony has political implications that are not necessarily present in cultural domination. In other words, cultural hegemony is a specific type of cultural domination that applies to situations where the distribution and reproduction of power in public life is at issue. Cultural hegemony hence pertains specifically to customs and practices which support the stratification of one social group with respect to another. Clitoridectomy, because it is a social practice that cuts across several stratified groups, would not qualify as a form of cultural hegemony.

This distinction between cultural domination and cultural hegemony, however, does not undermine the very important contribution made by Raymond Williams to a critical interpretive theory. I have shown in my discussion of Williams and Thompson that the instrumental logic of production supported by structuralist versions of Marxism is unable adequately to grasp the communicative process through which human co-subjects constitute and reproduce the social world. A critical interpretive theory must mediate and grasp the multivocality of the symbols in which human actions and power constraints are objectified.

Conclusion

Of the two Marxisms that I have discussed, the structuralist interpretation no longer predominates in contemporary anthropology, as it once did in the past. However, many anthropologists, following Godelier, Meillassoux, and Terray, have found their emphasis on political economy to be useful for understanding such problems as state formation, peasant rebellions, long-distance trade, cash cropping, and the process of proletarianization. That is, the categories of political economy appear to be particularly suitable for critically analyzing the social processes with which contemporary anthropologists are confronted. Meanwhile Hindess and Hirst, while less influential within anthropology, have raised important questions with respect to empiricism, rationalism, and the coherence of Marxist categories, which are all too often taken for granted.

While structuralist Marxism is not represented in the Anglo-American rationality debates, its leading proponents have certainly addressed issues that are important to interpretive theory. The intent of structuralist Marxist methodology, in contrast to the intersubjectively verifiable hypotheses of the neo-Popperians Jarvie and Horton, is to disclose the underlying structure or rationality that is concealed by the superficiality of appearances. While

Godelier, for example, shares with Jarvie, Horton, and Lukes an interpretive theory based upon the logic of one unified science, he maintains, unlike them, that there is a multiplicity of rationalities which characterize economic and social systems. According to Godelier, the formation and reproduction of social life is not reducible to a single human nature or logic; this is precisely what makes cross-cultural comparison possible. The structuralist-Marxist emphasis on modes of production and processes of appropriating surplus labor, moreover, challenges the implied reciprocity of the hermeneutic perspective and the relativity of Winch's unmediated language games and forms of life.

Although structuralist Marxism has made its contribution to the development of a critical interpretive theory, it generates many problems by virtue of its nonreflexive and ahistorical orientation. The degree of deemphasis on the significance of the human subject in structuralism is variable, but it is clear that the subject is at most a conduit for structures and their conjunctures. This view of the subject can be traced back to Durkheimian sociology, where the individual is presented merely as an expression of the social and hence has no constitutive or formative significance. Furthermore, Marxist structuralism posits a social formation as a collection of interrelated virtual systems, thereby privileging synchronic relations over process or history. Hindess and Hirst, for example, conclude that history and sociocultural contingencies are superfluous to the logic of the social sciences. By disregarding historical process and the sociohistorical contingencies through which actions and events obtain their substantive identity, the Marxist structuralists not only are unable to account for how the relations which they consider to be primary came to be but also fail to address the hermeneutic relation of their own theory to the social life-world out of which it is generated. Consequently, the critical potential of structuralist Marxism collapses into one of two forms: the self-confirming rationalism of Althusser and his many disciples, or the idealist solipsism of Hindess and Hirst.

A critical theory, on the contrary, is reflexive in that the theoretician reconstructs the relation of epistemological claims for validity to concrete sociocultural processes. Humanity is a contingent being whose knowledge claims, if they are to be critically or dialectically apprehended, must be identified with their constitutive interests:

> Thus, a critical Marxism must always operate at two levels, identifying both the contradictions in our conceptions and aspirations and their roots in the underlying social reality. If it tries to abandon the first level and to develop a "science" of society which would make no reference to conceptions and aspirations as integral to or partially constitutive of our institutions, then it becomes just another would-be positive science. ... (Kortian 1980: 15)

It is the human contingencies of knowledge claims that enable anthropologists to grasp indigenous societies as truly other while reflexively comprehending the uniqueness or sociohistorical particularity of their own society.

While the categories of political economy appear to present the social scientist with a critical perspective from which to mediate social formations where the market predominates, I have argued that the absolutizing of homo faber by the structuralist Marxists, as in Althusser's "last instance," interferes with our understanding of the multivocality of human interactions and social relations. As I have shown, human practical activity in the form of labor is based upon the knowledge-constitutive interest of instrumental rationality, or technical rules of procedure for the objectification and control of reality (Habermas 1970a). These technical rules, being non-reflexive, are inadequate for the reconstruction of the mutually intelligible norms and expectations that are at the basis of culture and all human activity in the world. Human actions and social relations are, as I showed in my discussions of Winch, Gadamer, and Ricoeur, intrinsically communicative in that their objectification, and hence being for others, is in the medium of symbolic, ordinary language communication. The sociocultural contingencies of production, whether in the form of capitalist work discipline or Trobriand incantations, are informed by the constitutive and formative process of communicative rationality. It is therefore not possible to use labor in its instrumental sense as a general characterization for the communicative rationality of all social relations. Godelier's discussion of indigenous societies, furthermore, in which kinship is equated with the relations of production, tends to universalize what is particular to the capitalist social formation.

Although the structuralist Marxist position exposes the limitations of an exclusively hermeneutic perspective through its emphasis on the mode of exploitation, the hermeneutic position, as articulated by Gadamer and Ricoeur, challenges in turn the putative equation of the totality of social relations with the labor process. I have therefore argued that the Marxist notions of production and reproduction must be reconceived to incorporate the hermeneutic emphases on the determinations of cultural tradition as embodied in the symbols of ordinary language communication. In the works of E. P. Thompson, whose influence in anthropology has increased markedly since the 1970s, along with the importance of history more generally, a more comprehensive notion of production is articulated. He incorporates the essential thrust of hermeneutics in his notion of the dialectics of social being and social consciousness. He maintains that the possibility of material social interaction in the world, whether in the form of production or otherwise, is dependent upon its "organizing concepts and expectations." Human participation in the world is not reducible to mere physical movements of the body, nor are there, as Jarvie, Horton, and Lukes have asserted, extraconceptual criteria of truth. This is not to say that Thompson believes that historiography or social science description should be equated with the informant's self-understanding. He contends, contrary to Althusser and his disciples, that the experience of human co-subjects is primary in the shaping of their world and hence that their self-understanding should not be undervalued. The self-understanding of informants must be evaluated in the light of adjacent historical evidence and thereby integrated into the developing narrative or totality which constitutes a critical grasp of social reality.

The notion of production has hence been reformulated by Thompson to incorporate the self-formative activity of human co-subjects in the light of mutually intelligible concepts and expectations. The notion of production as the dialectic of social being and social consciousness is, moreover, directly connected to the process of reproduction. Marx believed that the human species not only produces itself through the process of social labor but also reproduces itself through the institutionalization of the relations of production. For Marx, therefore, production is reproduction. Thompson's expanded notion of production as material interaction, including its organizing concepts and expectations, accounts not only for the constitution of social reality but also for its reproduction in institutionalized social relations and internalized cultural norms. Production and reproduction are hence hermeneutic concepts for Thompson, in that he asserts that humanity's being in the world and the processes through which it forms itself are permeated by sociocultural and historical contingencies and determinations.

The dialectic of social being and social consciousness also provides Thompson with an original and powerful perspective from which to conceptualize different circuits of social control as they are manifested in the lived experience of concrete historical subjects. This perspective, while incorporating the hermeneutic emphasis on social and cultural contingencies, transforms the phenomenology of the social life-world into an interpretive theory that is critical. The predominant emphasis of Marx's work was the critique of political economy, particularly in relation to understanding the origin, genesis, and uniqueness of the capitalist social formation. Thompson argues that Marx was concerned primarily with exploitation or the circuit of power most directly related to control of the production process. Thompson maintains, however, that the social relations of production do not exhaust the totality of capitalist social relations; hence there are other circuits of power, based upon alternative logics of production, with which a critical interpretive theory must contend. The implications for anthropology are profound. If exploitation does not exhaust the circuits of power that can exist in a society, then Marxist anthropologists must not hasten to conclude that domination cannot exist in indigenous societies with redistributive economies.

Although Thompson incorporates most of the central tenets of the hermeneutic perspective, his close association with British empiricism has prevented him from fully absorbing the communicative and reflexive potentials of hermeneutics. For this reason I turned to the Marxist cultural theory of Raymond Williams. Williams has become increasingly more important to anthropologists as the discipline seeks once again to center itself on the concept of culture. The importance of Williams's contribution to our consideration of rationality and interpretive theory lies in his bridging of the dichotomy between material existence and consciousness and his application of Gramsci's notion of cultural hegemony to the critique of social life. Williams, like Winch, Gadamer, and Ricoeur, has been thoroughly influenced by the linguistic turn in social theory, and hence he interprets the dialectical-materialist concept of social being as a process of signification. He does not, however, locate the source of critique within the objectified internal relations of human actions understood as a text, since he shares Thompson's conviction that sociocultural formations develop through human agency and must be grasped historically. Williams's position is unique because he not only treats human actions and events as intrinsically communicative but also mediates their significations with respect to power through the notions of selective tradition and cultural hegemony. For Williams, the sense of the whole that emerges through the dialectical concept of totality must focus on the partiality of self-representation and how the internalization of this partiality contributes to the production and reproduction of elite rule. Because he relates political power to culture, Williams, like Thompson, opens up new avenues of research with respect to forms of domination that are not immediately generated from or necessarily related to control of the labor process.

The historical-culturalist perspective, represented by Thompson and Williams, should not be expected to address all issues and problems that may arise in the course of interpreting human actions and events. As I argued in my discussion of hermeneutics, human existence in the world is finite and contingent and so, therefore, is the process of interpretation which it informs. The historical-culturalist trajectory in Marxism, however, does provide a critical framework that integrates a communicative concept of culture and human interaction with the historical determinations of a totality and its circuits of power. The process of cross-cultural interpretation is itself symbolically constituted and constituting and therefore cannot be equated with isomorphic statements about reality or a priori universal categories of logic. The instrumental rationality of the logic of one unified science modeled on the explanatory natural sciences, because it is informed by technical rules for the objectification and control of reality, does not lend itself to the reflexive reconstruction mandated by the multivocality of human actions and events. It is for this reason that adherents to the historical-culturalist perspective have argued that a critical science must be suitable to its object of knowledge, which in the human sciences is always an intentionally constituting co-subject.

That I have argued for the integration of hermeneutics and Marxism in the historical-culturalist perspective does not vitiate the important contributions made by the participants in the rationality debates. Their limitations are due mainly to the privileging of the mutually exclusive epistemological frameworks of explanation and understanding and the inability of Winch, Jarvie, Horton, Lukes, and MacIntyre to mediate critically the sociocultural, political, and economic constraints to which human actions are subject. To their credit, however, all of the participants in the debates have to various extents confronted the problematics of social science interpretation rather than conceal epistemological questions behind the veils of a facile method. We can therefore regard the rationality debates as an important contribution, if by no means complete, to the proliferating literature on the epistemology and praxis of the social sciences.

8 Modernism and Postmodernism in Anthropology

The publication of Dell Hymes's *Reinventing Anthropology* in 1969 was an important contribution to what has been called the anthropology of anthropology.[1] The contributors to this edited volume, drawing largely from the Marxist tradition, advanced a reflexive anthropology that sought to disclose or mediate the anthropological mode of inquiry and to shape its practice into a self-conscious critique of capitalist hegemony and the exploitation of indigenous peoples.[2] However, the project initiated by this volume, particularly the epistemological critique, no longer dominates the landscape of critical anthropology. Rather, this terrain now has two principal competitors: one informed by the metanarrative of political economy and its emphasis on the self-formation of the human species through systems of social labor, and the other informed by the postmodernist emphasis on discourse and the representation of the "other" through the writing of ethnography.[3]

I explore in this chapter what I perceive as avowedly competing claims of political economy and postmodernism to define the critical project of anthropology. The postmodernist emphasis on representation can provide a powerful corrective to positivist social science and the tendency in some versions of political economy to reduce symbolically mediated social action to the instrumental process of labor. However, the grounding of reflexivity in the metaphor of representation as "dialogical" comes dangerously close, I would argue, to a contemplative stance by ignoring praxis and the plurality of subjects that negotiate the historical and political process. Apart from the introduction and conclusion, I have organized this chapter into four sections. The first section gives a brief account of the dispute between Jürgen Habermas and Jean-François Lyotard over the significance of rationalization in advanced capitalist society. The issues raised in this dispute are then utilized to create a broader context by which to evaluate critically the postmodern emphasis in anthropology on the representation of the "other" through ethnographic writing. The second section puts forward the argument that Marcus and Fischer's anthropology as cultural critique is fully commensurate, especially with respect to their emphasis on relativism and small narratives, with Lyotard's vision of the postmodern condition. Examples of "small narratives" are drawn selectively from ethnographies discussed by Marcus and Fischer as well as from the important invention of tradition literature of the late 1980s and 1990s. This section also highlights the importance to critical anthropology of a reflexive approach to ethnographic writing. The third section discusses the metatheoretical presuppositions that inform political economy in general and Marxist anthropology in particular. The self-formative properties of social labor and the concept of totality are presented as an alternative to the postmodern vision of a fragmented social world and the ubiquity of power. Finally, the fourth section appeals, as did the preceding chapter, to Jürgen Habermas's theory of social action as communicative to illustrate the limitations of the Marxist concept of labor as a general theory of action and the problems ensuing from the small relativistic narratives that reputedly typify the postmodern condition. Although no new synthesis is proposed here, I suggest that a communicative metatheory grounded in the historical process offers the most promise by which to recast critically the postmodern emphasis on representation. Such a theory, if attentive to concrete social interaction and the problematics of advanced capitalist society, would also go a long way towards engaging constructively the critical concerns of political economy.

The Postmodern Controversy

While postmodernism does not constitute a school in any conventional sense, owing especially to its rejection of paradigms in the Kuhnian (1962) sense, its general trajectory has been well articulated by Jean-François Lyotard in his often-cited *The Postmodern Condition* (1984). Lyotard boldly proclaims, against the tradition of modernist social theory and its emphasis on foundations or universal criteria of truth, that knowledge generated through the medium of grand or metatheory has lost its legitimacy as either a speculative or an emancipatory narrative.[4] For Lyotard, as for most postmodern theorists, to continue to believe in the emancipatory potentials of grand theory is to be seduced by the logocentric pretense of the Enlightenment. Lyotard argues that metatheory has declined in importance because of the development of new technologies and specialized discourses that have relativized and rendered superfluous its normative foundations. The decline of metatheory is marked, in Max Weber's terms, by a shift from substantive to technical rationality whereby means dominate over ends. Furthermore, the redeployment of advanced liberal capitalism has led to what Lyotard calls the "elimination of the communist alternative and the valorization of the individual enjoyment of goods and services" (1984: 37–8). Lyotard contends, against all foundational theories and their universal standards, that the legitimation of knowledge claims can only arise from "their own linguistic practice and communicational interaction" (1984: 41).

Lyotard's version of the postmodern condition has been forcefully challenged by, among others, Jürgen Habermas (1981, 1984) and Andreas Huyssen (1981, 1984). While Huyssen indicts postmodernism for its "gleeful neglect of history except as text,"[5] Habermas contends that the research plan of postmodernism is essentially conservative in that it provides no standards by which to question the relativity of language games and their possible association with domination. Habermas argues that although the project of modernity represented by the critical rationality of the Enlightenment remains unfulfilled it can be realized through a reorientation of societal modernization, so as to limit "the internal dynamics and the imperatives of an almost autonomous economic system and its administrative complements" (1981: 13).

While Habermas recognizes in Enlightenment rationality – the very rationality of which postmodernists are suspicions – the potential to ground social relations in rational consensus, his challenge to the above-noted autonomy of the economic system as it encroaches on public life comes from his effort to develop a theory of communicative action.[6] This theory seeks to identify universal conditions, such as mutual comprehensibility, sincerity, truthfulness, and appropriateness, which are presupposed in communicative action and which mark the reciprocal process by which competing knowledge claims are advanced and mutual understanding or consensus achieved (Bernstein 1983: 185–6). Habermas's concept of communication oriented towards mutual understanding is also a theory of evolution in that the process by which competing knowledge claims are advanced and deliberated also serves the progressive learning capacity of the human species to solve problems and self-reflexively to monitor human action. Habermas thus suggests, in a manner reminiscent of Hegel and the rationalist tradition, that the history of the human species has become one of increasing self-transparency, whereby a growth in the reflexive potential has facilitated the solving of societal problems and the ability to put forward mutually binding truth claims grounded in rationality. In short, against the relativity of language games and fragmented world described by Lyotard, Habermas has proposed a reconstructive metatheory. This theory links the possibility of emancipation and the critical review of knowledge claims to practical action viewed from the ideal of communication free from domination.[7] Although there is little doubt that Habermas's project will appear abstract in relation to the practical concerns of the fieldworker, and perhaps even ethnocentric in that, as a reconstructive theory of social evolution, it draws upon developmental psychology to distinguish the cognitive learning potentials of indigenous and modern societies (not to mention its essentially western conception of rational consensus), it nonetheless has the merit of bringing relativistic knowledge claims and societal meanings into critical focus.[8]

The dispute between Habermas and his postmodernist adversaries, especially Lyotard, is important not simply from the point of view of epistemology but also because it is a commentary on the possibility of a critical praxis in the context of advanced capitalist society. Lyotard appears to believe that societal rationalization or, in common parlance, modernization, has in a positive sense produced not only a whole range of new technologies but also a concomitant horizon of new modes of inquiry whose logics are internal to their distinct communicational practices. The understanding of physics, jurisprudence, or the new informational technologies, for example, should proceed from reconstructing rules which are internal or shared by the practitioners of these respective sciences. From a more anthropological perspective, such a view would accept the incommensurability of language games across cultures and reject the possibility of a single translational language, or more importantly, a basis from which these incommensurable language games can be evaluated. Societal rationalization has, for Lyotard, shattered the possibility of creating a unified or even coherent metanarrative that could legitimize knowledge claims in their plurality. Furthermore it has linked knowledge to the ubiquity of power. For Lyotard, it is power rather than truth or appropriateness that has become the standard of the postmodern condition. Lyotard's view of contemporary social life seeks to render antiquarian the critical notion of social totality both in the epistemological and ontological senses.[9]

Habermas does not deny that there is in societal modernization a tendency to produce a fragmented social world, as described by Lyotard and other postmodernist theoreticians, nor the fact that there is an important link between knowledge and power under conditions which are historically variable. Rather, it is the seeming inevitability of the fragmentation of social life and the dominance of instrumental rationality that Habermas challenges. Habermas has a profound belief in the emancipatory potentials of Enlightenment rationality and an equally strong conviction that the abstract review of autonomous language games or forms of life leaves the world unchanged. His long-term project is, as I have indicated, to develop and refine a metatheory of universal pragmatics that utilizes the ideal speech situation as a model for human action free from domination. This theory not only seeks to correct the instrumentalist bias in historical materialism – the transformation of the intersubjectivity of culture into the instrumental process of labor – while preserving Marx's emphasis on a theory with practical intent, but it also strives to establish a foundation by which the legitimacy of knowledge claims can be evaluated. Habermas is not satisfied with a social theory that accepts the world as it is, as I believe should be the case with critical anthropology, but rather he seeks to present a reconstructive theory that offers to reconnect political action to the moral intent of rational consensus.[10]

Postmodernism and Anthropology

The development of a postmodern perspective in anthropology has paid insufficient attention to the debate between Lyotard and Habermas regarding the significance of societal modernization. This, I argue, has had the unfortunate consequence of creating an overly narrow conceptualization of what constitutes critique in anthropology. Rather, the anthropological contributors to the postmodern movement have sought to exploit its critical potentials through identifying representation as the key feature of reflexivity. This point of view is perhaps best exhibited, but by no means exclusively, by Marcus and Fischer's *Anthropology as Cultural Critique*, and by selections from the *Writing Culture* volume (1986) edited by Clifford and Marcus. Consider, for example, the following statement from the former of the two works:

> Modernism relied for much of its effect on mere shock, but there is nothing shocking anymore, so postmodernism now attempts to transform the strategy of defamiliarization into a prolonged, sophisticated discourse that engages the reader or viewer. Anthropology searches for similar solutions through changes in its modes of ethnographic representation. (Marcus and Fischer 1986: 161–2)

Marcus and Fischer go on to claim that experimentation with modes of representation in ethnographic writing is the means through which we can best bring our own cultural assumptions into question. They argue that the measure of a critical anthropology is an "engaged relativism" that brings together the concerns of interpretive anthropology and political economy with a sensitivity to local context. Although they claim to distance themselves from postmodernism, the project outlined by Marcus and Fischer is fully conversant with that of Lyotard in that it promotes the small narratives of ethnographic inquiry, rather than grand theory, as the basis of cultural critique.

Before advancing further with what I perceive to be the limitations of postmodernism as represented by Marcus and Fischer in particular, I think it important to consider the positive implications of this now common trajectory in anthropology. This is especially the case in light of the controversy, misrepresentation, and outright rejection to which postmodernism has been subject. An impulsive rejection of postmodernism risks overlooking the central problem of representation to which postmodernists have drawn our attention, and therefore the possible contribution of a theory of representation to critical anthropology.[11]

The critical project that Marcus and Fischer outline for anthropology is not, as they admit, entirely new. The comparative method has always been used to relativize and to challenge the avowed universality and superiority of western values and social practices. One has only to recall, for example, Rousseau's use in the eighteenth century of the "savage" as a critique of civil society (see Rousseau 1964) or Margaret Mead's (1950) early twentieth-century field research in New Guinea as a challenge to universally held gender stereotypes. The list of examples could go on indefinitely. What is interesting about Marcus and Fischer's approach, one which they share with a wide range of anthropologists who have been influenced by the postmodernist textual turn, discourse theory, and the numerous variants of literary criticism, is their self-conscious effort to utilize writing as a critical theory of representation. Marcus and Fischer argue, and I believe quite rightly, that the process of writing is not, as positivists have long contended, a means of reproducing isomorphically one's experience of the world.[12] Rather, writing, as a form of social action, is constitutive in that it is an important medium through which the "other," ethnographically speaking, is represented.

The recognition that the writing of ethnography is constitutive enables us to grasp the representation of the "other" in anthropology as not only potentially liberating in terms of cross-cultural comparison but also as potentially mystifying, if not an outright source of domination. This argument has been forcefully advanced, for example, by Edward Said (1979) in his exploration of the ideological uses of orientalism and by Johannes Fabian (1983) in his provocative account of domination as the denial of coevalness.

Said contends that the genre of orientalism, which is widely employed in writing about eastern societies, glosses over important differences between the plurality of eastern cultures and therefore represents what is diverse as homogeneous. Said's principal point is that there is a connection between the representation of the East as homogeneous and efforts to subject the east to western hegemonic and civilizing processes. Fabian, on the other hand, takes us to the heart of anthropology in his contention that the "other" has often been denied a temporality that would enable us to recognize indigenous societies as our contemporaries. Fabian maintains that the largely unreflected-upon temporal devices of anthropology, such as participant observation and the "ethnographic present," are built right into its very discourse and practice. Consequently, the discourse of anthropology tends to contrive the "other" in terms of temporal and spatial distance and therefore unwittingly transforms the intersubjectivity of ethnographic experience into objectified written accounts of informants. Fabian believes that the resolution of this problem is not so much epistemological as political in that anthropologists must strive to change the praxis and politics of anthropological research and writing.

Writing is not, therefore, simply a literary abstraction subject to the vicissitudes of taste and disengaged from the "material world." Rather it is, as Marcus and Fischer insist, a social praxis engaged in the construction and dialectical reformulation of the "other." This is not to say that the "other" is the passive product of a semiotic process, since surely there is a creative tension between written accounts and the autonomy of the "other" that co-determines the representation advanced. However, as is often the case under conditions that are historically variable, the representations offered through ethnographic and historical accounts become integrated into the self-identity of the "other" as a reinforcement or intensification of their otherness. This point has been made forcefully by Herzfeld (1987) in arguing that hegemonic representations originating in the Greek nation state and reproduced discursively in theoretical anthropology have served to shape the play of Greek national identity between the poles of western authenticity and eastern otherness. While Herzfeld's example is particular to Greece, it resonates with examples elsewhere and confirms the assertion that there is a central connection between the process of representation and power.[13]

Marcus and Fischer suggest that self-consciousness about the process of writing, along with experimentation in ethnographic writing, are the ways to further the project of a critical anthropology as cultural critique. As a model of self-consciousness or reflexivity, Marcus and Fischer have in mind Hayden White's highly controversial *Tropics of Discourse* (1978). White, a leading opponent of positivist historiography, suggests that the writing of history should be evaluated stylistically or through literary genres such as tragedy, comedy, irony, and satire.[14] White is convinced that the rhetorical persuasiveness of a work is reinforced by the literary genre employed. Marx, for example, is seen as employing a tragic narrative, which White believes accounts largely for its power. White argues, furthermore, that the failure to recognize the intrinsic rhetorical persuasiveness of a written work bestows an undeserved authority upon it that serves to mask its ideological appeal.

Marcus and Fischer contend that experimentation with ethnographic writing, beginning with the new ethnographies of the late 1960s and early 1970s, challenges the authority of ethnographic description and the claims of authors to speak for their co-subjects of knowledge. In short, they argue, as do all the contributors to the *Writing Culture* volume (Clifford and Marcus 1986), that having been there is not sufficient to justify one's claim to know another culture. Rather, the rhetorical use of the first-person pronoun masks the ideological or theoretical interests of the author, a factor that consequently is not overcome by the confessional style of the new ethnographies. Marcus and Fischer argue, and once again I am with them here, that ethnographic writing must open itself to a plurality of voices. In other words, Marcus and Fischer are calling for a style of ethnography that decenters the authority of the anthropologist by allowing a multiplicity of different perspectives to emerge in the ethnographic account itself. We are told by Marcus and Fischer that the decentering of authority involves much more than simply reporting what informants have disclosed.

Marcus and Fischer are very explicit, in their *Anthropology as Cultural Critique*, about what constitutes a decentered ethnography in that they identify a wide range of innovative works that are multivoiced or multivocal. Marcus and Fischer classify these innovative works according to genre or type of textual strategy pursued by the ethnographer. These genres, to name just a few, include psychodynamics, life histories, modernism and, perhaps of most importance to our consideration of critical anthropology, world historical political economy.

Psychodynamic ethnographies are innovative, Marcus and Fischer say, because they seek new ways to synthesize Freudian theory with cross-cultural materials. They have in mind here Obeyesekere's celebrated *Medusa's Hair* (1981), where Freudian theory is utilized to analyze the dream images and trance states of Sri Lankan priestesses.[15] Obeyesekere's strategy is to probe the life histories and unconscious psychological processes of his priestess informants to show how personal meaning is attributed to cultural experience and public symbols. This strategy, although problematic in its ethnocentric implications, nonetheless allows the informants to assume a forceful presence in the ethnographic narrative.

The life history genre, on the other hand, makes use of modernist textual strategies in drawing the ethnographer and the reader of the ethnographic text into a joint venture of interpretation. Marcus and Fischer discuss, among others, Shostak's *Nisa: The Life and Words of a !Kung Woman* (1981). This work, like the ethnographies of Radin and Griaule, is based upon countless hours of interviews with a single informant which are then extensively edited by Shostak for publication. Nisa's oral history is remarkable for its candor and the challenge that it provides to the conventional wisdom on !Kung society. The great appeal of this work has been, in Geertz's terms, its "distance near" style – a style that appears to foreground the voice of the informant over that of the ethnographer.

Marcus and Fischer believe that the genre of world historical political economy has much to contribute to an anthropology as cultural critique since it seeks to integrate the concerns of interpretive anthropology with those of political economy. While Marcus and Fischer discuss several works, it is Taussig's *The Devil and Commodity Fetishism* (1980) that attracts their attention because it describes local responses to the penetration of capitalist social relations into the community. It is precisely local-level cultural process in relation to capitalist penetration that Marcus and Fischer believe to be absent in the conventional accounts of political economy.

Taussig's strategy of exploring these responses permits the Colombian small peasants and Bolivian tin miners discussed in his book to assume a place in the ethnographic narrative as full subjects rather than as object or conduit for the world economic system. Taussig portrays the Colombian small peasants of his first case study as caught between the cultural logic of subsistence production on their own lands and the cash economy of the plantation system. According to the peasants, money is sterile and those who have acquired it are likely to have made a pact with the devil. In similar fashion, the Bolivian tin miners who serve as Taussig's second case study are also caught between pre-capitalist beliefs and those emerging from the system of capitalist exploitation. Tio, the male spirit that controls the mineral wealth of the mountains, assumes for the tin miners the role of symbolic mediator between that over which the miners have control and the control exerted over their lives by foreign capital. Tio's mediating role thus becomes a source for the elaboration of cultural meanings.

Although not addressed by the Marcus and Fischer edited volume, the "invention of tradition literature" is, with some exceptions, likewise representative of the postmodern emphasis on relativistic, localized narratives. The publication of Hobsbawm and Ranger's *The Invention of Tradition* (1983) contributed significantly to the rethinking of essentialist concepts of tradition that had long dominated in anthropology by arguing that tradition was not passed continuously from generation to generation unchanged. Rather, tradition in most communities is a product of invention, as contemporaneous communities look to the past to address political and cultural issues of the present. Trevor-Roper (in Hobsbawm and Ranger 1983) recounts how, for example, the Scottish kilt, which most people associate with Scottish national culture, along with the bagpipe, was introduced from the outside by a Quaker industrialist; it thus had nothing to do with the indigenous Scottish culture of the Highlands and Lowlands. The kilt only became a symbolic marker of Scottish national identity when the Scottish upper classes sought to distinguish themselves culturally from hegemonic English rule. What is important to note theoretically is that Hobsbawm maintains that although the invention of tradition is important to demystifying current claims to long-standing historical continuities of culture and social practice, there is nonetheless a real past to which invented traditions can be compared.

Hobsbawm's characteristically *modernist* assertion that there is a *real* past to which invented tradition can be compared has led to postmodern critiques on the part of authors such as Jocelyn Linnekin (1992) and Allan

Hanson (1989). Linnekin, whose work has largely addressed invented Hawaiian traditions (see Linnekin 1983, 1991) has argued that all culture is a social construction and thus there is no *real* past to which presently constructed historical narratives can be compared. Linnekin also challenges the Marxist critique of ideology by suggesting that the decentering of postmodernism emphasizes complexity, difference, and multiplicity over what she regards as the Marxist dismissal of quotidian views as "false consciousness." In a manner reminiscent of James Clifford's (1988) work on ethnographic authority, Linnekin (1992: 257) maintains that:

> The Postmodern "decentering" project is thus a more radical and a more fundamental challenge to the dominant social-science paradigm than Marxist or anticolonial analysis, for its target is not a particular authorship but the very premises of narrative authority and unitary point of view.

Linnekin also argues that not only do all communities invent tradition but so do scholars as well. This point is well illustrated by Hanson's (1989) celebrated but nonetheless controversial article on the invention of Maori tradition. Hanson relates that there are two competing versions of the Maori settlement of New Zealand, one known as the "grand fleet theory," which emphasizes canoes coming from Tahiti, and a second that ties Maori origins to a pre-European "esoteric cult" devoted to a supreme god Io. Hanson shows brilliantly that both of these versions are artifice, the former likely attributable to the scholarship of Percy Smith. With respect to the invention of tradition, Hanson (1989: 898), like Linnekin, regards the logic of cultural invention as a process of "sign substitutions," a view consistent with postmodern anti-essentialism and the emphasis on past and present as polyphonic or consisting of a plurality of narratives.

The invention of tradition literature as represented through Linnekin, Hanson, and others too numerous to mention here has no doubt been important to demystifying continuous and univocal visions of tradition and to grasping the often ingenious reconstructions of tradition in the present to justify nationalist claims virtually everywhere. However, Linnekin appears to overlook the political, economic, and cultural processes of often global import that both enable some and prevent others from advancing their constructed narratives as authoritative, even though she cites Raymond Williams (1977) for his concept of "selective" tradition. This oversight is not, however, particular to Linnekin but rather, as indicated earlier with reference to Clifford and Marcus, it is shared by postmodern theory more generally.

It is no doubt true that the ethnographies to which Marcus and Fischer appeal, and here one could include postmodern invention as well, have opened ethnographic narratives to a plurality of voices that challenge conventional ethnographic representation, and by extension historical and nationalist representations. But it is my view that this opening to a plurality of voices, compounded by their defense of relativism, complicates rather than resolves the issue of ethnographic authority. This takes us to a head-on confrontation with the other leading competitor in critical anthropology, that is, political economy.

Political Economy

> the world of humankind constitutes a manifold, a totality of interconnected processes; and inquiries that disassemble this totality into bits and then fail to reassemble it falsify reality. (Wolf 1982: 3)

Apart from the critique of capitalist hegemony and the exploitation of indigenous peoples, there is no single vision which captures in totality the contribution of political economy to the project of critical anthropology.[16] Furthermore, political economy itself has a wide range of articulations, from the structural variants of the French Marxist school, with its emphasis on the economic base and ideological superstructure, to Anglo-American neo-Marxism emphasizing the relative autonomy of culture from the process of production and reproduction.[17] Generally, anthropologists informed by the perspectives of political economy have been interested in issues such as the proletarianization of the peasantry, social transformations on the local level as linked dialectically to national and international markets, the resistance to capital accumulation or capital penetration, state and class formation, second economies in socialist societies, and the origins of gender inequality, to name just a few examples. Anthropologists working within the tradition of political economy have produced, furthermore, a number of works that have been highly influential in the discipline as a whole. One only has to think of Eric Wolf's *Europe and the People without History* (1982) and Sidney Mintz's *Sweetness and Power* (1985). Both of these works have won praise not only because of their command of regional social history but also because they make international connections between political economy and power that far transcend the usual areal orthodoxy.

Wolf's book commences with a survey of the world in the year 1400 and seeks to account for the historical and social dynamics by which Europe would eventually assert its dominion. However, in the year 1400, European states were only weakly organized and not very powerful. Europe would have to await the ascendancy of northern Italian mercantile centers such as Genoa and Venice before the tide would begin to turn. These centers would play an important role in funding the warfare carried on by European monarchs and in supplying the capital for European expansion abroad. Wolf is careful to point out, though, that it was not the circulation of commodities alone that launched Europe on its new destiny but rather gradual transformations in the social relations of production upon which the circulation of commodities depended. Wolf distinguishes in great detail the alternative paths of development followed by the tribute-taking states of Portugal and Spain, precariously dependent on foreign capital, from those of France and England. In contrast to a world systems approach where local dynamics are all too often overlooked, Wolf creates a historical narrative that tacks back and forth between international political and economic processes and the small-scale populations that are normally the subject of anthropological inquiry. In this way, he hopes to cast light on those peoples usually left in history's shadow.

Mintz pursues a similar strategy in the creation of what he calls the anthropology of modern life. Like Wolf, Mintz argues that any study that fails to incorporate the relation between metropolis and colony is flawed. It is Mintz's objective, therefore, to outline the triangle of sugar trade that emerges in the seventeenth century between Europe, Africa, and the New World. Mintz maintains that this triangle linked the fate of plantation slaves to that of the European working classes as sugar became transformed from a luxury commodity to the "kingly commodity of commoners." Sugar not only came to symbolize modern life – the fast fix – but it also played a role historically, argues Mintz (1985: 180), in provisioning and satiating farm and factory workers, thus reducing the cost of creating and reproducing the proletariat.

Although these works are somewhat different in their historical scope, Wolf and Mintz base their historical accounts equally on the logic of political economy. Apart from linking broad historical connections to local dynamics, each author claims to address what he perceives to be the overemphasis in anthropology and cultural studies on the autonomy of culture. Mintz, for example, criticizes Geertz's notion of culture as "webs of significance" by arguing that the generation of meaning is always constrained and profoundly shaped by social class relations – a factor which he believes to be apparent in the different historical experiences of sugar on the part of the upper and working classes. The view of culture as constrained by social class is given further support by Wolf, who maintains that it is modes of production specifically that condition human consciousness:

> Contrary to those who believe that Mind follows an independent course of its own, I would argue that ideology making does not arise in the confrontation of Naked Man thinking about Naked Nature; rather, it occurs within the determinate compass of a mode of production deployed to render nature amenable to human use. (Wolf 1982: 388)

It is clear that the force of their historical argumentation, as well as their discussion of power itself, comes from the assumption of Wolf and Mintz that it is labor that establishes the context of human self-formation and transformation and so it must be to the historical conditions of labor that we turn for critique and a vision of human emancipation. This, however, requires elaborating what is presupposed in utilizing labor as the foundation of a critical anthropology, especially since postmodernist anthropologists also claim to be interested in many of the historical questions normally associated with political economy.

Political economy in the Marxist tradition operates on both the level of the concrete and the level of metatheory. On the level of the concrete, political economy aims to disclose what is hidden by the appearance of things: the specific logic of a social formation and its determinant social relations of production. On the level of metatheory, however, the logical reconstruction of social formations proceeds from the ontological presupposition of socially constitutive labor. In other words, for political economy, it is social labor that serves as a universal model of human action and that accounts for the self-formation of the human species in particular. The relation between the concrete and the universal in the Marxist tradition provides a framework that is sensitive to variations in local context while challenging and transcending the dilemmas of legitimation raised by relativism and postmodern fragmentation.

Just as Habermas's ideal speech event distinguishes reciprocal communicative interaction from that which is subject to domination, so it is also the case that political economy, informed by the metatheoretical concept of socially constitutive labor, distinguishes reciprocal from exploitative human interaction. However, in the case of political economy, it is not symbolic exchange but rather the material process of labor and the historical conditions of its expropriation and alienation that provide the critical edge to social analysis.

Marx elevated labor to a general theory of action in maintaining that labor is the formative and transformative activity of the human species.[18] Against the long-standing division in western philosophy between subject and object and the essentially contemplative stance towards the world that this dichotomy implies, Marx argued for a view of labor as praxis, or a synthesizing of subject and object, in that its formative activity upon the world was simultaneously a moment of human self-transformation. He referred to this synthesizing or dialectical process as the "humanization of nature and the naturalization of man" (1967a: 177). Furthermore, the formative activity of labor upon the world was also recognized by Marx as labor's objectification or embodiment in its own products as well as a means through which subjective inner life could be given an objectivity in the world. An identification was thus advanced between the labor of subjects and the labor embodied in products grasped reflexively as their own.[19] This was not conceived to be a facile or static identification but rather one marked by temporality as Marx believed that labor is thoroughly socialized and socializing, that is, intersubjective to the core.

A Marxist political economy offers, therefore, a critical theory with universal and practical application, since it links the standard of evaluation or critique directly to a general condition of humanity, that is the ontology of labor. The universal standard by which the reciprocity of social relations can be determined is contained in the reconstruction of the meta-rules of social labor as formative and transformative, as well as in the identification of products with their products of labor. More specifically, it is the degree to which producers share in the products of their labor as a consequence of historically specific social relations of production that enables us to identify exploitative social relations across a wide range of different social formations.

The reconstruction of the concealed logic of a social formation from the ontological presupposition of socially constitutive labor would appear not only to afford a powerful cross-cultural and trans-historical means of critique but also to present a challenge to the postmodern conception of fragmentation and the self-legitimation of the small discourses of humankind. From the perspective of political economy, the fragmentation of the social world is not intrinsic to the nature of contemporary social relations and modes of knowledge but rather is part of their appearance or mystification. It was Lukács (1971), for example, who showed perhaps more convincingly than any modern social theorist in his celebrated, "Reification and the Consciousness of the Proletariat", that the alienation of workers from the products of their labor gives to the products of labor the appearance of a life of their own.[20] Lukács argued, in turn, that the alienation of workers is not distinct from the alienation or reification of consciousness that gives to modes of inquiry or specialized sciences an appearance of independence from the social relations of their production. The seeming independence and unrelatedness of specialized discourses of humanity is for the political economist a consequence of the concealed logic of the capitalist social formation and the dissemination of its commodity form.

The fragmentation, therefore, which postmodernists such as Lyotard have identified as intrinsic to the development of the contemporary world is for political economists a fragmentation only at the level of appearance. From the point of view of political economy, fragmentation serves not the emancipation from seductive reason but rather the hegemony of capitalist social relations through making power appear as diffuse and ubiquitous, that is, banal or ordinary.[21] In other words, by making what is extraordinary and particular appear as ordinary, the process of fragmentation can actually reinforce, rather than challenge, the rationalization of the social system. The critical analysis of the various fragmented discourses of humanity will disclose, to the contrary, their profound interconnection, the fact that these discourses are the product of historically specific social relations, and the commodity form which social relations have assumed in the period of advanced monopoly capitalism. For the political economist, as suggested by reference to Lukács above, wage labor and production exclusively for exchange have transformed labor itself into a commodity and, with the maturity of capitalism, this form has been generalized to all social relations. The development of the commodity form as a general model for social relations is foremost a question of power, as not only does it serve the expropriation of surplus value but it also tends to dissociate the consciousness of workers, and those of the oppressed in general, from the objective conditions of their exploitation.

Political economists have come to recognize the commodity form as not only a model for exploitative social relations in capitalist society but also as a model of hegemonic cultural production and reproduction. Following in the Marxist tradition, political economy has tended to view human consciousness and cultural products in material terms, even when rejecting Marx's own distinction between economic base and ideological superstructure. That is, culture and human consciousness have come to be seen as a form of material praxis itself.[22] All cultural products are produced and transformed within the context of historically conditioned social relations of production. If in fact these social relations have assumed the general form of the commodity, then it is no surprise, as many critical theorists have argued, that cultural products and human consciousness appear to participate in a disembodied, free system of exchange.[23]

The principal point of tension between the postmodernist anthropologists and their political economy colleagues arises, therefore, from how human action and cultural products are understood in the context of a social world conceived to be fragmented. In short, postmodernists appear to have accepted the self-legitimating small discourses of humanity and fragmentation that ensue from a thoroughly relativized social world.[24] This, as we shall see shortly, has led within the discipline of anthropology to a view of ethnography as collage. Political economy, on the other hand, interprets fragmentation, I believe correctly, as produced in the context of social relations that have assumed the commodity form. Fragmentation exists only in appearance and serves to reinforce, therefore, the rationalization of capitalist social relations. Furthermore, for the political economist, it is taking reputedly self-legitimating discourses from the context of their production, and not the reconstruction of their internal rules, that lays bare their legitimacy. Just as the postmodernists believe that metatheoreticians have been seduced by the universal claims of reason to render social life transparent on the basis of recognizable foundations, so the political economists would argue that postmodernists, in accepting the self-legitimation of small discourses, have fallen subject to the reification of consciousness and its logic of the commodity form.

Logics of Production and Metaphors of Representation

The emphasis in postmodern anthropology on representation of the "other" is not only a function of privileging small narratives over those of grand theory. It is also a consequence of a perceived failure on the part of political economy to adequately address the relation between the symbolic process and human action. This point has been advanced not only by Marcus and Fischer but also by Taussig (1987) in an article that, among other things, reviews Wolf's and Mintz's aforementioned celebrated works. Taussig takes the political economists to task for relegating human subjects and the cultural meanings that they produce to the margins of history in spite of their claim to cast light on those normally left in history's shadow. He contends that concrete human subjects, the key producers of culture and history, are subordinated by Wolf and Mintz to the univocal narrative of capitalism. Taussig hence believes that we learn very little from either Wolf or Mintz about micropopulations and how their cultural products both resist commodification and yet are subject to its penetration. History thus becomes an "Archimedean point," or phantom of itself, in that in being a narrative removed from "lived experience" history simply tells itself. Taussig concludes that the eclipsing of contextual human praxis by Wolf's and Mintz's respective appeals to the singular logic of production tends, contrary to their objective, to reify history by making what is an abstract narrative appear to be concrete.[25] Consequently, it has been to neo-Hegelian revisions of Marxist social theory, to interpretive anthropology, and to literary criticism that most postmodern anthropologists have turned in their effort to forge an "anthropology as cultural critique".[26]

Postmodern anthropologists have not rejected the claims of Marxist political economy that there is an inextricable relation between theory, politics, and praxis, since they themselves have argued that the process of writing in general, and ethnography in particular, is a political activity. Rather, it is the elevation of labor to a general theory of action that has appeared most problematic to postmodernists, a point of view that they share with neo-Marxist and interpretive anthropologists as well. Because I have outlined in considerable detail previously (see chapter 7) the principal objections to taking labor as a general model for the formative and transformative activity of the human species,[27] I only briefly summarize the argument here.

Perhaps more than any contemporary social theorist, Habermas has assumed the task of reconstructing historical materialism by addressing the problem of taking labor as a general theory of action. Beginning with his early *Knowledge and Human Interests* (1971), Habermas has sought to show that the activity through which the human species forms itself, solves problems, and self-reflexively monitors its own action, is dependent on a communicative framework that is distinctively broader than that implied in the Marxist notion of production and reproduction through labor. Furthermore, Habermas argues that the logic of inquiry that follows from a productivist logic is insufficient to serve the emancipatory interest of a reconstructivist social theory with practical intent. This is the case because emancipation not only involves understanding the genesis of exploitative social relations but, for Habermas, emancipation must also establish a means of reconnecting politics to a public life grounded in rational consensus.[28]

Habermas's argument against taking labor as a general theory of action rests largely upon distinguishing the cognitive interest that informs labor from that of social interaction. Habermas asserts that the human species forms and reproduces itself through labor and interaction and that these activities are grounded in technical and practical cognitive interests, respectively. Cognitive interests, furthermore, shape both actual and potential objects of knowledge and determine "the categories relevant to what we take to be knowledge, as well as the procedures for discovering and warranting knowledge claims" (Bernstein 1976: 192). For Habermas, therefore, there is a direct connection between knowledge and social action as formative.

While Habermas would agree with Marx that labor is the activity through which human populations transform the natural world to meet socially established needs, he would not agree that this self-same activity can also account for the reproduction of social relations. This is the case because Habermas believes that human labor is limited to a technical cognitive interest in that through labor human subjects constitute or objectify the natural world towards the end of technical control. From the point of view of the cognitive interest of labor, the natural world becomes posited as an object of human appropriation and use. This is to be distinguished, argues Habermas, from social interaction upon which the reproduction and transformation of social relations is based. Social interaction is informed by a practical cognitive interest in that it is characterized by norms of mutual expectation as embodied in symbolic, ordinary language communication. Social interaction is the arena, furthermore, in which knowledge claims are advanced and social and cultural identities negotiated and forged. As opposed to the technical rationality of labor, the objective of social interaction is communicative in mutual understanding and mutual consensus.

While it may be the case, as some critics of Habermas have argued, that technical and practical cognitive interests, and the rationalities of the systems of action that they avowedly inform, are intertwined in actual human praxis and therefore can only be distinguished at the most abstract level,[29] it is nonetheless his intention to show that the logical reconstruction of symbolically mediated human activity in social interaction cannot proceed from meta-rules of actual and potential objectification and control.

Habermas maintains, not unlike Clifford Geertz, that all human activity, whether instrumental or communicative, is symbolically constituted. Consequently, although having a rationality oriented towards the objectification and control of the natural world to meet humanly established ends, the sociability of labor and its reproduction are fundamentally dependent on a process of symbolic or communicative exchange. As Marx (1967a: 178) himself realized, in an observation redolent with cultural implications, it is the concept of a project prior to its execution that distinguishes human labor from the mere physical activity of a bee. The reconstruction of the social contexts under which all human action unfolds must follow, therefore, the logic of a hermeneutic science designed to interpret the density or opacity of symbolically constituted human action. A hermeneutic science postulates the process of understanding as a synthesis between the categories, assumptions, and expectations of the critical theorist and those of the object/subject of inquiry. This process, furthermore, is ongoing and hence the knowledge that arises from the inquiry is subject to continual revision. The purpose of this hermeneutic science, which Habermas raises to a critical theory of society, is not simply the elaboration of meaning along the lines of an interpretive anthropology or sociology of knowledge but rather the clarification of the contexts of mutual intelligibility and the social constraints to which action oriented towards mutual understanding is subject.

The fact that the instrumental process of labor is inadequate on its own to serve as a reconstructive science of symbolic human action does not render its critical intent superfluous. On the contrary, a critical theory tied closely to the category of labor is important for grasping the social constraints to which symbolic exchanges are subject. This assertion is supported, as world systems theory in particular has shown, by the recognition that it has been ever-expanding capitalist markets and hegemonic political diplomacy informed by economic interests that have assumed a leading role in shaping and transforming the relations between "civilized," "peasant," and "primitive" in the modern world – not to mention their importance in terms of the birth of anthropology. However, it is equally important to keep in mind, as Gramsci (1975) and more recently Thompson (1978) and Williams (1977) have reminded us, that social control, inequality, and the constraints of social interaction in general are not simply a function of the expropriation of surplus value or economic exploitation but perhaps, more importantly, of symbolically rooted cultural practices and their reproduction. According to these authors, there is a cultural or symbolic foundation of power even with respect to what appear as merely economic imperatives. Consequently, the call for a critical theory of representation on the part of postmodern anthropologists resonates with importance.

Although Marcus and Fischer and those who follow in the postmodern trajectory have drawn our attention to the necessity for a critical theory of representation, the creation of an anthropology as cultural critique remains in its early stages. Much of what postmodern anthropologists have to say is suggestive only in that they have neither successfully integrated the concerns of interpretive anthropology and political economy nor been very precise in identifying exactly how political economy serves as a constraint on symbolic or communicative exchange. Although postmodern anthropologists have encouraged the decentering of the ethnographic account, preferring the democratizing metaphor of the collage or plurality of voices to the singular voice of the ethnographer, they seem to have forgotten the hermeneutic lesson of Gadamer (1975) and other hermenenticians. The authority of the account rests with the fusion of the author's voice and a plurality of informants within a social world that is profoundly historically interconnected. In other words, the foregrounding of the informants' voices does not settle the issue of authority, since these voices are not autonomous but rather stand mediated by the social conditions of their production and the audiences to which they are addressed. This is not to say that postmodernists have substituted the reproduction of existing social conditions for the critical process of representation. However, in their attempts, at least in some anthropological variants, to scrutinize ethnographic writing, they have left the social world curiously "as is," thus betraying the practical intention of the tradition of critical theory.

I suspect that Marcus and Fischer are somewhat ill at ease with their idea of representation as an "engaged relativism" since they argue that representation must be sensitive to the concerns of political economy. I take this statement to mean, as indicated above, that representation itself may be constrained by historically specific modes of power embodied in the system of social labor. Even if we accept Marcus and Fischer's claim that Marxism is fundamentally a form of representation – a claim that is designed to relativize the special critical authority of Marxism – this does not absolve us from questioning the disclosures of our informants nor the forms of power that may reside in their opaque discourses and social relations.

The infusion of a multiplicity of voices into the ethnographic narrative, no matter how positive, is not a substitute for the critical grasp of social reality and hence leaves the authority of the ethnographic account incomplete. If anthropology is to be true to its emancipatory potential, which is not to deny that it has played a role in history as a medium of oppression, it must not rest satisfied with the representation of social meanings in their multiplicity. Rather, it must be prepared to probe beneath appearances through reconstructing reflexively the sociohistorical process to which they owe their origin.[30] A critical anthropology with practical intent must be prepared to do more than merely relativize our own social practices through the comparative method. On the contrary, it must go beyond the relativizing of narratives to challenge exploitative and hegemonic: social practices and social formations among our co-subjects of anthropological inquiry. I maintain that such a critical stance is based upon a vision of human emancipation not subject to compromise – the very assertion that is rejected by postmodernists.

Conclusion

It is impossible in a single chapter or perhaps even a book to do complete justice to the diversity of theoretical positions within postmodernism, not to mention its anthropological variant, or for that matter the equal diversity in Marxist scholarship. Rather, I have selected a more limited objective in choosing to identify the principal points of tension between these two leading competitors to a critical anthropology and to argue that each trajectory as it stands alone is insufficient as a basis to theorize the socio-cultural terrain. I contend that political economy must not only broaden its critical focus through questioning its productivist logic but should also strive to appropriate other metaphors of understanding. Such an effort, as for example initiated through Habermas's communicative reconstruction of historical materialism, would assist us to better understand the historical relations between culture, power, and systems of labor in their relative autonomy.[31] A communicative framework, furthermore, offers to enrich our understanding of the local dynamics of the world capitalist system through elaborating how those subject to capitalist hegemony both invent and make use of cultural conventions as a means of self-formation and resistance. If it is true that facts are socially constructed, as antipositivist social science has maintained, and that anthropology as a mode of inquiry is socially constitutive, then there is much that we can learn from the critical appropriation of a communicative or literary metaphor – an appropriation that discloses, as postmodernists and culture theorists alike have argued, the proximity of our discipline to the art of storytelling.

The postmodern tradition in anthropology, along the lines of cultural critique as articulated by Marcus and Fischer, remains inadequate as the definitive project of critical anthropology because in their efforts to explore the process of representation in ethnography they have advanced a notion of theory that is insufficiently connected to praxis and a grasp of the social world as a totality. This has led some anthropologists, such as Nicole Polier and William Roseberry (1989), to argue that postmodern anthropologists, while seeking to explore the "other" have merely found themselves.

While I believe that the postmodern emphasis on the representation of the "other" through the writing of ethnography is not without merit, it could be given a more substantial critical base if engaged seriously by the political and social issues raised in the Lyotard and Habermas dispute. That is to say, the critical evaluation of the process of representation, including its emancipatory potential, must unfold not simply within the confines of an experimental ethnography but rather from a broader consideration of how the process of representation itself and the plurality of our narratives in general articulate with societal rationalization and the problematics of advanced capitalist society. Such a consideration not only offers an alternative to Marcus and Fischer's engaged relativism, but it also offers to ease the impasse that has developed between political economy and postmodern theories of representation. With this admonition in mind, it seems appropriate to conclude where I began, that is, with Lyotard and Habermas.

The principal point of tension between Lyotard and Habermas, as I indicated previously, has to do with whether or not the social conditions that supported grand theory continue to be germane to understanding the contemporary human condition in its plurality. Lyotard argues that our advanced stage of capitalism has produced, through a process of societal rationalization, a whole range of new technologies and discrete narratives based upon their own linguistic practice. If we believe that the fragmentation of knowledge is actual rather than apparent, as Lyotard's vision of the social world would suggest, then we need only rely upon small narratives that are attuned to the internal problematics of their own linguistic practice. If it is true, however, as I believe Habermas is correct in arguing, that societal rationalization in the service of capitalist expansion and hegemony is a totalizing process that affects the human condition on a worldwide scale, then it seems a metanarrative is warranted that links together superficially fragmented discourses and social practices.

The danger of postmodernism, one which is as much political as epistemological, is that rather than recognizing the underlying historical unity of societal rationalization as the basis for creating a critical theory of society with practical intent, it takes the apparently discrete linguistic practices of small narratives, themselves the products of societal rationalization, as the basis for critical engagement. The avowedly critical narratives that arise within the context of discrete linguistic practices have no means, however, to account reflexively for their own generation and hence their probable connection to other discourses of humanity. Without a theory that links these discrete products of rationalization, we are left with a fragmented understanding of the social world and therefore an ineffective praxis that risks reproducing the very conditions of societal rationalization. In this regard, one can only agree with Habermas that postmodernism, at least as formulated by Lyotard, presents us with a conservative view of theory that neutralizes the critical potentials of praxis.

The criticism that I have directed to postmodernism is by no means intended as an outright rejection. Rather, like Huyssen, I stand in a position of ambivalence to its critical spirit. Postmodernists have made important contributions to social theory in pointing to the consequences of societal modernization and the connection of at least one sense of Enlightenment rationality to cultural domination. Furthermore, the emphasis of postmodernism on social action as a text, or in Tyler's (1986) sense discourse, and the process of ethnographic writing does in fact relativize some of the unrecognized critical potential of the anthropological mode of inquiry. However, for postmodernism ever to realize its own critical intention it must not accept a praxis informed by a fragmented social world or simply call for a sensitivity to political economy. It must seek instead to develop a reflexive and integrative vision of the social world and its emancipatory potentials grounded dialectically in the historical process. This, I admit, is a suggestion that cuts against the very grain of postmodern critique.

9 Bounded Cultures – Bounded Selves: The Challenge of Cultural Diasporas

The majority of the contributions to the Anglo-American rationality debates prior to and since the publication of this book's first edition assume an essentially epistemological perspective. That is, the objective of contributors from Winch to Jarvie and Horton, and even more recently Tambiah (1990), is to discuss the possibility of cultural comparison and ultimately cultural translation by pursuing the question of how we come to know the "other." The assumption here, and one that is not completely erroneous, is that societies or cultures are substantive *bounded* entities. These bounded entities have culturally particular rituals, social practices, beliefs, kinship structures, and so on that may be, as Winch asserts, incommensurable. For example, how does one make sense of Zande practices of consulting oracles or witchcraft accusations from an ethnographic standpoint where western notions of causality and empirical evidence predominate, or for that matter Australian kinship systems in light of a western family structure where the nuclear unit appears to be ubiquitous? According to the original contributors to the rationality debates, the theoretical options available to the researcher are to pursue the internal logic or language games of a defined "speech" community or to assume the logic of one "unified" science as the basis for cross-cultural translation. The former model assumes the autonomy of incommensurable "life-worlds" while the latter presumes that "difference" can be subsumed under a common set of assumptions and logical principles that we share as human.

I presented an alternative to the above theoretical options in chapter 6 through the hermeneutics of Gadamer and Ricoeur, one, like that of Tambiah (1990), that approaches cross-cultural understanding as dialogical; that is, a conversation with a co-subject where the pursuit of constituted meaning unfolds on epistemological grounds that are ever historically shifting. Societies as "bounded entities" are not, as the legacy of structuralism and functionalism asserts, prefixed and unchanging but, on the contrary, are *fashioned* by, in Marx's terms, formative and transformative human action

(See Marx 1973). However, and this is the critical point, even formative and transformative human action and the dialogical encounter of co-subjects, does not in any way challenge the now provincial assumption of society and culture as "bounded" substantive entities. This is less surprising once one recognizes the long-standing continuities of the subject–object relation, albeit variously formulated, in western culture and the primacy, at least within the construct of modernity, of the "bounded" knowing ego.

According to Agnes Heller (1981), the concept of the self that is often taken as a universal in modern philosophy and psychology owes its origins to the Renaissance of the seventeenth century. Heller regards the Renaissance as pivotal in the individualization of self and the incipient ascendancy of the individual over the collective narrative of community, a process that she regards, like her mentor of long ago Georg Lukács (1972), as informed largely by political economy but represented formatively in the art and literature of the seventeenth century. As I suggested in chapter 4 with respect to MacPherson's (1962) analysis of the political philosophy of Hobbes and Locke, and by extension to a critique of Jarvie's theory of possessive individualism, the argument for a bounded and possessive self can also be linked, as Heller suggests but MacPherson argues more directly, to the formative properties of rural capitalism, which would eventually come to surpass and fundamentally undermine the collective, albeit stratified, ethos of the past. Moreover, as we shall see, the history of western colonialism and now neo-colonialism accounts for and in turn can be used to deconstruct the primacy of bounded culture and the bounded ego at the heart of the subject–object relation as traditionally formulated, including anthropology's identification with the non-western "other."

All of the participants in the rationality debates operate, therefore, with a culturally and historically conditioned sense of knowing as bounded and with a concept of other cultures as univocal, non-differentiated, and likewise bounded. The implicit assumptions of boundedness are not only dated but they are an obstacle to understanding some of the most pressing social issues faced by the human sciences today, especially the problematic representation of "self" and "other." Thus, I argue in this concluding chapter, that postcolonial diasporas, what Arjun Appadurai (1991) refers to as "ethnoscapes",[1] and the apparent growing significance of globalism transcend and challenge the "bounded" epistemological assumptions and perhaps even ontological concerns at the core of the rationality debates and cross-cultural interpretation more generally. Stated more concretely, I suggest that the resolution of the subject–object formulation is ultimately, as Johannes Fabian (1983) asserts, a matter of ethnographic and I would add political praxis, and that ethnographic interpretation should be informed theoretically and methodologically by a process akin to what George Marcus (1998) has called "multi-sited" research.

Pursuing, however, an alternative to the "bounded" assumptions of the rationality debates through the challenges and pathways of globalism and multi-sited research is not a simple task, and so this chapter takes a somewhat indirect route. First, I establish as problematic the assumptions of bounded culture through invoking a commonly encountered example of identity and cultural diaspora. Next, I link, as noted above, the development of circumscribed field sites to European colonialism and the predominance of structural functionalism. Global models, especially world systems theory, are presented as a promising although not unproblematic alternative to bounded culture and circumscribed field sites, although these theoretical models are at fault for disregarding human agency. Finally, as a possible resolution to the shortcomings of world systems theory, I turn to the considerable merits of multi-sited research, a form of ethnographic praxis that appears to articulate well with the challenges of mobile populations and reconstructed identities. As we shall see, although it is an important step in transcending the limits of the "bounded" self as ethnographer, multi-sited research does not necessarily lead to collaboration between colleagues, nor does it address directly the question of power that informs ethnographic praxis and representation more generally. Nevertheless, taking on the challenges that globalism poses to bounded selves and bounded others is important to articulating the rationality debates with contemporary political, economic, and cultural issues. To that task, we proceed.

Bounded Cultures – Bounded Selves

In the spring of 1989, I returned to France to continue with a field research project on southwest French wine cooperatives that I had initiated in the Dordogne in the early 1980s and now had extended to the Médoc, north of Bordeaux. It was an interesting period to conduct field research in France because of the lively debate over plans of the European Union (EU) to liberalize trading relations among member nations, beginning in 1992. Some of my winegrowing informants were worried that liberalized trade would open French markets to copious amounts of less expensive European wines, thus affecting their livelihoods adversely. Moreover, EU initiatives offered to introduce a more comprehensive political agenda that included among other things facilitating the ability of Europeans to live and work in any of the member countries, a seemingly welcome option for all. However, as Mary Douglas (1966) has reminded us in a classic work that incorporates the theme of "matter out of place," albeit a theme that has rather conservative Durkheimian implications for the social order, permeable boundaries can lead, especially when human populations are on the move, to anxiety about the integrity and security of the individual body as it participates in metaphorical exchange with the social body. This appeared to be the case in France, since newspapers often reflected a popular concern that changes implemented through the European Union could affect the autonomy and thus the avowed integrity of disparate cultural practices, such as the length of the hunting season or the strict legislation that regulates and preserves the production of quality wine.[2] While these may not seem of much significance in comparison to pressing social issues such as unemployment and farm subsidies, the length of the hunting season and how wine is made are regarded as symbolic markers of being French. This has become especially so in light of English replacing French as the international language of commerce, and a growing sense that France could lose its reputed cultural leadership among western nations unless the French are vigilant in protecting French culture and social practices.[3] The movement of human populations across national borders, and the perceived challenge to the dominion of French culture, made fertile ground for the anti-foreigner politics of Jean Marie le Pen, itself a legacy of French colonialism and the diaspora of former French colonial subjects. It was in this social and political climate that a national debate arose over the now "infamous" chador incident.[4] The event takes on renewed significance given the French public's recent embracing of French Open winner Mary Pierce, born in Canada of a French mother but currently living in the United States.[5]

In late summer, at the beginning of the 1989 school year, a young Parisian girl of North African descent was sent by her parents to the local lycée wearing the traditional Islamic chador, a large cloth worn as a head covering. Paris has a sizable North African population, especially from Algeria and Morocco, and so women wearing the chador is by no means an unusual sight. On this particular morning, the school officials decided to send the young girl home, indicating that the chador was not appropriate school dress. The action of the school officials, as noted above, generated a rather wide-ranging public discussion on national identity, or what it means to be French, that resonates with similar debates that have occurred throughout Europe and North America, especially with respect to immigrant populations. As elsewhere, the reaction in France was emotionally charged and polarized.

The national papers covered the incident extensively and the public discussion that ensued. One well-represented view blamed the young girl's parents, insisting that they should conform to "French customs" and that the school officials had acted appropriately. The rhetoric characteristic of Le Pen, such as the slogan "France for the French," altogether overlooked the question of what it means to be French. Another view equally common suggested that French schools should be more tolerant and so should accommodate differences in dress and custom. In fact, this was the predominant liberal view. Occasionally, there was a third reaction, which was to raise the question whether or not there was anything that amounted to a uniform set of French customs and social practices, an attitude that was nevertheless in the minority because it challenged generally unrecognized institutional inequalities and social practices.

The theoretical challenge that the chador event poses to the "bounded culture" assumptions that inform the rationality debates epistemologically follows, as we shall see, from recognizing that national identities are malleable constructions generally open to dispute in reaction to shifting political and historical circumstances. The chador event shows how the present contesting, even if unintentional, of French national identity is brought to the fore by the symbolic play of permeable borders and boundaries – a play precipitated by postcolonial disporas – and how national identity is defended hegemonically by an invented national culture.

Permeable boundaries and contested identitied are typical as the above example illustrates, of what anthropologists encounter in field research virtually everywhere today. Permeable boundaries place in question the idea of a bounded "French culture" encountering a bounded "North African culture" as "other." The North African girl in question was born in France of parents who were immigrants. She spoke French like any other child and, apart from her dress on one particular day, there was nothing remarkable about her behavior at school that would lead one to single her out as a topic of national debate. If anything, she represented the increasing diversity and changing cultural landscape of French society. But she also represented a situation that provoked a sense of "bodily" insecurity – in this case manifested by the exclusion of "oriental" dress[6] – which was felt by those who were nostalgic for a reputedly more homogeneous and glorious French past.

In fact, as Eugen Weber (1976) has argued, the expansion of "French" national culture throughout the country is relatively recent, dating from the end of the First World War. According to Weber, prior to the First World War regions in France were distinct and French itself was only spoken in the countryside by the village clergy and local elites. For Weber, creating a national culture followed from improved transportation and travel, the institution of a uniform educational system, and military conscription to serve the nation in time of war – thus largely fulfilling Benedict Anderson's (1983) image of civic culture in the imagined community. However, even today France is, like most nation states, marked by diversity in regional dialects, histories, and even cuisines. Thus the "French" to which one appeals in opposition to the "difference" that the chador ostensibly represents to some is the exclusive civic or metropolitan culture of the bourgeoisie, which is often advanced as an icon for French culture in general.[7]

While the above example is not exhaustive, nor is it intended to be so, it does raise through broad parameters a typical circumstance with which many field researchers are presently faced. That is to say, there are no isolated cultures, since virtually everywhere societies of all sorts have been drawn into at the very least what Roger Keesing (1992) called regional systems and more often into economic and cultural exchange at the levels of the nation state and beyond. The pressing question here is how then did the "bounded" culture of an earlier period of ethnographic inquiry become the paradigm for field research more generally, and what implications does this have for the scope of the Anglo-American rationality debates and their primary theme of cross-cultural interpretation?

It is generally acknowledged that Malinowski was the first anthropologist to conduct intensive and long-term field research. Moreover, Malinowski's commitment to rigorous field research often under difficult and challenging circumstances has long set the standard for sociocultural anthropology. Contrary to many of his anthropological predecessors, Malinowski, in the early part of the twentieth century, spent considerable time among the indigenous populations of the Trobriands taking systematic and extensive field notes. As Eric Wolf (1999: 284) remarks, the fieldwork tradition of functionalist anthropology challenged the broad universalist evolutionary assumptions of a "primitive mentality" represented in the speculative writings of figures such as Sir James Frazer. Malinowski believed, furthermore, that mastery of the local language was key to gaining a comprehensive understanding of indigenous society in the social round. In fact, the limits of Malinowski's functionalism have often led scholars to overlook, myself included, his emphasis on and understanding of indigenous languages and the importance of language more generally to cross-cultural interpretation. However, the tradition of rigorous field search that Malinowski arguably initiated cannot be grasped in only methodological terms but requires rather a critical analysis within the overall context of the colonial era of which it was a part. That is, fieldwork as the method of cultural anthropology cannot be grasped as technique or in technical terms without falling subject to the positivist tautology of accounting for science in scientific terms. Rather, a cultural and historical perspective is required if we are to have any hope of understanding, in the sense of Foucault (1973), a disciplinary practice so fundamental to the identity of anthropology. (See also Gupta and Ferguson 1997.)

The tendency to romanticize the challenges of fieldwork persists in the image of the anthropologist living at the margins of "the familiar" while undertaking field research in distant or "exotic" places. Moreover, contrary to disciplines where collaborative work is the standard, social anthropologists generally conduct their research by themselves and make their professional reputations through single-authored ethnographies.[8] Given the image of the lone researcher it is then no surprise that the "bounded" culture became the unit of analysis conventionally studied by anthropologists. After all, it seems only reasonable to expect a lone scholar to master a circumscribed social terrain; anything more would likely be superficial. There is some truth to the belief that what one can address or manage to do in the field is limited, as anyone who has done field research would concur. Coming to understand the complex dynamics of any community, small or large, is a considerable undertaking, which, as Geertz (1973) asserts, never really gets to the bottom of things. In addition, most communities can be at some level typified by shared customs, beliefs, social practices, and even histories. However, while practical circumstances of working in far away or remote corners of the globe in combination with the cultural assumptions of the possessive individual – the bodily or natural assumptions of genius – may explain in part why researchers work alone, they do not necessarily provide good historical explanations of why the bounded culture has most typically prevailed as the unit of analysis.[9]

In a 1991 essay that sought to explain the marginality of the anthropology of Europe to field research conducted among indigenous populations of the Third World, I argued that there was a relation between the political objectives of European and North American nation states and the privileging of the non-western "other" as the predominant subject-object of anthropological research. The argument itself was by no means novel, since similar arguments had been advanced earlier in Dell Hymes's edited volume, *Reinventing Anthropology* (1969), and most specifically in Talal Asad's edited volume, *Anthropology and the Colonial Encounter* (1973). Taken collectively, these works sought to reconstruct critically the history of anthropology towards the end of forging a new anthropological praxis. I will leave aside for the moment the question of whether or not a new praxis has been forged and rather direct our attention to the often overlooked political issues that have historically shaped the practice of anthropology, and which I believe are significant to the theoretical positions assumed in the rationality debates.

It can be argued that the earliest anthropological accounts were written by explorers, traders, and missionaries who, like Captain Cook described by Sahlins (1985), traveled far and wide in pursuit of material resources and wealth that would in the long run contribute to the expansion and building of European empires. Although lacking the rigor of a Malinowski these early accounts were significant for what they revealed of both their European authors and the indigenous populations they encountered.[10] Apart from the "civilizing" intentions of early Europeans with respect to indigenous populations, which concealed the potential for commercial exploitation, the early contacts with indigenous populations were transparent in comparison to what would follow in the pursuit of ethnographic science. Even ethnographers such as S. F. Nadel (1942), who wrote a very good account of the Nupe kingdom of Nigeria, never disclosed that his anthropological research was in direct service to his other role as colonial administrator. In fact, the ethnographies of the period rarely addressed the context in which the research was conducted or the relationship of the ethnographer to the population being studied, outside of a few introductory remarks in the preface or introduction. The relation therefore between the formative period of field research and the intentions of European colonialism are obscure because of the potential of the former to be concealed in the ostensibly neutral cannon of science.

I want to make it clear, however, that the vast majority of field research conducted form the early twentieth century through the political end of the colonial era in the 1960s was not undertaken by anthropologists with the direct objective of subjugating and managing indigenous populations. On the contrary, anthropologists such as Evans-Pritchard, Leach, and Fortes, to name just a few, were sympathetic to the indigenous people they studied and their struggles to maintain cultural integrity amongst rapidly changing political and economic circumstances.[11] Nevertheless, the funding for field research originated from the colonial governments and the knowledge procured from the study of indigenous social and political orders was invaluable to the hegemonic administration of native peoples through the colonial office. Moreover, the theoretical paradigms of functionalism, structural functionalism, and structuralism that emerged to study indigenous populations, as I suggested at the outset of this chapter, were well attuned, albeit unknowingly, to the task of administering to these people and thus fitted better within the parameters of instrumental rationality discussed in this book. As we shall see, by eclipsing the central importance of the historical agent, which went hand in hand with a circumscribed and unchanging unit of analysis, the above theoretical paradigms constituted the "other" as an object rather than a subject of social life; they therefore are in accord with the cognitive interest of instrumental rationality in constructing the natural and social worlds as objects of technical control.

In an important essay on Europeanist anthropology that is relevant to our concerns here, John Cole (1977) argued, as I have above, that the colonial era was among other things the period in which anthropology became methodologically more rigorous. It became so by establishing long-term field work, participant observation, and cross-cultural comparison as trademarks of sociocultural anthropology. Likewise, Cole maintains that in spite of a comparative emphasis, field research conducted by anthropologists during the period of colonialism was essentially limited to single villages or societies studied in isolation. Anthropologists sought to describe their field sites in terms of the local ecology, the kinship system, including patterns of descent, alliance, and residence, and to render transparent economic, political, and religious systems.

Cole's argument regarding circumscribed field sites during the colonial era is given empirical support through Terence Ranger's (1983: 254) essay on invented tradition in colonial Africa. According to Ranger, the colonial office had an interest in limiting the customary fluid movement of individuals and ideas. Colonial officials were concerned that mobile populations could widen the African focus and thus increase the possibility of resistance to colonial rule. The invention of formalistic rituals and bounded small-scale societies was thus encouraged by the colonial office and then ironically reproduced by anthropologists as natural units of research and analysis.

The theoretical framework that was developed to study small-scale societies was structural functionalism. Cole concludes, as I have, that structural functionalism as the dominant theory of the colonial era articulated well with the study of indigenous societies as isolates. Structural functionalists, with few exceptions – most notably Leach – privileged synchronic over diachronic social relations. They created a static model of small-scale societies as resistant to change in that these societies were posited in Malinowski's sense as operating teleologically to meet the biological and psychological needs of their members. According to Cole (1977: 357), the emphasis in structural functionalism was not on individuals as agents in the making of their own social world but rather on institutions from which individuals derived rights and obligations.[12]

As Third World independence movements materialized, structural functionalism and its variants became suspect because they emphasized the atemporality of social systems and so were unable to account for social change except as introduced from outside the system. Consequently, argues Cole, anthropologists began to shift their framework away from static systems to the evaluation of factors that promote or retard change. While the emphasis on social change was a welcome theoretical advance, it did little to transform the image of the single village or society as the unit of analysis nor did it do much to challenge the essentially static view of small-scale societies represented by structural functionalism and the colonial view of the "other." Rather, the new emphasis on social change made use of the history of European modernization to explain Third World poverty and underdevelopment in technology, government, and social organization. Anthropologists employed a Eurocentric framework in attributing the blame for this underdevelopment to tradition or culture rather than the historical influence of the world system of political economy. By a "Eurocentric" framework, Cole has in mind theories such as Lewis's "culture of poverty," Banfield's "amoral familism," Horton's "open and closed societies" (see chapter 4) borrowed from Karl Popper, and Foster's "image of the limited good," to name just a few of the most influential. All of these frameworks imply, in one way or another, that if the Third World would remove the fetters of tradition and follow the European course of modernization, these presently impoverished nations would enjoy the prosperity and enlightened social organization of Europe and North America.

Cole has argued, in short, that the failure of anthropologists to engage seriously with the regional, interregional as well as international systems of political economy that have shaped profoundly the histories of virtually all societies has not only led to studies of small-scale societies as isolates but has also introduced into the discipline of anthropology reified notions of tradition and societal modernization. That is to say, the specific attributes of tradition that anthropologists have so often seen as continuous with the past and therefore as unchanging are themselves produced historically in response to political, economic, and social dynamics going beyond the purview of the local community and often the nation state. Moreover, modernization is, like tradition, particular even though it has been advanced as universal by anthropologists and other scholars. That modernization is often experienced in uniform ways throughout the world is the consequence not of necessity but the progressive ability of western capitalist societies to limit and shape the options of Third World development through political diplomacy, violence, and control of world markets and financial institutions. Although I will have more to say about resistance with respect to a discussion of globalization that follows, this is not to assert that Third World societies cannot through political, economic, and cultural resistance forge a future different from our own.

The relationship between colonialism and structural functionalism, inclusive of its analogs, as discussed by Cole is not causal nor is there an identity intended between Malinowski's functionalism, Radcliffe-Brown's structural functionalism, or for that matter the structuralism of Lévi-Strauss. Such an identity would surely be reductive and a causal relation would betray the very historical association that we are trying to establish here, one that must include, as noted, functionalism's challenge to late-nineteenth-century social evolution. However, one principal feature that the above theories share is an absence of historical agency. As I argued in chapter 2, although Malinowski has an emphasis on individuals not found in the very Durkheimian tradition that inspired functionalism, the individuals represented by Malinowski are ultimately driven by the biological and psychological necessities of adaptation. Under such circumstances culture becomes instrumental and the social order mechanical, the parts functionally interrelated to support the continuity of the whole. Contrary to Malinowski, Radcliffe-Brown envisioned the social order in terms of enduring pre-established institutional arrangements in the context of which individuals are substitutable. Individuals come and go but institutions essentially remain the same. With structuralism, we are directed away from the material interactions of human subjects to the underlying organizational principles and the "digital" logic of mind which the species shares in general. For all three distinct theories, individuals as part of collective life are mere conduits for the expression and realization of inborn needs, order, and logic.

I have argued throughout this book that the eclipsing of human agency in its plurality, especially historical agency, transforms what potentially could be the mutuality of communicative exchange into the more instrumental formulation of the human subject as "object" of ethnographic practice and science. This is one reason that I supported Winch's use of Wittgenstein's language games against the Neo-Popperians Jarvie and Horton and identified hermeneutics as a potential dialogical solution to some of the shortcomings of ordinary language philosophy. Functionalism, structural functionalism, and structuralism preclude a vision of social reality where subjects make choices that matter, struggle with one another over what is meaningful, and engage in the formation and reproduction of ever-changing possibilities of the shared life. To invoke a reflexive model, such options and choices involve recognizing the agency in others as part of a process of recognizing one's own agency. Like the theories with which it articulated, colonialism was a political, economic, and cultural ordering of the social world through violence, co-optation, imposed discipline, in Foucault's (1978) sense of disciplinary practices, and forced acquiescence that ultimately involved denying the "humanity," or more concretely stated, the subject in the object.

Denying a history to human subjects, such as we find with functionalism, structural functionalism, and structuralism, draws the narrative of human subjects closer to natural history (so it is no surprise to discover, with few recent exceptions, indigenous peoples and their artifacts represented in natural history museums) in that humans are throught to be moved ultimately by both internal and external ordering principles that are conterminous, if not convergent, with supposed laws of nature. This is regardless of the evident fact that early anthropological theorists in the structural functional traditions were suspicious of other than documented history. Nevertheless, to disregard that history is made and a "making" on the part of human subjects is to deny them a present and future of their own, or as Johannes Fabian (1983) has stated so well through the "denial of coevalness," to place them in a time ordering sequence other than our own, that is, as non-contemporaneous. Once human subjects become merely the objects of the anthropological "gaze" they are constituted in a manner not unlike the objects of natural science, that is, towards the end of, or at the very least amenable to, technical control. In this sense, the theories of functionalism, structural functionalism, and structuralism are no strangers to the technical or instrumental reason that informed the colonial process.

The disregard for human agency and for the making of history on the part of structural functionalism and its analogs of the colonial era contributed significantly to the ethnographic practice of "circumscribed cultures" and "circumscribed selves." Again, apart from the research limitations of the lone anthropologist on what can be practically managed, the disregard for history amounts to what Foucault would see as its total embracing by creating a system of classification that placed indigenous selves, in Fabian's sense, as outside history.[13] Ignoring history precludes the analysis of process that is necessary to grasp the interrelation of local cultures, regional systems, and nation states. That is, the limitation of functionalism, structural functionalism and structuralism was that in emphasizing the continuity of internal dynamics they largely ignored how what one encounters inside a community is profoundly related to the influence of the outside world. Moreover, by glossing over historical dynamics broadly conceived, ethnographers also discounted the very historical dynamics that informed their own research practice, thus the bounding of selves.

The above observation takes us back by a somewhat circuitous route to what was illustrated by the chador incident. The end of colonialism realized in many world areas by the end of the 1960s did not grant former colonies the type of independence that one might imagine or that is generally associated with colonialism's demise. While many former colonies gained their political independence as formally sovereign nations, they remained economically dependent on former colonial states such as Britain, France, and the United States and continued to live with a legacy forged by colonialism. In Africa, for example, postcolonial ethnic strife was often precipitated, and continues to be so, by the colonial partitioning of Africa by Britain, France, Germany, and Italy, through the Treaty of Berlin in 1895. To avoid potential conflict, European colonial states agreed to divide the African continent into exclusive areas of dominion. This went hand in hand with the European role in creating African states and territories that cut across ethnic and tribal boundaries, not to mention the creation of reservations to which the Azande of the rationality debates were subject. Moreover, the economic dependency of former colonial states continued, since Third World plans for development depended on loans from institutions such as the World Bank. These loans were generally contingent on following capitalist lines of development, which amounts to subordinating agriculture and the interests of rural populations to the building up of large-scale industry and a national infrastructure that privileges life in the city.

The economic restructuring of capitalist society after the Second World War and the growth of multinational corporations have enhanced, furthermore, the dependency of the Third World on capitalist nations and, as Arturo Escobar (1995) argues, has forged development policies as mechanisms of control. Third World nations are often regarded economically by centers of finance capital and multinational corporations as sources of raw materials, plantation agriculture, and cheap labor. This has deepened class divisions in the Third World, especially in rural areas, and for many peasants and indigenous populations it has threatened their livelihoods altogether. One consequence of this process has been a continuing migration of individuals from Third World peripheries to European and North American centers of finance capital. As immigrants from the Third World establish roots in North American and European societies they make claims and challenges to the national identities of their host countries as well as to those of their country of origin. This confounds what is often taken in simple terms to be self-evident national identity and renders antiquarian any notion of a "bounded" culture or "bounded" self.

It would be wrong to conclude that the above-described process of economic restructuring and the cultural diasporas produced by moving populations is new. Rather, the extent and contemporaneity of the situation only makes it more apparent, especially in the context of the nation state and nearly ubiquitous conflicts over national identity. However, in the early twentieth century, when the ideas that supported functionalism came to fruition, there was considerable exchange – economic and cultural – between the societies conventionally studied by anthropologists. I suggested, for example, in chapter 3 that the very Zande society that served as the focus for the Anglo-American rationality debates was itself forged from conquest and the bringing together of a number of formerly decentralized indigenous peoples. The continuous and ongoing exchange between indigenous populations of all types is also implicit in Morton Fried's (1975) challenge to essentialist notions of "tribe" in that the concept of the tribe often overlooked diversity to emphasize the homogeneity of cultural traits and cultural types, not to mention that tribal names were often created by the colonial office to identify a group of people subject to administration. Bounded cultures and bounded selves are thus the historical product of the ascendant proprietary rights of the individual, as argued by Heller and MacPherson, and the administrative logic of ethnographic science as it matured during the period of European and North American colonialism.

To return to the rationality debates, I asserted earlier in this chapter that the primary participants argued largely from an epistemological perspective. That is, they asked how a knowing subject can come to understand the "other" as object. The process of cultural diaspora and the claims that multi-ethnic populations advance on the agenda of national and transnational identities renders a strictly epistemological perspective ineffective in grasping the pressing issues of contemporary cultural theory in anthropology and other disciplines as well. Moreover, as Foucault (1973) has argued with respect to humanity more generally, and Gadamer (1975) similarly with respect to the primacy of the self through hermeneutics, the knowing subject is itself a product of historical discourses that undermine any claims to a foundational status. With subjects and objects in flux and epistemology rendered suspect, with what theoretical options are we left to pursue the shifting grounds of culture and identities? Surely one potential option is globalization, because of the commanding breadth of its theoretical and historical terrain.

Globalization and Fields of Power

Globalization is arguably the most widely used icon of the multifaceted processes that bring present-day societies of all sorts into sustained economic and cultural exchange. Globalization is employed rhetorically by environmentalists to cultivate a critical awareness of the fate we share as inhabitants of a planet with a threatened ecosystem, and by anthropologist Arjun Appadurai (1991) to refer to the potential of subaltern populations to imagine alternative lives as a consequence of their increasing exposure to the media. Globalization has been invoked in higher education to support diversified curriculums in expectation that students will live and work in a world where awareness of cultural difference is akin to civic responsibility. Moreover, even multinational firms such as IBM have employed the image of globalization to indicate that although there are many different cultures quite remote from one another geographically, we all share one culture when it comes to our dependency on technology and communications. The implication of this later reference is the universal applicability of science and technology to the building of a global awareness and a global culture. What is omitted is specific reference to capitalism and the economic restructuring of the globe in the last half of the twentieth century, which transformed industrial nations of the West and East into centers of finance capital. This transformation, which is ongoing, includes the mobility of multinational corporations and the cultivation of Third World nations by centers of finance capital as sources of cheap agricultural and manufacturing labor (see Jameson and Miyoshi 1998). In short, the multi-vocality of globalization appears to point both to the continuing expansion and hegemony of capitalism and to the potential for an articulated awareness of interconnections of the variety needed to transcend the limitations of "bounded culture." We shall see, however, that these seemingly opposed senses of globalization do have some common terrain, which leads us to reconsider its theoretical utility for grasping critically historically contingent interregional relations.

World systems theory remains for many anthropologists the dominant theoretical tradition that addresses the formation of capitalism on a global scale. It links theoretically reputedly distinct areas of the world and thus distinct cultures in terms of an inequality structured through an international political economy. However, in spite of this considerable merit, there is the tendency on the part of global analysis, as I suggested above, to participate in the very theoretical claims that one would expect it to criticize and supersede. I will therefore direct our attention to potential problems that global analysis shares with the very theories, such as functionalism and structural functionalism, with which it is implicitly at odds, while also acknowledging its considerable merits. To provide a concrete casting to the discussion which follows, I draw illustratively on the aforementioned ethnographic material that comes largely from my own field research on southwest French wine cooperatives.

Through my southwest French research I faced the daunting challenge of demystifying a tradition of French scholarship that tended to "naturalize" the privileged position of elite Bordeaux wines while relegating, in Derrida's (1974) sense, the account of wines produced by small growers to the margins of history. That is, tomes on French winegrowing history by Pijassou (1980) and Dion (1977), for example, tend to attribute the preeminent position of Bordeaux wines to favorable natural conditions and thus overlook social and historical factors that contributed to their ascendancy. Consequently, one has to look obliquely to what is concealed in these influential texts rather than the principal narratives themselves to discover the history of subaltern winegrowers, a methodological insight that suggests the rhetorical nature of writing history. That historical texts conceal as much as they reveal is by no means unique; Marx recognized early on the tendency of capitalism to mask social relations through the "fetishism of commodities," a theoretical insight that when pursued opens the study of commodities, as Sidney Mintz (1985) has noted, to the anthropology of modern life. Once we analyze critically the contemporary fascination with commodities we uncover different historical processes of power and domination through which social labor is appropriated (Wolf 1999). The narratives of the producers and the processes of domination and resistance occupy much of the terrain of differentiation covered by contemporary anthropology and present-day life.

Global or interregional analysis provided the theoretical insights needed to reconstruct an alternative historical narrative of southwest French wines to what was traditionally presented in numerous French tomes and reproduced likewise through popular wine guides. In my *Vintages and Traditions* (1996: 46), I demonstrate that the reputed superiority of elite Bordeaux wines over those produced in the interior, most noteworthily in Périgord, Agen, Toulouse, and Quercy, was not, as claimed, based upon favorable climate and soil, but instead unique historical circumstances that arose as a consequence of the English occupation of southwest France from the twelfth to the fifteenth centuries. In fact, prior to the English occupation, interior wines enjoyed a higher reputation than those produced in the vicinity of Bordeaux. These wines, like those of Bordeaux, were shipped to northern Europe, especially England, through the lively coastal port of La Rochelle, which enjoyed a significant wine culture. However, La Rochelle fell to the

French king, Louis VIII, in 1224, and he closed the port to English merchants. The English were thus forced to search for an alternative through
which they could ship wine to northern Europe. The importance of this
wine commerce to the English crown is not to be underestimated, since even
English warships of the time measured their size in the amount of wine they
could transport, or in *tonneaux*, a *tonneau* being 900 liters of wine.
Bordeaux to the south became the likely candidate to replace La Rochelle
because its location on the Gironde River gave merchants access to the
Atlantic Ocean.

   Bordeaux's transformation into the principal port for southwest France
had significant consequences for surrounding areas such as the Médoc,
arguably the most renowned of the Bordeaux winegrowing regions. In the
early part of the twelfth century, the Médoc was polycultural and much of
the land was covered with forests. As wine commerce through Bordeaux
began to mature in the second half of the thirteenth century, entrepreneurial
growers began to clear the forests to plant vineyards. However, the most
significant contribution to the reputation of Bordeaux wines followed from
concessions that the Bordeaux councillors received from the English crown
in exchange for acquiescing to English rule. The crown granted special
privileges to wine produced in the immediate vicinity of Bordeaux, which
gave Bordeaux growers and merchants considerable advantages over wines
produced in the southwest French interior. For example, Bordeaux wines
were exempt from the taxes levied on the wines of the interior. Moreover,
protective legislation designed to support Bordeaux growers prevented
interior wines from entering the city of Bordeaux before November 11.
Thus the superior reputation of Bordeaux wines owes, at least initially,
more to the English hegemony and the city's economic history than to any
special claim for climate and soil.

   While the above example is unrelated to the conventional "village" study,
it does show that a privileging of the local, in this case climate and soil, can
be demystified through interregional historical analysis. In fact, as I have
shown elsewhere (Ulin 1996), the hierarchical relationship of French winegrowing regions today and the particular circumstances of wine cooperatives are dependent upon and thus intelligible through their articulation
with a global political economy. That is, what one discovers on the local
level in terms of social relations and winegrowing culture reflects the very
historical circumstances of interregional exchange that begins with the
English occupation and arguably even earlier. How else can one explain
wines of distinction which have come metonymically to stand for the
Médoc and perhaps French culture in general in contrast to wines of the
interior that with few exceptions have long abandoned any claim to distinction and in some cases pride themselves on their generic reputations.[14]
Stated simply, and I am by no means alone in this claim, local culture is,

contrary to Geertz's (1983) formulation, marked and interpenetrated by associations with a world system of political economy and the political economy of the sign. This is surely what John Cole (1977) means in saying that there is little that is traditional in tradition, since all tradition is a product of political economic forces of global importance. I would add that tradition is likewise a product of cultural forces, an argument – as I maintain in the conclusion of this chapter-that cuts sharply against the possibility of "bounded cultures" being grounded in autonomous language games or, for that matter, being universally driven rationalities of local adaptation.

Although I have established the importance of a world systems or global perspective to the local terrain often inhabited by anthropological research, like all terrain, the grounds are frequently shifting and so this is the case with world systems and global theories. Some of the most significant critiques of this perspective have come from the very scholars, such as Eric Wolf (1982) and Sidney Mintz (1985, 1987), who clearly have theoretical positions of their own which are sympathetic to the very influential world systems theory of Immanuel Wallerstein (1974). Whether we are fully in accord with Wallerstein's argument for the role of merchant capital in the formation of an economic system that advanced wage labor as dominant is another question. Mintz's *Sweetness and Power* (1985) established the dialectical connections between Africa, the Caribbean and Europe while Wolf's *Europe and the People without History* (1982) clearly showed that there can be no European history without considering the peoples in the margins through whose exploitation European empires were constructed. Nevertheless, both Mintz and Wolf have argued that world systems theory eclipses the local dynamics that enable us to understand resistance and the mediums through which people on the local level struggle to forge their own destinies. To invoke a nearly forgotten figure of the Marxist tradition, that is, Louis Althusser (1970), there is a sort of "overdetermination" of the local on the part of the world systems theorists. This does not mean that Mintz and Wolf believe that we should atavistically resort to a local or circumscribed unit of analysis. Rather they are indicating that critical research in anthropology must examine how the global is present in the local and the local in the global.

An example that resonates theoretically with critical research in anthropology is Taussig's discussion of recently proletarianized workers in Bolivian tin mines in his *Devil and Commodity Fetishism in South America* (1980). Taussig shows that those who worked in the tin mines had few other work-related options and little control over their destinies. However, their strongest cultural resource was an ethos that stigmatized individuals for the very sort of characteristics that Max Weber (1958) thought to be so significant to the Protestant ethic and the culture of capitalism. That is, those individuals who were perceived by their peers as making more money and getting ahead, acting out of self-interest, were thought to have made a pact with the devil, a pact that could be taken as a symbol of resistance. Taussig's example is not idiosyncratic but resonates with my own experiences of cooperative growers struggling against, and sometimes borrowing from, the cultural capital of elite growers and the forces of multinational corporations.

World systems theory and global analysis, for all their considerable merits, have the tendency to overdetermine the local and thus eclipse human agency as constitutive. That is, without some appreciation of formative activity on the local level, human agents risk becoming simply a conduit for the realization of the global system. Politically speaking, this places human agents, whether willing or not in accordance with the broader economic objectives of global capitalism and on the practical level presents them as mere victims of capitalist hegemony and economic dominion. I believe that eclipsing human agency is not unique to world systems theory but rather is intrinsic to all systems theory and its predecessors in structural and functional analysis. Structural analysis borrows significantly, as does systems theory in general, from formal linguistics, emphasizing the interrelationship of component units within a self-contained and finite system. Units in themselves have no value but in relation to other units; the scenario is by now familiar. While systems theoretical and structural approaches are a strong corrective to Jarvie's methodological individualism (see chapter 4), they overlook praxis in a manner analogous to formal linguistics. Praxis incorporates the concrete activity through which human subjects engage each other in the collective formation of the social world. Contrary to systems and structural theory, the praxis position accounts for the capacity of human subjects, albeit not always consciously, freely, or deliberately, to shape their own destinies, and thus opens the analysis of the social world to historical processes, the constancy of change. In fact, it is generally argued that social change and history are made superfluous by structural theories, in the case of Lévi-Strauss's structuralism epiphenomenal to the universality or singular logic of mind.

To counter the charge that structural analysis is ahistorical and indifferent to human agency, Marshall Sahlins (1985) has suggested that culture as structured prefigures human experience. This is how we come to understand the Hawaiians' identification of Captain Cook as the god Lono rather than a wayward mariner, when he arrived at the beginning of their annual ritual cycle devoted to Lono. Sahlins believes that the prefiguration of human experience is not absolute, otherwise we would never be able to account for anything new. On the contrary, he argues that experience has the potential to transform the cultural code. What Sahlins argues is not remote from Winch's reconceptualization of Wittgenstein's language games and

Gadamer's assertion that "language speaks us." All three cases are strong arguments against knowledge commencing from a *tabula rasa* or sense sensations à la Hume in that they place a primary emphasis, albeit differently formulated, on the way collective life, through language, determines individual experience. Nevertheless, I believe that in spite of the intelligence Sahlins has applied to resolving the perennial problems of structural, and by extension system's analysis, that he too falls subject to a formalism that equates culture with a univocal code. Thus Sahlins presents culture, as Bill Roseberry (1989) has argued, as something *enacted* rather than *acted*, a consequence that places human subjects outside of the process of history-making. Sahlins's view of culture is thus complicitous with the very theories and historical process of globalization of which it is meant to be a critique.

It can be legitimately objected that Wallerstein's world systems theory and global analysis more generally, both of which are informed largely by structural and systems theoretical perspectives, do not participate in the erasing of history. After all, how can one raise questions concerning the formation of capitalism or the interrelation between core, semi-periphery and periphery without invoking historical analysis and process at some level? However, there is more to historical analysis than the self-evident contention that things change. Without the potential to point to the choices with which human actors are faced and how they go about making choices that are interwoven and textured by history, we arrive at social and historical narratives, as Taussig (1987) has argued, that seem to tell themselves. Stories that tell themselves contribute, as I mentioned previously, to what Johannes Fabian (1983) calls the "denial of coevalness" and thus align world systems theory with the very historical negation associated with structuralism and Europe's colonial legacy. The subject of anthropological research is placed out of the time framework of the anthropologist, an epistemological move with political consequences. Moreover, unless attentive to the particulars of a constitutive human agency, it is all too easy to represent culture as epiphenomenal, as is the case of some variants of structural and systems analysis, or to incorporate culture but in a fashion that ignores significant distinctions and disputed areas. That is, we have a clear picture from Immanuel Wallerstein, and his theoretical predecessor Andre Gunder Frank (1969), of societies as class-stratified and of how elites profit at the expense of subordinates. However, the metaphorical geometry or mechanics of the system that postulates core, semi-periphery, and periphery risks essentializing local culture as non-differentiated, in contrast to the relational positions in the global economy of which it is a determined part.

Let me re-emphasize that the above criticism is not a dismissal of global analysis, a position that would be indefensible in light of my own use of interregional economic connections as essential to grasping the formation of the southwest French winegrowing hierarchy and the past struggles and contemporary plight of wine cooperatives. Let me suggest rather that ethnographic inquiry must proceed from recognizing how the region and beyond is present in the local and how the local can in turn be, as for example Mintz illustrated with respect to sugar, in a transcending field of action. Since I have presented the argument in detail elsewhere (Ulin 1996), I will for economy's sake summarize the salient illustrative details here. I argue that the formation of the southwest French winegrowing hierarchy arose not only from economic initiatives that linked southwest France to Northern Europe and more distantly America and Russia, but also to an invented sense of tradition that established in the nineteenth century symbolic and cultural ties between a nascent bourgeoisie and a reputedly superseded nobility. Bourgeois owners of Médoc estates built their homes as small-scale replicas of the celebrated medieval French châteaux in order to distinguish themselves and their wines culturally from the peasant masses. These same elite proprietors were involved, along with the winegrowing associations over which they often presided, in the creation of the 1855 classification of Bordeaux wines, initiated at the invitation of the Universal Exposition held in Paris in the spring of 1855. Thus the ranking of wines from first to fifth growths as illustrative of a culturally distinct group of proprietors contributed commensuratively to the distinctiveness of French national culture. Small growers in the Médoc to this day have tried to appropriate the considerable cultural capital and commercial advantage of the elite estates of this region. Because the grapes brought to the wine cooperative come from the multiplicity of members' properties throughout a delimited region, in comparison to the more consolidated properties of the elite growers, these selfsame small proprietors have sought to negotiate a narrative of winegrowing history that presents their wines as the "authentic" ones of the region.

The example of the southwest French winegrowing hierarchy points to three important theoretical issues that can go a long way towards improving the theoretical and practical importance of global and interregional analysis, without the risk of reproducing the nefarious implications of globalization more generally. First, contrary to the economic teleology, or in terms of the rationality debates, instrumental rationality, of global analysis, it is important to recognize the relative autonomy of culture from political economy as well as their historical interdependency and interpenetration in certain circumstances. Elite growers, as did small proprietors, worked within the context of international political economy in building a cultural and symbolic construction that was *distinctive*.[15] Second, contrary to systems and structural analysis, local culture is never reducible to a code to be enacted but rather must be recast to account for the plurality of voices that are woven into the social fabric, sometimes at the center and sometimes at the periphery. As Lila Abu-Lughod (1991) has argued, culture employed to distinguish between self and other, the homogeneity of codes and shared practices, overlooks the intrinsic hierarchy of the culture concept. The claims to the "authenticity" of wine are illustrative of the contested discourse that contributes to the plurality of winegrowing culture. Finally, it is important to recognize concrete human actors who struggle individually and collectively over the terms of their own existence. These actors must be recognized as operating in fields of power that position human agents differentially in constructing the social world, an insight that forces us to pay attention to the competing narratives and social practices of history. With these three correctives in mind – the relative autonomy of culture, the importance of human agency, and the recognition of differentiated fields of power in which and through which individuals and collectivities forge their social existence – it is evident that global analysis continues to have importance to a critical understanding of both past and contemporary human affairs.

Multi-sited Analysis

The above qualifications of global and world systems analyses take us full circle to the issue of bounded cultures and bounded selves. It should now be apparent that bounded cultures and bounded selves are not only theoretical and methodologically produced but also have a significant tie to the formative period of anthropology and especially its colonial legacy. While a global approach surely seems to overcome many of the limitations of a bounded study in seeking to link local-level social processes to those of the region, nation state, and beyond, the integrity of the lone researcher and the epistemological assumptions that support solitary ethnographic research remain unexamined and therefore unchallenged. What then can a multi-sited analysis offer that is not taken up in global or world systems approaches?

George Marcus has perhaps been foremost in advancing the theme of multi-sited analysis in a collection of essays entitled *Ethnography through Thick and Thin* (1998), the title being an apparent play on Clifford Geertz's notion of thick description.[16] However, Marcus has something quite different in mind with thick description than Geertz's formulation as the elaboration of local meanings. In fact, Geertz is an interesting point of contrast, even with respect to the impact of globalization on local cultures, in that he does not believe that the dissemination of new technologies and communication systems is resulting in a growing uniformity of cultural practices worldwide. This belief seems to be supported ethnographically by Susan Rogers (1991), who demonstrates how the penetration of capital among an

Aveyronnais community has reinforced rather than challenged the reproduction of an extended or stem family, in contrast to the assumption that
capitalism or "modernization" promotes the universalization of the nuclear
family. Rather, Geertz believes that universal processes are refashioned to
meet local intentions and local contexts. Nevertheless, neither Geertz's more
general assertion nor Rogers's concrete ethnographic example raise the type
of theoretical and methodological concerns that are at the heart of Marcus's
appeal to multi-sited analysis; in fact, both Geertz and Rogers embrace the
concern for local-level analysis and the methodological assumptions of
"boundedness" that have traditionally informed field research in sociocultural anthropology.

There are a number of provocative ideas that Marcus has in mind with
multi-sited field research that challenge the assumptions of both bounded
cultures and bounded selves and which, with the exception of his emphasis
on small narratives,[17] transcend some of the limitations of postmodernism
discussed in the previous chapter. According to Marcus:

> Thinking in terms of multi-sited research provokes an entirely different set of
> problems that not only go to the heart of adapting ethnography as practices of
> fieldwork and writing to new conditions of work, but challenge orientations
> that underlie this entire research process that has been so emblematic for
> anthropology. This thinking arises from the very practical need that anthro-
> pologists confront all the time these days to resignify habits of thought about
> fieldwork and adapt their emblematic method to objects of study that are not
> simply "peoples" in topical arenas that do not readily define themselves in
> terms of sites available for sustained participant observation. For me, it has
> been the multi-sited character of the challenges – the need in any project to
> keep in view and mind two or more ethnographically conceived sites juxta-
> posed – that has made the difference, that has raised new provocation beyond
> the trenchant critiques of anthropological practice of the 1980s, which none-
> theless occurred within a sustained *mise-en-scène* of traditional research im-
> aginary. (1998: 3–4)

An important issue raised here, one that opens the possibility of constructing research subjects as active – what I refer to earlier in this book as co-
subjects – rather than simply as objects of knowledge, is Marcus's assertion
that field research can arbitrarily circumscribe a community in a manner
that is not commensurate with how research subjects define and signify
themselves. The long-dominant and continuing tradition of the cultural area
in anthropology, the mapping of contiguous cultural traits, and their dissemination from cultural centers, and compilations based on such methodological assumptions such as Murdock's *Human Relations Area Files*,
make a case in point. So also is the aforementioned tendency of the African
colonial office to bestow names on populations for administrative purposes

rather than seek to identify how populations define themselves (Asad 1973). The mapping of cultural areas, and the concept of cultural area itself, tend to create a pseudo-identity between geography and culture, thus impeding the pursuit of diasporas that dominates thematically today. Moreover, this tradition is reproduced in the writing of ethnographies in that most ethnographers signify those they write about, and apart from working with informants rarely collaborate with others in the writing of the ethnography itself.

We do not know precisely how classic and contemporary ethnography would change if in fact informants had an opportunity to shape how they are represented, as well as participating in the writing of the ethnography itself. The atypical ethnographies, in which informants do speak for themselves, such as Griaule's *Conversations with Ogotemmeli* (1965), Andrew Strathern's translated *Ongka: A Self-account of a New Guinea Big-man* (1979), or Kevin Dwyer's *Moroccan Dialogues: Anthropology in Question* (1982), are well known. All three of these ethnographies, especially Strathern's, have a manifestly different rhetorical intention from the average ethnographic account, in that by foregrounding informants' views they ostensibly bring us closer to the "lived experience" of the "other." Surely, Winch's use of Wittgenstein's language games comes to mind as Winch argued that ethnographers must extend their uses of language to incorporate that of informants. Addressing the challenge of who represents whom is clearly a hermeneutic undertaking and potentially offers to place ethnographer and informants discursively as co-subjects.

The above terrain has nearly become pedestrian in cultural anthropology, since virtually every ethnographer today makes some effort – one could argue in part as a consequence of the influence of Clifford and Marcus's *Writing Culture* – to foreground informants' voices even if they fall considerably short of the ideal of collaboration. However, it is Marcus's specific reference to juxtaposition of field sites that demands further elaboration in light of its potential to build upon and thus transform the limits of global or world systems analysis. What kind of critical tension between sites does he have in mind beyond the self-evident working in more than one world area? We have a partial answer to this question through Marcus's (1998: 44–5) critique of Paul Willis' *Learning to Labor*. Marcus commends Willis for illustrating how global capitalism can make itself felt on the local level through the accommodation and resistance of working class lads to schooling. Marcus (1998: 53) maintains that the juxtaposition of sites enables the ethnographer to focus on "emergent discourses," or oppositional practices, and not just ones which are dominant. However, Marcus believes that Willis's ethnography would have been significantly more complex if juxtaposed with the shop floor, bars, or even street culture. Juxtaposition can occur even within a relatively circumscribed field arena. However, juxtaposition can be cast in wider terms as well. Again, because of its familiarity,

I will appeal to my own research as illustrative of one type of juxtaposition that I believe Marcus has in mind.

My original formulation of a field project on southwest French wine cooperatives was largely conventional in that I identified an area in southwest France – the Dordogne – that would be the locus of my research with the usual time commitment that has become typical of field research. I selected a village near Bergerac where one cooperative was located and was also in proximity to a second, where I thought it important to pursue research in order to preclude idiosyncratic examples and interpretations. My planned research was somewhat distinctive in that an institution rather than a village or community was the topic, although the members of the cooperative are concretely located in geographical space of consequence. Because there was a focus on the institution as well as the growers I pursued links of both sorts. Like most field researchers, my introductions both inside and outside of the cooperative were made through my winegrowing informants. However, I was also interested in the cooperative's administration, and so made contacts with professional directors and through them to institutions, mostly of the marketing variety, beyond. This is surely one sense of multi-sited to which Marcus refers: I sought to incorporate a wide range of voices both inside and outside the cooperatives, voices that were on occasion in accord but often had objectives that were at odds. The village was my home site but the multifarious connections led me widely throughout the south of France and on occasion to Paris. The challenge that I faced, again like most ethnographers, was to mediate discordant voices – a task that is sometimes passed over in favor of conveying the "culture of a given peoples."

The field research that I conducted in the Dordogne on wine cooperatives largely sought to give a voice to small-scale growers whom I discovered to be rather marginal to the historical accounts written about wines, winegrowing, and the wine trade. Most of these accounts (see Ulin 1987) tended to celebrate the famous estates and their proprietors as icons of French national culture. Generally, a work of 600 or more pages devoted one or two pages to cooperatives, mostly to indicate that cooperatives had facilitated the quality of wine produced by small growers. However, little was said about their quotidian existence. I fell prey to what has become an occupational hazard in cultural anthropology by focusing on small growers to the exclusion of the elite wines, a serious but fortunately correctable mistake. In other words, I initially tended to disregard the juxtaposition of discourses between elite growers and those producing wines that drew little attention beyond a very local area of consumption.

As noted, I decided to return to France in the late 1980s to research cooperatives in the elite winegrowing region of the Médoc, north of the city of Bordeaux. The intention of the second phase of research was to pursue what I had earlier ignored, to learn more about the critical tension between elite and so-called ordinary wines, a tension that can be experienced within the Médoc region as well, owing to the proximity of elite estates to those owned by cooperative growers. The decision to study wines in an elite region proved to be crucial because it enabled me to understand historically how wine came to be regarded as a "natural" product and an icon of French elite culture, thus how the social processes were concealed by which the French winegrowing hierarchy was forged and reproduced. The juxtaposition of field sites, in the sense proposed by Marcus, thus enabled me to comprehend the symbolics of power and the different fields of power in which French winegrowers operated.

With the juxtaposition of field sites one can be sensitive to local dynamics that are often overlooked in global analysis, and escape the limitations inherent in traditional research in bounded cultures – though these limitations may be due only to practical considerations. As Marcus notes, often the most interesting questions to be researched by ethnographers take them beyond a single domain, both in terms of populations and geographical/cultural area, and thus can lead to collaboration with a diverse group of informants. All of this makes a lot of sense especially in light of the historical, political, and economic circumstances that have long shattered the feasibility of studying locally circumscribed cultures and have thus provoked anthropologists to look carefully at cultural diasporas such as that noted earlier in this chapter.

In spite of considerable merits, there are a number of important issues which are not taken up in Marcus's provisional formulation of multi-sited fieldwork. It seems clear to me that the collaboration that Marcus suggests in fieldwork is still between an anthropologist and his or her informants, even if the informants are located in a number of different sites. This leaves the structure of the bounded self intact as it does not promote collaborative work between anthropologists. In fact, I have come to believe increasingly that the method by which we confer degrees in anthropology – all of which celebrates the individualization of intellect – and thus establish a model for future research, is antiquated. Even when exploring local or circumscribed sites field researchers often have limited access to the larger population because of a number of factors, especially gender. A more feasible way of conducting research, which admittedly complicates the first fieldwork of the doctorate, is to work in teams both at local sites and between sites where there is some critical degree of tension. Although conducted at the mature stage of a career, Gudeman and Rivera's (1990) joint field research in Columbia is representative of such collaboration across sites. I have no doubt that my work would have been enriched locally by collaborating with a female anthropologist able to work with greater ease with female informants, especially older female informants, and with colleagues working on the numerous sites characteristic of the geographically extensive commerce in wine.

There is also the ubiquitous issue of power, which is not resolved through Marcus's vision of multi-sited research, although this fault, as we shall see, is not his alone. Whether anthropologists establish their research terrain in terms of circumscribed populations or ones that are diasporic, there is a common epistemological issue; there is also a political one, that of defining the research "object/subject" and the terms through which representation in general is negotiated. As noted in the previous chapter, this is likewise a problem with the postmodern foregrounding of informants' voices, in that foregrounding can give the illusory, albeit compelling, impression that informants speak for themselves.[18] Nevertheless, critical ethnographic research must be directed to power embedded in local sites, the juxtaposition of local sites and their articulation with a global system, and to power which ensues from a mode of scholarship where the "other," even co-subject "other," is generally the represented rather than the representer.[19] The epistemological and political issues that are generated by juxtaposed field sites, as I have noted, raise questions that were never addressed in the original rationality debates. I will therefore conclude with a brief reconsideration of the rationality debates in light of current critiques represented above of bounded cultures and bounded selves.

Reconsidered Rationality

The emphasis on diasporas throughout this chapter does not mean that this is the only issue that concerns cultural anthropologists, although its importance to questions of nationalism and identity more broadly should be apparent. However, diasporas present and past do render suspect the way the discipline embraces, theoretically and methodologically, "bounded cultures" and "bounded selves" as central to its historically created identity and distinctiveness. On the other hand, globalization is not, as we have seen, a facile panacea to the limitations of the conventional culture concept, since globalization has come to mean everything from how the local articulates with the region, national state, and beyond, to a belief in the merits of universalizing capitalist economies, cultures, and reputedly democratic institutions. While not unproblematic itself, multi-sited analysis seeks to focus our attention on juxtaposed sites, local and global, and the importance of human agents in the making and reproduction of the social world.

The above identified issues surely were not paramount when the original rationality debates of Winch, Jarvie, Horton, and others were commanding our attention throughout the 1960s and 1970s in particular. Rather, as we recall from chapter 3, Winch was interested in exploring independent life-worlds and constituted meaning in the face of a potentially dismissive instrumental logic, one that was predominant in the natural sciences and advocated by some scholars as paradigmatic of understanding social life more generally. For Winch, it was the task of the anthropologist to grasp indigenous beliefs and social practices through extending western uses of language to incorporate those employed collectively by informants. There is, as I argued originally and believe presently, much merit to Winch's employment of Wittgenstein's theory of language games and forms of life; the theory of language games preserves an image of the human condition as diverse and moreover emphasizes human subjects as active in the construction of their social world. As Renato Rosaldo has argued in his *Culture and Truth* (1989), the potential for treating indigenous informants as equals or co-subjects resides in part through recognizing that human subjects are not simply moved by forces beyond their control – economic, historical, unconscious, biological, or otherwise – but are actively engaged in what it means to be human in particular.[20] Consequently, from Winch's point of view, anthropologists must be open to ways of thinking and being that may be incommensurate with their own.

As I suggested in my review of Winch's work, reconstructing or ultimately translating informants' language games and forms of life does not mandate that the ethnographer and informants agree on their significance or general import. There are few, if any, ethnographers who would be willing to abandon the drawing of conclusions that may differ from those of informants. However, Winch maintains, through invoking the example of psychotherapy – psychotherapy and field research sharing an emphasis on knowing through discourse – that the anthropologist and informants must at the very least have some mutual understanding of what the informants are up to. One could object that knowing or agreeing to what we know on the local level is less problematic than the altogether different challenge of knowing how global processes interrelate with those which are local, thus presupposing that informants do not have a very good grasp of global processes. Such a conclusion, however, would overlook how informants on the local level symbolize, appropriate, transform, and resist global processes, all of which is of paramount interest to anthropologists and requires in Winch's sense the capacity to extend our categories and to be open to new ways of thinking and being. That Bolivian tin miners symbolize capitalist social relations in terms of the "devil" is important to both understanding local level social relations and capitalism itself (Taussig 1980). The examples in the anthropological literature are extensive and far-reaching.

Although I have once again come to Winch's defense, I still maintain that his account of language games and forms of life is essentially contemplative. Winch's ultimate objective is to review language games and forms of life, and therefore he does not address the constraints and controls which real positioned actors, sometimes with opposing interests, exert on each other through language games and forms of life. The notion of cultural diaspora and cultural borders, of those living in contiguous cultural areas, makes this limitation apparent because diasporas and borders are often, as the chador incident discussed earlier illustrates, the very grounds for dispute over national identities for individuals and groups with unequal social capital in the hegemonic sense developed by Bourdieu (1984). In a manner analogous to Geertz's semiotic formulation of culture,[21] Winch presupposes a homogeneous language community and therefore does not take on the struggle for mutual recognition that is, as Jürgen Habermas (1984) has shown, central to the formation of language games and discourse as social practice. To accommodate a nuanced and differentiated conceptualization of culture, Winch's vision of language games would have to move beyond the anthropologist's and informant's incommensurable social meanings, or in phenomenological terms "life-worlds," to a focus on the very communicative social action and social actors to which he argues that the theory of language games and forms of life is indispensable.

Winch has, in short, much to offer anthropology and interpretation theory more generally through recognizing that human logic and more importantly the identity and meaning of social action are particular, what Clifford Geertz (1983) refers to as the essential components of "local knowledge." Contrary to some implications of globalization, especially the belief in the inevitable universalization of capitalist institutions and social relations, local cultures have the capacity to preserve their distinctiveness and to continue to contribute, as they have in the past, to a reflexive understanding of western ways of thinking and being and the diversity of the human condition. However, as I noted earlier, there is something problematic in Winch's epistemological assumption that "knower and known" constitute independent and perhaps incommensurable life-worlds, because this assumption is based on the specious principle of "bounded culture." The challenge to Winch is to rethink the theory of language games to accommodate the shifting but unequal grounds on which culture is constantly negotiated.

With respect to the rationality debates in particular, Winch is not alone in presupposing that the anthropologist and informants stand as independent epistemological entities, even though, as I argued in chapters 4 and 5, the views of Jarvie, Horton, Lukes, and MacIntyre are generally critical of Winch. As we may recall, Jarvie and Horton appeal to the general foundation of natural science in supporting a concept of causality and a context-independent notion of rationality. However, the underlying assumption beyond the mechanics of their epistemology, especially Jarvie's emphasis on causality – human agents being moved by forces they do not comprehend – is that a bounded anthropologist representing western culture tries to come to terms with bounded informants representing a wholly distinct culture. While Winch preserves the independence and intentionality of indigenous cultures, Jarvie and Horton ultimately translate difference into similitude, the common logic that underlies difference.

Again as we may recall, Lukes takes a Durkheimian perspective to critique Jarvie's concept of methodological individualism. The critique is cogent because it shows the historical and thus relative character of the assumed "bounded self" and places an emphasis on the institutional and public nature of social life. Lukes is also critical of Winch in that he maintains that not all criteria of truth and rationality are context-dependent, for to assume so is to preclude the possibility of mutual understanding between anthropologist and informants. Nevertheless, Lukes, like Winch and the Durkheimian tradition he follows, assumes that culture is homogeneous, and contrary to Winch's emphasis on the intentional, Lukes views culture as a social fact. Therefore, from Lukes's perspective, it is not possible to pursue how culture is negotiated on the local level or the global issues that go hand in hand with cultural diasporas.

As noted earlier in this book, MacIntyre's position is more subtle than that of Jarvie, Horton, and Lukes and thus his critique of Winch is more refined in that, like Winch, MacIntyre supports the idea that criteria of truth and rationality have a history. In arguing this, MacIntyre establishes a social arena in which human subjects are active and thus there is considerably more potential for tracking the mediations of culture on the local and global levels. Regrettably though, MacIntyre invokes an evolutionary framework in his concept of history and by extension resorts to an objectivist sense of meaning in historical reconstruction. Like Winch, Jarvie, Horton, and Lukes, MacIntyre makes his fundamental question and pursuit of inquiry that of how we come to know, the classic epistemological formulation that does not take us very far in understanding the history of modes of knowing or the social conditions through which human actors pursue their own options in life.

The hermeneutic perspective, on the other hand, especially through Gadamer, presents us with a significantly different formulation of the rationality question in that the emphasis here is ontological rather than specifically epistemological. That is, for Gadamer, and likewise for Ricoeur even though his theoretical contribution is deliberately methodological, the primary concern following Heidegger is to grasp the general conditions of understanding from the perspective of "being." Admittedly, the concept of being is abstract in relation to the largely empirical pursuits of the social sciences. However, not unlike Foucault who takes his philosophical cues from Nietzsche rather than Heidegger, Gadamer does not assume the singular ego, reflective or otherwise, as foundational but rather views humanity individually and collectively as a product of discourse. According to

Gadamer, it is not so much that "we speak a language as language speaks us" (1975: 421). His emphasis on an ontology of language places human experience and human action within the collective communicative determinations of the past, which establish the possibilities for the present and future. While the self-reflective ego of epistemology is replaced by the determinations of language embodied in historical speech communities, the sense of discourse proposed by Gadamer appears to be non-differentiated and thus would not be able to account for the struggles over identity that take place within and between speech communities. The emphasis on the determinations of communicatively embodied and mediated collective experience is refreshing in light of the dominant theme of the bounded self but falters when it comes to the politics of cultural differentiation.

As I argued in chapter 6, Ricoeur's version of hermeneutics is distinguished from Gadamer's by virtue of his emphasis on a methodology critically appropriated from the structuralist tradition. Ricoeur's hermeneutic method was especially influential in anthropology throughout the 1980s for the analogy that it drew between the interpretation of texts and human action, an analogy that was designed to foreground the multivocality of symbolic action, the sedimentation of meaning, and the historical character of interpretation itself. Of special importance to Winch's argument is Ricoeur's claim that we must distinguish between intentions, which may be deliberate and individual, and meanings which are collective and often opaque, hence the need for a method of interpretation. However, like Gadamer and Winch, Ricoeur does not connect multi-vocal meanings to a potentially differentiated public. Thus Ricoeur's method falls short of the critical intentions which he claims to advance.

To transcend the limitations of "bounded cultures" and "bounded selves" as represented in much of conventional anthropology and the Anglo-American rationality debates, it is necessary to employ a theoretical and methodological framework that accounts for fields of social action whereby social actors are recognized as differentiated and where the issues of power are made apparent. This is surely not an easy task and likely to be one that is partial on the individual level and requires an ongoing conversation on the collective level. That is, whether we employ Marxist, neo-Marxist, Geertzian interpretive perspectives, or a remade structuralism à la Sahlins, the consequences for understanding cultures in their plurality and ever-changing arenas of action is likely to be limited or circumscribed by the horizon of questions advanced. This is not so much a liability of social theory or scholarship more generally but rather it is representative of the localization of scholarship and scholars in time and space, perhaps an ironic claim in light of what I have argued about cultural diasporas. However, we need not take circumscribed scholarship in its most individual or idiosyncratic terms, but rather can look to Gadamer and his recognition that as historical beings our most pressing questions are always framed in critical tension between past and an emergent present, a point incidently that is made cogently by Joan Vincent (1991) with respect to the history of anthropology. We could perhaps qualify Gadamer's insight by adding that there are a multiplicity of pasts that engage a multiplicity of possible presents and futures, a qualification that would allow us to account for scholarship as positioned and advancing potentially competing questions and competing claims. Moreover, recognizing that scholars are positioned and circumscribed enables us to confront intellectual inquiry reflexively and therefore critically.

The challenge that cultural diasporas pose to bounded cultures as perhaps the most pressing intellectual concern in contemporary anthropology brings the issue of power to the forefront both theoretically and practically. Although relevant here, I will not review the terrain covered in chapter 7 with respect to the synthesis of practical and critical reason as represented in various versions of neo-Marxism. Suffice it to say that most Marxists have come to accept the critique of instrumental reason as applicable to the Marxist concept of labor and surely understand the necessity of grasping the play of power through cultural mediums in addition to the social relations of production. Eric Wolf's *Envisioning Power* (1999) is a good example in that on the one hand he appeals to Bourdieu's theory in arguing for culture as a communicative framework where human actors are positioned, but nevertheless emphasizes, in a manner consistent with his Marxist framework, the determining moments of power as the "deployment and allocation of social labor" (1999: 5). Wolf's proclaimed intention is to understand the complex interrelations between power and ideas and he believes in doing so through elaborating comparatively the case studies of the Kwakiutl, the Aztecs, and National Socialist Germany. To his credit, Wolf's discussion is densely textured with historical and theoretical insights and he presents power ultimately as a multifarious process inextricably interwoven with all social relations.

The issue of deploying social labor aside, recognizing that social actors are positioned is, as I have repeatedly emphasized, a key omission from any of the contributors to the Anglo-American rationality debates, including Gadamer and Ricoeur's elaboration of a communicative theory of society and inter-cultural understanding. Moreover, focusing on the identity of social actors as a component of their positioning provides a medium of analysis that is concrete, forcing us to look closely not just at individuals but differentiated collectivities as they interrelate in space and time. For Wolf, the determining moment of this interrelation, as noted above, derives from the control of social labor, a theoretical move that restricts other practical options through which real actors historically connect with one another (see Abu-Lughod

1991). That is, he believes that gender inequalities or those structured through religion are ultimately shadowed by labor deployment, a theoretically decisive move that gives insufficient autonomy to culture or ideas.

Human agents operate in numerous fields of social action and thus it is important to recognize how human possibilities are created, reproduced, and circumscribed within these diversified domains of practice. These fields of social action are sometimes institutional and serve to define the significant associations of human agents, while at other times fields of social action may take the form of ethnicity, class, or gender, to name just some of the possibilities. The metanarrative of social labor may in fact structure human possibilities within certain fields of action but to assume or assert that labor structures all fields of action is to ultimately reduce what I have argued is communicative to instrumental reason and practice. Such a theoretical move also has consequences for how we understand power. Although not strictly prescriptive, the concept of power as allocated and deployed labor tends to portray a process where power is viewed only as the control of human populations structured by control of the labor process, even if that control, as Wolf shows, is orchestrated through religious idioms. Such a view of power overlooks, as Hannah Arendt (1958) has argued, the difference between "the power over" and the "power to." The former of these conceptualizations is significant to grasping human associations or social relations involved in the construction of political and civic life. That is, human agents not only make use of power in multiple ways to control others but they also empower through having a sense of a life shared. This distinction in the use of the concept of power would no doubt help in understanding the associations and cultural forms that link human actors in their resistance to the very sort of power that is implicit in exploitation and domination as instrumental processes.

Locating human actors within differentiated fields of social action enables us to reformulate the subject–object relation at the core of the rationality debates and to open field research to a mode of inquiry that transcends the limitations of bounded selves and bounded cultures. Human actors engage with each other not as essentialist actors, ideal types, or systemic units, but as concretely positioned. This is as much true for anthropologists as it is for co-subjects studied. Moreover, employing a concept of fields of action necessarily leads to a different sense of a fieldwork as multi-sited and thus enables us to follow the diasporas of peoples and cultures that to a large degree occupies our attention. However, these parameters of cross-cultural understanding do not bring a final resolution to the rationality debates, for if there is such a resolution – a dubious assumption – it is likely to be couched in political terms.

All of the participants in the rationality debates have the common goal of understanding other cultures. The points of differences are essentially theoretical with some potential consequences for method. However, the arguments that I have advanced here for "fields of social action" and multi-sited field research would not lead to the achievement of the coeval ideal proposed by Fabian (1983), even if the theory and practice of anthropology were restructured and included informants as active collaborators in writing and research. This is not to undermine Fabian's argument, since he is right in believing that the conceptual devices of anthropology, our classificatory logic of modern and traditional, etc., place the peoples we study in a time outside of the anthropologist, a time that is non-contemporaneous. Moreover, this is evident not only in the logic of classification but in widely diverse theories that eclipse the constitutive activity of those we study, including the self-interpretations that they provide of their own experiences and life-world. Fabian's vision of a theoretically and practically remade anthropology has much to offer in the humanizing of the social sciences and more importantly in the recognizing of our mutual humanity.

Fabian does not, however, take up the larger issue of global politics although I believe this issue is latent in the historical materials he presents and surely is a continuous theme in the aforementioned works of Eric Wolf. That is, anthropology as a discipline, including the subject/objects studied by ethnographers, was created through both accommodation to and critique of the growth of western colonial societies, colonialism itself being a significant phase in the emergence and maturation of global capitalism. While we admittedly live in the postcolonial, perhaps neo-colonial, era the presence of a global capitalism, even a disorganized one as suggested by Scott Lash and John Urry (1987), continues to establish the intellectual and practical contexts from which scholarly problems are formulated and research interests are pursued. In short, anthropology, like culture, has an autonomy that is only relative. As a disciplinary practice, anthropology is inextricably intertwined with the history of capitalism and its present and future are likely to be profoundly influenced by – even if the tension is critical – the emergent political economic structures and cultural contradictions of an arena that is global. It is this very global context that presents cultural diasporas as demanding our attention and which likewise renders obsolete models of social research with assumed "bounded selves and bounded cultures" as foundational. The prospects of a practical and critical coevalness, one that "truly" transforms subjects and objects into co-subjects and establishes research as collaborative, resides therefore not in the academy but in the broader geo-political domain.[22]

It is a long and somewhat circuitous route from Evans-Pritchard's Zande witches as discussed by Peter Winch through ordinary language philosophy, to the critiques of Winch from methodological individualism and universal logic, to hermeneutics and neo-Marxism and finally to postcolonial diasporas as illustrated here through the French chador event. Nevertheless, this is a route that must be followed in order to move the Anglo-American rationality debates from the circumscribed epistemology of "bounded selves" and "bounded cultures" to confronting the larger political, economic, and cultural issues that play themselves out globally, and which are seminal to the important research questions and research agendas that presently command our attention in anthropology and the comparative human sciences more generally. As noted previously, this is not entirely new territory, as even Evans-Pritchard's classic work on the Azande, while not about contested identities and cultures on the move *per se*, is nonetheless suggestive of cultural diasporas and power in that Zande society and Zande witchcraft likely resulted from the conquest of formerly decentralized peoples by an incipient Zande state (see chapter 3). Zande nobles could accuse commoners of witchcraft and commoners could accuse each other but commoners could not direct their accusations to the nobility. If Evans-Pritcahrd's classic work on the Azande is exemplary, as I believe it is, one would expect to find similar embodied evidence of cultural diasporas and power in the vast majority of circumscribed ethnographies of the past that potentially offer us new narratives in the present, which is more than simply old wine in new skins.

The phenomenological and communicative frameworks of Winch, Gadamer, and Ricoeur, not to mention the Hegelian phenomenology of Marx, can be essentially preserved through the emphasis on human agency, fields of power, and multi-sited field research as presented here. In fact, in spite of the trenchant critiques of the above theoretical positions throughout this work, with the exception of neo-Marxism, this book stands as a testimony to the enduring importance of phenomenology, albeit not in the conventional manner of the transcendental ego or abstract notions of being. The most cogent argument in favor of phenomenology is that by emphasizing "constituted meaning" phenomenology offers a vision of the social world where human subjects define themselves and what they value. While this may not be the conclusive point of critical social analysis, it is not possible, as Fabian (1983) and Rosaldo (1989) have argued, to enter into mutual relations with informants, coeval or otherwise, without emphasizing their self-determinations. Moreover, the phenomenological trajectory in all of its senses enables us to entertain, as Winch maintained in the rationality debates, alternative ways of being, a concept that does not preclude the presence of the global in the local and which strongly counters the over determination of local cultures by hegemonic global systems.

Fields of power provides a conceptual framework from which to grasp identity in its ever-changing and negotiated multiplicity while simultaneously understanding the local, regional, national, and global constraints under which human agents forge their ties and construct their social lives. Methodologically and theoretically, multi-sited field research offers the best

potential to tracking and grasping critically cultural borders, cultural diasporas, and the shifting terrains of both social research and those populations that engage us; it is a challenge to bounded selves and bounded
cultures. To invoke the aforementioned wisdom of Clifford Geertz (1973),
one never gets to the bottom of any study: an argument against totalization
and a humble reminder of the limits and situational basis of "knowing"
which, in my view, support the critical, theoretical, and disciplinary practices advanced in this book.

Notes

1 Introduction

1 Grand narratives can take many different forms. The theory of social evolution is a grand narrative because it is both comprehensive and teleological as is Marx's theory of the self-production and transformation of the human species through social labor.

2 I take up the theme of globalism in chapter 9. In short, globalism has come to mean everything from an awareness of profound international ties with critical potentials to attempts on the part of advanced capitalist countries to impose their plans for economic and social development on former colonies and the Third World more generally.

3 Some of my colleagues in archaeology and physical anthropology have complained that the American Anthropological Association is really an association of cultural anthropology. Their evidence is the few sessions at the annual meetings of the AAA where archaeology and physical anthropology are represented.

4 For a discussion of Boas as a social activist, particularly in relation to challenging racist immigration policies, see chapter 2. Mead is perhaps best remembered for raising critical questions about gender identity.

5 The sociobiology debates are a good example of the continuous disagreement in the human and social sciences over the influence of nature and culture.

6 Alfred Schutz and Maurice Natanson were foremost among the phenomenologists in applying a framework of meaning to the realm of human affairs during a period of the 1960s and 1970s when positivism was well articulated in the social sciences.

7 One apparent reason that Evans-Pritchard is not identified with historical anthropology is the absence of this perspective in his numerous ethnographic works. However, his collected essays (1962) contain an essay on anthropology and history that anticipates many of the issues presented by Bernie Cohen (1987) in an often cited work on historical anthropology.

8 I believe that this is well recognized by most anthropologists seeking to deconstruct the privilege of scientific knowing, from Marilyn Strathern's (1988) outright critique of nature/nurture to Donna Haraway's *Primate Visions* (1989).

9 While Jarvie has remained committed to methodological individualism, Karl Popper's *Objective Knowledge* is a significant move away from methodological individualism and towards a more institutional perspective.

10 It is not uncommon to hear scientifically inclined colleagues in anthropology argue that we should be committed to the scientific paradigm because it works, it simply explains nature as it is. The implication is that nature is lawful and science best captures its regularities of which human nature is an extension. Interestingly, many practitioners of science would reject such a view and would likely embrace Popper's vision of the tentative nature of scientific truths.

11 This is not to say that hermeneutics is the only influential theoretical position. Clearly the foregrounding of informants' voices in the writing of ethnographies has been profoundly shaped by the Marxist discourse theory of Mikhail Bakhtin (1986).

12 Ricoeur's (1970) book on the continuing relevance of Freud to the human and social sciences is a case in point, especially in light of the outright rejection of Freud on the part of scientific psychology. Ricoeur argues that human consciousness and symbolism are opaque; so we have much to learn about the interpretive process from Freud in that Freud drew out attention early in the twentieth century to the multivocality of symbols and the density of human consciousness.

13 In this respect, Gadamer departs from the hermeneutics of Dilthey that established different modes of knowing for the human and natural sciences on the basis of their respective different objects of knowledge.

14 Conservative think tanks such as the Heritage Foundation have been foremost in arguing for the triumph of capitalism. This does not, however, address in the slightest the continuing cycles of crisis in capitalism, both economic and cultural, nor what appears to be the eclipsing of the public realm – what Habermas sees as the colonialization of the life-world in the most profound terms.

15 Even if I have some theoretical disagreement with Wolf over the relation between culture and power (see chapter 9), I continue to have enormous respect for his erudition. Wolf's command of historical details in numerous world areas is impressive.

16 Neo-Marxism is generally attributed to scholars who seek to make political economy responsive to a theory of culture often through an appeal to Hegel or phenomenology more generally. Apart from the Frankfurt School (Adorno, Horkheimer, Benjamin), scholars such as Lukács and Gramsci are often regarded as central to the emergence of a neo-Marxist perspective and continue to be widely read by scholars seeking a cultural alternative to political economy.

17 Lawrence Kohlberg developed a theory of cognitive development implying that a child's ability to reason increased as it aged and matured. Habermas borrows what is particular to the developmental stages of humans, psychologically conceived, and applies this to the cognitive and reasoning potentials of human society. That is, he believes that human societies have matured cognitively in a manner analogous to inborn psychological processes of reasoning. The key juncture for Habermas is the Enlightenment because this is a period when ostensibly reason could be utilized to question societal assumptions and thus advance the project of human emancipation. It is important to note, however, that Habermas regarded the Enlightenment transition and the potentials it offered to emancipation in historical and social rather than innate and psychological terms.

18 Habermas, like Marx, also fits the image of the public intellectual in that he frequently writes for German newspapers addressing such crucial issues as the German revisionist historians who have tried to cleanse the atrocities of National Socialism.

19 The emphasis on local discourses does open the possibility for subaltern populations to tell their stories, a factor that is often overlooked in the hegemonic discourses of nation states.

20 One clear advantage of foregrounding is the manifest presence of women's voices in ethnographies. In some of the older ethnographies, there was a tendency to learn about women of other cultures through men or through the lone voice of the ethnographer.

21 In all fairness to Winch, Jarvie, MacIntyre, Horton, and Lukes, it is always easy retrospectively to fault scholars for not addressing certain themes or issues. At the time of the original rationality debates, few scholars were raising challenges to the concept of culture by invoking globalism and cultural diaspora.

22 This is a point that is generally overlooked in Wallerstein's world systems theory. For Wallerstein, local communities of the Third World, theorized as the periphery, are regarded as overdetermined by their relationship to dominant and hegemonic core areas.

23 George Marcus (1998) has championed multi-sited research although I believe that his dismissal of grand narratives undermines the potential political force of his argument. I address this issue more substantively in chapter 9.

24 It is, however, important to note that when a paper in the natural sciences has a plurality of authors there is an implicit hierarchy with the first author being considered principle. This is not a custom that holds in anthropology for co-authored works.

25 In fact, I was fortunate to be affiliated with a center for regional historical studies at the University of Bordeaux that enabled me informally to discuss my work with historians who had considerable years of experience conducting research in this area. However, this falls short of a more comprehensive collaboration where I would be sharing materials and conclusions with others working in the field on a common set of issues.

2 Anthropological Ancestors and Interpretation Theory

1 It was Kant's thesis that the categories of the human mind are determinant in organizing both experience and knowledge of the world. While there is a strong parallel between Boas's unconscious laws and Kant's determinant categories, the influence of Bastian places Boas's notion within a more clearly developed psychological medium rather than the Kantian transcendentalism. I contend that Kant's categories, which constitute the world through the monological subject, and Boas's concept of the constitution of cultural phenomena through the determinations of psychological laws that are also monological are both historically symptomatic of transformations in western ideas following the destruction of communal life and the rise of civil society. See, for example, C. B. MacPherson's

interesting portrayal of Hobbes as the architect of modern society in *The Political Theory of Possessive Individualism: Hobbes to Locke* (1962).

2 The fact that Lévi-Strauss claims to be indebted to Boas's emphasis on the unconscious generation of cultural phenomena shows that I am not alone in my interpretation of Boas as having a psychologically oriented concept of the subject. See Lévi-Strauss's essay "Introduction: History and Anthropology" (1963). Evans-Pritchard (1962) also draws our attention to the influence of introspective psychology on eighteenth-and nineteenth-century anthropological theory; see especially pp. 44–5.

3 The tradition that follows from Emile Durkheim (1965) is the flip side of the coin from that represented by the monological contract theorists. While the Durkheimian tradition emphasizes the primary of the social over the individual, it cannot account for how the social comes into existence or how it is transformed or maintained. Social facts thus become equivalent to natural facts.

4 By guiding interests, I have in mind both the political conditions under which British social anthropology developed and knowledge-constitutive interests in Jürgen Habermas's (1971) sense.

5 By dialectical, I mean the mediation of the superficiality of reality and reflection upon the knowledge-constituting interests of the inquiry.

6 I am referring here to the early Dilthey; see, for example, Richard E. Palmer (1969).

7 I have in mind here the dialectical character of all knowledge, in which the engaging of the radical other makes transparent our own historical finitude. The radical other, either as native informant or event, poses questions to the investigator. The investigator must seek to discover to what questions, in R. G. Collingwood's sense, a given event or cultural representation is the answer.

3 Peter Winch and Ordinary Language Philosophy

1 The *Tractatus* was published in 1921 and was Wittgenstein's doctoral dissertation. Wittgenstein's early work, which attracted the admiration of Bertrand Russell, was an attempt to solve all philosophical problems through the formal clarification of language.

2 Apel's work parallels the recent attempts of Jürgen Habermas to create a transcendental pragmatics of language or a theory of language games. Apel's recent work, as well as that of Habermas, is faulted by an ethnocentric evolutionism. His work on language, however, is a very useful and powerful critique of positivism and scientism.

3 By reification, Winch implies that the communicative nature of witchcraft practices, which gives them their specific cultural identity, is reduced to a "thing like" object. By treating meaningful human activity as a thing, science is unable to comprehend the process through which the meaning of human activity is constituted. The nonreflexive dimensions of science make it an activity that is unable in the end to account for the constitution of scientific facts.

4 The relation between psychoanalysis and language games has also been developed in Paul Ricoeur's (1970) exciting work on Freud. Ricoeur gives an excellent

argument for a communicative interpretation of Freud's energetics. Jürgen Habermas (1971) also applies the communicative insights of psychoanalysis to a potentially emancipatory social theory.

5 This shows that Malinowski's (1961) notion that the Trobriand Islanders suffer from the Oedipus complex is nonsensical. The Trobrianders do not have the prerequisite institutional structure to support the possibility of an Oedipus complex, which means that this Freudian complex cannot be present in the linguisticality or concept of their social interaction.

6 I am not implying that sin is a primary feature of all universal religions; Buddhism would certainly be an exception. I am claiming that the concept of law, which is endemic to the Judeo-Christian covenant, is a necessary prerequisite of a concept of sin. Sin cannot exist, therefore, prior to the development of universal religions. Indigenous societies, on the contrary, recognize the transgression of custom or contagion. See, for example, Stanley Diamond's essay "The Rule of Law versus the Order of Custom" (in Diamond 1974).

7 In this regard, Winch's thesis clearly provides an alternative to the classification of categories such as that which occurs in ethnoscience.

8 Winch in this respect equates the rationality of languages to the Greek concept of logos.

9 Scientism looks upon prescientific aspects of social life, such as class or politics, as obstacles to objective knowledge. We shall see in chapter 6 that these prescientific aspects of social life are precisely what makes knowledge a priori possible.

10 Casati and Schweinfurth are the two historical sources cited by Evans-Pritchard (1962), which makes his failure to treat the sociopolitical dimensions of the Azande all the more disappointing. The fact that a great deal of the documentation of Zande society is in Italian or German makes historical research on this society difficult for those who lack a facility with languages.

11 The only anthropological source I have been able to discover which mentions (in passing) the disparity between nobles and commoners is Paul Radin's *The World of Primitive Man* (1971).

12 Since ideology and power relations are to be understood communicatively, I refer to a misconceived self-understanding as distorted communication. I am indebted to Jürgen Habermas for the concept of distorted communication; see, for example, *Knowledge and Human Interests* (1971), especially the chapters on Freud.

13 This does show that no simple equation can be made between the meaning of social practices and self-understanding.

14 Literature seems to imply that the European witchcraft craze was a form of misogyny involving competition between men and women over occupations traditionally held by women. See, for example, Barbara Ehrenreich and Deirdre English, *Witches, Midwives and Nurses: A History of Women Healers* (1973). What European and Zande witchcraft have in common is that they are both expressions of domination, although based upon very different historical circumstances and principles of social integration.

15 I have in mind historically specific political and economic interests as well as Jürgen Habermas's (1971) notion of knowledge-constitutive interests.

16 The *benge* substance is the poison administered to a fowl as part of the oracle process.

17 For the development of this point with respect to the eschatology of Francis Bacon, see William Leiss's *The Domination of Nature* (1974).

4 The Neo-Popperians and the Logic of One Science

1 Although I have strong objections to Jarvie's characterization of anthropological praxis, I agree with much of the spirit of *The Revolution in Anthropology* (1964) insofar as it is addressed to a critique of induction and the identification of being an anthropologist with having done fieldwork.

2 Kant's alternative to native empiricism was the structuring of all sensations and experience according to the a priori universal categories of mind. The anthropological version of Kantian philosophy without the transcendental subject is best exemplified by the rationalism of Claude Lévi-Strauss.

3 See Jürgen Habermas (1970a: 92). Purposive rational action is concerned with deductive, alternative strategies for achieving a desired goal or end.

4 See Stanley Diamond (1974: 3) for a fully developed argument concerning the relation between power and the written word.

5 Marcuse's (1964) observations are important in that the universalization of scientistic or technical rationality can become embodied in societies following capitalist or socialist development. The universalization of technical rationality as a form of domination should be a warning to socialist countries of the Third World whose plans for modernization or development include the sacrifice of the peasantry to rapid, large-scale industrialization.

6 This position is most clearly developed in William Leiss's *The Domination of Nature* (1974). The implication of Leiss's analysis is that the degradation of the environment, following capitalist market principles and technical rationality, parallels the degradation of human community and the domination of men.

7 Even a cultural ecologist such as Julian Steward, who was tied to a more modest Boasian program of historical particularism, anticipated a period in which generalized laws would be established.

8 The concept of leading interests of knowledge or knowledge-constitutive interests or guiding interests is used by Habermas (1971) to refer to the transcendental processes through which objects of actual and potential experience are constituted. This enables Habermas, for example, to relate the methods of science epistemologically to the universal formative process of humanity in objectification and control, or what he refers to as instrumental rationality. It is important to note that interests of knowledge are not subjective motives or goals but are implicit in the modes of rationality through which the human species forms and transforms itself through interaction.

I have used Habermas's concept throughout this book in a less transcendental sense. I believe that interests are rooted in the formative capacity of human co-subjects but that these interests are subject to historical, socio cultural, and domination contingencies.

9 My claim clearly contrasts with Malinowski's interpretation of magic, whereby culturally specific languages and rituals can be utilized to bring about a desired outcome. Malinowski and Horton are not wrong in contending that control is a principal feature of primitive magical systems, but are mistaken in equating the control of magic with the technical rationality of science. The control of science, on the contrary, involves a subjective self-assertion that would be inconceivable to a native immersed in the bonds of community and tradition. Native peoples thus do not attempt to employ their gods and ancestors as means towards realizing subjectively conceived ends nor as deductively arrived-at strategies. Neither Malinowski nor Horton have seriously considered the concrete historical and social preconditions that are the source of the constitution of indigenous cosmologies and modern western science.

10 I am arguing here for a dialectical relationship between types of sociocultural integration and modes of thought. From this perspective certain social prerequisites necessary for the development of modern science are not intrinsic to the social order of indigenous societies. Furthermore, if we view the social order from the perspective of communicative interaction, then it is easy to see the relation between sociocultural integration and the realm of ideas. The relation of ideas or forms of representation to types of societies is brilliantly portrayed by Georg Lukács in *The Theory of the Novel* (1972). In this short book, Lukács discusses, for example, why certain types of literature (e.g., the epic novel) are correlated with specific forms of sociocultural integration (e.g., community, civil society). This dialectical perspective gives him a trajectory from which to argue why the novel cannot develop in just any society with writing. The novel form interiorizes the lost totality of community life, as exhibited by the main character and plot. According to Lukács, the novel form can only develop in a society where community and traditional life are waning.

11 This important book, edited by Imre Lakatos and Alan Musgrave, covers, the Kuhn–Popper controversy over the nature of scientific research.

12 See Georg Lukács (1971), especially the essay "Reification and the Consciousness of the Proletariat."

13 In other words, value orientations for Horton have no relation to the social constitution of reality. What he considers to be reality is unchanging and static.

5 Ordinary Language Philosophy in Question

1 Marvin Harris's *Cultural Materialism* (1979) takes Stanley Diamond's praxological anthropology to task for not adhering to science as the criterion of objective truth. Harris, like most social scientists who appeal to science as the sole criterion of truth, has an instrumentalist notion in mind; science, or more accurately scientism, is grounded in a correspondence theory of truth with no moral or practical intent. Diamond's praxological notion of anthropology recognizes a communicative as well as an instrumentalist concept of truth; it privileges the reflexive and hermeneutic preconditions of anthropology as well as the importance of the historical subject in the constitution of cultural phenomena.

Contrary to what Harris claims, Diamond's concept of anthropology does include a notion of truth, but one more in concert with the broad range of the human condition and therefore more authentically anthropological. Treatises on truth, however, have not been the central concern of anthropology even though a concept of truth is always implicit in anthropological theories and methods.

2 See, for example, Robin Horton's comments on Leach in an essay entitled "Lévy-Bruhl, Durkheim and the Scientific Revolution" (1973a: 5). J. H. M. Beattie's views in relation to truth and ritual are discussed in his essay "On Understanding Ritual," in Bryan Wilson (1971).

3 Methodological individualism is ideological because it claims to be universal yet conceals the historically particular contractual basis of social relations in civil society.

4 The strength of British social anthropology, which admittedly is also its weakness, rests on this particular dictum of Durkheim's. The British social anthropologists have tended always to emphasize the collectivity over the individual.

5 The fact that truth can be intrinsic to the intersubjectivity of cultural traditions presents the anthropologist with an alternative to an ethnocentric scientism and therefore with a more comprehensive vision of human possibilities.

6 Whorf shows that the Hopi have no verb tenses that refer to past, present, or future yet are capable of accounting for all events. In some respects, Whorf contends, there are parallels between the Hopi conceptions and modern relativity theory. What is implied here is that language does not simply label the world but, on the contrary, accounts for its constitution and meaning. This should be a warning to anthropologists to take discourse seriously in fieldwork encounters.

7 This once again supports the notion that critical reflection can be grounded in the communicative rationality of ordinary language rather than the instrumental rationality of scientific linguistics.

8 Scientistic anthropology has adopted the concept of causality from the natural sciences. Anthropologists operating within this framework seem to ignore the fact that the objects of inquiry are also subjects and hence follow intentional rules.

9 The socially created basis of human needs is self-evident once the subject/object problem has been solved.

10 The universality of the nuclear family has been put forward by George Peter Murdock (1949). Even if we accept Murdock's thesis (which I regard as questionable), we cannot overlook the different principles of social organization that provide the context and hence define the nature of the nuclear family in primitive versus modern societies (e.g., the absence of social classes and private property in pre-state societies versus the primacy of social classes, private property, and contractual relations in civil society). There is a great deal of recent Marxist literature that is critical of Murdock's thesis (e.g., Reiter 1975). This debate, however, goes beyond the point that I am making here.

11 I should add, however, that a very different sense of use is implied in the functionalist thesis.

6   Beyond Explanation and Understanding

1 During the latter part of his career, Dilthey moved away from a specifically psychological hermeneutic. My comparison of Winch and Dilthey only takes into consideration Dilthey's early period. For an informative introductory discussion of Dilthey, see "Dilthey: Hermeneutics as Foundation of the Geisteswissenschaften," chapter 8 of Richard E. Palmer's *Hermeneutics* (1969).

2 The unity of the diverse Anglo-French philosophies is also argued forcefully in Peter Gay's *The Englightenment: An Interpretation* (1968).

3 The relation between critical-emancipatory reason and the hermeneutics of cultural traditions is at the basis of the Habermas–Gadamer controversy. For Paul Ricoeur's interpretation of this controversy, see his article "Ethics and Culture: Habermas and Gadamer in Dialogue" (1973a).

4 The debates concerning the nature of culture are viewed by scientistic anthropology as of only historical interest. This is because the Sapir–Kroeber debates failed to operationalize the concept of culture. Current discourse on the concept of culture has followed upon a growing fragmentation of anthropology. Consequently, it is only within symbolic and interpretive anthropology, with few exceptions (e.g., Jules Henry's *Culture against Man* (1965)), and now "postcolonial studies," that culture remains a lively topic of concern and inquiry. Within symbolic anthropology, there have been few attempts to link culture to the inherent linguisticality of social relations or to the mediative process of critical anthropology. Current anthropology could be strengthened through a reintegration of its various, fragmented modes of inquiry around the concept of culture.

5 It is the hermeneutic circle as an ontological precondition that is rejected by scientism in its scorn for the prescientific life-world. Hence, the notion of value-freedom is abstract and idealistic.

6 The hermeneutical elucidation of anthropology does not provide the ethnographer with a technically usable method but, on the contrary, illuminates the ontological preconditions of anthropological understanding, both in the narrow sense of the discipline of anthropology and in the larger sense of western culture.

7 Bios is a concept that Ricoeur absorbs and modifies from classical Greek philosophy. Bios in classical Greek philosophy was used to refer to life itself, in contrast to nous or intellect and logos or reason. Ricoeur uses the concept of bios to refer to the undifferentiated force of life itself before it becomes culture or human convention. The force of life differentiates itself only as it becomes manifest in different regions of human existence such as religion or psychoanalysis.

8 Mary Douglas's approach is deeply ahistorical in that it does not, for example, account for differences in principles of social organization. This leads her to conclude that some indigenous societies can be as aritualistic as modern society. She does not consider that ritual, which is based upon the principle of community, is absent in modern society because of the atomism of the contractual basis of civil society. While I cannot explain why ritual would be de-emphasized in certain native societies, it makes no sense to universalize the preconditions of modern civil society.

9 This is why Boas's rejection of the native's interpretation is untenable. We cannot arrive at an interpretation of the meaning of culturally specific actions without working through the immediacy of self-understanding.

10 In other words, the ontological dimensions of sociocultural life have been eclipsed by a purely modern view that humanity makes, and therefore controls, all that we associate with the sociocultural realm. Ricoeur's theory of symbols gives us a position from which we can recognize how tradition shapes much of what we associate with the actual and possible.

11 The epoché is central to Edmund Husserl's transcendental phenomenology. It is an abstract method that "brackets" the empirical ego so that the constituted object of knowledge can be examined in its multiple appearances and its noema or essence ascertained. See, for example, his *Cartesian Meditations* (1973).

12 It is because social phenomena owe their constitution to the universal operation of reason that Lévi-Strauss contends in *The Savage Mind* that it does not matter whether we think the savage or whether the savage thinks us. According to Lévi-Strauss, the meanings of social phenomena in native and modern societies are ultimately reducible to the logic of a uniform process of rational structuration.

13 The pervasiveness of this concept in structuralism can also be seen in the various archaeologies of Michel Foucault (1970, 1973), where the history of the species is reconstructed as a series of constituted discourses. It is, however, a discourse without empirical interlocutors.

14 This is implicit in Marx's methodology as shown in the first volume of *Capital*. While Marx discloses the concealed logic of the capitalist system, he does so by concretely examining its history. Only in this way does he exhibit the uniqueness of capitalism with respect to other social formations.

15 This is in some senses comparable to the concept of language game developed by the later Wittgenstein (1953). The language game emphasizes that language is an activity and hence that meaning arises from use in context.

16 The constitution of the life-world through a solipsistic ego is attributable to the early work of Husserl. Phenomenologists such as Merleau-Ponty were responsible for bringing the phenomenological tradition into a fully intersubjective and critical framework.

17 Power does not always have to imply the domination of one group over another. As Hannah Arendt (1958) has shown, power also arises from the cooperation and consensus of the body politic.

7   Hermeneutics and Critical Anthropology

1 In the expressive concept of totality, no distinction is made between the degree of determination of different social practices. Althusser (1970: 206–8) introduces the concept of overdetermination to describe the uneven relationships of contradictions in the complex whole. Each contradiction not only reflects in itself the uneven relationships of the whole but also its place in the structure of dominance.

2 This is particularly true with their concept of mode of production in *Pre-Capitalist Modes of Production*. While they emphasize the mode of extraction

of surplus labor as a key feature of any mode of production, we discover that it is absent, for example, in their discussion of the slavery, Asiatic, and feudal modes of production.

3 While Hindess and Hirst use the language of phenomenology (e.g., "constitution"), they make no reference to either a transcendental or an empirical subject.

4 By dismissing epistemology, Hindess and Hirst not only reject a subject/object dichotomy but also fail to raise questions concerning the grounds of valid knowledge claims. They are thus left with a method that is commensurate with scientism, in that it is self-validating and cannot account for its own formation.

5 In some versions of rationalism, as Hindess and Hirst relate, the relations between concepts are supposed to be the cause of the real.

6 In their view, Althusser's distinction is a priori because it is made in advance of theoretical articulation.

7 See, for example, Rod Aya (1976), Talal Asad and Harold Wolpe (1976), and Maurice Dobb (1976).

8 This could be a valuable contribution to political anthropology if developed, since most anthropologists take political life as a cultural universal. Unfortunately, politics is all too often conceived in its instrumental sense as the control and allocation of principal resources.

9 See, for example, Claude Lévi-Strauss's essay "History and Anthropology," in his *Structural Anthropology* (1963).

10 The analysis is implicit in the method of *Capital* and in Marx's somewhat ambiguous reference to the anatomy of the ape in the *Grundrisse* (1973: 105).

11 This is a vision of economic anthropology supported by the formalists. It has its origins with Herskovits and its recent reconceptualization through Robbins and Samuelson. The substantivist theory, on the other hand, as articulated by Polanyi, connects the economy to historically and culturally variable objectives of the social system. Although Godelier is sympathetic to the substantivist theory, he argues that the substantivist and formalist theories converge when it comes to the definition of principal economic categories such as value, wages, profit, and price (1972: xv).

12 Leopold Pospisil argues from a formalist point of view in his *Kapauku of Western New Guinea* that this group of pastoralists is capitalist. He bases this claim, in part, on a superficial etymology of the word *capital* from *cattle*.

13 While it is beyond the scope of my project to elaborate on Baudrillard's notion of emancipation, he does argue that the critique of political economy is tied to the productivist logic of capitalism and hence its problematics. He suggests that a critical theory of capitalism must be concerned with its process of signification. It is the control of the code that ensures capitalist hegemony. Baudrillard, however, is unable to account for how the code is produced and hence reproduced because his level of analysis is embodied in a virtual system.

14 There is a very important work by Perry Anderson (1980) which supports the structuralist theory against Thompson's privileging of the human subject. I only refer the reader to this work, as any discussion of its content would lead us astray into yet another series of debates whose roots are in Thompson's break from the *New Left Review*.

15 Periodicity or chronology establishes historical periods on the basis of famous battles, rulers, and the fall or rise of state societies. It often eclipses the history of those who have been subordinated and the social processes through which the chronology is generated.

16 Thompson, for example, says the following about history as process with respect to the English working class:

> This book has a clumsy title, but it is one which meets its purpose. Making, because it is a study in an active process, which owes as much to agency as to conditioning. The working class did not rise like the sun at an appointed time. It was present at its own making. (1966: 9)

17 The example of the Methodist Church also exhibits Thompson's sensitivity to the multivocality and complexity of historical phenomena. He not only shows how the Methodist Church provided a context for working-class resistance but also how this same institution served the ends of capitalist socialization.

18 Thompson says the following with respect to the concept of class:

> By class, I understand an historical phenomenon, unifying a number of disparate and seemingly unconnected events, both in the raw material of experience and in consciousness. I emphasize that it is an *historical* phenomenon. I do not see class as a "structure", nor even as a "category", but as something which in fact happens (and can be shown to have happened) in human relationships. (1966: 9)

19 See C. B. MacPherson (1962), who outlines the relationship between bourgeois notions of property, civil society, and possessive individualism. The effects of possessive individualism on the public realm are also discussed by Hannah Arendt (1958) and Jürgen Habermas (1973).

20 Politics in its classical sense was concerned with the establishment of the just or moral society through which right action in its citizens would be cultivated. In modern capitalist societies and bureaucratic socialist societies, this classical notion of politics has been eclipsed by an instrumental version. The instrumental version of politics substitutes the decisions of party elites and government administrators for the consensus of the governed. Often these decisions are made and carried out in secrecy, as in the case of the veil of national security in the United States.

21 The distinction between the in-itself and the for-us was central to Hegel's critique of Kant – a critique that was accepted, then recast, by Marx in historical materialism. The essence of the argument is that an object of knowledge is always an object of some consciousness, hence for-us.

22 Thompson's loss of the reflexive potentiality of historiography only reflects his comments on the ontology of past events. His actual historical research is demonstratively reflexive. Part of the difficulty in interpreting Thompson's theoretical work is the fact that he is a dialectician in an empiricist cultural and intellectual tradition. These contingencies are reflected in some of his comments on theory.

23 It is this point in particular which distinguishes the historical-culturalist notion of totality from the structuralist concept of social formation as a hierarchy of levels.

24 See, for example, Max Horkheimer and Theodor W. Adorno (1972), Jürgen Habermas (1975), Max Weber (1964), and Robert N. Bellah (1975).

25 It has been the tendency of vulgar Marxism to view the political realm, in the form of the state, as an agency of the ruling class. This univocal notion of politics overlooks other dimensions of political activity that lead to consensus, legitimation, and the cultivation of right action.

26 It is beyond the scope of this chapter to develop fully an analysis of the capitalist form of domination. I have merely used Thompson's notion of circuits of power to show that there are areas of social control that have their own logic of reproduction and hence do not operate as a reflex of the economy.

27 Although Herder regarded culture as distinct patterns of life that distinguish one people from another, his notion of culture was dissociated from lived material practices.

28 Edward Said argues in his *Orientalism* that the imperialist relation of West to East has generated a distorted discourse that constitutes the East as a singular tradition. Said claims that this is even true with respect to Marx's notion of oriental despotism.

29 See, for example, Karl Polanyi's *The Great Transformation* (1957).

8   Modernism and Postmodernism in Anthropology

1 Bob Scholte, one of the contributors, was one of the early figures to call for a critical examination of the epistemological foundations of anthropology.

2 A reflexive anthropology is self-conscious of its origins and development. Mediation, on the other hand, is a process of disclosure that seeks to make apparent what is concealed in a science's claim to objectivity. Reflexivity and mediation work together to disclose the social and political interests that are embodied in the history of anthropology and which continue to influence its discourse and practice.

3 For the purpose of this chapter, I limit my discussion of critical anthropology to political economy and postmodernism as this is a current source of tension and debate. It is also clear that the feminist trajectory in anthropology constitutes an important part of the critical project of the discipline; one merely needs to recall the challenge to the division of public and private or the challenge to "male voices" represented through informants, ethnographers, and even theory as a whole. However, in order to do justice to the so called "postmodern controversy" in particular I leave the elaboration of feminist theory to others more able to comment extensively on its complexities and internal tensions.

4 It was the intention of all grand theory informed by Enlightenment rationality, whether in the form of Kant, Hegel, Marx, or Darwin, to provide grounds for knowledge claims that were indubitable. It is the indubitability of knowledge claims, often referred to as foundationalism, that Lyotard believes is no longer applicable in the contemporary world.

5 In the 1981 essay, Huyssen is largely critical of postmodernism for its reduction of historical process to the inscription of text. Postmodernism, like poststructuralism, turns its back on the human subject, which it regards as just another

discourse of humanity. However, in the 1984 essay, Huyssen seems to have become more accepting of postmodernism's critical potential.

6 Habermas believes that the economy in advanced capitalist societies is often regarded as operating autonomously, establishing its own imperatives and goals. The avowed autonomy of the economy, argues Habermas, then threatens to undermine the capacity of an informed public to reach goals and objectives based upon consensus.

7 Habermas believes, unlike the postmodernists, that reciprocal interchange, rather than power, is the normal condition of social interaction. Therefore, he represents speech as its ideal.

8 For a critical review of Habermas's use of developmental psychology, see the essays edited by John B. Thompson and David Held (1982).

9 The notion of totality has always been a central part of critical theory both in its Frankfurt School version and for those who have followed Lukács. However, with the work of Habermas, the notion of social totality has fallen into disfavor.

10 There is no doubt that Habermas's project will strike some readers as highly idealistic. However, if rational consensus is the obstacle, one can at least see the merit of political action that is informed by a moral or practical, in the sense of praxis, intent.

11 I have in mind here the outrageous claims of Steven P. Sangren (1988) that Marcus and Fischer, not to mention other postmodern anthropologists, are a kind of "gang of four" seeking to impose their hegemony on anthropology departments all over the country. This needs to be compared with the thoughtful criticism from the political economy camp by Polier and Roseberry (1989).

12 The idea that writing merely reproduces the social world actually far predates the positivists in that it can be found in association with Platonic conceptualizations of language. For an excellent critique of the realist notion that writing actually reproduces reality, see Richard Rorty's *Philosophy and the Mirror of Nature* (1979).

13 Herzfeld's example has some parallel with my own fieldwork on southwest French wine cooperatives. In spite of the important role played by cooperatives in successfully commercializing the wines of small growers who compose their membership, I discovered a near absence of historical and ethnographic accounts of those who forged the wine cooperative movement. Rather, countless books and articles have been written documenting – and sometimes celebrating – the history of the châteaux and the labor attached to these noted estates. I believe, as I have argued elsewhere (Ulin 1987, 1996), that the long-term association of French wine with the clergy, aristocracy, and later, wealthy merchants, served during the nineteenth century – the period of the formation and expansion of French national culture – to elevate the quality wines of the châteaux, rather than the table wines of the small peasant producers, to the quintessential representative of French national culture. Consequently, small growers and the wines which they produce have lived in the historical shadows of the esteemed French châteaux. The view of the cooperative wines as secondary in importance was confirmed by informants at the cooperatives who questioned why I had come to study their wines when those of the famous Bordeaux châteaux were so near by.

The writing of winegrowing history, or history in general, from the point of view of the elites eclipses the multiplicity of voices that constitute the historical record.

14 While White's work is no doubt important for drawing our attention to the poetics and power of the historical record, a factor that I have discovered independently with respect to my own fieldwork on French winegrowers (Ulin 1987, 1996), it shares the neo-Kantian and now postmodern problematic of not being able to account reflexively and historically for its own categories of analysis. Consequently, we are left with the impression that the literary genres of tragedy, comedy, irony, and satire are themselves eternal, living outside the historical process, yet self-reproducing.

15 While I believe that Marcus and Fischer are correct in pointing to the imaginative features of this work, I believe that they are not sufficiently critical of its use of Freudian theory. It appears to me that its ethnocentric implications, not to mention its gender bias, greatly hinder Obeyesekere's objective of understanding how Sri Lankan spirit mediums give personal significance to public symbols.

16 For an excellent review of the current state of political economy in anthropology, see William Roseberry's (1988) essay in the *Annual Review of Anthropology*.

17 I had believed that the French school of Marxist anthropology had abandoned the distinction between economic base and ideological superstructure. However, the time I spent in the late 1980s as a participant in the Franco-Espagnol seminar on social change has led me to conclude to the contrary. Through getting to know a number of French and Spanish anthropologists, I can assure the reader that structural Marxism is alive and well on the continent. Many members of this seminar identify social change almost exclusively with transformations in the economic base. This is quite distinct from Anglo-American variants of Marxism that are sensitive to the relation between culture and production.

18 There is little doubt that anthropologists and political economists who accept a Marxist methodology will probably feel ill at ease with its metatheoretical or ontological presuppositions. Nonetheless, if we are to accept the universal applicability of the method, then we must acknowledge the universal presuppositions on which the method rests.

19 Those familiar with Marx's theory of alienation will immediately recognize the importance of the identification of workers with the products of their labor. It is particularly the case in capitalism that the workers lose their identification with their products. These products then appear merely as things and therefore subject to the laws of circulation of capitalist markets. It is the project of Marxist political economy to demystify the reification of commodities.

20 In a provocative edited work entitled *The Social Life of Things* (1986), Arjun Appadurai recreates the reification argument by implying that commodities have a biography of their own. While I understand that it is his intention to get beyond a strictly productivist model to one that is more cultural or semiotic, the idea of separating biography from its usual sense of human agency risks separating culture from its embodiment in social relations.

21 The idea that power is ubiquitous actually owes its origin to the poststructuralism of Michel Foucault. In his archeology of the human sciences, Foucault tried to show that power was intrinsic to the constitutive process of subjectless discourses. Foucault's work has made a measurable mark on postmodern

anthropology. While recognizing the significance of Foucault's claim, I prefer to follow Hannah Arendt's more refined use of the concept of power. Arendt distinguished between the "power over" and the "power to." The first of these concepts is how the notion of power is usually employed, that is, in the sense of coercion or social control. However, Arendt gives a political twist to the concept in arguing that power also has to do with human association oriented towards common ends. It is this specifically political dimension of power as distinct from coercion that is lost in the unrefined employment of the concept in poststructuralism and now postmodernism.

22 The largest influence here has come from a Hegelianized revision of traditional Marxism that has tried to articulate a relation between culture, politics, and domination as an expansion of the exploitation model in political economy. The influence here has come largely from the works of Gramsci, the Frankfurt School, Williams and Thompson. It is not clear, though, that the Hegelianized version of political economy, if it can be called that, is acceptable at all to those close to a Marxist orthodoxy.

23 This is generally the complaint made by Marxist social theorists about a semiotic understanding of the social world: semiotics appears to present a process of semiosis that renders superfluous human praxis; for semiotics, the human subject itself can become just another sign system with no special epistemological or ontological privilege.

24 As a discipline, it can be argued that anthropology, in spite of its modernist roots in the Enlightenment, has contributed greatly to the relativizing of the social world.

25 While Taussig is no doubt correct in pointing out in Wolf and Mintz the absence of a consideration of concrete subjects, I believe that his objection is overstated in that it is not the interest of Wolf or Mintz to provide a standard or, for that matter, an unconventional ethnography. Rather, the questions that they pose in these books necessitate the level of abstraction pursued.

26 It should be noted that the revision of Marxist social theory predates considerably the postmodern challenge. Rather, attempts to make Marxism responsive to cultural hegemony arose from the failures of Marxism to explain why socialist transformations did not occur and the inability, especially in the United States, of the working class to develop an identity of its own or to forge its own existence. Apart from Lukács, who has been mentioned, it has been Gramsci and members of the Frankfurt School who have contributed most to a cultural theory of Marxism.

27 In chapter 7 I discuss the general problematic of mode of production analysis. Here, I focus on only the implicit rationality of labor as a model of human action.

28 Habermas is not alone in arguing that Marx had an insufficiently developed notion of politics in spite of the critical intent of his theory. Habermas wishes to explore the general process of political life that would ensue from a socialist revolution. The idea of the dictatorship of the proletariat lacks a normative foundation in a broad general consensus.

29 See, for example, the essays in the volume edited by John B. Thompson and David Held (1982). It is also not clear that Habermas himself any longer supports the neo-Kantian implications of two systems of human activity supported

retrospectively by instrumental and communicative rationality. Nonetheless, the critics of Habermas would support him in maintaining that symbolically constituted human action cannot be reduced to the instrumental process of labor.

30 Anthropology is profoundly tied to the modernism of the Enlightenment. This takes, on the one hand, the form of a rationality whose cognitive interest is control and objectification, while, on the other hand, presenting a sense of rationality tied to emancipation. It is my assertion that anthropology has not outgrown its modernist origins in that the historical problematic of modernism is still with us.

31 It is not my intention to hold up Habermas as the only possible alternative to historical materialism. There are a number of contemporary scholars who also address the problems of the logic of production from a communicative framework. Pierre Bourdieu (1977) comes to mind as well as the work of Jean Baudrillard (1975). Of the two, I prefer Bourdieu because he does not reduce human praxis to an autonomous semiotic system. Habermas is discussed to the exclusion of others because he has been foremost in challenging Lyotard and because of the comprehensiveness of his communicative theory.

9 Bounded Cultures – Bounded Selves

1 The concept of ethnoscape, a neologism that invokes the visual landscape, is nonetheless for Appadurai a concept that includes concretely the movement of persons across borders and the reconstitution of ethnic identities. Appadurai's work is also interesting for its assertion that globalism has become more generally a process by which all peoples and cultures imagine other lives, an insight which has important implications for ethnographic research.

2 The French were not the only Europeans to express concern over European Union proposals. Germans were worried, for example, that EU regulations would undermine the long-standing purity laws that prevent additives and preservatives from being added to beer.

3 One pastime that I enjoyed while traveling to my multiple field sites was listening to French talk shows. While the information is surely anecdotal and partial, I often heard expressed by individuals who called into the station a real concern with the diminishing role of French culture globally and the sense the EU regulations would undermine local cultural autonomy. The growth of English as the dominant commercial language was also a common complaint on the part of callers.

4 This is not to say that the chador incident was the first or only precipatator of national debate over French identity. Such debates go hand in hand with the formation of the nation state and are ever present in France with respect to regional autonomy and regional identity. However the conservative politics of Le Pen and incidents of ethnic prejudice and violence against both French of North African descent and immigrants tend to keep the debate over being French current and lively.

5 Mary Pierce was the women's champion of year 2000 Roland Garos tennis championship. There has not been a "French" champion at Roland Garos since

1970 or before. The French, believing that Mary Pierce is their best hope in women's tennis, have claimed her as one of their own in spite of the fact that Pierce was very nervous about having to give a speech in French if she won Roland Garos. The contrast to the young North African girl and the chador incident is remarkable.

6 I sensed from the beginning that the rejection of the chador as appropriate dress for French schools had something to do with what Edward Said (1978) has referred to as orientalism: regarding the East as homogenous and exotic, yet subordinate to the dominion of western ways and values. In a more violent sense, the exclusion of the "orient" is what led the Serbs to destroy the university library in Sarajevo, since the library contained documents that seemed to substantiate the considerable eastern influence on that region of the world.

7 The Comaroffs (1992) have pointed out that inhabitants of the European countryside were often regarded by the metropolitan centers of Europe as if they were indigenous populations in the colonies. In France, inhabitants of the countryside are often a subject of ridicule by ostensibly cultivated city dwellers, who make country-dwellers the analog of the non-western "other."

8 There are numerous examples in anthropology of collaborative work, such as the Harvard Project among the Kung, but generally in the form of accomplished scholars training their graduate students in the field. Conventionally, a doctoral dissertation is supposed to be an original work based on an original research agenda, both of which are individualized.

9 I believe that apart from the practical exigencies of funding and working in far-away places, there is in the notion of the doctoral thesis – making an original contribution that carries forward a field of knowledge – an implicit idea of genius, itself a natural component of select individuals. Consequently, creative work is often seen in western societies as based on individual effort, on utilizing the unique qualities of the individual. Again, this is likely to be an idea that emerges with the prioritizing of the individual over that of community.

10 Whether or not one agrees with Sahlins's (1985) account of Cook's reception and eventual fate, Sahlins is unique in seeking to present the fateful encounter from the "native's point of view."

11 It is the case that the Azande studied by Evans-Pritchard lived on a reservation and that the Nuer presented a challenge to the colonial office as a consequence of political unrest. This would surely qualify to some degree the "sympathy" of the anthropologist. However, I want to avoid the direct attribution of instrumental motives on the part of anthropologists who conducted field research during the colonial era. The context of this research was generally complex, with mixed motives and expectations.

12 The relationship I (and Cole) establish between structuralism, colonialism, and instrumental rationality is not meant as a dismissal of the important challenge made by British social anthropologists to historical accounts informed by evolutionary theory.

13 I am here thinking of Foucault's treatment of Victorian sexuality. In contrast to most scholars, Foucault believes that Victorians were obsessed with sexuality, and this is evidenced by social arrangements of space and action that created separate domains for men and women. One could argue the same for colonial

anthropology in the sense that the denial of history was its hegemonic embracing.

14 I conducted field research initially at a Dordogne wine cooperative located in the interior. The director of this cooperative told me that it was the cooperative's objective to produce wines that did not vary at all in taste from year to year, much like Coca Cola. This idea is very foreign to Médoc cooperatives, where it is expected that variation in the taste of wine from year to year is a component of its distinction.

15 I am indebted to Pierre Bourdieu's celebrated *Distinction* (1984) in coming to grasp the winegrowing hierarchy and differences between wines through the concept of "cultural capital." This concept, with its emphasis on differentiated symbolic power, provides a valuable insight to and critique of wine and winegrowing as a "natural" process.

16 That anthropologists should conduct field research in more than one locale, perhaps tracing the relations between disparate sites, is not a new idea. However, I believe that Marcus deserves credit, as we shall see, for bringing some fresh thought to this research potential.

17 This is most evident from Marcus's rebuke of Mintz for employing the "grand narrative" of Marxism (1998: 91). Nevertheless, Marcus does seem to appreciate Mintz's tracing of broad interconnections and consequences associated historically with the sugar trade between Europe, Africa, and the Caribbean.

18 The foregrounding of informants' voices is rhetorically powerful and seductive in that readers are given the impression that informants speak directly. What is not always apparent is that informants' voices are prefigured through the ethnographer's writing, translation, and selection of material presented in the text.

19 This is even the case with indigenous anthropologists in that their training and scholarship places them in a position of representing the populations they study even though there may be a close association on cultural grounds.

20 One is also reminded of Geertz's (1973) witticism that what we have in common (as humans) is also what sets us apart.

21 Geertz's (1973) emphasis on signification and thick description, while a monumental improvement on Tylor's classic "complex whole," still reproduces the notion that culture is shared and homogeneous. What is missing in most of Geertz's compelling ethnographic accounts is the struggle of human actors over what amounts to "contested meanings." Contested meanings are in fact the real density of thick description.

22 I want to be clear that I do not believe that anthropology has no role to play in the creation of civic discourse and the critique of hegemonic social relations. However, academics sometimes believe that in writing for their peers that they are transforming the social world when in fact their influence is often regrettably marginal.

Bibliography

Abu-Lughod, Lila. 1991. "Writing Against Culture," in Richard G. Fox (ed.) *Recapturing Anthropology: Working in the Present*. Sante Fe, NM: School of American Research Press.

Adorno, Theodor W. 1976a. "Introduction," in *The Positivist Dispute in German Sociology*, Theodor W. Adorno et al., pp. 1–68. New York: Harper and Row.

—— 1976b. "On the Logic of the Social Sciences," in *The Positivist Dispute in German Sociology*, Theodor W. Adorno et al., pp. 105–22. New York: Harper and Row.

Afigbo, A. E. 1972. *The Warrant Chiefs: Indirect Rule in Southeastern Nigeria 1891–1929*. New York: Humanities Press.

Althusser, Louis. 1970. *For Marx*. New York: Vintage Books.

Althusser, Louis and Balibar, Etienne. 1970. *Reading Capital*. New York: Pantheon Books.

Anderson, Benedict. 1983. *Imagined Communities*. London and New York: Verso.

Anderson, Perry. 1980. *Argument within English Marxism*. New York: Schocken Books.

Apel, Karl-Otto. 1967. *Analytic Philosophy of Language and the Geisteswissenschaften*. Dordrecht: D. Reidel.

—— 1972. "The A Priori of Communication and the Foundation of the Humanities." *Man and World 5* (February), pp. 3–37.

—— 1977. "Types of Social Science in the Light of Human Interests of Knowledge." *Social Research* 44 (Autumn), pp. 425–70.

Appadurai, Arjun (ed.) 1986. *The Social Life of Things*. Cambridge: Cambridge University Press.

—— 1991. "Global Ethnoscapes: Notes and Queries for a Transnational Anthropology," in Richard G. Fox (ed.) *Recapturing Anthropology: Working in the Present*, Sante Fe, NM: School of American Research Press.

Arendt, Hannah. 1958. *The Human Condition*. Chicago: University of Chicago Press.

Asad, Talal (ed.) 1973. *Anthropology and the Colonial Encounter*. New York: Humanities Press.

Asad, Talal and Wolpe, Harold. 1976. "Concepts of Modes of Production." *Economy and Society* 5/4, pp. 470–505.

Aya, Rod. 1976. "Review of Barry Hindess and Paul Q. Hist: *Pre-Capitalist Modes of Production." Theory and Society* 3/4, pp. 623–9,

Bakhtin, Mikhail. 1986. *Speech Genres and Other Late Essays*, translated by V. W. McGee. Austin: University of Texas Press.

Banji, Jairus. 1970. "Description, Meaning and Social Science." *Journal of Anthropological Society Oxford* 1/3, pp. 110–13.

Barthes, Roland. 1967. *Elements of Semiology*. New York: Hill and Wang.

—— 1975. *The Pleasure of the Text*. New York: Hill and Wang.

Baudrillard, Jean. 1975. *The Mirror of Production*. St. Louis: Telos Press.

Bauman, Zygmunt. 1978. *Hermeneutics and Social Science*. New York: Columbia University Press.

Beattie, J. H. M. 1971. "On Understanding Ritual," in Bryan R. Wilson (ed.) *Rationality*, pp. 240–68. New York: Harper and Row.

Bellah, Robert N. 1975. *The Broken Covenant: American Civil Religion in Time of Trial*. New York: Seabury Press.

Bernstein, Basil. 1971. *Class, Codes and Control*. London: Routledge and Kegan Paul.

Bernstein, Richard J. 1976. *The Restructuring of Social and Political Theory*. Philadelphia: University of Pennsylvania Press.

—— 1983. *Beyond Objectivism and Relativism: Science, Hermeneutics and Praxis*. Philadelphia: University of Pennsylvania Press.

Boas, Franz. 1889. "On Alternating Sounds." *American Anthropologist* 2, pp. 47–53.

—— 1940. *Race, Language and Culture*. New York: Macmillan.

Bourdieu, Pierre. 1977. *Outline of a Theory of Practice*. Cambridge: Cambridge University Press.

—— 1984. *Distinction: A Social Critique of the Judgment of Taste*. Cambridge, MA: Harvard University Press.

Bowden, Ross. 1970. "Winch and the Social Determination of Truth." *Journal of Anthropological Society Oxford* 1/3, pp. 113–25.

Clifford, James. 1988. *The Predicament of Culture: Twentieth-Century Ethnography, Literature and Art*. Cambridge, MA: Harvard University Press.

Clifford, James and Marcus, George E. (eds.) 1986. *Writing Culture: The Poetics and Politics of Ethnography*. Berkeley: University of California Press.

Coates, Peter. 1971. "Problem of Paradigm Discrimination." *Journal of Anthropological Society Oxford* 2/3, pp. 137–45.

Cohen, Bernard S. 1987. *Anthropologist among the Historians and Other Essays*. New Delhi: Oxford University Press.

Cole, John W. 1977. "Anthropology Comes Part-Way Home: Community Studies in Europe." *Annual Review of Anthropology* 6, pp. 349–78.

Colletti, Lucio. 1975. "Marxism and the Dialectic." *New Left Review* 93, pp. 3–92.

Collingwood, R. G. 1956. *The Idea of History*. Oxford: Clarendon Press.

Comaroff, John and Comaroff, Jean. 1992. *Ethnography and the Historical Imagination*. Boulder, CO: Westview Press.

Crick, Malcolm. 1971. "Anthropology and the Philosophy of Science." *Journal of Anthropological Society Oxford* 1, pp. 18–32.

—— 1973. "Two Styles in the Study of Witchcraft." *Journal of Anthropological Society Oxford* 4/1, pp. 17–31.

Culler, Jonathan. 1976. *Structural Poetics: Structuralism, Linguistics, and the Study of Literature*. Ithaca: Cornell University Press.

Derksen, A. A. 1978. "On an Unnoticed Key to Reality." *Philosophy of Social Sciences* 8 (September), pp. 209–25.

Derrida, Jacques. 1974. *Of Grammatology*. Baltimore: Johns Hopkins University Press.

—— 1978. *Writing and Difference*. Chicago: University of Chicago Press.

Diamond, Stanley. 1974. *In Search of the Primitive: A Critique of Civilization*. New Brunswick, NJ: Transaction Books.

Dion, Roger. 1977. *Histoire de la vigne et du vin en France*. Paris: Flammarion.

Dobb, Maurice. 1976. "Review of *Pre-Capitalist Modes of Production.*" *History* 61/201, p. 91.

Douglas, Mary. 1966. *Purity and Danger: An Analysis of the Concepts of Pollution and Taboo*. London: Routledge and Kegan Paul.

—— 1973. *Natural Symbols*. New York: Random House.

Dupré, Georges and Rey, Pierre-Philippe. 1973. "Reflections on the Pertinence of a Theory of the History of Exchange." *Economy and Society* 2/2.

Durkheim, Emile. 1965. *The Elementary Forms of the Religious Life*. New York: Free Press.

Dwyer, Kevin. 1982. *Moroccan Dialogues: Anthropology in Question*. Baltimore: Johns Hopkins University Press.

Eco, Umberto. 1979. *A Theory of Semiotics*. Bloomington: Indiana University Press.

Ehrenreich, Barbara and English, Deirdre. 1973. *Witches, Midwives and Nurses: A History of Women Healers*. Old Westbury, NY: Feminist Press.

Emmet, Dorothy. 1960. "How Far Can Structural Studies Take Account of the Individual?," *Journal of the Royal Anthropological Institute of Great Britain and Ireland* 90, pp. 191–200.

Escobar, Arturo. 1995. *Encountering Development: The Making and Unmaking of the Third World*. Princeton: Princeton University Press.

Evans-Pritchard, E. E. 1937. *Witchcraft, Oracles and Magic among the Azande*. Oxford: Clarendon Press.

—— 1956. *Nuer Religion*. New York and Oxford: Oxford University Press.

—— 1962. *Social Anthropology and Other Essays*. New York: Free Press.

—— 1965. *Theories of Primitive Religion*. Oxford: Clarendon Press.

Fabian, Johannes. 1971. "Language, History and Anthropology." *Journal for the Philosophy of the Social Sciences* 1/1, pp. 19–47.

—— 1983. *Time and the Other: How Anthropology Makes its Object*. New York: Columbia University Press.

Firth, Raymond (ed.) 1970. *Man and Culture*. New York: Humanities Press.

Flaubert, Gustave. 1964. *Madame Bovary*. New York: New American Library.

Foucault, Michel. 1970. *The Order of Things: An Archaeology of the Human Sciences*. New York: Random House.

—— 1973. *The Birth of the Clinic: An Archaeology of Medical Perception*. London: Tavistock Publications.

—— 1978. *Discipline and Punish: The Birth of the Prison*, translated by Alan Sheridan. New York: Pantheon.

Fox, Richard G. (ed.) 1991. *Recapturing Anthropology: Working in the Present*. Sante Fe, NM: School of American Research Press.

Frank, Andre Gunder. 1969. *Capitalism and Underdevelopment in Latin America*. New York: Monthly Review Press.

Fried, Morton H. 1975. *The Notion of Tribe*. Menlo Park, CA: Cummings Publishing Company.

Gadamer, Hans-Georg. 1975. *Truth and Method*. New York: Seabury Press.

—— 1976. *Philosophical Hermeneutics*. Berkeley: University of California Press.

Gay, Peter. 1968. *The Englightenment: An Interpretation*. New York: Random House.

Geertz, Clifford. 1973. *The Interpretation of Cultures*. New York: Basic Books.

—— 1976. "From the Native's Point of View: On the Nature of Anthropological Understanding," in Keith Basso and Henry Selby (eds.) *Meaning and Anthropology*, pp. 221–37. Albuquerque: University of New Mexico Press.

—— 1980. *Negara: The Theatre State in Nineteenth Century Bali*. Princeton: Princeton University Press.

—— 1983. *Local Knowledge: Further Essays in Interpretive Anthropology*. New York: Basic Books.

Geras, Norman. 1972. "Althusser's Marxism: An Account and Assessment." *New Left Review* 71, pp. 57–86.

Glucksman, Andre. 1972. "A Ventriloquist Structuralism." *New Left Review* 72, pp. 68–92.

Godelier, Maurice, 1972. *Rationality and Irrationality in Economics*. New York: Monthly Review Press.

—— 1973. "Structure and Contradiction in Capital," in Robin Blackburn (ed.) *Ideology in Social Science*, pp. 334–68. New York: Vintage Books.

—— 1977. *Perspectives in Marxist Anthropology*. Cambridge: Cambridge University Press.

—— 1999. *The Enigma of the Gift*, translated by Nora Scott. Chicago: University of Chicago Press.

Goffman Erving. 1961. *Asylums*. Garden City, NY: Doubleday.

Gramsci, Antonio. 1975. *The Modern Prince and Other Writings*. New York: International Publishers.

Griaule, Marcel. 1965. *Conversations with Ogotemmeli*. London: Oxford University Press.

Gudeman, Stephen and Rivera, Alberto. 1990. *Conversations in Colombia: The Domestic Economy in Life and Text*. Cambridge: Cambridge University Press.

Gupta, Akhil and Ferguson, James (eds.) 1997. *Anthropological Locations: Boundaries and Grounds of a Field Science*. Berkeley: University of California Press.

Habermas, Jürgen. 1970a. *Toward a Rational Society: Student Protest, Science and Politics*. Boston: Beacon Press.

—— 1970b. "Towards a Theory of Communicative Competence." *Inquiry* 13, pp. 360–75.

—— 1971. *Knowledge and Human Interests*. Boston: Beacon Press.

—— 1973. *Theory and Practice*. Boston: Beacon Press.

—— 1975. "Towards a Reconstruction of Historical Materialism." *Theory and Society* 2 (Fall), pp. 287–300.

—— 1976. "The Analytical Theory of Science and Dialectics," in *The Positivist Dispute in German Sociology*, Theodor W. Adorno et al., pp. 131–63. New York: Harper and Row.

—— 1977. "A Review of Gadamer's *Truth and Method*," in F. Dallmayr and T. A. McCarthy (eds.) *Understanding and Social Inquiry*, South Bend: Notre Dame Press.

—— 1979a. "History and Evolution." *Telos* 39 (Spring), pp. 5–44.

—— 1979b. *Communication and the Evolution of Society*. Boston: Beacon Press.

—— 1981. "Modernity versus Postmodernity," *New German Critique* 22 (Winter), pp. 3–14.

—— 1984. *The Theory of Communicative Action*, vol. 1: *Reason and the Rationalization of Society*. Boston: Beacon Press.

Hanson, F. Allan. 1970. "Understanding in Philosophical Anthropology." *Journal of Anthropological Society Oxford* 1/2, pp. 61–81.

—— 1989. "The Making of the Maori: Cultural Invention and Its Logic," *American Anthropologist* 91, pp. 890–902.

Haraway, Donna. 1989. *Primate Visions: Gender, Race, and Nature in the World of Modern Science*. New York: Routledge.

Harris, Marvin. 1979. *Cultural Materialism*. New York: Random House.

Hegel, Georg W. F. 1967. *Hegel's Philosophy of Right*. London: Oxford University Press.

Heller, Agnes. 1981. *Renaissance Man*. New York: Schocken Books.

Henry, Jules. 1965. *Culture against Man*. New York: Random House.

Herder, Johann Gottfried. 1966. "Essay on the Origin of Language," in *On the Origin of Language: Two Essays by Jean-Jacques Rousseau and Johann Gottfried Herder* translated by John H. Moran and Alexander Gode, pp. 87–176. New York: Frederick Ungar.

Herskovits, M. J. 1952. *Economic Anthropology*. New York: Alfred A. Knopf.

Herzfeld, Michael. 1987. *Anthropology through the Looking-Glass: Critical Ethnography in the Margins of Europe*. Cambridge: Cambridge University Press.

Hilton, Rodney (ed.) 1978. *The Transition from Feudalism to Capitalism*. London: Verso.

Hindess, Barry and Hirst, Paul Q. 1975. *Pre-Capitalist Modes of Production*. London: Routledge and Kegan Paul.

—— 1976. "Mode of Production and Social Formation in *PCMP*: A Reply to John Taylor." *Critique of Anthropology* 2/8, pp. 49–58.

—— 1977. *Modes of Production and Social Formation: An Auto-Critique of Pre-Capitalist Modes of Production*. Atlantic Highlands, NJ: Humanities Press.

Hjelmslev, Louis. 1963. *Prolegomena to a Theory of Language*. Madison: University of Wisconsin Press.

—— 1966. *Le Language, une introduction*. Paris: Editions de Minuit.

Hobsbawm, E. J. 1973. "Karl Marx's Contribution to Historiography," in Robin Blackburn (ed.) *Ideology in Social Science*, pp. 265–83. New York: Vintage Books.

Hobsbawm, Eric and Ranger, Terence. 1983. *The Invention of Tradition*. Cambridge: Cambridge University Press.

Hodge, Joanna. 1977. "Hermeneutics in Anthropology." *Journal of Anthropological Society Oxford* 8/2, pp. 74–83.

Hogan, John. 1976. "Gadamer and the Hermeneutical Experience." *Philosophy Today* (Spring) pp. 3–12.

Hollis, Martin. 1967. "The Limits of Irrationality." *Archives Européennes de Sociologie* 82, pp. 265–71.

——1972. "Witchcraft and Winchcraft." *Philosophy of Social Sciences* 22, pp. 89–103.

Hookway, Christopher and Pettit, Philip (eds.) 1978. *Action and Interpretation: Studies in the Philosophy of the Social Sciences*. Cambridge: Cambridge University Press.

Horkheimer, Max. 1972. *Critical Theory*. New York: Seabury Press.

Horkheimer, Max and Adorno, Theodor W. 1972. *Dialectic of Enlightenment*. New York: Seabury Press.

Horton, Robin. 1971. "African Traditional Thought and Western Science," in Bryan R. Wilson (ed.) *Rationality*, pp. 131–72. New York: Harper and Row.

——1973a. "Lévy-Bruhl, Durkheim and the Scientific Revolution," in Robin Horton and Ruth Finnegan (eds.) *Modes of Thought*, pp. 249–305. London: Faber and Faber.

——1973b. "Paradox and Explanation: A Reply to Mr. Skorupski I." *Philosophy of Social Sciences* 3/3, pp. 231–56.

——1973c. "Paradox and Explanation: A Reply to Mr. Skorupski II." *Philosophy of Social Sciences* 3/4, pp. 289–312.

Horton, Robin and Finnegan, Ruth (eds.) 1973. *Modes of Thought: Essays on Thinking in Western and Non-Western Societies*. London: Faber and Faber.

Husserl, Edmund. 1970. *The Crisis of European Sciences and Transcendental Phenomenology: An Introduction to Phenomenological Philosophy*, translated with an introduction by David Carr. Evanston, IL: Northwestern University Press.

——1973. *Cartesian Meditations: An Introduction to Phenomenology*. The Hague: Martinus Nijhoff.

Huyssen, Andreas. 1981. "The Search for Tradition: Avant-Garde and Postmodernism in the 1970s," *New German Critique* 22 (Winter), pp. 3–14.

——1984. "Mapping the Postmodern." *New German Critique* 33 (Fall), pp. 5–52.

Hymes, Dell (ed.) 1969. *Reinventing Anthropology*. New York: Random House.

——1974. *Foundations in Sociolinguistics: An Ethnographic Approach*. Philadelphia: University of Pennsylvania Press.

Idhe, Don. 1971. *Hermeneutic Phenomenology: The Philosophy of Paul Ricoeur*. Evanston, IL: Northwestern University Press.

Jackson, Michael. 1998. *Minima Ethnographica: Intersubjectivity and the Anthropological Project*. Chicago: University of Chicago Press.

Jameson, Fredric and Miyoshi, Masao (eds.) 1998. *The Cultures of Globalization*. Durham, NC and London: Duke University Press.

Jarvie, I. C. 1964. *The Revolution in Anthropology*. Chicago: Henry Regnery Company.

——1967. "On Theories of Field Work and the Scientific Character of Anthropology." *Philosophy of Science* 34/3, pp. 223–42.

——1972. *Concepts and Society*. London: Routledge and Kegan Paul.

Jauss, Hans Robert. 1975. "The Idealist Embarrassment: Observations on Marxist Aesthetics." *New Literary History* 7/1, pp. 191–208.

Jules-Rosette, Bermetta. 1978. "The Veil of Objectivity: Prophecy, Divination and Social Inquiry." *American Anthropologist* 80 (September), pp. 549–71.

Keesing, Roger. 1992. *Custom and Confrontation: The Kwaio Struggle for Identity.* Chicago: University of Chicago Press.

Kekes, John. 1973. "Towards a Theory of Rationality." *Philosophy of Social Sciences* 3/4, pp. 275–88.

Kolakowski, Leszek. 1971. "Althusser's Marx." *Socialist Register,* pp. 111–28.

Kortian, Garbis. 1980. *Metacritique: The Philosophical Argument of Jürgen Habermas.* Cambridge: Cambridge University Press.

Kosik, Karel. 1969. "The Concrete Totality." *Telos* 4 (Fall), pp. 35–54.

Kuhn, Thomas. 1962. *The Structure of Scientific Revolutions.* Chicago: University of Chicago Press.

Lakatos, Imre and Musgrave, Alan (eds.) 1970. *Criticism and the Growth of Knowledge.* London and New York: Cambridge University Press.

Lash, Scott and Urry, John. 1987. *The End of Organized Capitalism.* Madison: University of Wisconsin Press.

Lefort, Claude. 1978. "Marx: From One Vision of History to Another." *Social Research* 45 (Winter) pp. 615–66.

Leiss, William. 1974. *The Domination of Nature.* Boston: Beacon Press.

Lenhardt, Christian K. 1972. "Rise and Fall of Transcendental Anthropology." *Philosophy of Social Sciences* 2/2, pp. 231–46.

Lévi-Strauss, Claude. 1963. *Structural Anthropology.* New York: Basic Books.

—— 1974. *Tristes Tropiques.* New York: Atheneum.

Lévy-Bruhl, Lucien. 1965. *The "Soul" of the Primitive.* London: George Allen and Unwin.

Linnekin, Jocelyn. 1983. "Defining Tradition: Variations on the Hawaiian Identity," *American Ethnologist* 10, pp. 241–52.

—— 1991. "Cultural Invention and the Dilemma of Authenticity," *American Anthropologist* 93, pp. 446–9.

—— 1992. "On the Theory and Politics of Cultural Construction in the Pacific," *Oceania* 62, pp. 249–63.

Llobera, Josep R. 1978. "Epistemology: The End of an Illusion?," *Critique of Anthropology* 3/12, pp. 89–95.

Löwith, Karl. 1949. *Meaning in History.* Chicago: University of Chicago Press.

Lukács, Georg. 1971. *History and Class Consciousness.* Cambridge, MA: MIT Press.

—— 1972. *The Theory of the Novel.* Cambridge, MA: MIT Press.

Lukes, Steven. 1970. "Methodological Individualism Reconsidered," in Dorothy Emmet and Alasdair MacIntyre (eds.) *Social Theory and Philosophical Analysis,* New York: Macmillan.

—— 1971. "Some Problems about Rationality," in Bryan R. Wilson (ed.) *Rationality,* pp. 194–213. New York: Harper and Row.

—— 1973. "On the Social Determination of Truth," in Robin Horton and Ruth Finnegan (eds.) *Modes of Thought,* pp. 230–48. London: Faber and Faber.

Lyotard, Jean-François. 1984. *The Postmodern Condition: A Report on Knowledge.* Minneapolis: University of Minnesota Press.

MacIntyre, Alasdair. 1971a. "Is Understanding Religion Compatible with Believing?" in Bryan R. Wilson (ed.) *Rationality,* pp. 62–77. New York: Harper and Row.

—— 1971b. "The Idea of a Social Science," in Bryan R. Wilson (ed.) *Rationality*, pp. 12–30. New York: Harper and Row.

MacPherson, C. B. 1962. *The Political Theory of Possessive Individualism: Hobbes to Locke*. London and New York: Oxford University Press.

Malinowski, Bronislaw. 1961. *Argonauts of the Western Pacific*. New York: E. P. Dutton.

Marcus, George E. 1998. *Ethnography through Thick and Thin*. Princeton: Princeton University Press.

Marcus, George E. and Fischer, Michael M. J. 1986. *Anthropology as Cultural Critique*. Chicago: University of Chicago Press.

Marcuse, Herbert. 1964. *One Dimensional Man*. Boston: Beacon Press.

Marwick, M. G. 1973. "How Real is the Charmed Circle in African and Western Thought?," *Africa* 42/1, pp. 59–71.

Marx, Karl. 1964. *The Economic and Philosophic Manuscripts of 1844*. New York: International Publishers.

—— 1965. *Pre-Capitalist Economic Formations*. New York: International Publishers.

—— 1967a. *Capital*, vol. 1. New York: International Publishers.

—— 1967b. "On the Jewish Question," in Lloyd D. Easton and Kurt H. Guddat (eds.) *Writings of the Young Marx on Philosophy and Society*, pp. 216–48. New York: Anchor Books.

—— 1973. *Grundrisse*. New York: Random House.

Marx, Karl and Engels, Frederick. 1970. *The German Ideology*. New York: International Publishers.

Masterman, Margaret. 1970. "The Nature of a Paradigm," in Imre Lakatos and Alan Musgrave (eds.) *Criticism and the Growth of Knowledge*, pp. 59–91. London and New York: Cambridge University Press.

Mead, Margaret. 1950. *Sex and Temperament in Three Primitive Societies*. New York: New American Library.

Meillassoux, Claude. 1960. "Essai d'interpretation du phénomène économique dans les sociétés traditionelles." *Cahiers d'Études Africanes* 4.

—— 1964. *Anthropologie économique des Gouro de Côte d'Ivoire*. The Hague: Mouton.

—— 1969. "Introduction," in Claude Meillassoux (ed.) *Development of Indigenous Trade and Markets in West Africa*, pp. 49–85. London: Oxford University Press.

—— 1976. "Social and Economic Reproduction in Pre-Industrial Society." Unpublished paper.

Melton, Lawrence C. 1973. "Is Belief Possible?," *Journal of Anthropological Society Oxford* 4/3, pp. 143–51.

Mészáros, Istvan. 1972. *Lukács' Concept of Dialectic*. London: Merlin Press.

Mintz, Sidney 1985. *Sweetness and Power*. New York: Penguin Books.

—— 1987. "Author's Rejoinder," *Food and Foodways* 2: 171–97.

—— 1996. *Tasting Food, Tasting Freedom: Excursions into Eating, Culture and the Past*. Boston: Beacon Press.

Morgan, Lewis Henry. 1972a. *Ancient Society*. Palo Alto: New York Labor News.

—— 1972b. *League of the Iroquois*. Secaucaus, NJ: Citadel Press.

Murdock, George Peter. 1949. *Social Structure*. New York: Macmillan.

Nadel. S. F. 1942. *A Black Byzantium: The Kingdom of Nupe in Nigeria.* London: Oxford University Press.

Natanson, Maurice Alexander (ed.) 1969. *Essays in Phenomenology.* The Hague: Martinus Nijhoff.

——(ed.) 1973. *Phenomenology and the Social Sciences.* Evanston, IL: Northwestern University Press.

Needham, Rodney 1972. *Belief, Language and Experience.* Oxford: Basil Blackwell.

Nielsen, Kai. 1974. "Rationality and Relativism." *Philosophy of Social Sciences* 4/4, pp. 313–31.

Obeyesekere, Gananath. 1981. *Medusa's Hair: An Essay on Personal Symbols and Religious Experience.* Chicago: University of Chicago Press.

Palmer, Richard E. 1969. *Hermeneutics.* Evanston, IL: Northwestern University Press.

Piccone, Paul. 1969. "Structuralist Marxism." *Radical America* 3/5.

Pijassou, René. 1980. *Le Médoc: Un grand vignoble de qualité,* 2 vols. Paris: Tallandier.

Pitkin, Hanna Fenichel. 1972. *Wittgenstein and Justice.* Berkeley: University of California Press.

Polanyi, Karl. 1957. *The Great Transformation: The Political and Economic Origins of Our Time.* Boston: Beacon Press.

Polier, Nicole and Roseberry, William. 1989. "Tristes Tropes: Postmodern Anthropologists Encounter the Other and Discover Themselves." *Economy and Society* 18/2.

Pollner, Melvin. 1974. "Mundane Reasoning." *Philosophy of Social Sciences* 4/1, pp. 35–54.

Popper, Karl. 1966. *The Open Society and Its Enemies,* 5th edn. London: Hutchinson.

Pospisil, Leopold. 1963. *The Kapauku Papuans of West New Guinea.* New York: Holt, Rinehart and Winston.

Rabinow, Paul. 1973. *Reflections on Fieldwork in Morocco.* Berkeley: University of California Press.

Radcliffe-Brown, A. R. 1965. *Structure and Function in Primitive Society.* New York: Free Press.

Radin, Paul. 1971. *The World of Primitive Man.* New York: E. P. Dutton.

Radnitzky, Gerard. 1970. *Contemporary Schools of Metascience.* Chicago: Henry Regnery Company.

Ranger, Terence. 1983. "The Invention of Tradition in Colonial Africa," in Eric Hobsbawm and Terence Ranger (eds.) *The Invention of Tradition.* Cambridge: Cambridge University Press.

Reiter, Rayna R. (ed.) 1975. *Toward an Anthropology of Women.* New York and London: Monthly Review Press.

Ricoeur, Paul. 1969. *The Symbolism of Evil.* Boston: Beacon Press.

——1970. *Freud and Philosophy: An Essay on Interpretation.* New Haven: Yale University Press.

——1971. "The Model of the Text: Meaningful Action Considered as a Text." *Social Research* 38/3, pp. 529–62.

——1973a. "Ethics and Culture: Habermas and Gadamer in Dialogue." *Philosophy Today* 17 (Summer), pp. 153–65.

—— 1973b. "The Task of Hermeneutics." *Philosophy Today* 17 (Summer), pp. 112–28.

—— 1974. *The Conflict of Interpretations: Essays in Hermeneutics.* Evanston, IL: Northwestern University Press.

—— 1976. *Interpretation Theory: Discourse and the Surplus of Meaning.* Fort Worth: Texas Christian University Press.

Robbins, Lionel Charles. 1935. *An Essay on the Nature and Significance of Economic Science.* London: Oxford University Press.

Rogers, Susan Carol. 1991. *Shaping Modern Times in Rural France: The Transformation and Reproduction of an Aveyronnais Community.* Princeton: Princeton University Press.

Rorty, Richard. 1979. *Philosophy and the Mirror of Nature.* Princeton: Princeton University Press.

Rosaldo, Renato. 1989. *Culture and Truth: The Remaking of Social Analysis.* Boston: Beacon Press.

Rosdolsky, Roman. 1974. "Comment on the Method of Marx's Capital." *New German Critique* 3 (Fall).

Roseberry, William. 1988. "Political Economy." *Annual Review of Anthropology* 17.

—— 1989. *Anthropologies and Histories: Essays in Culture, History and Political Economy.* New Brunswick, NJ and London: Rutgers University Press.

Rousseau, Jean-Jacques. 1964. *The Social Contract and Discourse on the Origin of Inequality.* New York: Simon and Schuster.

Sahlins, Marshall. 1972. *Stone Age Economics.* New York: Aldine Publishing Company.

—— 1976. *Culture and Practical Reason.* Chicago: University of Chicago Press.

—— 1985. *Islands of History.* Chicago: University of Chicago Press.

Said, Edward W. 1979. *Orientalism.* New York: Vintage Books.

Samuelson, Paul. 1973. *Readings in Economics,* 7th edn. New York: McGraw-Hill.

Sangren, Steven P. 1988. "Rhetoric and the Authority of Ethnography." *Current Anthropology* 29/3.

Saussure, Ferdinand de. 1966. *Course in General Linguistics.* New York: McGraw-Hill.

Scholte, Bob. 1966. "Epistemic Paradigms: Some Problems in Cross-cultural Research on Social Anthropology, History and Theory." *American Anthropologist* 68/5, pp. 1192–201.

—— 1974. "Toward a Reflexive and Critical Anthropology," in Dell Hymes (ed.) *Reinventing Anthropology,* pp. 430–59. New York: Random House.

Schroyer, Trent. 1975. *The Critique of Domination.* Boston: Beacon Press.

Schutz, Alfred. 1967. *The Phenomenology of the Social World,* translated by George Walsh and Frederick Lehnert. Evanston, IL: Northwestern University Press.

—— (ed.) 1970. *On Phenomenology and Social Relations.* Chicago: University of Chicago Press.

Searle, John. 1967. *Speech Acts: An Essay in the Philosophy of Language.* London: Cambridge University Press.

Settle, Tom. 1971. "Rationality of Science versus Rationality of Magic." *Philosophy of Social Sciences* 1/3, pp. 173–94.

Settle, Tom, Jarvie, 1. C., and Agassi, Joseph. 1974. "Towards a Theory of Open Criticism." *Philosophy of Social Sciences* 4/1, pp. 83–90.

Sharpe, R. A. 1974. "Ideology and Ontology." *Philosophy of Social Sciences* 4/1, pp. 55–64.

Shostak, Marjorie. 1981. *Nisa: The Life and Words of a !Kung Woman*. Cambridge, MA.: Harvard University Press.

Skorupski, John. 1973a. "Science and Traditional Religious Thought I and II." *Philosophy of Social Sciences* 3/2, pp. 97–115.

—— 1973b. "Science and Traditional Religious Thought III and IV." *Philosophy of Social Sciences* 3/3, pp. 209–30.

Stocking, George W., Jr. 1968. *Race, Culture and Evolution: Essays in the History of Anthropology*. New York: Free Press.

—— (ed.) 1974. *The Shaping of American Anthropology 1883–1911*. New York: Basic Books.

Strathern, Andrew. 1979. *Ongka: A Self-account of a New Guinea Big-man*, translated by Andrew Strathern. New York: St. Martins Press.

Strathern, Marilyn. 1988. *The Gender of the Gift*. Berkeley: University of California Press.

Tambiah, Stanley. 1990. *Magic, Science, Religion and the Scope of Rationality*. Cambridge: Cambridge University Press.

Taussig, Michael. 1980. *The Devil and Commodity Fetishism in South America*. Chapel Hill: University of North Carolina Press.

—— 1987. "History as Commodity in Some Recent American (Anthropological) Literature." *Food and Foodways* 2.

Taylor, John. 1975. "Review Article: *Pre-Capitalist Modes of Production*, Part I." *Critique of Anthropology* 1/4–5, pp. 127–55.

—— 1976. "Review Article: *Pre-Capitalist Modes of Production*, Part II." *Critique of Anthropology* 2/6, pp. 6–70.

Terray, Emmanuel. 1972. *Marxism and Primitive Societies*. New York and London: Monthly Review Press.

Thompson, Edward P. 1966. *The Making of the English Working Class*. New York: Vintage Books.

—— 1967. "Time, Work-Discipline and Industrial Capitalism." *Past and Present* 38 (December), pp. 56–97.

—— 1978. *The Poverty of Theory and Other Essays*. New York: Monthly Review Press.

Thompson, John B. and Held, David (eds.) 1982. *Habermas: Critical Debates*. Cambridge, MA: MIT Press.

Torrance, John. 1967. "Rationality and Structural Analysis of Myth." *Archives Européennes de Sociologie* 8/2, pp. 272–81.

Tyler, Stephen A. 1986. "Post-Modern Ethnography: From Document of the Occult to Occult Document," in James Clifford and George E. Marcus (eds.) *Writing Culture*. Berkeley: University of California Press.

Tylor, Sir Edward B. 1960. *Anthropology*. Ann Arbor: University of Michigan Press.

Uchendu, Victor C. 1965. *The Igbo of Southeast Nigeria*. New York: Holt, Rinehart and Winston.

Ulin, Robert C. 1987. "Writing and Power: The Recovery of Winegrowing Histories in the Southwest of France." *Anthropological Quarterly* 60/2, pp. 77–82.

—— 1996. *Vintages and Traditions: An Ethnohistory of Southwest French Wine Cooperatives*. Washington and London: Smithsonian Institution Press.

Veltmeyer, Henri. 1972. "Towards an Assessment of the Structuralist Interrogation of Marx: Claude Lévi-Strauss and Louis Althusser." *Science and Society* 72, pp. 68–92.

Vilar, Pierre. 1973. "Marxist History, a History in the Making: Dialogue with Althusser." *New Left Review* 80, pp. 65–108.

Vincent, Joan. 1991. "Engaging Historicism," in Richard G. Fox (ed.) *Recapturing Anthropology: Working in the Present*. Sante Fe, NM: School of American Research Press.

Wallerstein, Immanuel. 1974. *The Modern World-System: Capitalist Agriculture and the Origins of the European World-Economy in the Sixteenth Century*. New York: Academic Press.

Weber, Eugen. 1976. *Peasants into Frenchmen*. Stanford: Stanford University Press.

Weber, Max. 1958. *The Protestant Ethic and the Spirit of Capitalism*. New York: Scribners.

—— 1964. *The Theory of Social and Economic Organizations*. New York: Free Press.

Wellmer, Albrecht. 1971. *Critical Theory of Society*. New York: Seabury Press.

White, Hayden. 1978. *Tropics of Discourse*. Baltimore, MD: Johns Hopkins University Press.

Whorf, Benjamin Lee. 1956. *Language, Thought and Reality*. Cambridge, MA: MIT Press.

Williams, Raymond. 1962. *Communications*. New York: Penguin Books.

—— 1973a. "Base and Superstructure in Marxist Cultural Theory." *New Left Review* 82 (November–December), pp. 3–17.

—— 1973b. *The Country and the City*. Oxford: Oxford University Press.

—— 1977. *Marxism and Literature*. Oxford: Oxford University Press.

Willis, Paul. 1981. *Learning to Labor: How Working Class Kids get Working Class Jobs*. New York: Columbia University Press.

Wilson, Bryan R. (ed.) 1971. *Rationality*. New York: Harper and Row.

Winch, Peter. 1958. *The Idea of a Social Science and its Relation to Philosophy*. London: Routledge and Kegan Paul.

—— 1964. "Understanding a Primitive Society." *American Philosophical Quarterly* 1/4, pp. 307–24.

—— 1972. *Ethics and Action*. London: Routledge and Kegan Paul.

Wittgenstein, Ludwig. 1953. *Philosophical Investigations*. New York: Macmillan.

—— 1961. *Tractatus Logico-Philosophicus*. London: Routledge and Kegan Paul.

—— 1965. *The Blue and Brown Books*. New York: Harper and Row.

Wolf, Eric. 1962. *Sons of the Shaking Earth*. Chicago: University of Chicago Press.

—— 1982. *Europe and the People without History*. Berkeley: University of California Press.

—— 1999. *Envisioning Power: Ideologies of Dominance and Crisis*. Berkeley: University of California Press.

Wright, Georg Henrik von. 1971. *Explanation and Understanding*. Ithaca: Cornell University Press.

Index

Abu-Lughod, Lila, on culture, 224
action
    communicative, 53–4, 133–5, 140,
        155–7, 177–8
    considered as text, 126–31, 136
    conventionality and, 53–4
    fields of social, 233–6
    unconscious, 53; see also Winch,
        psychoanalysis and unconscious
        motives
Adorno, Theodor, on critique of
    positivism, 84
agency
    historical, 164, 214
    and praxis, 221
Althusser, Louis
    on generalities I–III, 142
    on last instance, 15
    on overdetermination, 248 n. 1
    on social formations, 142–3, 148–9
    on structural causality, 141
    on structures, 142–3, 169
    on theoretical mode of discourse,
        141
American Anthropological Association,
    2
anthropology
    critical, 119–20, 149–50
    as a four-field discipline, 2
    interpretive, 111–15, 118–19, 127;
        see also discourse; Gadamer, fusion
        of horizons; texts, as model for
        fieldwork; witchcraft, Zande
    reflexive, 251 n. 2

and scientistic perspective, 109–10,
    119, 137, 246 n. 8, 247 n. 4
anthropology, functionalist
    critique of, 42–5
    and theory, 41–2
anthropology, social
    British and self-criticism, 41–2
    and colonialism, 42, 44
    humanism, 42
    view of history, 43–4
Apel, Karl-Otto, 58, 242 n. 2, ch. 3
    on the early Wittgenstein, 49–50
Appadurai, Arjun
    on commodities, 253 n. 20
    on ethnoscapes, 205
Arendt, Hannah, 3, 159
    on power, 235, 254 n. 21
Aya, Rod, on Hindess and Hirst, 148
Azande
    historical background, 216
    rationality of beliefs, 47, 66–7; see
        also witchcraft

Balibar, Etienne, 141, 145
Barthes, Roland, semiotic theory of
    culture, 132–3, 172
Bastian, Adolf, influence on Boas, 30
Baudrillard, Jean, critique of
    productivist logic, 157–8, 169,
        249 n. 13
Beattie, J. H. M., 89
being and language, 117; see also
    Gadamer
Boas, Franz

early writings, 28–9
epistemological faults, 28, 31–5
on integrated cultural wholes, 28
and Kant, 29
linguistic writings, 29–30, 32
psychological view of human subject,
    29–30, 32–3
and scientism, 33–4
as social critic, 27–8
theory of interpretation, 29–30
views on history, 31–2
Bourdieu, Pierre, 19–20, 257 n. 15

causality
Horton's concept of, 76–8
limitation of the concept for social
    science, 101
MacIntyre's concept of, 100–2
chador and French national identity,
    207–8
Clifford, James and Marcus, George, on
    ethnographic writing, 21–2
clitoridectomy, 176
Cole, John
on modernization, 213
on structural-functionalism, 212
on village studies, 211
Collingwood, R. G., 161
Comaroff, John and Comaroff, Jean,
    256 n. 7
commodities, fetishism of, 218
contradiction in historical process,
    134
critique
Marxist-dialectical, 135
semiotic, 132–7
cultural traits, 27–8
culture
as bounded, 204, 206–17
and communicative rationality, 178
concept of, 27, 170–1,
    247 n. 4
and hegemony, 175–6
and logic of production, 148–9
semiotic theory of, 171–2
culture area, 225

Derrida, Jacques
concept of relation, 132–3
on discourse and writing, 136–7
development: see Cole, on
    modernization; see also Escobar
Diamond, Stanley, on Lévi-Strauss, 131
diaspora, 229, 231; see also nation and
    identity; chador
Dilthey, Wilhelm, 40–1, 107–9, 112–13,
    247 n. 1
discourse
and the fusion of horizons, 114–15;
    see also Gadamer
Hindess and Hirst on, 143–5
language and being, 117
and symbols, 125
theoretical mode of, 141
as world constituting, 126–7
Douglas, Mary, 124, 206–7, 247 n. 8
Durkheim, Emile, and social facts, 52–3,
    242 n. 3, ch. 2

emics, 137
Enlightenment
Anglo-French, 29–30
Habermas on, 184
against tradition, 109–10, 111–12
epistemology
Boas, 26
Evans-Pritchard, 26
Malinowski, 26
politics of functionalist fieldwork, 26,
    41–5
rationality, 251 n. 4
Escobar, Arturo, on development,
    215–16
ethnoscapes, 255 n. 1; see also
    Appadurai
etics, 137
European Union, 206
Evans-Pritchard, E. E.
challenge to Lévy-Bruhl, 46–7
critique of, 38–41, 42, 51–2
difference from Dilthey, 4, 40–1
distinction from Durkheimian
    tradition, 40–1, 51–2

Evans-Pritchard, E. E. (*cont.*)
  on ethnographic facts, 40–1
  on history, 40, 239 n. 7
  on language, 38
  and Malinowski in contrast, 38, 39
  view of culture, 39
  views on fieldwork and participant
    observation, 39, 71–2
explanation and understanding
    dichotomy, 83–4, 137–8

Fabian, Johannes, denial of coevalness,
    17, 187–8, 214, 222, 236
facts, Thompson's method of inquiry,
    165–6
fieldwork, 209, 211, 227–8; *see also*
    Marcus, on multi-sited analysis
formalist economic theory, 153
Fortes, Meyer, 121–2
Foucault, Michel, 17–19, 214–15,
    216
  on power, 253–4 n. 21
  on Victorian sexuality, 256–7 n. 13
fragmentation and postmodernism,
    195–6
Frankfurt School, 140, 169
Freud, Sigmund, and symbolic
    interpretation, 123–4
Fried, Morton, on tribe, 216

Gadamer, Hans-Georg
  Dilthey, critique of, 108–9
  effective historical consciousness,
    112–14, 140, 161
  on Enlightenment reason, 109
  explanation and understanding
    dichotomy, rejection of, 112
  fusion of horizons, 114–15, 118–19,
    139
  language and being, 11–12, 117, 125,
    232–3
  on method, 12
  on prejudices and prejudgments,
    111–12, 112–13, 128
  on Romanticism, nineteenth century,
    109–10

  on tradition, 108–11, 113–14, 139,
    216
  with Winch, comparison on language,
    115–16
Geertz, Clifford, 12, 121, 159
  on meaning as local, 224–5, 231
Geisteswissenschaften: *see* Dilthey
globalism, theories of, 23
globalization, 217–24
Godelier, Maurice
  anthropology, contribution to, 150
  anthropology and logic of one unified
    science, 154–5
  economic basis and ideological
    superstructure, 153–4
  on history, 150
  on internal logic of social formation,
    151
  rationality of economic systems, 152,
    157
  rationality of social systems, 152–4
  on structures, 153
  on theory and hypothetico-deductive
    method, 151–2
Goffman, Erving, total institutions and
    causality, 102
Gramsci, Antonio, 140, 173, 175
Guoro, 146–7

Habermas, Jürgen
  Gadamer and hermeneutics, critique
    of, 120
  on grand narratives, 21
  influence on anthropology, 16–17
    monological subject, critique of,
    31–2
  positivism, critique of, 84–5
  postmodernism, critique of, 184–5
  rationality, transcendental and
    science, 3, 101
  on reconstruction of historical
    materialism, 198–200
  self-reflection, 99–100
Hanson, F. Allan, on invented tradition,
    190–1
Harris, Marvin, 245–6 n. 1

Hegel, Georg W. F., 250 n. 21
hegemony, 139–40
Heidegger, Martin, 232
Heller, Agnes, on the self, 205
Henry, Jules, 247 n. 4
Herder, Johann Gottfried, 171
hermeneutics
  and determinacy of the past, 167–8
  hermeneutic circle, 112–13
  importance for anthropology, 108,
    139–40
  limitations, 139
  origins, 107–9
  philosophical hermeneutics and
    emancipatory interest, 119–20
  of suspicion, 125, 129, 132, 155
Herzfeld, Michael, 188, 252 n. 13
Hindess, Barry, and Hirst, Paul
  Althusser's rationalism, critique of,
    143–4
  on discourse and concepts, 143–5
  empiricism, rejection of, 143
  epistemology, rejection of, 143,
    249 n. 4
  Meillassoux, critique of, 146–7
  on mode of production, 144, 145–9,
    248–9 n. 2
  rejection of concept, 148–9
  on social change, 148
  on social formation, 147–8, 149
  theory, concept of, 145, 147, 148–50
historical materialism, 169, 171–2
historicism, Gadamer's critique of,
  108–9
history
  and contingency, 133–5
  and critique, 134–5
  as process, 112–13, 136–7, 250 n. 16
Hobbes, Thomas, contract theory,
  89–90
Hobsbawm, Eric, on invented tradition,
  190–1
Hobsbawm, Eric and Ranger, Terence,
  190
Horton, Robin
  on anthropological understanding, 84

  on consensus and scientific
    community, 80–1, 231–2
  continuity-evolution perspective, 72–3
  critique of, 77–8, 81–2, 84
  language, concept of, 9, 73–5
  open and closed societies, 9, 80, 81–3,
    110
  on theory, 75–7, 85
  on traditional society, 71–2
  on Zande witchcraft, 79
Husserl, Edmund
  on life-world, 3
  phenomenological epoché, 130–1,
    248 n. 11
Huyssen, Andreas, critique of
  postmodernism, 184
Hymes, Dell, 182
hypothetico-deductive method: *see*
  Jarvie, objectivist methodology

ideology
  critique of, 94–5, 133–4
  and superstructure, 154
illocutionary force, 135
indigenous societies, 82
institutions, 84–5, 91, 104
interpretation theory
  conflict of interpretations, 129
  critical, 140, 152, 173, 176
  neopositivist, 166–7
  structuralist, 130, 132, 141–60

Jarvie, I. C.
  on anthropological understanding, 84
  Durkheimian tradition, critique of,
    64–5
  induction, critique of, 63
  on literacy, 69
  methodological individualism, 8, 65,
    90
  objectivist methodology, 63–4
  on pluralism, 69–70
  on presuppositions, 64
  rationality, strong and weak sense, 67
  science as progress, 68–9, 70, 230–1
  situational logic, 65, 87–8

Jarvie, I. C. (*cont.*)
  on theory, 85
  Winch, critique of, 66–8, 69, 70

Kant, Immanuel, 241–2 n. 1, 244 n. 2
Keesing, Roger, on regional systems, 209
kinship and mode of production, 148–9, 154, 157–8
Kohlberg, Lawrence, 240 n. 17; *see also* Habermas
knowledge-constitutive interests, 158–9, 177–8
Kuhn, Thomas, on science, 80–1

labor
  as metanarrative, 235
  and political economy, 194–5
language
  and constitution of reality, 127
  label theory of, 49
  social control, 67–9
  and socialization, 73; *see also* Horton
  as a temporal system, 126–7, 130
  see also discourse
Lash, Scott and Urry, John, 236
Leach, Edmund, 89, 121–2
legitimation and the state, 169–70
Leiss, William, 70, 244 n. 17
Lévi-Strauss, Claude, 130–1, 141–2, 150, 152, 248 n. 12
  on Boas, 34, 242 n. 2, ch. 2
Lévy-Bruhl, Lucien, 71, 121
  on pre-logical mentality, 4, 46–7
linguistic turn, 5–7, 26; *see also* Wittgenstein, later period
Linnekin, Jocelyn, on invented tradition, 190–1
Löwith, Karl, 126
Lukács, Georg, 24, 94–5, 141, 168, 195, 245 n. 10
Lukes, Steven
  on context-independent criteria, 94–5
  contextual interpretation, critique of, 93–4
  on culturally specific criteria, 92–3
  on language, 95

language games, critique of, 93
  on methodological individualism, 9, 90, 92
  on social reality, 91–2
  on social role of ideology, 96
  on universal criteria of truth, 10, 92–3, 104–5
  on Winch, 232
Lyotard, Jean-François, on postmodernism, 21, 183–4

MacIntyre, Alasdair
  causality and meaning, 98–9, 100, 101–2, 129
  on cross-cultural interpretation, 103–4
  extracontextual criteria of truth, 97, 104–5
  on functionalist anthropology, 104
  history and critique of rationality, 10, 96, 97–8, 232
  on language, 103
  theory as contemplation, 105–6
  Winch's concept of meaning, critique of, 58, 99
MacPherson, C. B., critique of Hobbes, 205
magic and rationality, 245 n. 9
Malinowski, Bronislaw
  comparison with Boas, 35, 36
  critique of, 37, 38
  goal of ethnography, 35–6
  on history, 36–7
  on language, 209
  methodology, 37–8
  on social systems, 35–6
  on Trobriands, 155–6
Marcus, George
  critique of, 228–9
  on multi-sited analysis, 24, 224–9
  on Paul Willis, 226
Marcus, George and Fischer, Michael
  critique of, 200–1, 201–2
  on ethnographic representation and writing, 186, 188–9
Marcuse, Herbert, 70, 244 n. 5

Marx, Karl, 94–5, 149, 150, 155, 158, 161, 179, 194–5, 199, 248 n. 14, 253 n. 19
Marxism and critical theory revisited, 13–20
Marxism
  and concept of culture, 170, 171, 175
  historical culturalist, 143, 160–76, 180–1
  on social control, 61–2
  structuralist, 141–60, 171, 177–8
Mead, Margaret, 187
Meillassoux, Claude, mode of production among Guoro, 146
metaphor
  positivist theory, 121–2
  Ricoeur's theory, 121–3
methodological individualism: see Jarvie; Popper
Mintz, Sidney
  on commodities, 218
  on Geertz, 193
  on political economy, 192–4
  on world systems theory, 220
mode of production, 15–16, 144, 145–6, 146–7, 148, 151
modernism, 1–2
Morgan, Lewis Henry, 26
multi-sited fieldwork, 224–9
multivocality: see symbol, Ricoeur's theory of
Murdock, George Peter
  Human Relations Area Files, 225–6
  and nuclear family, 246 n. 10
myth, Ricoeur's view of, 131

Nadel, S. F., 210
narrative
  grand, 239 n. 1
  and history, 166–8
  see also Thompson, on historical interpretation
nation and identity, 208; see also chador
neo-Popperians, 170

Obeyesekere, Gananath, 189
oral traditions, 82–3
ordinary language philosophy, 87

participant observation, 26, 85–8
phenomenology, 237, 239 n. 6
Piaget, Jean, 73
political economy, 169–70, 176–7, 178, 192–7
politics, 250 n. 20
Popper, Karl
  methodological individualism, 65; see also Jarvie
  open and closed societies, 78–9, 110
  on science, 78–9
  situational logic, 65
  on truth, 8
postcolonial states, 215
positivism
  Adorno's and Habermas's critique of, 83–4
  defined, 84
  limits, 86
postmodernism
  and anthropology, 186–92
  the controversy, 183–6; see also Lyotard
  limitations of, 202–3, 251–2 n. 5
power, 229, 235, 253–4 n. 21; see also Arendt
praxis, 96, 196, 221
production
  and instrumental rationality, 158,176
  logic of as communicative, 155–6
proletariat and social control, 163, 164
propositional content, 135–6

Rabinow, Paul, 11
Radcliffe-Brown, A. R., concept of structure, 141
Ranger, Terence, invented tradition in Africa, 211–12
rationalism
  Enlightenment, 109
  neo-Kantian and Piaget, 75
  and structuralism, 131, 142, 151–2

rationality
  communicative, 76, 168–70
  and economic systems, 152–3
  instrumental, 76, 155–6, 158–9,
    168–70
  reconsidered, 229–38
  strong and weak: *see* Jarvie
  on universal criteria: *see* Lukes
rationality debates, 1, 26, 34–5, 180–1,
  204, 233
redistribution, simple and complex,
  146–7
reflexivity
  as critique of positivism, 85–8
  and cross-cultural understanding,
    43–4, 85–6
  self-reflection , 96–7
reification, 242 n. 3, ch. 3
Ricoeur, Paul
  actions and texts, 12–13, 126–32
  anthropology, importance for, 137–8,
    233
  on Freud, 240 n. 12
  Gadamer in comparison, 120–1
  hermeneutics of suspicion, 126, 129,
    155
  on language and discourse, 121–7
  on metaphor, 39, 120–3
  structuralists, distinction from, 132–3
  theory of symbols, 123–4, 125, 140,
    161
Rogers, Susan, on local autonomy,
  224–5
Romanticism
  consequences for anthropology,
    109–10
  nineteenth century and tradition, 110
Rosaldo, Renato, 230
Roseberry, William, critique of Sahlins,
  222
Rousseau, Jean-Jacques, 171

Sahlins, Marshall
  critique of instrumental rationality,
    157–9
  on structure and agency, 221–2

Said, Edward W., 20, 187, 251 n. 28,
  256 n. 6
Saussure, Ferdinand de, 126
Schmidt, Wilhelm, 27–8
Scholte, Bob 251 n. 1
science
  as conservative, 80; *see also* Kuhn
  and epistemology, 87, 97
  as ideology, 81–2; *see also* Horton,
    open and closed societies
  logic of, 51–2, 56–7
  as progress, 68–70, 90; *see also* Jarvie
Searle, John, speech acts, 135
semiotics
  and culture, 132–3
  as mediation, 128, 130, 132, 134–5,
    135–7, 139
Shostak, Marjorie, 189
social control
  domination, 103, 134–5, 136, 137,
    139–40, 163–4, 170, 175
  exploitation and domination
    distinction, 161–2, 169–70
social formation
  Althusser's concept of, 141
  Hindess and Hirst's concept of, 148–9
  see also totality
societies, open and closed: *see* Jarvie;
  Popper
Stocking, George, on Boas, 27, 29
structural-functionalism, critique of,
  213–14
structuralism
  and linguistics, 126–8
  Marxist, 141–60; *see also* Althusser;
    Godelier; Hindess and Hirst
  as method, 130–1
subjects, human, 30–1, 141
symbol, Ricoeur's theory of, 122–6

Tambiah, Stanley, 204
Taussig, Michael
  on local responses to capitalism,
    189–90
  on critique of political economy, 197,
    222, 254 n. 25

texts
  and human actions, 126–31, 136
  interpretation of, 133–4, 139
  as model for fieldwork, 112–13
theory
  classical notion, 42–3, 77–8, 105–6
  and common sense: see Horton
  as contemplation, 105
  contract, 53, 89–90
  critical, 141
  cultural, 173
  and modern science, 77–8
  neo-Popperian, 85
Thompson, E. P.
  on Althusser, 160, 164, 165
  on category of experience, 160, 164–5
  on exploitation and domination,
    162–3, 168–9, 170
  on facts and historical evidence,
    165–6
  on historical agency, 163–4, 169–70
  on historical interpretation, 160–1,
    165, 166–7
  historical logic and mediation, 166,
    167
  political economy, 169–70
  social being and social consciousness,
    165, 170
  on social formation, 168–9
  on social history, 162
  on time, 96
  on work discipline, 161–2
  on writing of history, 166
totality
  concept of in critical theory, 88, 141,
    167–9, 252 n. 9
  functionalist, 43–4
tradition: see Gadamer; Horton
  invention of, 190–2
  invention of critiqued, 191–2
Treaty of Berlin 1895, 215
Trevor-Roper, Hugh, 190
truth claims
  correspondence theory of, 89, 167–8
  extracontextual criteria: see
    MacIntyre

universal criteria of truth: see Lukes
Universal Exposition of Paris 1855, 223
utilitarian philosophy, 90

validity claims: see truth claims
Vincent, Joan, 234

Wallerstein, Immanuel, 220–1, 241 n. 22;
    see also world systems theory
Weber, Eugen, on French national
    identity, 208
White, Hayden, on writing of history,
    21, 188, 253 n. 14
Whorf, Benjamin Lee, 95–6, 246 n. 6
Williams, Raymond
  on cultural hegemony, 174–5
  culture, concept of, 171–3
  on interactions as material and
    communicative, 16, 172
  social being, 171, 172
  on tradition, 173–5
Willis, Paul, 226
Winch, Peter
  anthropology, contribution to, 62
  criticism of, 54, 57–62
  on cross-cultural interpretation, 57–8
  Evans-Pritchard, challenge to, 47,
    48
  forms of life, 55–6, 66–7
  Gadamer, comparison with on
    language, 116–17
  language games, 55–6, 67, 76–7, 230;
    see also Wittgenstein
  logic and category mistakes, 48–9, 56
  psychoanalysis and unconscious
    motives, 54–5, 99–100
  on rationality, 22
  social relations as communicative, 53;
    see also action
  Wittgenstein, distinction from , 54–5,
    58–9
  Zande interpretation, shortcomings
    of, 6–7, 58–60
wine on French cooperatives, 206
  Bordeaux, 218–19
  fieldwork on, 227–8

winegrowing hierarchy, 223–4,
  252–3 n. 13
witchcraft
  European, 243 n. 14
  Zande, 7, 46–8, 51–2, 58–60, 66–7
Wittgenstein, Ludwig
  early period, 49–50, 242 n. 1
  later period, 6, 48–9, 50–1, 55

Wolf, Eric
  on culture as autonomous, 234
  on functionalism, 209
  on political economy, 192–4, 234
  on power, 14;
  on world systems theory, 220
world systems theory, 217–18
  critique of, 220–1